MW01091958

The James Dean Collectors Guide

Featuring The Collection of
David Loehr

Text by
Joe Bills

Published by

L-W BOOK SALES
P.O. Box 69
Gas City, IN 46933

ISBN#: 0-89538-102-8

Published by: L-W Book Sales
PO Box 69
Gas City, IN 46933

Please write for our free catalog

Printed in the USA by Image Graphics

Table of Contents

"Jim Dean and Elvis were the spokesmen for an entire generation. When I was in acting school in New York, years ago, there was a saying that if Marlon Brando changed the way people acted, James Dean changed the way people lived. He was the greatest actor who ever lived. He was simply a genius." - - *Martin Sheen*

Meet James Dean

James Dean gave his all. On screen, on the racetrack, and in life, the totality of his effort set him apart. As an actor, Dean's genius was his unerring ability to broadcast honest human complexity through the lens of a camera. As an icon, he resonates through society on a much deeper level.

In the annals of American popular culture, there is no more enigmatic figure than Dean: his brow furrowed while his mouth smiles, face and body twisted in emotional contradiction. James Dean meant different things to different people. His story is one of conflicting information, divergent opinions and wild exaggerations. The triumph and tragedy that was Dean's life lasted exactly 9000 days-- culminating in an 18 month movie career that earned him immortality.

Perhaps on factor that most accounts for the separation of Dean from other young stars both of his own time and from other eras is his unique chronology. Essentially, Dean died and *then* had a career. Of his three starring film roles, only *East of Eden* had been released at the time of his death. In the minds of the public, a full two-thirds of James Dean's movie career "occurred" postmortem.

The scenario is a romanticist's dream. Already knowing the conclusion of Dean's tragic story, fans read ominous premonition into innocent and unrelated events. Watching *Rebel Without a Cause* , released soon after Dean's death, distraught viewers cringed when Jim Stark lamented to the juvenile officer at the police station, "I don't know what to do anymore, except maybe die." Later, during his first tender moment with Judy, Dean's character reflects, "You know something? I woke up this morning, you know? And the sun was shining, and it was nice and all that type of stuff. And then first thing I saw you, and, I said now, "Boy, this is going to be one terrific day, so you better live it up. Because tomorrow you might be nothing. And I almost was." To fans in mourning, it was all but impossible to avoid reading inferences of fate into these lines. In the movie, Dean's character had a near miss and was learning new appreciation of life. In the real world, the voice that had spoken the words was already gone.

The legend has outlasted the life several times over. James Dean has grown bigger in death than he ever was in life. Though he's been dead nearly a half a century, Dean's image remains one of the most recognizable in the world. As a symbol of the rebellious youth of postwar America, Dean is merchandised the world over. His estate today generates more income per month than the actor made in his entire life, mostly from advertising and the sale of memorabilia.

Quickly, the merchandise superseded its subject-- the commemoration grew to outweigh the man. The concept and look of James Dean became iconographic, infiltrating the collective unconscious in a way few contemporary figures ever do. To this day, college dorm rooms around the world are adorned with depictions of his slouching form, in many cases put there by teenagers who haven't seen the films, some who can't even name one. Eternally young and beautiful, Dean's face expresses his private demons, and in so doing opens a window upon our own. Ebbing and flowing behind his eyes are waves of confidence and fear, tragedy and rebellion, love and alienation that are at once personal and universal.

Advertisers are drawn to Dean because he offers them the best of two worlds. His image is at once nostalgic and contemporary, spontaneous and predictable. With his rebelliousness couched safely in the past, Dean is a risk-free advertising investment who will never embarrass his sponsors. For proof of Dean's continuing popularity, one need look no further than the list of companies that have licensed items or created ads using his likeness. The Bradford Exchange, Champion Spark Plug, Hallmark, Levi-Strauss, the MGM Grand Hotel, the San Francisco Museum of Modern Art, Pepsi and Reader's Digest are among those who have attempted to attach some portion of Dean's image to their products or services. James Dean is big business.

Death not only solidified Dean's corporate appeal, it also locked him into his public persona. Unlike Marlon Brando or Elvis Presley, whose images evolved (perhaps devolved) as they aged, Dean did not live long enough to contradict the characters he played. In each of his films, Dean portrays a vulnerable character reacting in opposition to an authority figure. Whether up against his overly pious father and absentee prostitute mother in *East of Eden,* his bickering, self-absorbed family in *Rebel,* or ranch boss Bick Benedict in *Giant,* Dean's characters sought acceptance and found rejection. His desperate and futile search for love invests an almost sexual tension into scenes with both male and female costars. Torn between his brother and his brother's girl, or between Plato and Judy, Dean embodied the very essence of teenage awkwardness and confusion. As he oscillated between adult and child, between affection and violence, young audiences felt they were seeing themselves realistically captured on screen as never before. And the timing was perfect.

In the years following World War II, teenagers emerged as a distinct and definable group for the first time in American history. Like never before, this underappreciated transitional phase took on a shape and form of its own. National prosperity had given these almost-adults their first experience with cars and money and leisure time. Hollywood was quick to identify the new market, and just as quick to set its sights upon it.

Like any business, the movie industry is dictated by the laws of supply and demand. Never has that scale been more lopsided than in the case of James Dean. The powers that be in the film industry had identified a new youth market and found a rising star who proved to be an instant grand slam. Then, just as audiences were clamoring for more, he was gone. Movie makers had no reason to believe Dean was irreplaceable, and left no stone unturned in their search for his successor.

Meanwhile, entrepreneurs helped out by keeping interest alive until the next sensation came along. Pictures and posters were printed in all shapes and sizes. Medallions, pendants, earrings and pins were made available through ads in popular magazines. One morbid innovator supposedly even marketed rings set with glass shards from the tiny windshield of Dean's Porsche. Five dollars would buy an "authentic" mask with which fans could"become" James Dean. It seemed everyone had an opinion or a story to share--during some months in the late 50's there were as many as twenty Dean articles on newsstands at the same time.

Many stars have been temporarily labeled "The New James Dean," but death has fixed Dean's character more firmly into his cultural moment than a living, growing person can ever manage to be. So the search continues. Paul Newman. Tony Perkins. Dean Stockwell. Carroll Baker. Horst Buckholz. Matt Dillon. Sean Penn. Luke Perry. Brad Pitt. Many have passed through the gap without filling it. And the list extends beyond the film industry. Elvis. Bob Dylan. Morrissey.

Dean is unique not so much because of the things he said and did, but because he was first to say and do them. Since no one else can ever be first, a true replacement will never be found. The search will continue, and continue to fail, because what is sought is not just an actor, but an actor whose roles and whose personality fit seamlessly into a complicated transitional phase of our cultural evolution. The time and mind-set that Dean has come to represent can not be reproduced. The proven ability of the Dean image to weather any and all shifts in public taste and style is a phenomenon of popular culture duplicated only by Elvis, Marilyn Monroe, and perhaps the Beatles.

James Dean has been dead nearly twice as long as he lived, and the legend shows no sign of fading. A glance through any fashion magazine turns up page after page of imitators. Many of Dean's gestures and poses have been so assimilated into the culture that it's easy to forget their origin. But they're there. Everywhere.

Mother's Boy

"In a certain sense, I am a (fatalist). I don't know how to explain it, but I have a hunch there are some things in life we just can't avoid. They'll happen to us, probably because we're built that way-- we simply attract our own fate, make our own destiny."
--Dean to reporter Jack Shafer

In July of 1930, the United States was in the midst of the Great Depression and Herbert Hoover's Presidency was nearing its end. That month, 19-year-old Mildred Wilson married Winton Dean, a dental technician who was two years her senior. James Byron, their only child, was born at home in the Seven Gables Apartments in Marion, Indiana on February 8, 1931. The name James was chosen after James Amick, chief dental officer at the Veteran's Administration Hospital where Winton was employed. Byron was selected not in deference to the great poet, but in honor of Thomas Byron Vice, Winton's best friend.

Mildred Dean fostered her son's creative side, dancing, drawing and acting out puppet shows with him. Mother and son were almost always together, and their intimacy must have occasionally caused Winton to feel like a third wheel in his own house. The family lived in several homes around Marion and Fairmount until 1936, when Winton accepted a transfer to a V. A. Hospital in Santa Monica, California.

On the West Coast, Jimmie started school but was not popular with his classmates. A pale and fragile child, he was subject to frequent nosebleeds. The teasing of his peers only intensified Dean's closeness to his mother. She was the only one who understood him, who saw what was special in him and loved him for it. If his mother was the foundation of his world, it was a foundation that was soon to be shaken. Mildred's moods grew darker until one day she did not get out of bed at all. She was sick. Doctors came and talked to Winton behind closed doors. As days turned to weeks, Grandma Emma Dean came from Indiana to help out. But there was nothing any amount of helping or praying could do. James Dean's mother died of uterine cancer on July 14, 1940, at the age of twenty-nine.

Financially devastated by his wife's illness, Winton was unable to make the trip back for the funeral. Fearing that he could not work his way out of debt and be a single parent at the same time, his father arranged for Jimmie to return with Emma Dean to Indiana where Winton's sister Ortense and her husband Marcus Winslow would look after him for a while. At every stop during the long cross-country train ride, Jimmie ran back to the car that was carrying his mother's casket to make sure she was still there. Within the space of a few days, Jimmie found himself back in Indiana with a surrogate family consisting of an aunt , an uncle and a cousin Joan, a couple of years older than him. The Winslows raised Jimmie as one of their own, loved him as he loved them. But in time when complete nuclear families were still the norm, the new addition to the Winslow family was unable to forget that in his new home, only he bore the last name Dean.

Talents Take Shape

"Those of us who worked with Jimmy Dean carry an image of his intense struggle for a goal beyond himself." - *Ronald Reagan*

The young actor's first stage performances were speeches delivered for the Fairmount chapter of the Women's Christian Temperance Union, to which his Aunt Ortense belonged. In the decades following the repeal of Prohibition, young people commonly read speeches denouncing alcohol and its effects at WCTU meetings. Later, he would joke about the WCTU, "The way they had it, you could go to hell for squashing a grape." But these earliest performances planted a seed in Jim Dean.

Around the same time, Jimmy's interest in speed was also in its formative stages. Winton's brother Charlie Dean was a car buff who imparted that love to Jimmy. On the farm, Dean learned first to drive a tractor, then a bicycle, and then a motorized bike called a Whizzer. During his sophomore year of high school, Jimmy traded up for a more powerful motorcycle. As his passion for motors and speed blossomed, nearby Carter's Motorcycle Shop became one of his favorite hangouts.

Competition and the drive to excel became increasingly important to Jimmy as he grew up. In later years, he would confide to friends that much of his ambition could be traced to a desire to prove to his mother that he was good and that she was wrong to leave him. While a young teenager, he worked hard to develop athletically, spending hours at the basketball hoop in the Winslow barn. Jimmy thrilled at being able to do things that no one else would dare even try. His obsession with impressing others was tempered only by an extreme fear of failure and public humiliation. To compensate, each and every stunt was practiced in private, over and over, until success was all but guaranteed. Only then would he perform. Dean pulled off many wild stunts, but they were not without a price. Several pairs of glasses were sacrificed to the cause, as were the youngster's front teeth, which were knocked out during a botched trapeze act. By the time he reached high school Dean was a good athlete, excelling in track and field, basketball, and baseball.

Although dramatics at first played second fiddle to athletics, Jimmy's priorities eventually began to shift, thanks in large part to his association with two people: high school drama coach Adeline Brookshire Nall and local Wesleyan minister James Deweerd. While in seventh grade, Dean asked for Brookshire's assistance on "Bars, " a piece he was performing at the WCTU. She took a liking to him and eagerly awaited his participation in her classes. Ms. Brookshire's appreciation of his talents sparked Dean's first serious interest in theater.

When he wasn't playing ball or practicing lines, Dean could often be found in the company of Reverend DeWeerd, a war hero and prominent member of the community. DeWeerd was one of the few members of the small farm community to have traveled the world. He regaled Jimmy with stories of bullfights in Mexico and of his acquaintance with Winston Churchill. He introduced Jimmy to the classics of music and poetry. DeWeerd encouraged his young friend to set high standards for himself, to aspire. As much as anyone, Reverend DeWeerd was responsible for turning Jim Dean into a young man who was hungry for all the world had to offer, who would not be satisfied by a simple life.

In 1949, his senior year, Dean won the Indiana State speech tournament, entitling him to enter the National Forensics League's nationwide contest in Longmont, Colorado. Dean used the same dramatic piece he had used in the state meet, an excerpt from Charles Dickens called "The Madman's Manuscript." Although in later press releases he would claim to have been victorious, Dean placed a respectable sixth in the national competition. He may well have finished higher, had he not been penalized for exceeding the time constraints of the contest. Several judges approached him following the contest to compliment his performance and offer him encouragement. He may not have won, but he got his first assurances that he wasn't just Ms. Brookshire's pet. He had talent by anyone's standards.

Following graduation, James Dean enrolled at Santa Monica City College, where at his father's urging, he agreed to confine acting to an extracurricular activity while pursuing a physical education major. It was not long, however, before he became something of a teacher's pet with the school's drama coach. In this case it was Gene Owen who spent hours with Jimmy, working on his diction. Although it had never been a problem in Indiana, in California Dean had become self-conscious about the combined impediment of his Hoosier twang and the dental plate he had worn since knocking out his front teeth. Several times a week, Dean would get together with Owen after classes, working through Shakespeare's "Hamlet," a play that would always interest Jimmy, though he never fulfilled his goal of performing the lead role.

When the school year ended, Dean occupied himself with summer stock work, appearing in a production of "The Romance of Scarlet Gulch" under the name Byron James. At about the same time he also reapplied to UCLA, where he had previously been denied admission. With a year of college under his belt, he was accepted.

Although ostensibly enrolled as a pre-law student, it was the UCLA theater department that attracted Dean. Jimmy stayed at the University for only one year, but during that time he scored his biggest acting job yet--the coveted role of Malcolm in a production of *Macbeth*.

Reviews in the school paper indicate in no uncertain terms that very little promise was seen in this newcomer. Jimmy had performed in front of his largest audience, but had, by most accounts, failed to impress. Dean felt good about his performance, however, and was sure he was headed in the right direction when a theater department connection landed him his first agent and a paid acting job- as one of a group of playful youths in a Pepsi commercial. His first professional dramatic role, in a nationally televised Easter play entitled "Hill Number One," followed soon thereafter.

On the heels of his part as John the Apostle, Dean received an unexpected honor. A group of catholic schoolgirls for whom the show had been required viewing formed the Immaculate Heart James Dean Appreciation Society , the first of many James Dean fan clubs. Honored, Dean even attended one of their meetings, soaking up the star treatment.

Through fellow student Bill Bast, Dean met and began dating Beverly Wills, a radio star and the daughter of comedienne Joan Davis. Although the romance was short-lived, it provided Dean with his first behind-the-scenes glimpse of the more successful side of Hollywood. Bast got Dean work parking cars in the CBS Radio lot, but Dean was not a conscientious employee, and did not keep the job. He was there just long enough to meet Roger Brackett, an acquaintance that would prove enormously beneficial to the young actor. Brackett was an influential advertising executive and radio producer who always had an eye for a new talent. Brackett's interest in Dean was more that platonic, but his desire to help was genuine. He took Dean under his wing, becoming a mentor as had Reverend DeWeerd back in Fairmount. Brackett had friends in high places: directors, producers, and artists of all sorts. He opened doors for his young protégé, gave him a place to live and kept him well fed. Brackett arranged for Dean to play roles on several of the radio shows he was producing. Classes with established actor James Whitmore kept Dean moving in the right direction, as did bit parts in the movies *Fixed Bayonets, Sailor Beware,* and *Has Anybody Seen My Gal?*

New York

"One of the deepest drives of human nature is the desire to be appreciated, the longing to be liked, to be held in esteem, to be a sought-after person." -*James Dean*

By October of 1951, Jimmy's career had lost momentum and he was growing frustrated with what he saw as limited opportunities to act in Hollywood. At Whitmore's urging with Brackett's support, he packed his bags and moved to New York. Television was the new kid on the block in the mid 50's, mostly live, low budget and experimental. It was a new medium that opened a new world of work to struggling actors.

Dean landed some minor roles in the new city, but was not working consistently enough to support himself. He scored about a half a dozen bit parts in television dramas in the first half of 1952, and at the same time worked behind the scenes of the game show *Beat the Clock* as a stunt tester. Finally, in August of 1952, Dean's luck took a turn for the better. Acting with his friend Christine White in a skit she had written, Jimmy won admission to the prestigious Actors Studio. The Studio and its Stanislavsky Method were sweeping the acting world, having risen to prominence along with its most famous student, Marlon Brando. At the time, Dean was among the youngest ever accepted.

Jimmy became romantically involved with Elizabeth "Dizzy" Sheridan, a dancer who has since become a successful television actress. College friend Bill Bast had also made the move to New York, and the three spent much time together, cohabiting in various combinations, pooling their resources, relying on the income of whichever of them was working. New York City was invigorating and alive, but it was also exhausting. When months of fruitless auditions had worn him down, Dean proposed that they hitchhike to Indiana. Bill and Dizzy laughed him off at first, but were swayed by promises of home cooked meals and comfortable beds. They were lucky enough to get a ride shortly after sticking out their thumbs, and within two days had settled in on the Winslow farm.

Good food and fresh air was invigorating, but within a week Dean received a phone call notifying him he'd been cast in his first Broadway play. After weeks of rehearsal and a brief trial run in Connecticut, N. Richard Nash's *See the Jaguar* opened at The Cort Theater on the third of December. The play was a flop, closing after five performances. Although critics panned the show, Dean's role--as a boy whose mother had kept him locked in an icehouse for years--was well received. The *New York Herald-Tribune* said Dean gave "an extraordinary performance in almost impossible role." The *Morning Telegraph* found him "overwhelming, " the *Daily News* "very good." Other reviewers made note of his work as "believable and unembarrassing," and "gently awkward." The *Daily Mirror* offered simply that James Dean stole the show.

Jobs came Dean's way a little more frequently following his brief stint on Broadway. By the end of November 1953, Dean had added at least 16 television dramas to his resume, and in December he learned that he was getting a second chance at Broadway. Ruth and Augustus Goetz had adapted Andre Gide's *The Immoralist* into a play that was expected to be a major hit. It proved to be just that, although most of the run would go on without James Dean. Despite critical acclaim for his role as Bachir, the corrupt Arab houseboy, Jimmy was unhappy with behind-the-scenes decisions and script changes, and gave his notice after the first week. Many insiders reacted with shock. What kind of an actor leaves a successful Broadway show over quibbles? It seemed to many that Dean had just made the biggest mistake of his life. A bad decision like that was almost certainly a career- killer. But, as with the stunts he loved to pull as a boy, Jimmy only appeared to be acting impulsively. While others scrambled to justify his actions, Dean knew he was destined for bigger and better things.

Success

"You're going to meet a boy, and he's going to be very strange to you., and he's going to be different. No matter what you see or what you think of him, when you see him on the screen, he's gonna be pure gold." --*Elia Kazan*

Although the news had not yet been made public, Jimmy knew before he gave his notice that he'd been cast as the lead in Elia Kazan's screen adaptation of John Steinbeck's novel *East of Eden.* There was no bigger director than Kazan, whose work with Brando and Montgomery Cliff had given him a reputation as a maker of stars. Now Dean was the new boy being prepped by the director with the Midas Touch. Toward the end of May, filming got underway on location in Mendocino, California. Cast and crew soon moved on to Salinas before settling down to complete the picture on the Warner Brothers lot in Hollywood. James Dean was on his way.

On the soundstage next door to *Eden,* an old New York acquaintance of Jimmy's, Paul Newman, was filming his debut as well--in a role Dean had turned down. Newman's costar in the Biblical epic *The Silver Chalice* was the beautiful young Italian actress Pier Angeli. Although Dean first visited the neighboring lot to visit Newman, Angeli soon caught his eye. They began dating in June, and a volatile five-month relationship ensued.

When *East of Eden* finished shooting in the early part of August, Jimmy returned to New York for good TV roles in "Run Like a Thief" and "Padlocks." Dean was also lobbying for the role of Jett Rink in George Stevens' *Giant,* a project that was on hold due to Elizabeth Taylor's pregnancy.

Dean traveled to the West Coast to work with Natalie Wood in a TV presentation of *I'm a Fool* by Sherwood Anderson. The show aired on the 14th of November. Ten days later, Pier Angeli married Vic Damone in a lavish ceremony at St. Timothy's Church in Hollywood. Legend has it that a distraught Dean revved his motorcycle across the street as the newlyweds appeared on the church steps. Regardless of whether the scene played out quite that way, Jimmy was deeply hurt and couldn't wait to leave Los Angeles. Just before returning to New York, Dean played a delinquent who burglarizes Ronald Reagan's home in a show called "The Dark, Dark Hours."

Jimmy had a growing interest in photography, and had become friendly with several photographers, all of whom were now eager to shoot Kazan's hot new star. Toward the end of December, Dean posed for Roy Schatt's famous "Torn Sweater" series, arguably the most famous of the Dean photos. A shot from this series was used as the backdrop for the stage show *Grease;* another as the basis for the 1996 James Dean postage stamp.

Dean gave his final New York acting performance during the first week of January 1955, appearing with Mary Astor in "The Thief." That same day, Warner Brothers announced that since *Giant* was still on hold, Dean had been cast in the lead role of Nicholas Ray's *Rebel Without a Cause.*

Since *Rebel* was not scheduled to start filming until the end of March, Jimmy had some time to fill. In February, *Life* magazine photographer Dennis Stock trailed Dean through visits to Fairmount and New York. The resulting article would be good publicity and Dean was excited by the idea of appearing in town with a photographer--a successful homecoming. He was seeing Fairmount for the last time.

Back in New York, Jimmy busied himself visiting old haunts and catching up with friends. Although success was impending, James Dean still went largely unrecognized on the streets of New York.

On March 6th, Dean returned to Hollywood. That week, Stock's photos appeared in *Life.* *Eden* was forecast as a huge hit, and by all indications Dean was poised to become the hottest property in Hollywood. To celebrate, he bought himself a Porsche Speedster.

Although he loved the attention and the adoration, the stress of all the acclaim was sometimes too much for him. When *East of Eden* premiered in Los Angeles on March 16th, celebrity guests included Marilyn Monroe, Marlene Dietrich, Celeste Holm, Terry Moore and Eva Marie Saint. Dean stayed away.

Ten days later, just before shooting was to start on *Rebel Without a Cause,* Dean entered his new Porsche in races at Palm Springs. He placed first in a preliminary race and second in the final. In high-speed competition, Dean found the perfect antidote to career stress. Coming off such a promising start, he was eager to race again.

The following months went by in a whirlwind of activity. *Eden* was shown at the Cannes Film Festival and soon after opened nationally. While still at work on *Rebel Without a Cause,* Dean placed third in a race at Bakersfield and appeared in the television play "The Unlighted Road." Warner Brothers announced that Dean would be appearing in MGM's *Somebody Up there Likes Me,* based on the life of middleweight boxing champion Rocky Graziano. The loan of Dean to MGM was payback for the use of Liz Taylor in *Giant.* An actor who was all but unknown a year ago was now considered an equal trade for one of the industry's biggest names. Dean had arrived.

By the time *Rebel Without a Cause* wrapped, principal filming had finally begun on *Giant.* Jimmy squeezed in one final race at Santa Barbara, working his way from the back of the pack up to fourth place before blowing his engine, then joined the rest of the cast and crew in Marfa, Texas.

By the time production moved to Hollywood in July, things were looking up for Dean. TV and movie offers were pouring in. He would have his pick of future projects and plenty of time to pursue racing between films. He started dating 19 year-old German starlet Ursula Andress, who had just been signed by Paramount. Plans for the future were solidifying, and when Dean leased a nice log home in Sherman Oaks, he insisted that the lease include an option to buy.

On September 17th, in what has proven to be one of the most ironic and prophetic moments in Hollywood history, Dean filmed a National Safety Council commercial promoting highway safety. The spot was done as an informal interview on the set of *Giant.* Dean, wearing cowboy garb, sits down with interviewer Gig Young and the two chat about racing and how fast Dean's car will go. Jimmy comments that he has become a much safer driver since confining his racing to the track, and urges viewers to be safe on the highways. In a now legendary ad-libbed line, Dean ends with the quip, "Take it easy driving. The life you save might be...mine." Then he smiles and is gone.

Though Dean's *Giant* contract forbade him from racing during filming, that didn't mean he couldn't be prepared. Jimmy had a Lotus sports car on order, but while awaiting delivery he fell in love with a Porsche 550 Spyder he'd found at a dealership in Los Angeles. He traded his Speedster toward the Spyder on September 21st, the day before his work on *Giant* was finished. The moment his contractual obligations were fulfilled, Dean made arrangements to enter the Spyder in a race in Salinas on the first of October.

The day before the race, everything seemed ready to go. The only lingering issue was Dean's concern that he had not yet put enough miles on the Spyder to properly break the car in. He had been planning to tow the Porsche to Salinas, but now had second thoughts. At the last minute he decided drive the car, taking along mechanic Rolf Wuetherich, whose services he had negotiated as part of the Spyder purchase. His friends Sandy Roth and Bill Hickman would follow in Dean's station wagon, towing the trailer for the return trip.

The End

"I don't think people should be subservient to movie idols... I would like to be a star in my own sense. I mean to be a very consummate actor, to have more difficult roles and to fill them to my satisfaction. But not to be a star on the basis of gold plating. A real star carries its own illumination, an inward brightness." *--Dean to reporter Aline Mosley*

At dusk on September 30, 1955, James Dean's low silver racer collided with a Ford Tudor driven by a college student. Donald Turnupseed banged his nose on the Ford's steering wheel but was otherwise fine. Rolf Wuetherich was thrown from the Spyder and suffered broken bones and the other injuries. Dean was trapped behind the wheel of the crumpled Porsche. He never regained consciousness and was pronounced dead upon arrival at Paso Robles hospital.

From the Ashes Arise

"No one came before [Dean], and there hasn't been anyone since." *--Martin Sheen*

"He died at just the right time. If he had lived, he'd never have been able to live up to his own publicity." *--Humphrey Bogart*

On October 8th, three thousand people gathered as James Dean's body was laid to rest in the Winslow family plot at Fairmount's Park Cemetery, about a mile from the farm where he'd grown up.

Warner Brothers was unsure how to proceed with *Rebel Without a Cause,* which was ready for release. Historically, movies featuring deceased stars had performed poorly at the box office. In October, the film was released without a big premiere or much advertising. Still, the film made a strong showing, grossing only slightly less than *East of Eden,* though it had cost much less to make.

Just over a year later, the release of *Giant* was accompanied by enough fanfare for two films. The big movie did big box office, becoming one of the highest grossing films of the time. Nominations from the Academy of Motion Picture Arts and Sciences for *East of Eden* and

Giant gave Dean the distinction of being the first actor posthumously considered for an Oscar, twice.

Before the decade was over, he had taken a place among the iconographic images of the fifties: tail fins on cars, hot rods, sock hops, drive-ins, rock'n'roll, Marilyn Monroe, Buddy Holly...and James Dean, from Fairmount, Indiana.

In the Years since, Dean has remained startlingly contemporary. Memorabilia is the peculiar immortality that society awards its popular heroes, a collective effort to recapture in some tangible form that which might otherwise be lost forever.

Getting Started

Many collections start almost accidentally. A t-shirt or poster is followed by a second, a third, and suddenly, "out of nowhere," a collection is born. Others consciously set out to accumulate particular favorite items or objects associated through a certain theme. No matter the reasons for beginning, collecting can be both entertaining and educational.

As with any worthwhile pursuit, it takes time and effort to develop the necessary skills to get the most from this hobby. Collectors must learn to protect themselves, and knowledge is the best protection. Knowledge of what to buy, of where to buy it, and, most importantly, of how to care for what is bought.

Where To Look

One of the wonderful benefits of collecting memorabilia is that there is no telling where items will turn up. Most collectors eventually come to rely heavily on at least one of three primary sources: collectible shops, auctions, and flea markets or yard sales.

Collectibles shops are stocked by dealers who are in the business of buying and selling. Dealers generally know what items are worth and set prices accordingly. They are professionals who have expenses to cover and reputations to protect. From a collector's standpoint, this can be both a positive and a negative. Although a buyer is unlikely to find bargain basement prices at such shops, those purchases can still be a great deal when the value of the dealer's research and knowledge are factored in. If money is not an issue, collectibles shops can be the fastest and easiest way to build a formidable memorabilia collection.

Auctions are more of a gamble, but sometimes pay great dividends. The most important tools for buying at auction are observation and self-restraint. Before bidding, beginners should sit in on an auction or two to develop a feel for how they operate. A savvy bidder can and will find great deals, but auctions present more risk of mistake than any other method of buying. Auction bids are legally binding and all sales are final. Even experienced auction-goers can get caught up in the excitement of a bidding war and end up paying far more than an item is worth. Most reputable auction houses will have a preview period before the auction gets underway. Attending the preview is one of the best defenses against auction accidents. Previews offer the opportunity to examine items up close and at a leisure. Depending on scheduling, there may even be time to research particular lots before they come up for auction. Take notes, if necessary, choosing items on which to bid and setting limits on how high to go. No one makes the right decision 100% of the time, but any serious collector will benefit from an effort to make every buying decision an educated one.

One of the biggest recent collecting advancements has been the success of Internet auctions. These cyber-sales work just like real-world auctions, but with bidding open to a much wider audience. One drawback to online purchasing is that there is no preview before the auction. To compensate for this, most auction houses have an agreed upon period during which items can be returned and sales voided if the buyer feels an item has been misrepresented. The neophyte should proceed with the same cautions as with any other auction, but by and large, online auction transactions are fast and dependable. Half a dozen Internet auction houses are already up and running, and their success likely means that others will not be far behind.

Flea markets and yard sales can be a real bonanza, but there will be a lot of misses for each hit. For the collector who doesn't mind sifting through a menagerie of valueless items in search of a treasure, these private, amateur sales be the source of some wonderful finds. Because in most cases the seller will not be a dealer or professional appraiser, flea markets and yard sales are the most likely sources for drastically underpriced items. Although documentation and assurances of authenticity are not generally available when buying from these sales, the low prices more than compensate for any risk.

Whenever possible, save all correspondence and all the bill of sale. Not only do these documents offer protection against dishonesty, they can be tremendously important as a continuation of an item's provenance. For flea market purchases or other special cases where documentation is not available, bringing new items to a reputable dealer for appraisal may be worthwhile. The earlier a paper trail can be started for each individual item, the better. As a collection grows in value, documentation becomes crucial for tax and insurance concerns. Reputable dealers will never balk at supplying a detailed bill of sale and guarantee of authenticity, but it is the buyer's responsibility to ask for it. When doing business with someone who is not a professional dealer, retaining all receipts and written information is doubly important. If documentation can't or won't be provided, find out why. Make sure the risk is worth taking.

Repair VS. Restore

Collectibles are, in essence, historical artifacts. Whatever is done to repair or restore an item should be the minimum necessary to retain its historical value. Because purely cosmetic treatments should be avoided, most collectors prefer repair to restoration.

A repaired paper document, for example, has tears and holes neatly filled with similar, but not exactly matching, paper. An observer will easily be able to tell which pieces have been added. When restored, a document is brought back to an approximation of its original condition. With paper patches matched exactly, missing writing replaced and damaged images reconstructed, work on a restored document is all but impossible to detect. Following restoration, an item will have the appearance of an untouched original. Besides obvious potential for trickery, the biggest difference from the collector's stand point is that while repair is always reversible, restoration often is not.

Care For Paper Items

Knowledge of proper care, repair, and storage of paper products is a must for almost every collector. Depending upon its composition and the conditions to which it is subjected, paper can be either incredibly durable or very short-lived, with most falling somewhere in between. Paper has many natural enemies, each of which must be thwarted if a collection is to survive.

Atmospheric conditions present many challenges. Paper fibers expand when moist and contract when dry. If paper contains particles of copper or iron, excessive moisture may cause areas of light brown discoloration called foxing. A lack of humidity is just as harmful, as it hastens the aging process by making paper brittle. Storing a collection in an attic or cellar, even for a short time, can have far-reaching negative effects. Ideally, paper should be stored at a temperature around 70°F with humidity in the mid-30s.

Light, especially UV-intensive sunlight, is another hard-to-avoid danger. Sunlight (direct or reflected) and florescent light cause inks and dyes to fade. Although incandescent light is less harmful, only total darkness offers real protection. Obviously, complete avoidance of light is incompatible with the desire to show items off. What good is having a rare movie poster if no one can ever see it? Clear, UV-filtering plastics can provide some degree of protection for items on display.

Although seemingly harmless, dust is a potent enemy, especially of books and non-flat paper items. Dust particles have sharp edges that penetrate paper over time, with a cutting and scouring effect. Some particles may also carry fungus spores that can infect paper. Solutions to dust-borne problems must be preventative. Once embedded, dust is all but impossible to remove without damage.

Not all threats to a paper collection are inanimate. Book-lice, silverfish, termites, woodworms and cockroaches are just a few of the insects for whom a paper collection seems a feast befitting a king. House pets, mice, and other larger animals have also been known to nibble where they shouldn't . Moth balls or cedar chips wrapped in cloth will deter some pests, but there is no fool-proof solution to critter catastrophes. Once that prized autograph is eaten, it's eaten.

Without a doubt, humans are in a class by ourselves when it comes to damaging paper. Each time a piece of paper is handled, it deteriorates a little. Sweat and skin oils cause damage that becomes visible over time. The obvious tortures of stapling, taping, folding, tacking and clipping have immediately apparent results. Avoid transference of skin contaminants by wearing light cotton gloves when handling delicate items. Folded or tightly curled documents should be flattened gradually. Forcing the correction will break paper fibers, hastening deterioration. Barring professional restorative work, creases and holes are irreversible.

As dangerous as paper's external enemies may be, they pale in comparison to paper's primary internal foe: acid. Derivative of the wood pulp from which most paper is made, acid slowly but steadily consumes its host from within. Because of wood acids, all paper preservation methods share a common first step: pH testing. If paper is found to be acidic, chemical stabilization and de-acidification must follow. Solvent-based solutions that add an alkaline base to paper are a quick fix, but can be harmful if misapplied. Many collectors wisely consider de-acidification a job for a qualified professional. If attempting the process at home, be sure to practice on a few non-essential items before tackling prized pieces.

Once paper has been de-acidified, long-term storage and preservation can be considered. For large, single-sided items like posters, backing with linen or canvas is one popular technique. Backing provides a durable base for restoration of missing parts and reduces the likelihood that the paper will be torn. On the down side, the process is expensive and time-consuming and offers no protection for the front of the poster. When having items backed, be certain that no permanent glues are used and that the process can be undone if later desired.

Lamination is less popular, although some collectors have had success with the process. When performed with an eye toward preservation, lamination is done with a tissue paper laminate, as opposed to the plastic more commonly used for objects like wallet cards. Plastic lamination is permanent and a sure-fire way to devalue any collection. Tissue laminates, however, are removable with mineral spirits. Tissue lamination can be applied to the back of a poster at very little risk as a means to repair tears and flatten creases. Use on the front is more risky, as even the best laminates alter color and contrast slightly and the reversibility of the process is questionable.

The safest and most effective form of long-term protection for paper collectibles is encapsulation. Encapsulation is a process developed by the Library of Congress through which an item is chemically stabilized and sealed in Mylar. The Mylar keeps the item dry and free of contaminants while allowing for double-sided visibility. Mylar is tough and can withstand routine handling for many years. Encapsulation is less expensive than backing, and because nothing is actually attached to the paper, the process is fully reversible.

Mylar is the wunderkind of the collecting world. The cautious collector should beware of vinyl products and polyethylene bags, as they contain plastic additives that can damage paper. The sheet protectors sold in discount and drug stores are most often made of vinyl. Archival quality storage materials will have very little scent; avoid supplies with a strong plastic smell. In the absence of Mylar, single sheets of acid-free tissue can be placed between items as a simple and inexpensive preventative measure.

Once protected, items can be stored flat in a box, allowing enough room for individual pieces to be removed without crowding or damaging others. The box provides another layer of protection and allows for easy storage on sealed wooden or enameled steel shelving. It is critically important that air be allowed to circulate, especially behind and under storage shelves. Never store boxes or shelves in direct contact with damp floors or walls.

Cleaning Paper

Smudges and marks can often be cleaned from paper using an India-rubber eraser. This process is abrasive, however, and can damage paper that is textured, soft or brittle. For fragile items, a fine, powdered eraser can be sprinkled on and gently rubbed. Even this slight abrasion inevitably removes bits of the surface along with the dirt. As a non-abrasive alternative, tacky kneadable rubber erasers can be applied and lifted from a surface without rubbing, smearing or leaving particles behind.

Other paper-cleaning techniques are risky and require skill to avoid irreversible damage to items. For the collector with a delicate hand, a scalpel can be used to very lightly abrade surface dirt before it is dusted away with a soft bristled brush. This process works especially well for waxy deposits and other nonerasable marks. Under strictly controlled conditions, paper can be wetted to aid in removal of stains and marks. Wet-cleaning presents tremendous opportunity for error and should not be attempted by a novice.

Care Of Clothing Items

Textiles are extremely perishable and, like paper goods, are sensitive to light, humidity, dust, body heat and oils. Because strain on an old garment can weaken or tear fabric, proper storage is important. Relatively lightweight clothing can be kept on padded hangers, but heavy garments should lay flat to avoid strain on the shoulders or waistband. Take care that fabric is not stored in direct contact with unsealed wood. Acids from wood will break down cloth fiber and greatly reduce the life-span of the garment. In the absence of properly sealed or acid-free storage, an unbleached white sheet is an acceptable temporary shelf or drawer liner. Always store clothing with wrapped packets of moth crystal or cedar chips to discourage snacking by insects and pests.

Photos

Publicity shots, film stills, or candids, photographs are among the most popular movie collectibles. Unlike paper items, photographs should be stored vertically, never flat or stacked. Acid-free envelopes make excellent storage for negatives and prints.

Matting photographs is a process whereby a print is surrounded by a protective border, often in preparation for framing. Whether having items matted professionally or doing the work independently, insist that only acid-free museum board be used. The photo must not be trimmed or tampered with, and no tapes, glues or pastes should be used. Removable dry mounting tissue is the ideal adhesive for attaching prints to mounting boards. Mounting tissues vary in quality, and are available in either self-adhesive or heat-sealing versions. Attach the print to the center of the mounting board and overlay it with a second piece of board with a hole just a hair smaller than the print cut out. Matting a photo before framing prevents contact between the print and the fronting glass, and maintains all-important air circulation.

"Magnetic" photo albums cause great damage and should never be used. For unframed, unmounted pictures that will be frequently viewed, enclosure in archival quality transparent sleeves is an ideal method of protection. For particularly fragile pieces, insert a piece of acid-free board or folder stock for support.

On The Road

If a collection is going to travel frequently, mount and storage boxes are an option worth considering. Also known as museum cases, portfolio cases or solander boxes, these portable containers hold items mounted on standard-sized cards. The boxes are lined with acid free paper and have a dust proof closure. The consistent size of the panels prevents movement of contents within the box; and the horizontal racking eliminates buckling and bending. The semi-rigid panels allow for handling, and with only slight alteration may be used to form an in-house display or travelling exhibition.

The Seven Habits Of Highly Successful Collectors

Alright. So now you are armed with all the information you could ever need to build a record-setting collection. Right? Well, almost. Before setting off on your own, file away the following dos and don'ts, intended to keep the beginner's eyes on the road and headed in the right direction.

Rule One. Collect What You Enjoy.

Generally, collections are a safe investment and it is unusual for quality items to decrease in value. But it can happen. If a collector's sole motivation is financial, there is always a risk that things won't work out. There are no guarantees. By collecting items that are enjoyable in and of themselves, the focus is shifted away from the financial and the collector's peace of mind is assured. If a beloved collection happens to appreciate in monetary value, so much the better.

Rule Two. Buy Only Items You Actually Want.

This is really a continuation of Rule One. It may seem like common sense, but it's not as simple as it sounds. Don't buy items just because your collection lacks them.If you don't like an object, you don't need it. As far as your collection is concerned, you decide what belongs and what doesn't.

Rule Three. Set Price Guidelines For Yourself.

Pre-determine what an item is worth to you and refuse to exceed that amount. Set a hard and fast rule not to exceed your top price on a given day. If confronted with new information that indicates the item may be worth more than originally estimated, think before acting. Sleep on it and come back the next day with a new top price. Do not underestimate the willpower this approach requires. While it is possible that a chance at a good piece may be lost while being overly cautious, the odds are good that any such losses will be more than compensated for by the bad buys that are avoided.

Rule Four. Buy The Best You Can Afford.

When there is a choice to be made, always go for the best item you can afford. It may sound obvious, but a quality item will always be a quality item. Today's fad, however, may well be tomorrow's landfill. One great item will always outshine two lesser pieces.

Rule Five. Be Methodical.

This ties back to Rule Three. Work slowly, setting goals and plotting the steps necessary to attain them. Advance at the pace that best suits you. Don't feel pressured to accumulate too much too fast. Be reasonable and enjoy yourself.

Rule Six: Anything That Seems Too Good To Be True Probably Is.

Cliché perhaps, but true nonetheless. This does not mean you should run if presented a great bargain. Quite the contrary. There are good deals out there, and a lucky collector will find many of them. Simply do as much research as you can about both the item and the seller, and follow your instincts from there. Insist on documentation whenever possible.

Which brings us to our seventh and final rule--undoubtedly the most important of them all:

Rule Seven. Make Your Own Rules.

The point of this whole collecting thing is to have fun, right? And as James Dean would have been among the first to attest, nothing is more fun than breaking the rules. Now that you know what you *should* do, you can do as you please and enjoy doing it. Use the rules when you need to, but don't let them ruin the fun. This is *your* hobby after all.

A Collector's Tale

Since 1955, hundreds of thousands of fans have ventured to Fairmount, Indiana in pursuit of James Dean. When David Loehr first made the trip in May of 1979, there wasn't much to see. The Winslow farm where Dean was raised. Park Cemetery where he is buried. A small exhibit at the town Historical Museum. The local motorcycle shop. The old high school.

David was a late-comer to the phenomenon surrounding the charismatic young actor: Dean was nearly twenty years dead when a friend gave Loehr David Dalton's book ***James Dean: The Mutant King.*** David read the book while traveling from New York, where he had studied at Parson's School of Design and the Lester Polokov School for Stage Design, to Pasadena, California.

"Not long after I read ***The Mutant King,*** I saw ***East of Eden*** for the first time. It was in Cinemascope on the big screen, and it just kind of knocked me out."

Later that year, David got the opportunity to see ***Eden*** again, along with ***Rebel Without a Cause, Giant*** and ***James Dean Story*** at a Los Angeles County Art Museum film series that featured Dean, Montgomery Clift, and John Garfield.

Following that film festival, Loehr began searching memorabilia shops, bookstores and flea markets for anything related to James Dean. He found photos, books,magazines and posters, along with many oddball items. Party favors, medallions, dolls, and statues. Dean had been gone 20 years, and memorabilia seemed pretty scarce. But things kept turning up. Before long the collection filed a cardboard box.

After five years in California, David returned to New York. Driving across the country, he planned his trip to allow for a stop in Fairmount. "I visited the Historical Museum, which at that time was located above the auto parts store on Main Street. I was greeted by Jimmy's high school drama teacher, Adeline Nall. I was impressed with the small hometown exhibit of memorabilia and artifacts.

"From there I visited the grave and then the Winslow farm. Jimmy's Aunt Ortense invited me in, and I could hardly believe I was there. That whole first visit to Fairmount lasted only three hours."

The rest of the way to New York, David's head was buzzing with thoughts of Dean and Fairmount. Before he was even back in the city, he was planning another trip to Indiana.

Over the next several years, Loehr visited the town with increasing frequency. He began hosting James Dean birthday parties at Manhattan nightclubs and organized a six-hour Walking Tour of James Dean's New York Hangouts. Both became popular annual events.

As the collection grew, people began to take notice. When Dalton set to work on ***James Dean: American Icon***-- a photographic sequel to ***The Mutant King --*** Loehr was hired on as a research consultant. It was Dalton who gave David the nickname that has become his unofficial, semi-serious title: The Dean of Deanabilia.

In 1986, he worked as a research consultant and guest speaker when the Museum of Broadcasting put together their symposium, "James Dean: The Television Years." It was one of the Museum's most successful events.

In time, Loehr started giving serious thought to how he could share his treasures with the public. Fairmount seemed the logical place for such a tribute. Together with his partner Lenny, David began looking for a building that could be turned into a museum. A beautiful, turn of the century Victorian house that had once been a funeral parlor was available on Main Street. It would be a huge step, a tremendous commitment.

Could they do it? Should they do it? One night, still uncertain, David pulled his car off the road near a cornfield behind the Winslow farm. He had traversed these roads many times, but the area still held a special charge for him--the land where James Dean grew up. He got out of the car and stood in the cool night air, looking up at the sky from a spot whereDean may well have done the same thing. "Should I be doing this, Jimmy?" he questioned the heavens. He had barely spoken the words when a shooting star blazed across the sky. And he had his answer.

On September 22, 1988, the James Dean Memorial Gallery opened in that 12-room house on Main Street. The local high school band played at the opening ceremonies, and Adeline Nall cut the traditional ribbon with a switchblade lent by Hollywood artist Kenneth Kendall.

For more than a decade, David Loehr's James Dean Memorial Gallery has been Fairmount's newest location of pilgrimage. The collection is the largest of its kind in the world, and David is frequently sought out as a research consultant and/or photo editor for books, articles, films and videos. The Gallery has been featured on shows like *Current Affair, 20/20, Entertainment Tonight, The Joe Franklin Show, Across Indiana, and Personal FX.*

Along the way, he has acquired some truly extraordinary items. Have you ever wondered what happened to the James Dean head from the old Coney Island Wax Museum? You can see it at the Gallery. Can't imagine what the basketball shirt Dean wore in elementary school looked like? The Gallery has one. The brown trousers from ***Rebel Without a Cause*** brought tough bidding at a Sotheby's auction. Another treasure from that film came much easier. During a visit to Los Angeles, David and some friends were making a tour of the few remaining James Dean sites. When they arrived at the alley where several scenes of ***Rebel*** were filmed, the fence over which Jim Stark first calls to Judy had been taken down and was in a pile on the sidewalk, awaiting the garbage truck. The trousers and the fence are both on display at the Gallery.

Few items can be had for free, of course, and maintaining the Gallery has been an uphill battle. But Loehr's dedication is unwavering and the collection continues to grow. For a quarter of a century, he has been archiving, collecting and chronicling Dean's short life. David smiles at the thought that he's gone overboard. "I'm obsessed. I don't think there is anything wrong with it. I'm hoping to keep his memory going. It's a tribute."

Film & Video

James Dean was presented to the world on screen. As such, film and video form an integral part of most Dean collections. Since video did not exist in Dean's day, it can be assumed that there is a film master to any video item. Only in the case of recently produced documentaries and tributes is this sometimes not the case. Dean's three starring movie roles are generally easy to come by, available for rent or purchase at most video stores. Though a legal dispute between Warner Brothers and the estate of author John Steinbeck has made *East of Eden* hard to find in recent years, the film will surely be made available again when the case is settled.

Both of Dean's television commercials, the Pepsi spot that marked his first paid and first filmed performance and the traffic safety announcement done on the set of *Giant,* can still be found, each in several differently edited versions. *Sailor Beware* (Paramount, 1951), *Has Anybody Seen My Gal?* (Universal, 1952) and *Fixed Bayonets* (20th Century Fox, 1951), *Has Anybody Seen My Gal?* (Universal, 1952) and *Fixed Bayonets* (20th Century Fox, 1951), in which Jimmy had small parts, are unavailable commercially but still make the rounds of cable TV and late night movies. Most collectors will have little trouble turning up watchable copies.

While 17 of the 32 television plays that comprise the core of James Dean's acting experience are known to exist in some recorded form, the others have seemingly been lost to the ages. Television dramas from this early period in the 1950's were usually rehearsed for about a week in preparation for live performance before the cameras. The signals were broadcast, but not recorded. Every show was literally a one time only event. No repeats, no cuts, no corrections. Luckily for today's collector, some foresightful folks thought to aim a camera at their television screen and create recordings of the broadcasts.

The resulting kinescopes, as they are called, are often of low quality. It is in this form that most of Dean's early television work is preserved. To cut on expenses, the only shows that were filmed in studio were those intended in advance for syndication. In Dean's television résumé, only the two commercials and the roles in *Hill Number One, Trouble With Father, I'm a Fool,* and *The Unlighted Road* are recorded on first generation film. For that reason, the circulating tapes of these performances tend to be of much higher quality than those of his other shows. Several of the shows have been marketed commerically, others remain available only through trade with private collectors.

Dean's television appearances present a unique challenge to the collector because new material, though rare, continues to surface. In recent years, recordings of a previously unknown appearance in *The Evil Within* and a bit part in an episode of the popular series *Trouble With Father* have been discovered. With the current interest in television nostalgia and film preservation, it is likely that at least a few more Dean discoveries will be made amongst the inventories of the industry's many huge, uncataloged film vaults.

These early dramas, in which the young actor can be seen evolving and honing his craft are great, but there are other TV treasures to be collected as well. Although never one for gala events, brief shots of Dean at the televised opening of *A Star is Born* and in the audience at the 1954 Academy Awards have been uncovered by eagle-eyed fans. On March 10, 1955, Dean was featured in a live interview segment before the airing of an episode of Lux Video Theater. Another gem that may someday be discovered is footage of Dean on *Beat the Clock.* Occasionally his behind the scenes stunt testing job on that show was extended to include the performance of gags to warm up the live audience before the broadcast. As yet no recordings have surfaced, but you never know.

In high school, during his college years, at the Actors Studio, and both on and off Broadway, Dean appeared in at least twenty-two plays and staged readings. No recording of any of these performances is known to exist.

There is a limited amount of footage to be had of James Dean on film and video, but a collection can grow without limit if expanded to include items **about** the young actor. In 1956, Steve Allen and Ed Sullivan competed to be the first to bring a Dean special to their respective programs. Since then, there have been seemingly countless documentaries and Dean-inspired dramas produced. Robet Altman's *The James Dean Story* started the ball rolling in 1957. In the years since, more than a dozen full documentaries have been produced, along with hundreds of smaller pieces on news or entertainment shows. Dean biopics have had a rougher go of it, with most dying before making it to the filming stages. Of the few that have made it to the screen, none has really succeeded in capturing Dean's presence. Far more successful have been movies that play on the legacy without requiring Dean's presence on screen. Altman's *Come Back to the Five and Dime, Jimmy Dean, Jimmy Dean* and Kevin Reynold's *Fandango* are two of the best among these.

Film

At the time James Dean's films were being made in the 1950s, some of the biggest changes in the history of motion pictures were occurring. Changes not just in terms of what the audience saw on screen, as blacklisting terrorized, television threatened and Method acting flourished; not just behind the scenes, where the Hollywood studio system crumbled and actors became free agents; but physically, mechanically, in the ways movies were filmed and in the very film on which they were captured.

Competition from television inspired innovation in Hollywood. In the age of black and white TV broadcasts, color was one advantage on which movies increasingly relied. The three-color Technicolor process that had been introduced in Disney's 1932 animated short *Flowers and Trees* was gradually phased out in favor of much simpler chromogenic color processes. WarnerColor, in which Dean's three starring roles were produced, is a version of the chromogenic color dye system.

In addition to color, the motion picture industry of the 1950s experimented with various types of gimmickry to entice audiences back to theaters. These were the days of 3-D, Smell-O-Vision and many variations on widescreen formats. Among the latter was CinemaScope, which was used in the filming of *East of Eden* and *Rebel Without A Cause.* First used by 20th Century-Fox in 1953's *The Robe,* CinemaScope involves filming with a lens that compacts a wide image onto 35mm film. The film is then decompressed through another lens during playback. The resulting visual image can be as much as twice as wide as a normal movie picture.

The very film on which these processes were produced was also changing. Nitrate-based film stock, previously the norm, was largely phased out in favor of an acetate base. Unlike nitrate film, the acetate stock was non-flammable. It was also thought at the time to have a longer shelf life than nitrate, which had already deteriorated significantly in the case of many older films. With the increased use of color came the additional problem of rapid fading, with some films showing noticeable color loss in ten years or less. The instability of organic color dyes, like the decomposition of nitrate and acetate film stock, results from a chemical process. All film is subject to fading, which is impossible to stop entirely, but small changes in storage conditions can have huge effects on life expectancy. Warmth and humidity accelerate fading and decomposition, cool and dry conditions slow the reactions.

The problems that were becoming apparent to the film industry in the 1950s are the same ones confronting today's collector. Whether on acetate or nitrate stock, film deteriorates quickly. It is a far from permanent medium that requires much care to prolong its lifespan. If film must be handled, it should be held by the edges to avoid leaving oily deposits on picture and sound areas. Films should always be wound evenly, and never too tightly, always with the emulsion side out. Metal film storage cans or plastic boxes should be uniform in size, stored flat, and never stacked more than twelve inches high. Don't put paper or any other loose material in the container with a film. Decomposing films, which often give off a scent similar to vinegar, should be separated from each other and stored apart from healthier reels.

Video Tape

While relatively few collectors are likely to amass film libraries, virtually every collection will include video taped material. Video tapes are still a very new technology. With only a few decades of existence to base research on, the resulting information is considerably less concrete than that pertaining to film.

What is known for certain is that magnetic tape is organic and eventually decomposes. As with film, the life expectancy of a tape depends upon the rate of disintegration of its chemical components: the plastic base, polymer binders, back-coating materials and lubricants. If kept at a constant temperature around sixty degrees Fahrenheit and a relative humidity between 40 and 60 percent, tapes can average a life span of 15 years without significant degradation. Fluctuations in temperature will cause the base film to expand and contract, which expedites breakdown. Under normal household conditions, tapes will likely begin to show visible and audible wear after about ten years. Frequently viewed videos may not last that long.

To protect important tapes, make copies from a good master every three to five years. Although down a generation, copies provide protection against failure or loss of the original. Tapes that are seldom viewed should be wound once a year to prevent adhesion or print through between windings. When transported from a colder to a warmer environment, moisture can condense on the tape. Since a damp tape may sick to the recorder heads if placed in a VCR, tape should always be allowed to "warm up" before viewing.

A few simple precautions should be observed when storing videos. Keep tapes out of direct sunlight and away from magnetic fields. The mechanism inside a cassette is delicate, and rough handling can cause a malfunction. The tape itself should never be touched by bare fingers. Broken tapes should not be spliced and reused, since the splice can damage the VCR heads. Excessive use of functions like slow motion, freeze frame, and fast forward search will also accelerate tape wear.

Even more so than with other collectibles, the challenge of the film and video collector is one of preservation of a temporary resource. The recent emergence of DVD and other digital technologies may well be the long awaited "permanent" motion picture medium. Little of Dean's work has yet been made available in these new formats, but they will surely play host to the next round of Dean video collectibles.

Television Appearances

This list includes all currently known appearances, with the date of the original airing, the name of the series, and the name of the episode. An asterisk after the episode title indicates that copies of the show circulate in some recorded format.

DATE OF ORIGINAL AIRING	SERIES TITLE	EPISODE TITLE
December 13, 1950		Pepsi-Cola Commercial*
March 25, 1951	Family Theater	Hill Number One*
October 29, 1951	Bigelow Theater	T.K.O.
January 27, 1952	CBS Television Workshop	Into The Valley
February 1952	Trouble with Father	Jackie Knows It All*
February 20, 1952	The Web	Sleeping Dogs
March 3, 1952	Westinghouse Studio One	10,000 Horses Singing*
March 17, 1952	Lux Video Theater	The Foggy, Foggy Dew
May 21, 1952	Kraft Television Theater	Prologue to Glory
May 26, 1952	Westinghouse Studio One	Abraham Lincoln*
June 2, 1952	Hallmark Hall of Fame	The Forgotten Children
January 15, 1953	The Kate Smith Show	The Hound of Heaven
January 29, 1953	Treasury Men In Action	The Case of the Watchful Dog
February 8, 1953	You Are There	The Killing of Jesse James
April 14, 1953	Danger	No Room
April 16, 1953	Treasury Men in Action	The Case of the Sawed-Off Shotgun
May 1, 1953	Tales of Tomorrow	The Evil Within*
July 17, 1953	Campbell Soundstage	Something for a Empty Briefcase
August 17, 1953	Westinghouse Studio One	Sentence of Death*
August 25, 1953	Danger	Death Is My Neighbor
September 11, 1953	The Big Story	Rex Newman*
October 4, 1953	Omnibus	Glory in the Flower*
October 14, 1953	Kraft Television Theater	Keep Our Honor Bright*
October 16, 1953	Campbell Soundstage	Life Sentence*
November 17, 1953	Armstrong's Circle Theater	The Bells of Cockaigne*
November 23, 1953	The Johnson's Wax Program	Harvest*
March 30, 1954	Danger	The Little Woman
September 5, 1954	Philco TV Playhouse	Run Like a Thief
November 9, 1954	Danger	Padlock
November 14, 1954	General Electric Theater	I'm A Fool*
December 12, 1954	General Electric Theater	The Dark, Dark Hour
January 4, 1955	United States Steel Hour	The Thief*
May 6, 1955	Schlitz Playhouse of Stars	The Unlighted Road*
September 17, 1955		Highway Safety Commercial

East of Eden
Warner Home Video1005
color - 105 minutes
USA - 1982

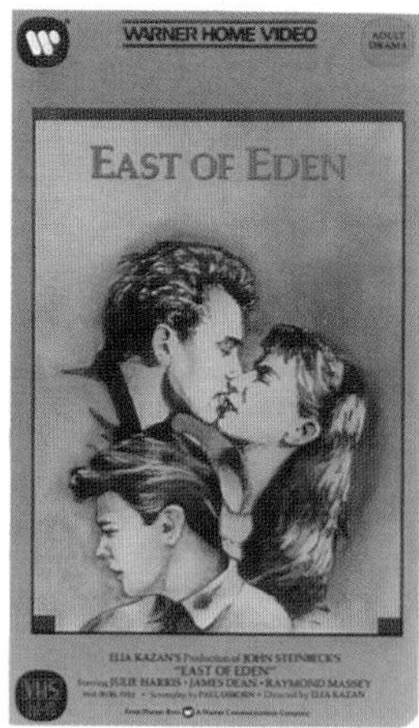

East of Eden
Warner Home Video 1005
color - 115 minutes
USA - 1985

East of Eden
Warner Home Video1005
color - 115 minutes
USA - 1987

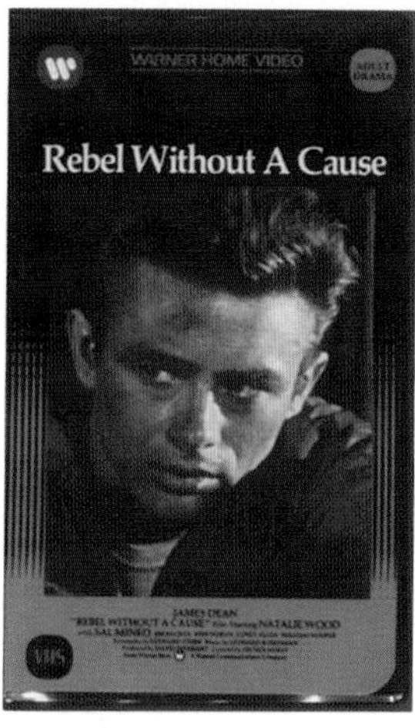

Rebel Without A Cause
Warner Home Video 1011
color - 105 minutes
USA - 1983

Rebel Without A Cause
Warner Home Video 1011
color - 111 minutes
USA - 1985

Rebel Without A Cause
Warner Home Video 1011
color - 111 minutes
USA - 1986

Rebel Without A Cause
Warner Home Video 14069
color & black/white - 150 min.
USA - 1996

Giant
Warner Home Video 11414
color - 201 minutes
USA - 1985

Giant
Warner Home Video 11414 A/B
color - 202 minutes
USA - 1987

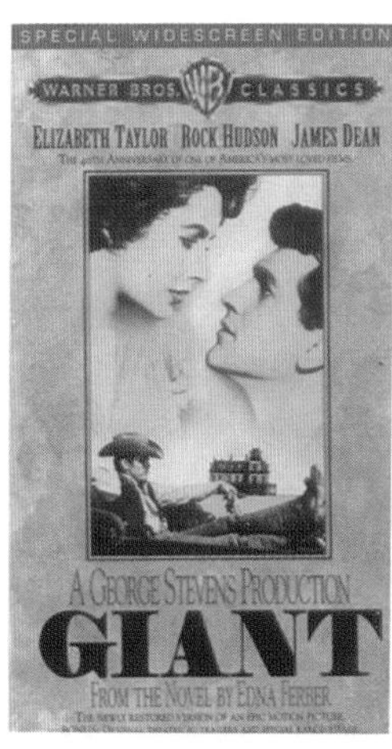

Giant
Warner Home Video

The James Dean Story
Pacific Arts Video Records #543
black & white - 80 min.
USA - 1983

James Dean Story
Celebrity Showcase #10001
black & white - 80 min.
USA - 1988

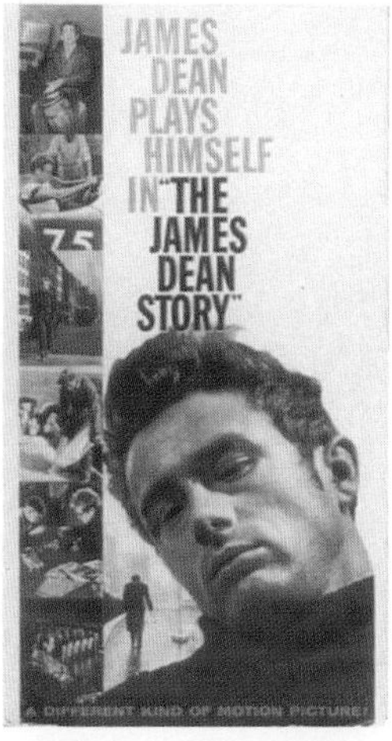

The James Dean Story
Goodtimes #9163
black & white - 79 min.
USA - 1990

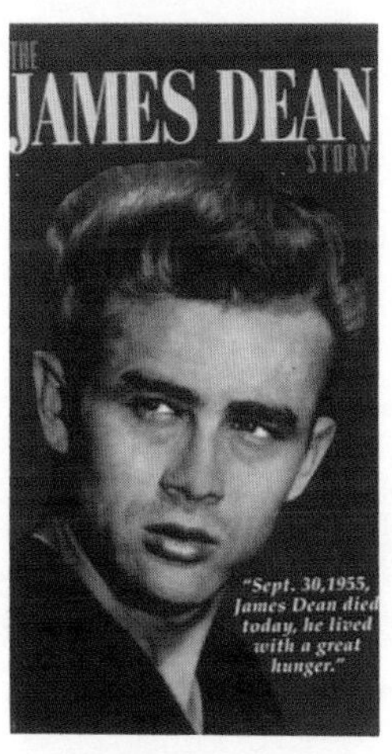

The James Dean Story
Front Row Ent. #5766
black & white - 80 min.
USA - 1996

The James Dean Story
Delta Entertainment #83017
USA - 1998

James Dean
The 1st American Teenager
Vid America #891
color & black/white - 83 min.
USA - 1982

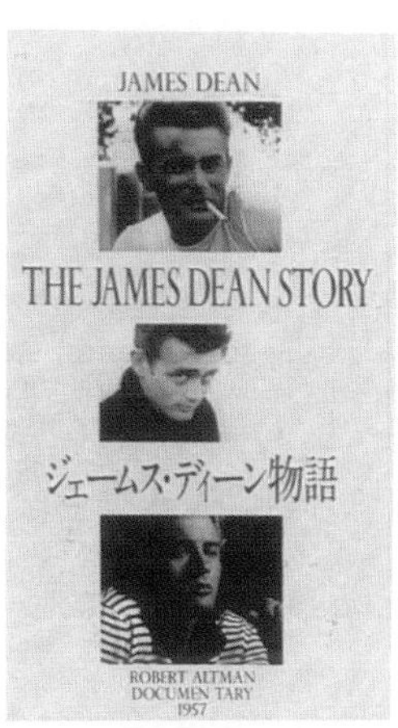

The James Dean Story
Japan

Idol The Story of James Dean
Labyrith Video LML 0247
color & black/white - 92 min.
United Kingdom - 1995

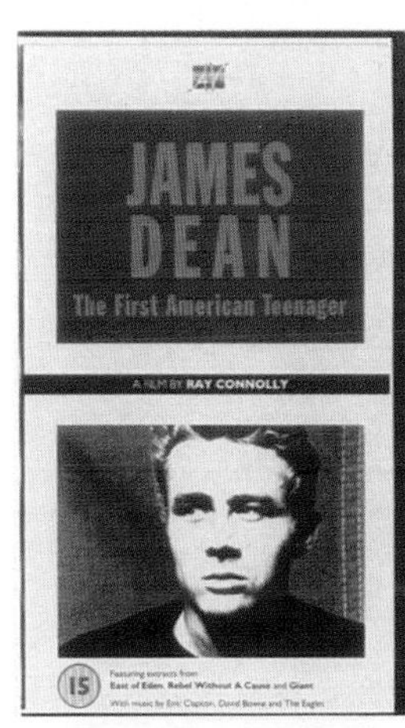

James Dean The First
American Teenager
Academy Video #CAV039
color & black/white - 75 min.
United Kingdom

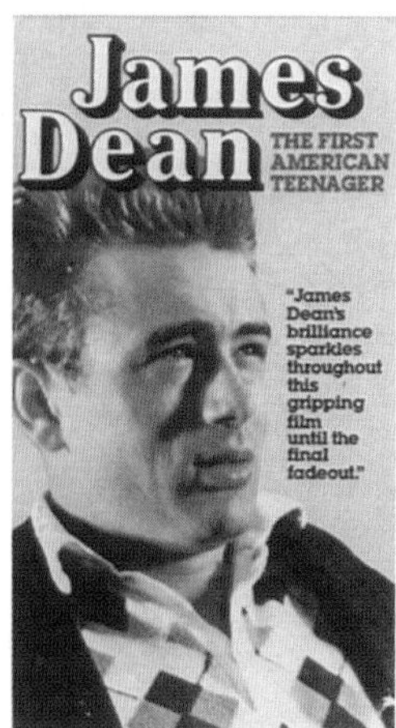

James Dean The First
American Teenager
Vid America #891
color & black/white - 83 min.
USA - 1985

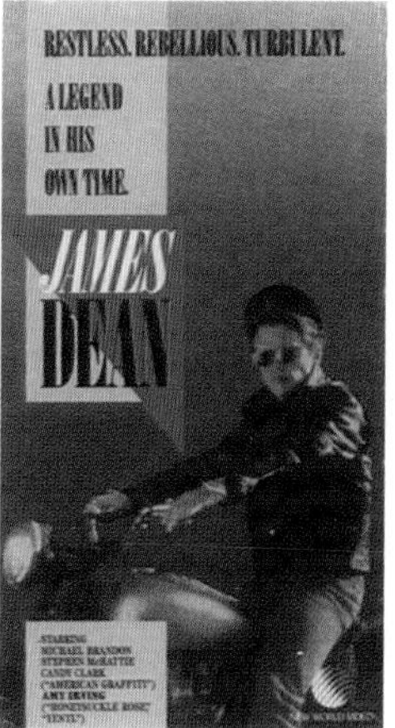

James Dean
New World Video #C95770
color - 99 minutes
USA - 1987

The Rebels: James Dean
Kartes Video Comm.
color - 90 minutes

James Dean: A Portrait
White Star #1766
color - 55 minutes
USA - 1995

James Dean And Me
Nineteenth Star
color & black/white - 48 min.
USA - 1996

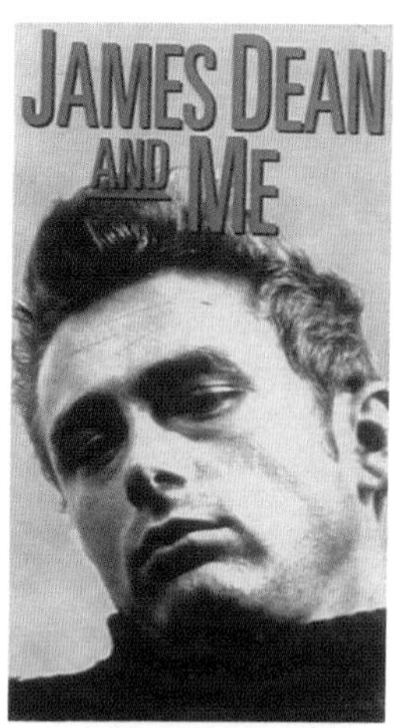

James Dean And Me
Kultur/White Star #1774
color - 50 minutes
USA - 1996

Forever James Dean
Warner Home Video #11816
color & black/white - 69 min.
USA - 1990

Hollywoods Leading Men
James Dean
Video Specials #066
color & black/white - 30 min.
USA - 1992

James Dean at High Speed
Kultur/White Star #1775
color - 50 minutes
USA - 1997

Hill Number One
Rhino Home Video #2010
black & white - 57 min.
USA - 1991

Hill Number One
Front Row Entertainment #5805
color - 57 minutes
USA - 1996

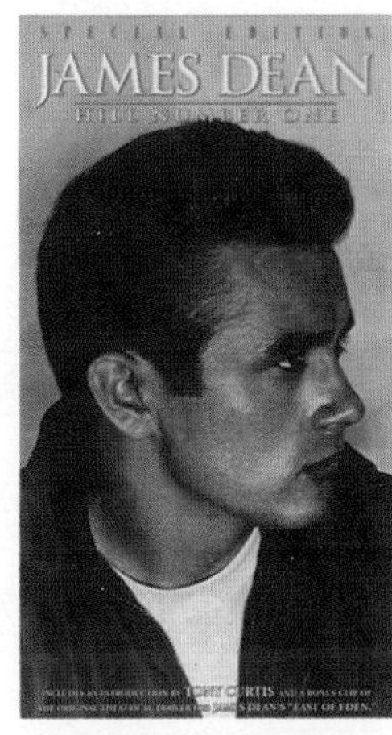

Hill Number One
Delta Entertainment #83 016
USA - 1998

The Bells of Cockaigne
Front Row Ent. #5767
black & white - 30 min.
USA - 1996

The Bells of Cockaigne
I'm A Fool
Delta Entertainment #83 018
USA - 1998

Harvest
Front Row Ent. #5668
black & white - 57 min.
USA - 1996

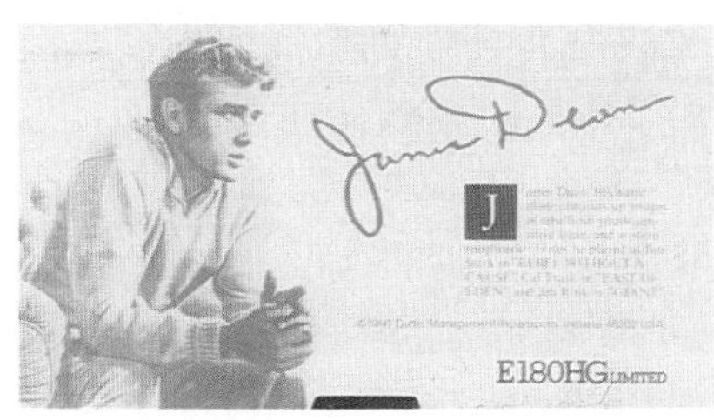

James Dean
Blank Video Tape #E180HG Limited
Japan - 1990

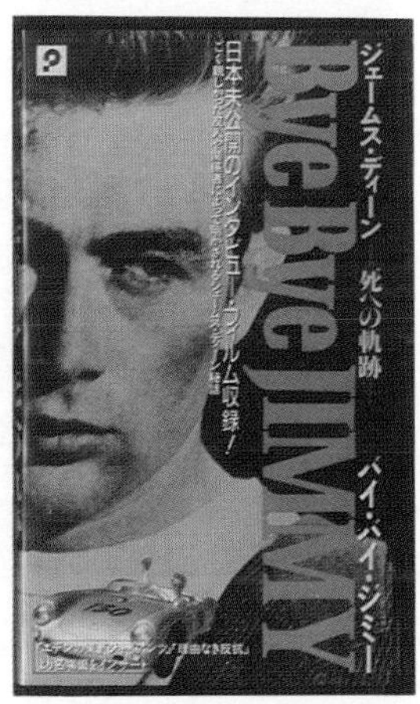

Bye Bye Jimmy
Japan - 1988

James Dean
Private File
Japan
Date unavailable

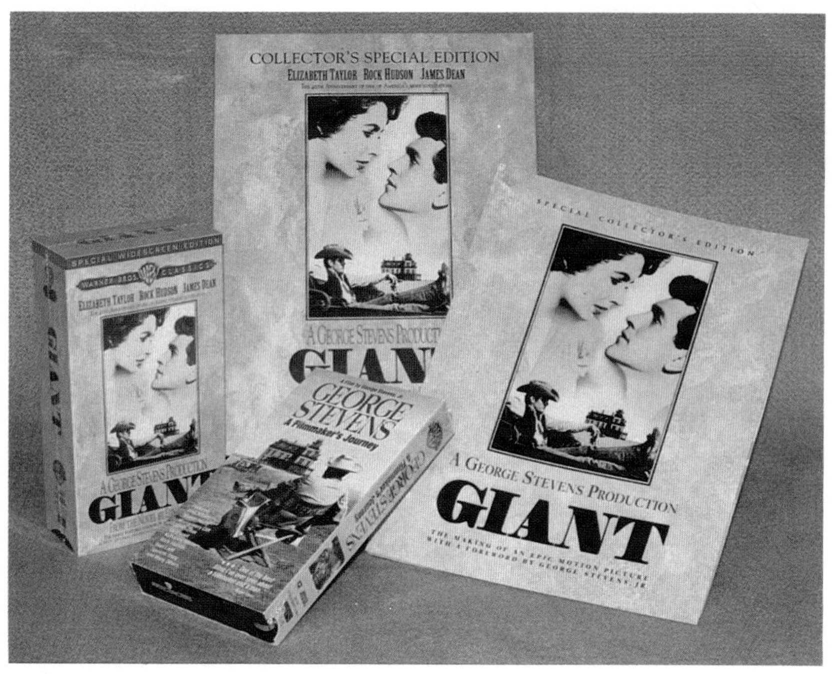

Collectors Special Edition
Warner Brothers #36135
80 Page Book and 3 Videos
USA - 1996

The Dean Legacy (4 Tape Set)
East of Eden, Rebel Without A Cause, Giant
Warner Brothers - USA - 1985

The recent revelation that Dean acted in the science fiction drama The Evil Within was an important addition to his list of credits. But the role also bears a unique distinction. Playing a scientist's lab assistant, Dean wears glasses throughout the show. With the exception of a few scenes of Rebel Without a Cause that were cut from the final film, The Evil Within represents the only acting role in which Dean, who was extremely nearsighted, could actually see what he was doing.

RUMOR:

Amongst Dean's screen credits was a bit part in the John Wayne vehicle Trouble Along The Way.

FACT:

At the time Trouble Along the Way was being filmed in Hollywood, Dean was in New York rehearsing for his Broadway debut in See The Jaguar. He was not in the film and never worked with John Wayne. Shortly before his death, however, Dean did meet with representatives of Wayne's production company to discuss the possibility of doing a film version of Barnaby Conrad's novel Matador.

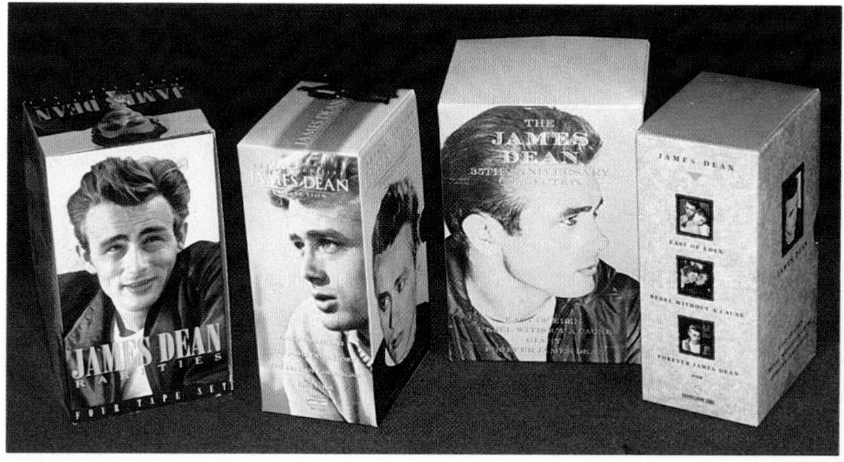

Left to Right:

1. James Dean Rarities, Front Row Entertainment #4043, USA - 1996
2. James Dean Collection (3 Tape Set), Delta Ent. Inc. #89-006, USA - 1998
3. 35th Anniversary Collection (4 Tape Set), Warner Bros. #35326, USA - 1990
4. James Dean (3 Tape Set), Warner Bros. #12534, USA - 1992

Forever James Dean - (DVD)
#CD-1-065
Japan

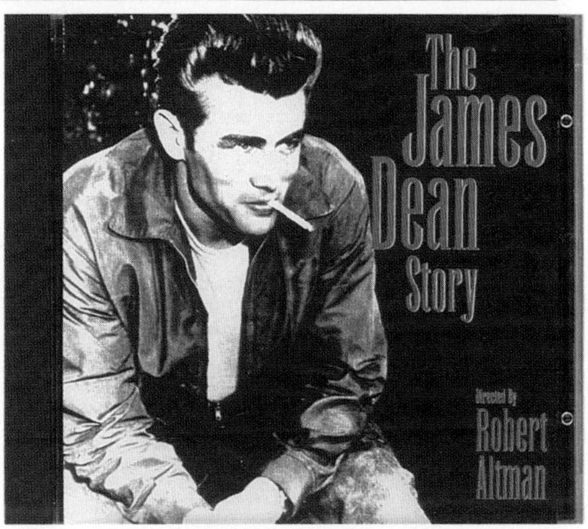

The James Dean Story - (DVD)
Valkerie Mktg. - USA - 1995

James Dean (DVD)
by Dennis Stock
Japan - 1996

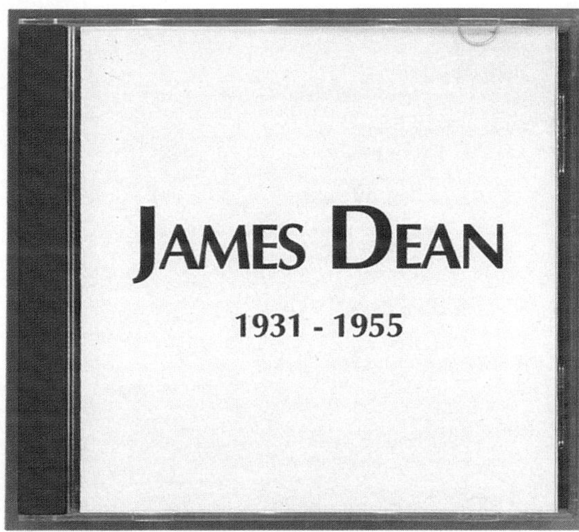

James Dean - (DVD)
Motion Picture & Television Archive
USA - 1995

East of Eden (Video Disc)
Warrner Home Video #03124
USA - 1983

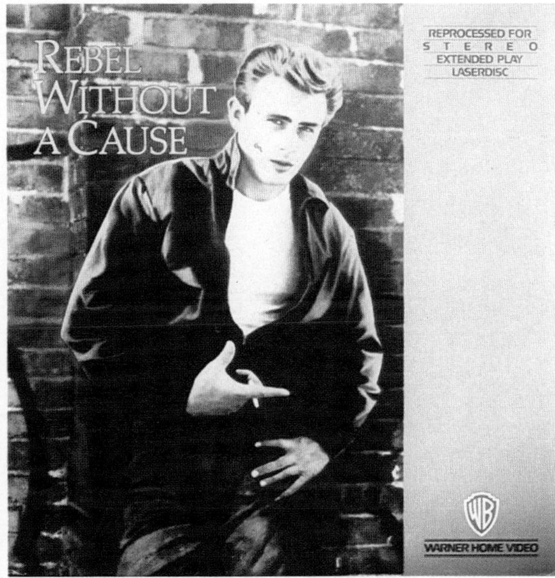

Rebel Without A Cause - (Laser Disc)
Warner Home Video #1011
USA - 1983

Giant - (Laser Disc)
Warner Home Video #NJEL 11414
Japan - 1984

> *"Those of us who worked with Jimmy Dean carry an image of his intense struggle for a goal behind himself."*
> *- - Ronald Reagan*

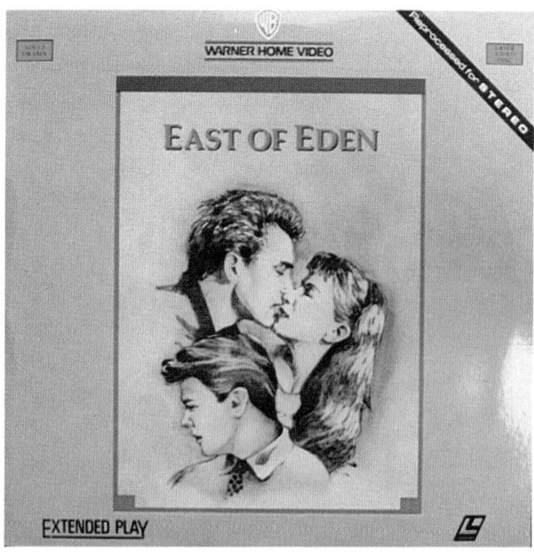

Laserdisc
East of Eden
Warner Home Video
USA - 1985

> *"Maybe publicity is important. But I just can't make it, can't get with it. I've been told by a lot of guys the way it works. The newspapers give you a big build-up. Something happens, they tear you down. Who needs it? What counts to the artist is performance, not publicity."*

Laserdisc
East of Eden
Warner Home Video
USA - 1993

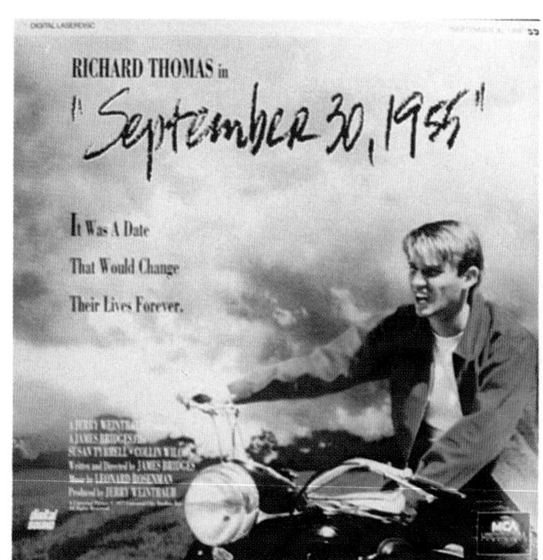

Laserdisc
September 30, 1955
MCA/Universal
USA - 1992

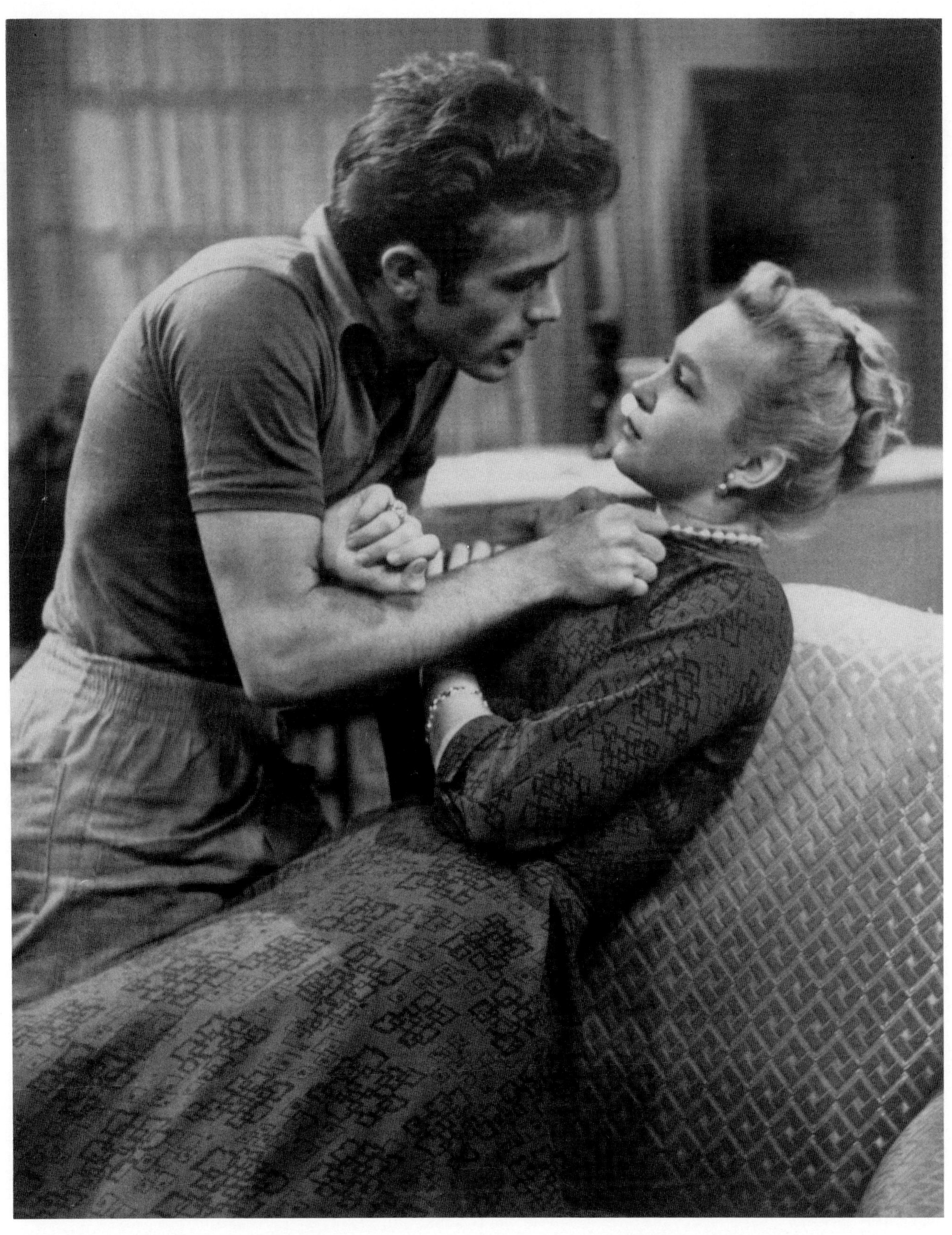

Scene from "Life Sentence" with Georgiann Johnson.
October 16, 1953 - Campbell Sound Stage - NBC

Music & The Recorded Word

One of the most interesting aspects of Dean's legacy has been his impact on music, particularly on rock and roll. Rock was still in its formative stages when Dean died, but he is credited, in source after source, as one of the most important influences on the style's development.

Rock was not Dean's music of choice. Asked by a journalist about his taste in records, Dean responded, "I collect everything from twelfth and thirteenth century music to the extreme moderns - you know, Schönberg, Berg, Stravinsky. I also like Sinatra's *Songs For Young Lovers* album." James Dean may have heard and enjoyed early rock, but his contribution to its evolution was conceptual rather than musical. The attitude and style that Dean embodied both on screen and in real life were widely emulated by musicians. Elvis Presley and Bob Dylan, two of the most influential performers of all time, both patterned themselves after their idol, James Dean.

Popular muscial allusions to Dean are far too numerous to list, but he has featured prominently in songs by everyone from Tommy Sands to Lou Reed, from Mott the Hoople to the Eagles, from Red River Dave to the Atomics. Don McLean. Larry John McNally. David Essex. John Mellencamp . . . .

Dean himself was not without musical talent. He could often be found practicing on bongo drums or his recorder and occasionally jammed with other musicians. One such tape recorded session was marketed after Dean's death by Romeo Records. The recording is murky and the music is not very good, but it is surely Dean, in his only commercially available musical offering.

According to author David Dalton in his extraordinary 1974 biography *James Dean: The Mutant King* (who in turn was quoting Howard Smith of *The Village Voice),* Dean does actually hve a song to his credit. Robert Bowden, an established rock composter of the period, claims to have corrusponded with Dean starting in 1954. Dean sent him a sheet of lyrics for which Bowden composed a tune. The result was a song entitled 'Will You Miss Me Tonight.' The song, which has never been released, is listed with BMI under only Bowden's name, although he claims Dean is acknowledged on the copyright in Washington and that Dean's estate will receive half of the royalties from the song, if ever there are any.

Amoung non-musical audio items, one of the hardest to find is an interview recorded on the set of *Rebel Without A Cause* that was included in the September 1957 issue of *Hear Hollywood* magazine on a 45 rpm cardboard insert. Included on the same disc is an interview with Tony Perkins. The magazine itself is fairly common, but significantly rarer with the record intact.

Dean was enamoured of the technology of tape recording, and he used a recorder both for recreation and to help him memorize his acting roles. The most famous of the informal recordings is the one Dean made with members of his family during his final trip home in 1955. Jimmy used a watch containing a hidden microphone to capture a conversation at the kitchen table. Discussing his great-grandfather, an auctioneer, Dean coaxes his grandfather into giving a sample of the auctioneer's banter. Jimmy briefly follows suit but breaks out laughing. Another great recording made later that year captures Jimmy on the set of *Giant,* laughing and yodeling and belting out a very off-key rendition of "Cattle Call." The few known recordings of Jimmy in casual moments are mostly in the hands of private collectors and rarely circulate. Offering rare glimpses into the actor's life, they are all but priceless to those who own them. Sadly, many tapes were supposedly burgled from Dean's Sherman Oaks, California home in the hours following his death and have never resurfaced.

Surprising in their complete absence from the category of Dean audio collectibles are the various radio shows in which he took part. Jimmy made his first radio appearance on February 13, 1949, during his senior year in high school, participating with classmate Barbara Leach in a debate against students from nearby Marion High. Leach and Dean argued that the President of the United States should be elected by a direct voit of the people. Their opponents spoke in support of the continued use of the Electoral College. At the debate's end, the Fairmount duo was declared the victors.

The next year, while enrolled at Santa Monica City College, Dean was a regular annuouncer on the college station. There is no record of any radio work at UCLA, but by 1951 Dean had befriended Rogers Brackett, an advertising executive and radio producer who used his influence to get the actor small parts on several of the shows with which he was affiliated. *Alias Jane Doe* is the program on which Dean appeared most often, with documented parts on July 28, August 11, September 15 and September 22 of 1951. During late 1951 and early 1952, it is also likely that Dean played roles on *Hallmark Playhouse, Stars Over Hollywood,* and *The Theatre Guild on the Air.* According to Donald Spoto's biography of Dean, the young actor performed in a live radio commercial for Toni home permanent sometime in 1951. While some of these performances can be verified through pay stubs and other documentation, no scripts or tapes of Dean's shows have yet been found.

Care of Records, Tapes, CDs

Cleaning and storage of recorded material is very straightforward. Like any plastic items, audio media should be kept out of direct sunlight and away from heat. Records should be stored in cardboard sleeves with paper liners and shelved in an upright position. The surface of the disc should be touched as little as possible. A soft cloth applied in a circular motion is generally maintenance enough for records. Audio cassettes are subject to all the same problems as video cassettes and should be kept in plastic cases when not in use. As with video, avoid touching the tape itself. Cassettes that are not frequently listened to should be wound occasionally to prevent adhesion and transference between windings. Compact discs are a sturdier medium, but still delicate. Because indentations in the blank side of the disc are read by lasers in the player, handle CDs by the edges and labeled side and store them in cases or sleeves when they are not in use. To clean a compact disc, run it under warm tap water. Using mild dish soap and a soft cloth, wipe the disc outward from the center rather than in a circular motion. Finish by rinsing well and drying completely with a clean cloth.

Sheet Music

The challenge of collecting Dean sheet music is that there simply isn't much of it. Although some of the tribute songs have been made available in this form, it is generally the music associated with the films that is of primary interest.

There is sheet music available for *Sailor Beware* and *Has Anybody Seen My Gal,* but there are no references or allusions to Dean. Music for *Fixed Bayonets* was never issued.

Dean went unmentioned on the sheet music for *East of Eden,* but was featured prominently in the releases for his final two films, as well as that for *The James Dean Story.* Two songs were published in 1956: "The Ballad of James Dean" by Jack Hammer and "A Boy Named Jimmy Dean" by Stanley Clayton, Ruth Roberts and Bill Katz. More recent additions to the field have included Allan Joy's "James Dean Still Lives East of Eden" and a full orchestral version of "As Summer Was Only Beginning" by Larry Daehn.

WHAT IF . . . .

It is a little known fact that Dean auditioned unsuccessfully for the part of Curly in the movie adaptation of the stage musical Oklahoma!

Romeo Records Magazine Ad in August 1957
with free charcoal sketch
available as a 45 rpm and a 78 rpm record

Giant
Boxed set of 4 - 45 rpm
Capitol EDM 773
USA - 1956

The James Dean Story
Boxed Set of 4 - 45 rpm
Capitol EDM881
USA - 1957

Mantovani Conducts Let Me Be Loved (Main theme from The James Dean Story) - 45 rpm
London 45 - 1761
USA - 1957

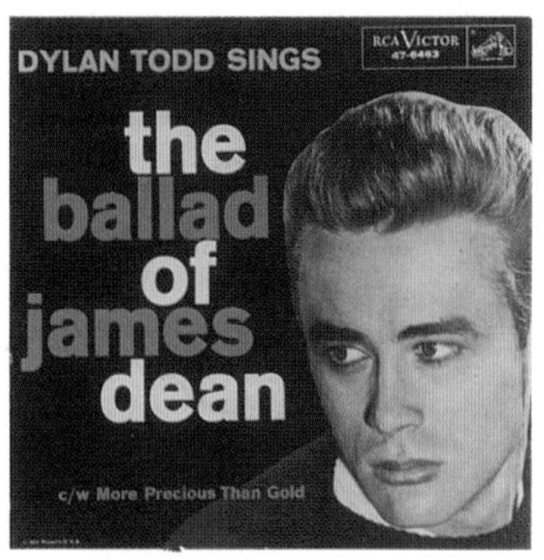

Dylan Todd Sings
The Ballad of James Dean
RCA Victor 47-6463
USA - 1956

A Tribute to James Dean
Theme Music From East of Eden &
Rebel Without A Cause
Ray Heindorf and the WB Orchestra
Columbia 4-40754
USA - 1956

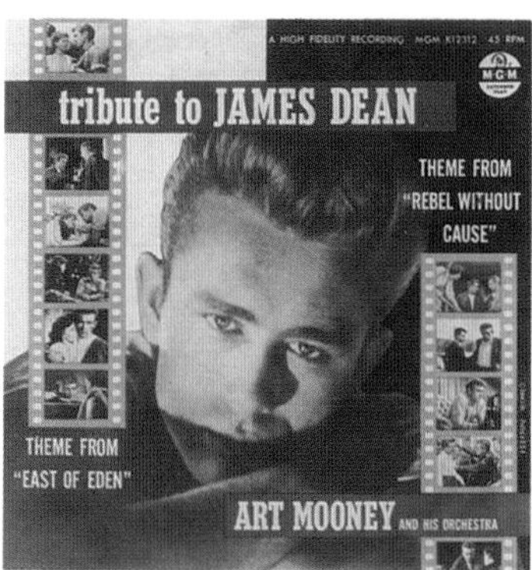

Tribute to James Dean
Theme Music From East of Eden
& Rebel Without A Cause
Art Mooney and His Orchestra
MGM K12312
USA - 1956

Red River Dave
James Dean Deck of Cards
Jimmy Dean is Not Dead
Hymn for James Dean
Home In Indiana
TNT Records - 45 rmp
USA - 1956

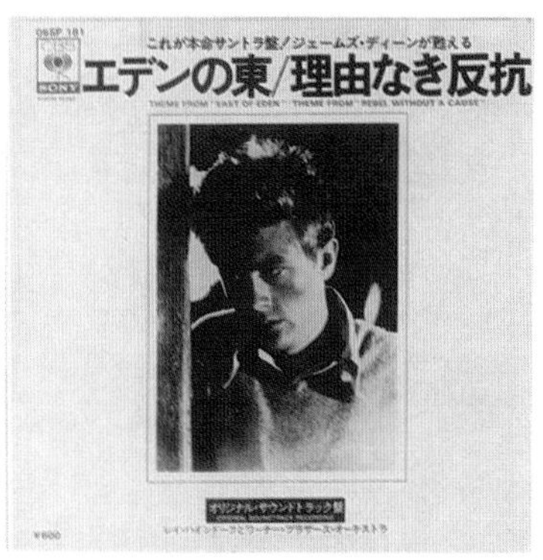

Theme From East of Eden &
Rebel Without A Cause
Ray Heindorf & The Warner
Bros. Orchestra CBS Sony - 06sP 181
- 45 rpm - Japan - 1977

Movie Parade Vol. 7
Giant and others
Decca DEP-132 - 45 rpm
Japan - 1966

Free Tear-Out Cardboard Record
from Hear Hollywood Magazine -
September 1957
Rainbow Records, Lawndale, CA

Themes from East of Eden &
Rebel Without A Cause
Ray Heindorf & The WB Orchestra
CBS/Sony #06SP 399 - Japan - 45 rpm

Only After Dark
Ghosts of Romance
Disclexia Records #DXL 001
45 rpm - England - 1982

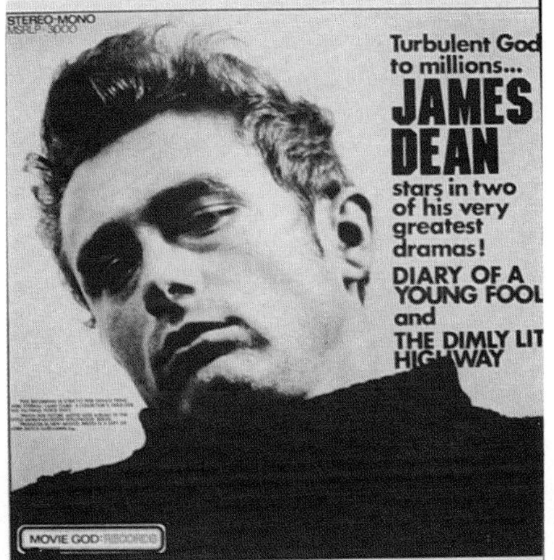

Turbulent God toMillions . . . James Dean
Dialog from 2 TV Dramas
Movie God Records #MSRLP-3000
33⅓ rpm - USA - 1976

James 1955 (Picture Disc)
Gary Hardier
Condor Classix Records #8807
Number Edition - 45 rpm
USA - 1986

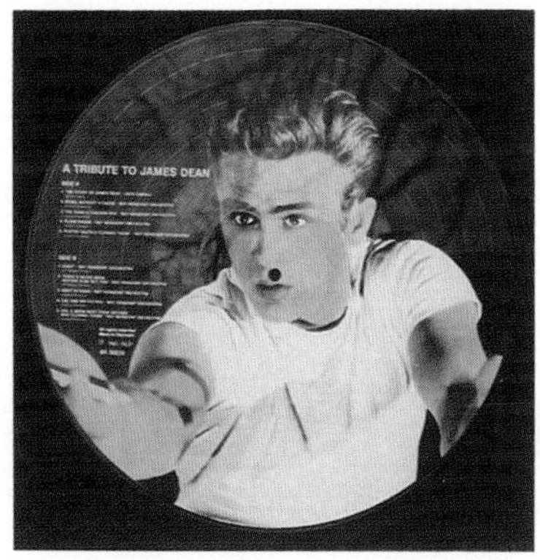

Tribute to James Dean
(Picture Disc) #AR30039
33⅓ rpm - Denmark - 1985

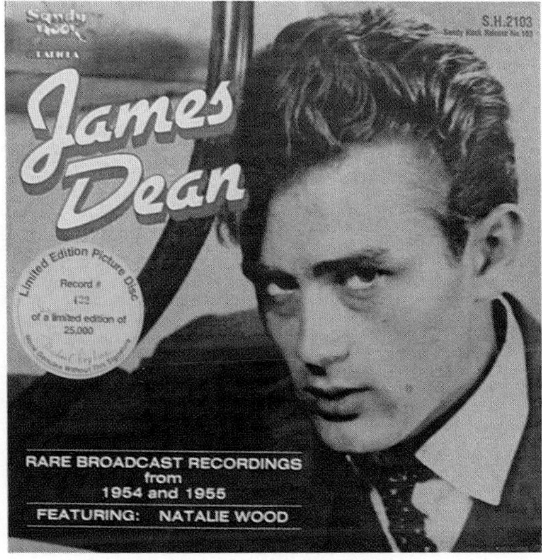

Cover of the Picture Disk
pictured at the right

James Dean On The Air
(Picture Disc)
Sandy Hook Records - SH2103
Limited Edition of 25,000
33⅓ rpm - USA - 1984

The Best Loved Screen Music
Readers Digest #R620025
Apollon Music - 33⅓ rpm
Japan - 1980

The James Dean Story
Coral Records #CRL 57099
331/3 rpm - USA

Music James Dean Lived By
Unique Records LP-109
331/3 rpm - USA - 1957

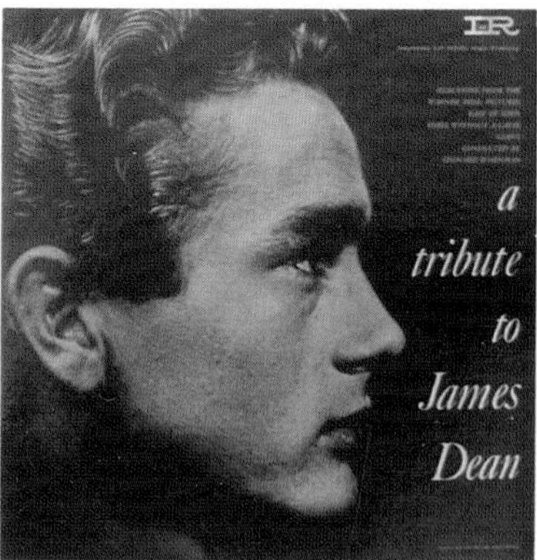

A Tribute to James Dean
Imperial Records #9021
331/3 rpm - USA

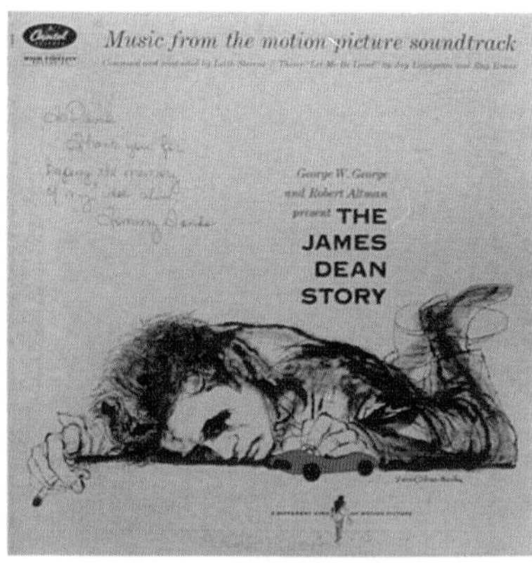

The James Dean Story
Capitol Records W881
331/3 rpm - USA - 1957

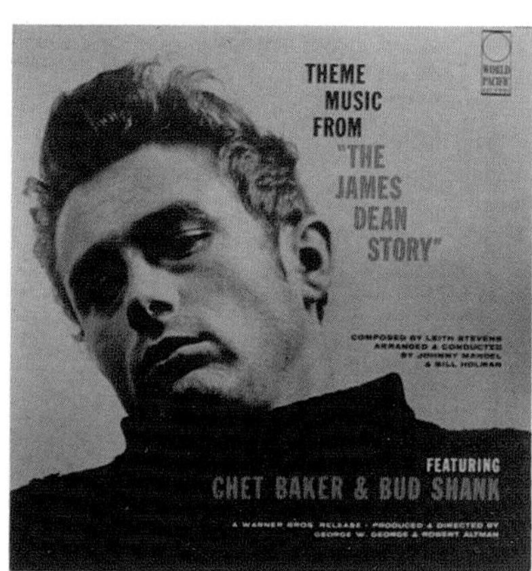

Theme Music from The James Dean
Story - World Pacific Records #P-2005
331/3 rpm - USA - 1957

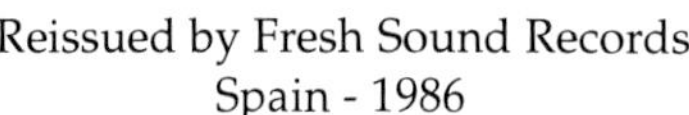

Reissued by Fresh Sound Records
Spain - 1986

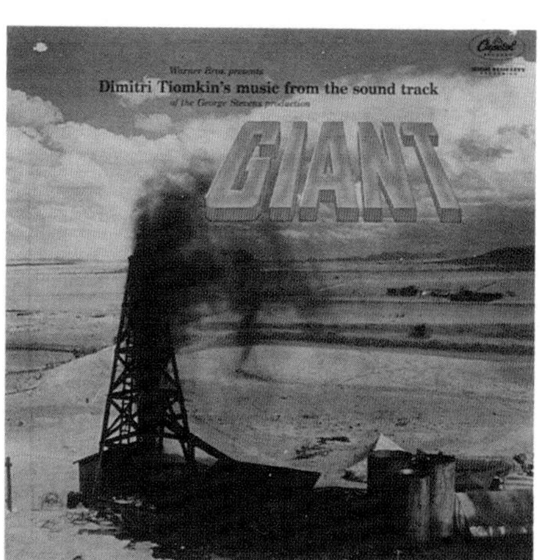

Giant Soundtrack
Capitol Records W773
331/3 rpm - USA - 1956

A Tribute To James Dean
Music From Giant
Columbia CL 940
331/3 rpm - USA - 1957

James Dean
Sony #25AP 738
Came with a 16 page album size
booklet inside - 331/3 rpm
Paper Sleeve - Japan - 1977

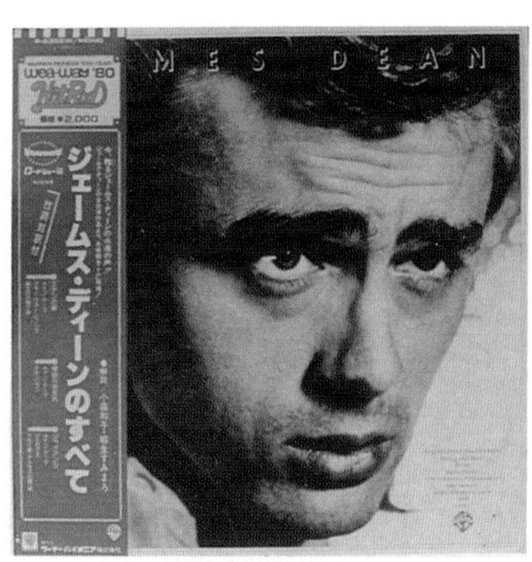

James Dean
Dialog & Music from his films
Warner Bros. BS2843
331/3 rpm - USA - 1975
Paper Sleeve - Japan

Records

James Dean "He Never Said Good-By"
Rod Wimmer
Caprice Records CALP-1006
331/3 rpm - USA - 1980

He's A Rebel Genie
Botts Records #9/12 - 12" Single
45 rpm - England

The Wonderful World of the Movies
Seven Seas Records #GXC 6009 10
331/3 rpm - Japan - 1976

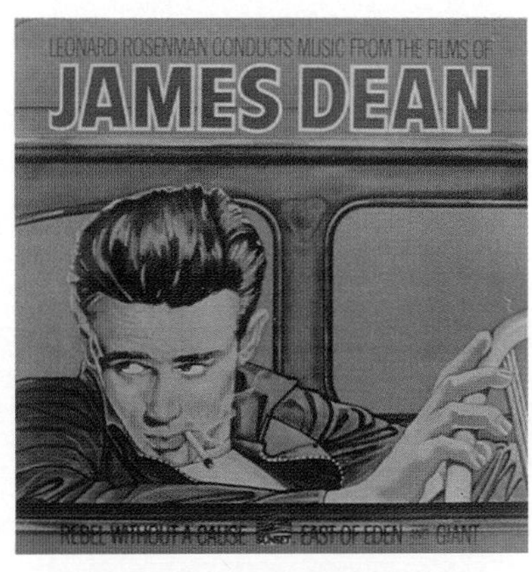

Leonard Rosenman Conducts Music
From The Films of James Dean
Sunset Records #SLS 50420
331/3 rpm - England - 1978

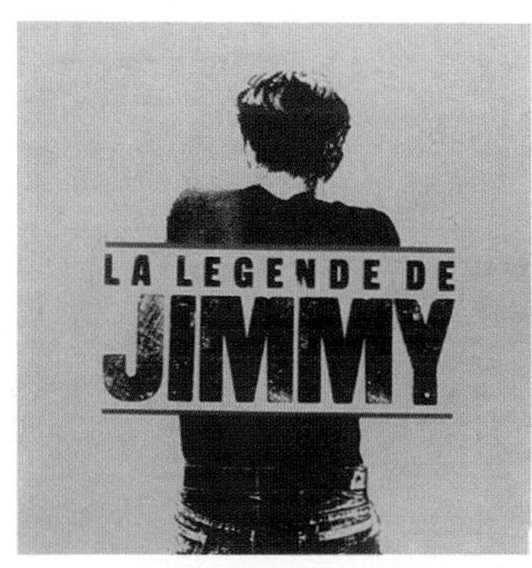

La Legende De Jimmy
Michel Berger & Luc Plamonden
331/3 rpm - France - 1990

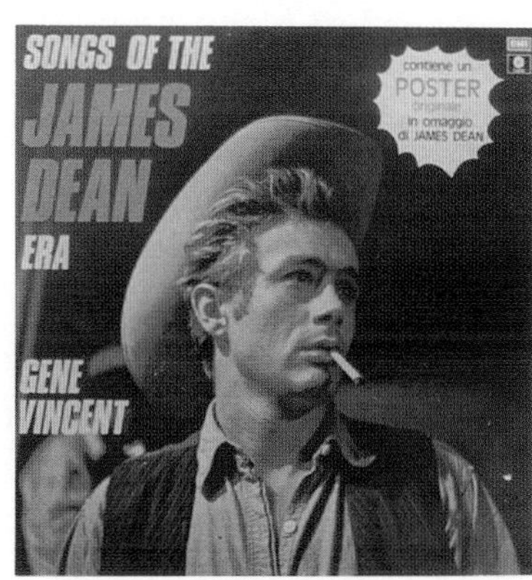

Songs of the James Dean Era
Gene Vincent
Capitol Records #3C 054 82021
(came with a large fold out poster)
331/3 rpm - Italy - 1975

Sound Track from 9/30/55
MCA Records #2313
331/3 rpm - USA - 1977

The Smiths
Big Mouth Strikes Again
Rough Trade Records RTT192
Available as a 7" & 12" single
45 rpm - England - 45 rpm

The Smiths
The Bad Boy From A Good Family
B & W Records #72388
331/3 rpm - Canada

A Tribute To James Dean
Sony #SRCS 7079
Japan - 1992

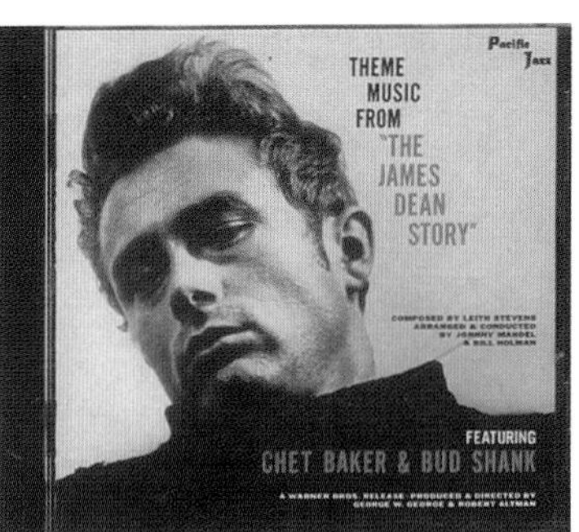

Theme Music From
The James Dean Story featuring
Chet Baker & Bud Shank
Pacific JA22 #WP-2005
Japan - 1990

Giant
Dimitri Tiomkin's
music from the sound track
Capitol #CDP 92056 2
USA - 1989

Giant Soundtrack
Tsunami #TSU-0106
Germany

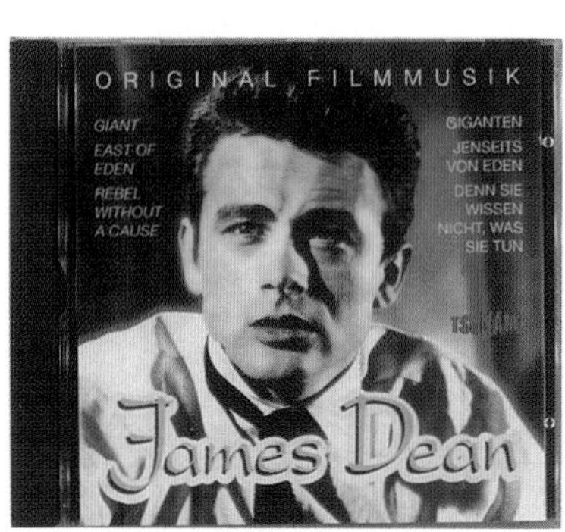

James Dean Original Filmmusik
Tsunami #TSU-0201
Germany

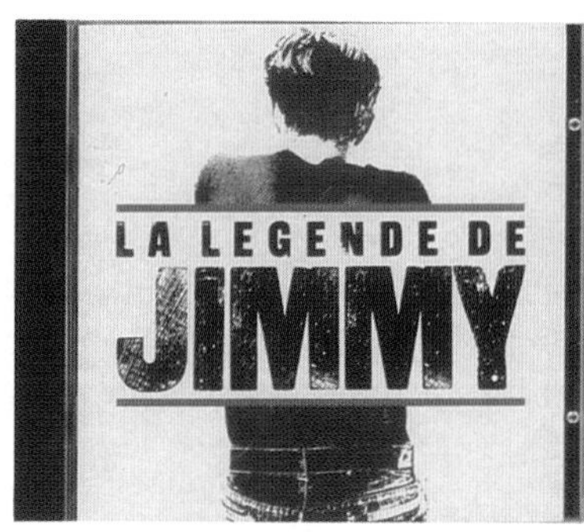

La Legende De Jimmy
Apache Disques #9031-73040-2
Germany - 1990

East of Eden
Soundtrack Recordings #535
USA - 1998

Leonard Rosenman
East of Eden & Rebel Without A Cause
Film Scores
Nonesuch #79402-2
USA - 1997

Rebel Music From
The Films of James Dean
Cinerama #MC:CIN 2206-4
Germany - 1993

James Dean Tribute to a Rebel
Compose #9923-2
USA - 1991

Cardboard CD Long Box

James Dean
Tribute to a Rebel
Compose 9923-4
USA - 1991

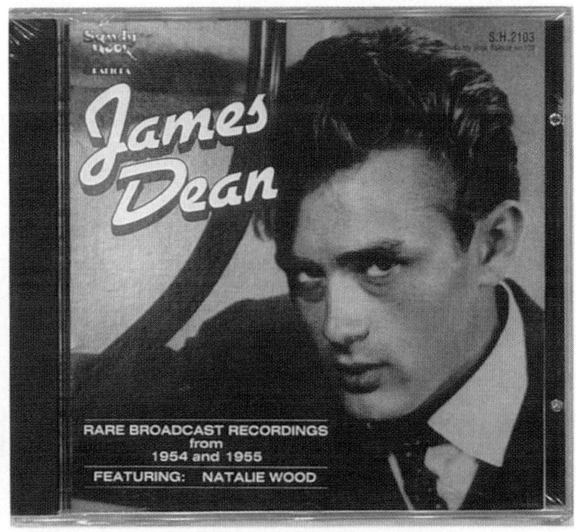

James Dean
Dialog from 2 TV Dramas
Sandy Hook Records #SH-403 - USA

James Dean on the Air!
Rare Broadcast Recordings
Sandy Hook Records - CSH-2103
USA - 1984

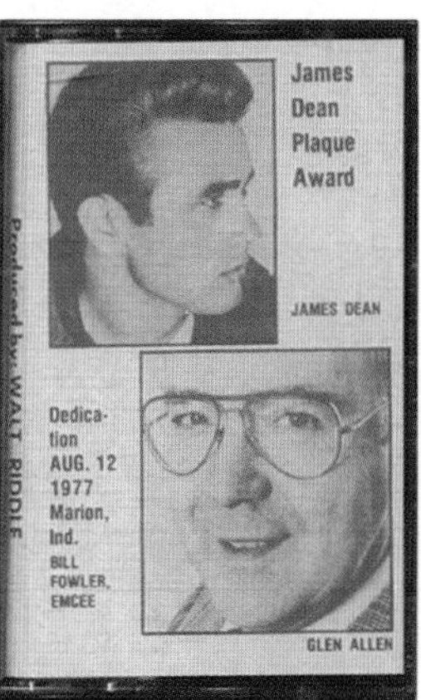

James Dean Plaque
Dedication
Marion, Indiana
1977

Billy Swan - I Used To Be James Dean
706 Records - USA - 1998

Efforts to avoid copyright and trademark infringement sometimes have humorous results. Among the most amusing items of Dean-related audio is a disc put out by Movie God Records in 1976. The album cover, which consists of a sheet of paper glued to a blank cardboard record sleeve, promises audio of Dean in two of his best television roles, "The Dimly Lit Highway" and "Diary of a Young Fool," and states that "This recording is strictly for Dean's-Teens and Eternal-Lamp clubs. A collector's issue for his faithful flock only." The producers were obviously depending on the fact that Dean's "faithful flock" would recognize their disguised offereings as The Unlighted Road and I Am a Fool. The same shows were released under their true titles by Sandy Hook Records a few years later.

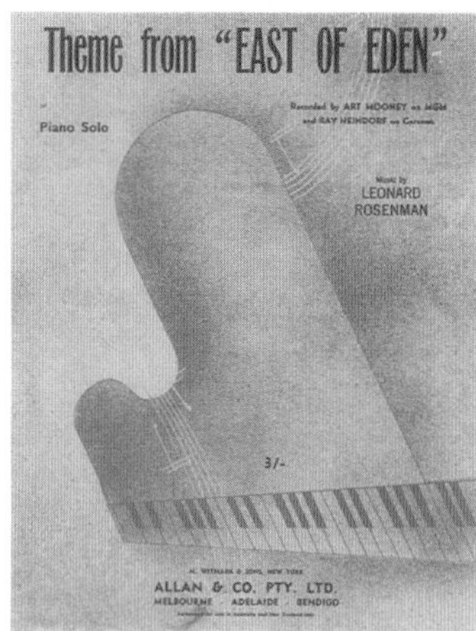

Theme from East of Eden
Allan & Co. Pty. Ltd.
Australia - 1955

Secret Doorway
M. Witmark & Sons
USA - 1955

There's Never Been
Anyone Else But You
M. Witmark & Sons
USA - 1956

Giant (This Then Is Texas)
M. Witmark & Sons
USA - 1956

Jett Rink Ballad
(The James Dean Theme)
Allan & Co. Pty. Ltd.
Australia - 1956

The Yellow Rose of Texas
Planetary Music Publishing Co.
USA - 1955

Let Me Be Loved
Livingston & Evans Music Company
USA - 1957

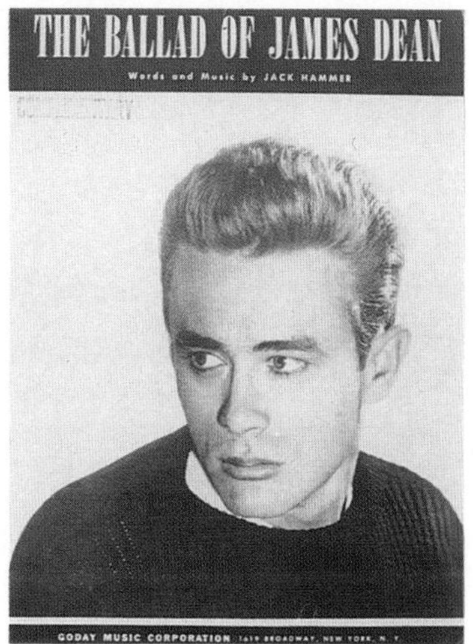

The Ballad of James Dean
Goday Music Corporation
USA - 1956

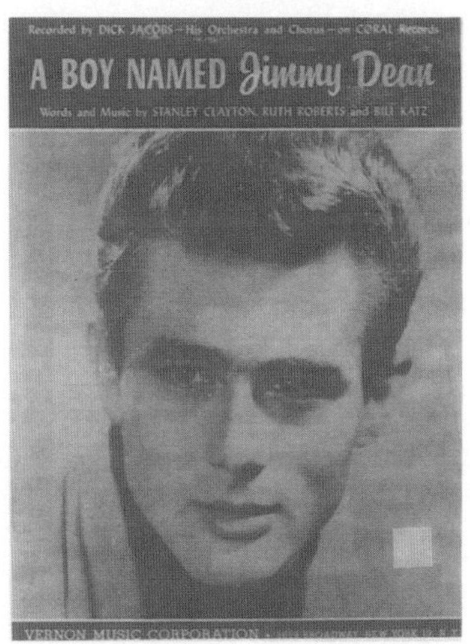

A Boy Named Jimmy Dean
Vernon Music Corp.
USA - 1956

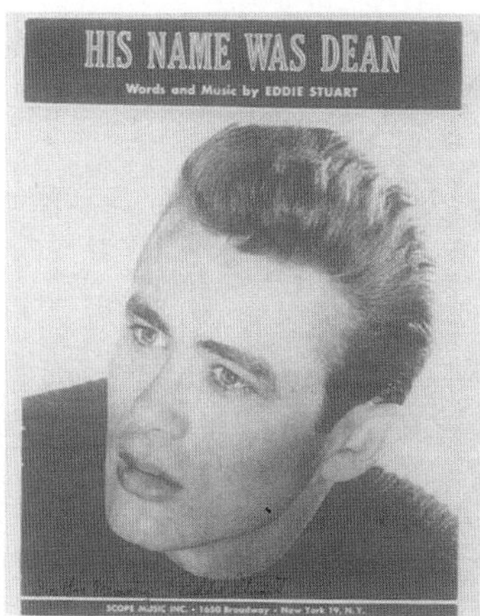

His Name Was Dean
Scope Music
USA - 1956

James Dean Still Lives
East of Eden
by Allen Joy
USA - 1982

As Summer Was Just Beginning
Daehn Publications
USA - 1998

Novelties

James Dean novelty items encompass the extremes of style and taste. For almost fifty years, Dean's likeness has been transferred, screened, printed, painted, pasted or otherwise affixed to all manner of items. Were he to return today, Dean would surely be amused by the miscellaneous forms of this material adoration. How would he react to the hundreds of stamps, postcards, trading cards, shirts, socks, pens, rulers, buttons and medallions? Would James Dean himself use a James Dean bookmark?

He might. Throughout his brief career, Dean stated openly that his aim was immortality. If this was the bravado of a confident, hopeful, yet insecure young actor, it was also his way of saying that he wanted to be good enough to be remembered. While Jimmy would undoubtedly get a good laugh out of some of the items that have borne his image, at the same time he'd be thrilled by the appreciation inherent in them.

Stamps

Of all the honors that can be bestowed upon a person, appearing on a stamp is among the greatest. Montserrat, a tiny island nation in the British West Indies, issued a set of nine legal tender James Dean commemoratives in a limited edition of a few thousand early in 1996. The stamps sold out almost instantly. In the years before and since, Dean has been featured on both legal tender and purely commemorative stamps by organizations and countries around the world.

The United States Postal Service released a legal tender commemorative James Dean stamp later that same year. Featuring artwork by Michael Deas based on a photograph from Roy Schatt's "Torn Sweater" series, the Dean stamp was the second in the USPS's "Legends of Hollywood" series that started with a Marilyn Monroe release the previous year.

Of 40 billion stamps minted annually by the Postal Service, the vast majority are definitives - stamps intended solely for use as postage. Definitives usually feature standard designs like flags or historical landmarks and are reprinted whenever need be, often in multiple runs spanning several years. Commemoratives, although functional as legal postage tender, are targeted at collectors and printed only once. Of the nearly 400 million James Dean stamps produced, the USPS estimates that 31 million were sold but not used, making it the most collected single issue of the year.

While some philatelists focus on unused specimens, others prefer stamps marked with a first day cancel. The Dean stamp set a precedent that is likely to be widely emulated by future "event" stamps: the use of an extended first day ceremony. The primary release took place at Warner Brothers Studios in Burbank, California, but more than one hundred Warner Brothers retail outlets each had their own cancel as well. Second day ceremonies followed in Dean's hometown of Fairmount, Indiana. With such variety, simply collecting the cancels presents a sizeable challenge.

Cards

Long before he graced a stamp with which to mail them, thousands of postcards bearing Dean photos or artwork had been sent to and from destinations all over the globe. Picture postcards originated in Europe in the late 1870s and first appeared in America in 1893. Card sizes, typically "standard" (3.5 x 5.5 inches) and "continental" (4 x 6 inches), have changed little over the years, although odd cards will vary in shape. By the 1950s when the first Dean cards were produced, printers had adopted the photochrome technology that remains the industry standard. While earlier cards may interest deltiologists for technical or manufacturing reasons, those from the modern era are collectible only for their subject matter. Dean issues, therefore, belong to the least valuable category of postcards. Despite their modest value, sheer quantity makes a comprehensive collection a challenge.

James Dean trading cards are not nearly as plentiful as postcards, and tend to be more valuable. One set has been devoted exclusively to Dean, and he has been featured on individual cards in several Hollywood and nostalgia collections. The general rules for paper preservation apply to postcards and trading cards. Mylar storage pages are available in various sizes to provide protection while allowing for double-sided visibility of the cards.

Fan Clubs

With their propensity for badges, membership cards, newsletters and the like, fan clubs have spawned a good number of Dean novelty items. The initial James Dean club was formed by a group of Catholic schoolgirls following the actor's very first television appearance. The Immaculate Heart James Dean Appreciation Society paved the way for dozens of groups that followed. Dean's Teens. The James Dean Memory Ring. The James Dean Widows Club. Dedicated Deans. Some were heartfelt tributes, others transparent attempts to make a quick profit. Most have quickly come and gone, but a few have thrived. By far the biggest and best of the current clubs is We Remember Dean International, founded by Sylvia Bongiovanni and Bill Lewis in 1978 and still going strong. WRDI continues to grow, and counts several Hollywood influentials among its members. The club newsletter has been a consistently entertaining source of information on all things Dean for more than twenty years.

Museum Days

The Museum Days festival in the actor's home town has likewise inspired the creation of many Dean items. In addition to promotional materials for the event itself, the festival has served as a gathering place for merchants and collectors, whoshowcase an assortment of new novelties each year. The festival always takes place during the last full weekend in September.

Clothing

Since image is such a major part of Dean's legacy, clothing is an obvious medium for commemoration. Several manufacturers have created replicas of articles Dean is known to have worn; many others have affixed his name or image to unrelated items. Stetson created a reproduction of the hat he wore as Jett Rink in *Giant.* Another company copied his eyeglasses. There have been boots and belts and socks and shorts and even a line of "Dean's Jeans." But in all the assortment of James Dean apparel, the red jacket from *Rebel Without a Cause* looms flipped-up collar above the rest.

In the years since his death, the red windbreaker has been second only to the car in which Dean died among the most sought after items. The Porsche Spyder has not been seen since 1960. The jacket, on the other hand, turns up everywhere.

Many people have claimed to have the real windbreaker, but there really is no one original. Frank Mazzola, who plays a gang member named Crunch in the film, bought several identical jackets at Mattson's clothing store. They came right off the racks, at $22.95 each. Of those who have laid claim to a jacket worn by Dean in the film, Sammy Davis, Jr. is one of the more credible, since he and Dean were acquaintances around that time. While a verifiable original would be among the ultimate Dean rarities, most fans and collectors must be content to own a replica. Several companies have intentionally reproduced the jacket, and many have marketed red windbreakers oblivious to Dean connection. Oddly enough, of the two groups, the inadvertent replicas are often the more authentic.

The windbreaker may be the most sought after of James Dean clothing items, but t-shirts are by far the most plentiful. With the advent of decals and screening technology, photo t-shirts have become a medium of public expression. Hundreds of Dean shirts have been created, with many more to come.

The variety of novelty items is all but limitless. Just when it seems that every angle has been pursued, that the creation of a new Dean product is simply impossible, someone steps forward to dispel that notion. They may not all be fore everyone, but more than any other category of memorabilia, novelties offered physical evidence of the continuing popularity of James Dean.

Grading Cards

Mint: A perfect specimen with no markings or wear of any kind.
Near Mint: Still sharp, though may show very minor fading.
Excellent: No bends or creases, no rounded or blunted corners. Cards may have been postally used, as long as markings are confined to the address side.
Very Good: Corners slightly blunted, with very minor bending or writing that does not detract from picture side.
Good: Corners blunt or rounded, with noticeable bends or creases.
Fair: Intact, but with soiling that affects picture. *Most collectors eschew postcards or trading cards that are in anything less than excellent condition, although specimens in lesser condition are sometimes acceptable as a space holder until a better card is found.*

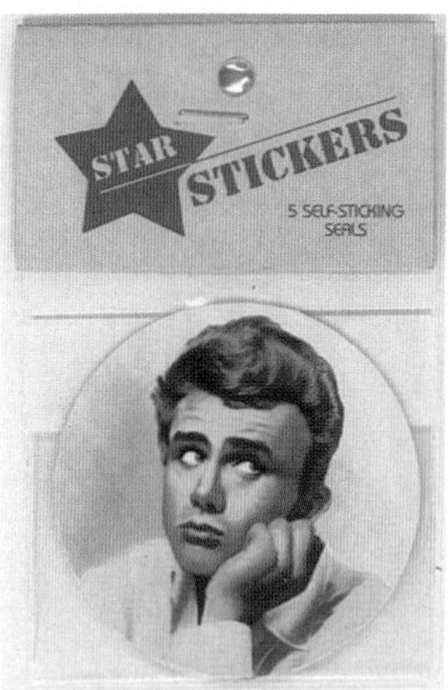

Star Stickers
Movie AD Corp.
USA - 1988

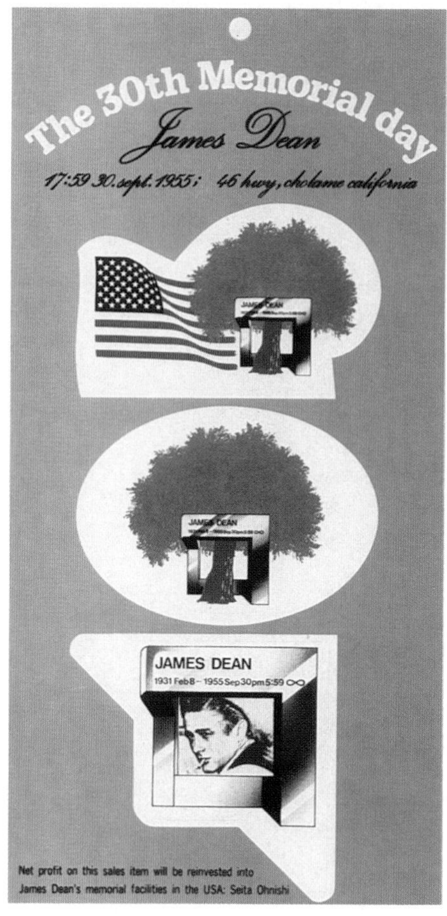

Souvenir Stickers from
Cholame, California
USA - 1985

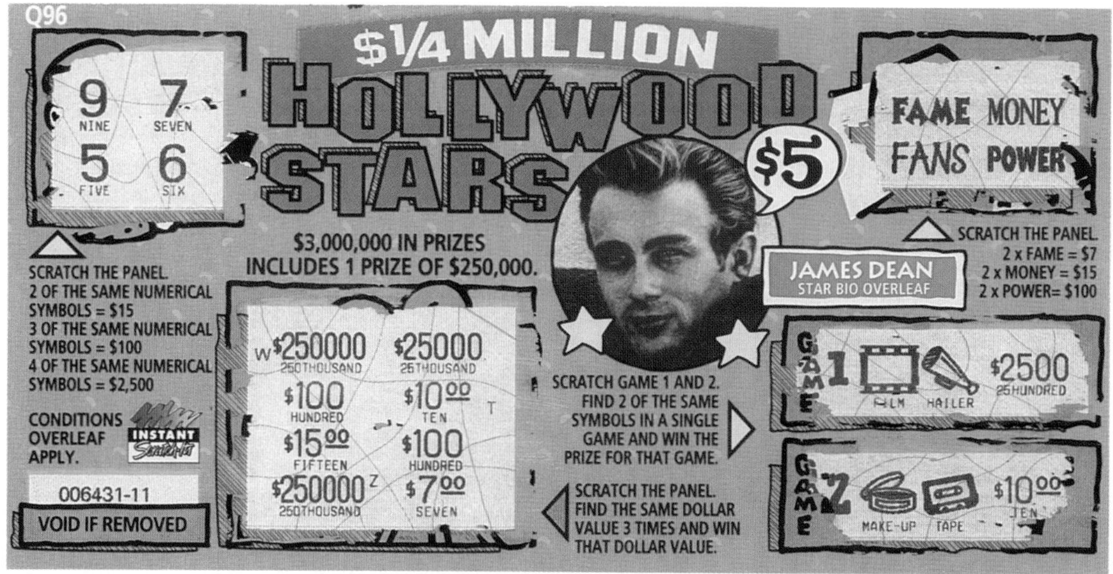

Scratch Off Lottery Ticket
California
no date available

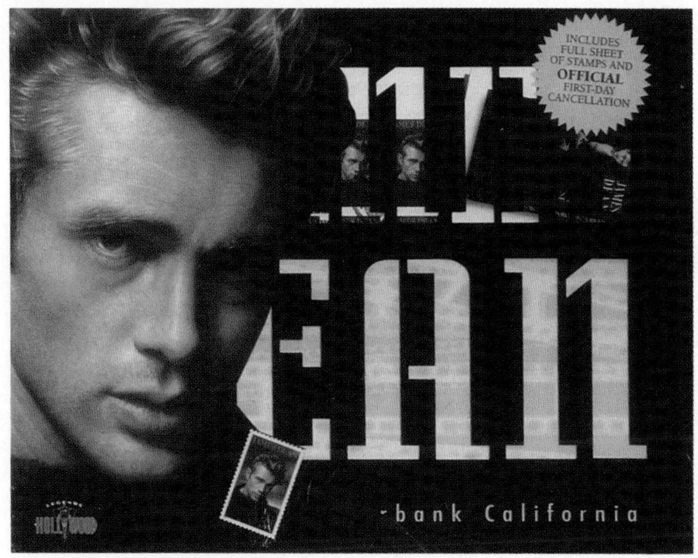

US Postal Service
First Day of Issue Souvenir
A folder with sheets of
twenty cancelled stamps
USA - 1996

US Postal Service
Counter Top Display and
Stamp Brochure - USA - 1996

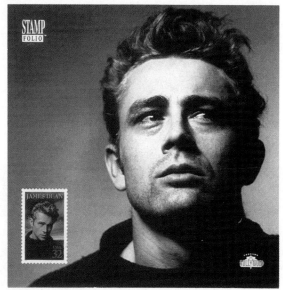

US Postal Service
Stamp Folio with Four Stamps
USA - 1996

US Postal Service
Six Foot Tall Lobby
Display and Brochure
Holder - USA - 1996

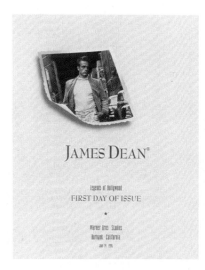

US Postal Service
Souvenir Program from
the Official Stamp
Dedication Ceremonies at
Warner Brothers Studios in
Burbank California
June 24, 1996

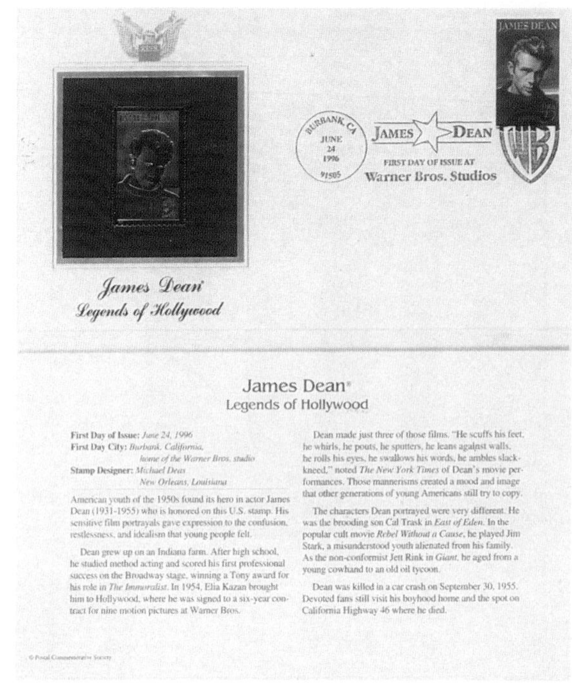

JAMES DEAN

BURBANK, CA JUNE 24 1996 91505

JAMES DEAN

FIRST DAY OF ISSUE AT
Warner Bros. Studios

James Dean®
Legends of Hollywood

James Dean®
Legends of Hollywood

First Day of Issue: *June 24, 1996*
First Day City: *Burbank, California, home of the Warner Bros. studio*
Stamp Designer: *Michael Deas New Orleans, Louisiana*

American youth of the 1950s found its hero in actor James Dean (1931-1955) who is honored on this U.S. stamp. His sensitive film portrayals gave expression to the confusion, restlessness, and idealism that young people felt.

Dean grew up on an Indiana farm. After high school, he studied method acting and scored his first professional success on the Broadway stage, winning a Tony award for his role in *The Immoralist*. In 1954, Elia Kazan brought him to Hollywood, where he was signed to a six-year contract for nine motion pictures at Warner Bros.

Dean made just three of those films. "He scuffs his feet, he whirls, he pouts, he sputters, he leans against walls, he rolls his eyes, he swallows his words, he ambles slack-kneed," noted *The New York Times* of Dean's movie performances. Those mannerisms created a mood and image that other generations of young Americans still try to copy.

The characters Dean portrayed were very different. He was the brooding son Cal Trask in *East of Eden*. In the popular cult movie *Rebel Without a Cause*, he played Jim Stark, a misunderstood youth alienated from his family. As the non-conformist Jett Rink in *Giant*, he aged from a young cowhand to an old oil tycoon.

Dean was killed in a car crash on September 30, 1955. Devoted fans still visit his boyhood home and the spot on California Highway 46 where he died.

© Postal Commemorative Society

First Day of Issue
Warner Brothers Studio
Cancellation with Gold Stamp Replica
June 24, 1996 - USA

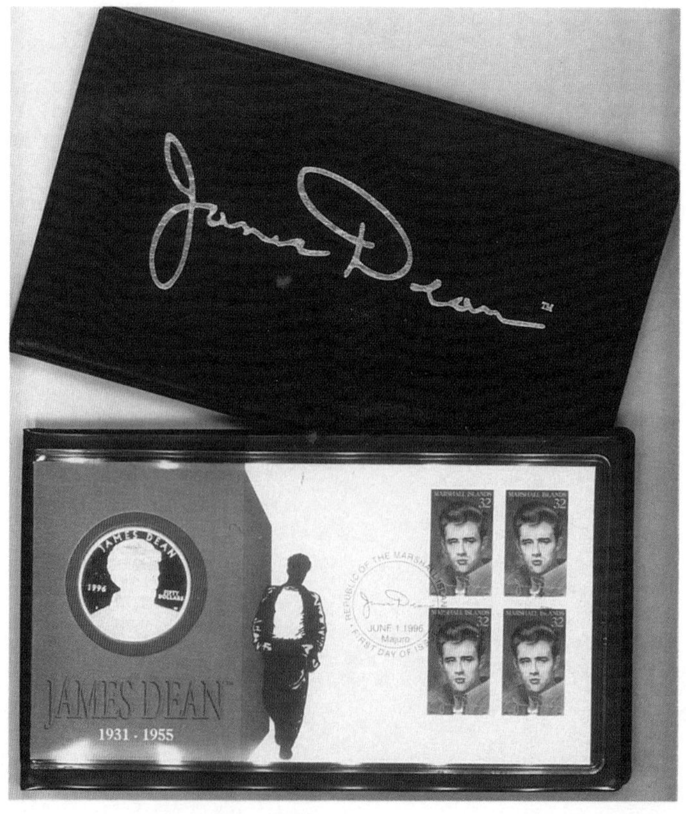

First Day Cover and $50 Silver Coin from
Republic of the Marshall Islands
June 1, 1996

Full Sheet of Twenty Stamps
signed by the artist Michael Deas
USA - 1996

Full Sheet of Twenty Stamps
Republic of the Marshall Islands
1996

Sheet of Nine Stamps
Monserat

Cancelled Stamp
Fujeira

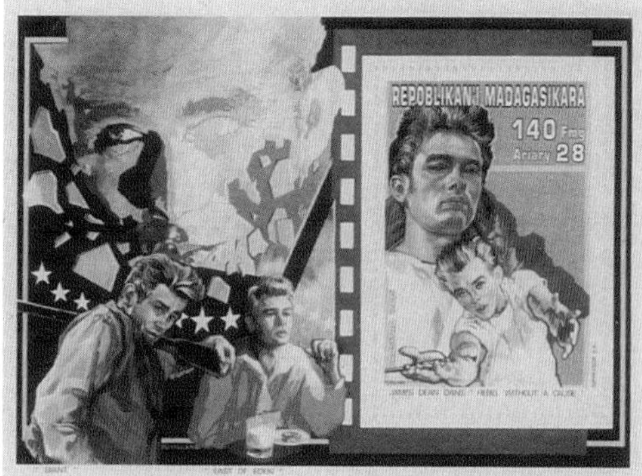

Republic of Madagaskar

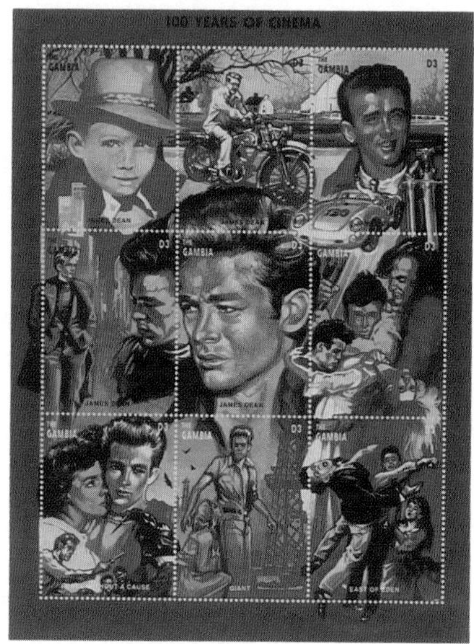

Sheet of Nine Stamps
Gambia

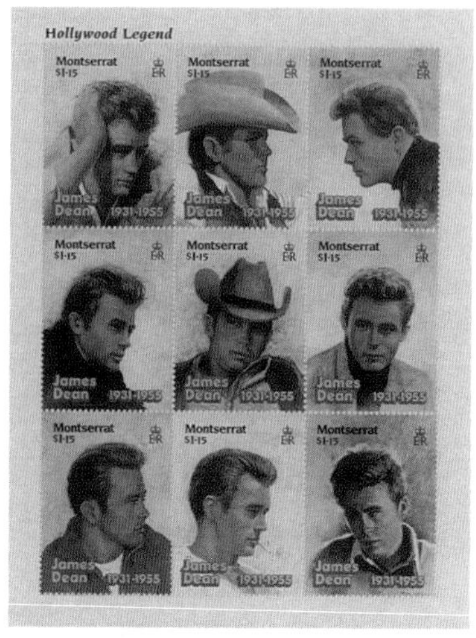

Sheet of Nine Stamps
Monserat

Novelty Art Stamps
Roger Cannon Productions
USA - 1980

Norman Patterson - South Africa - 1984

Gambia

S. Tome E. Principe

Monserrat

Tanzania

Republic of Madagaskar

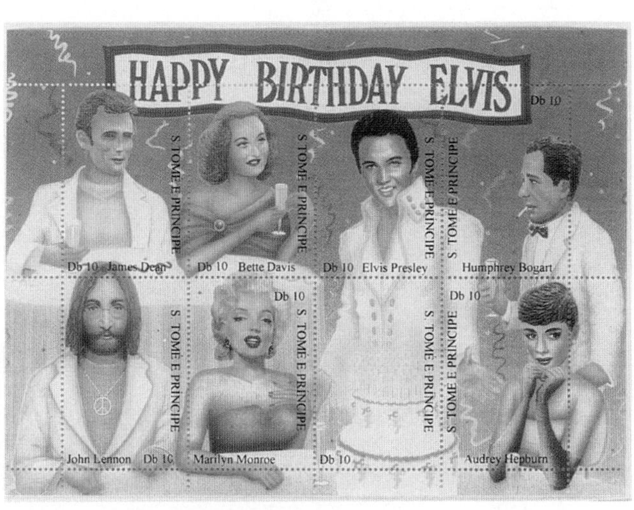

S. Tome E. Principe

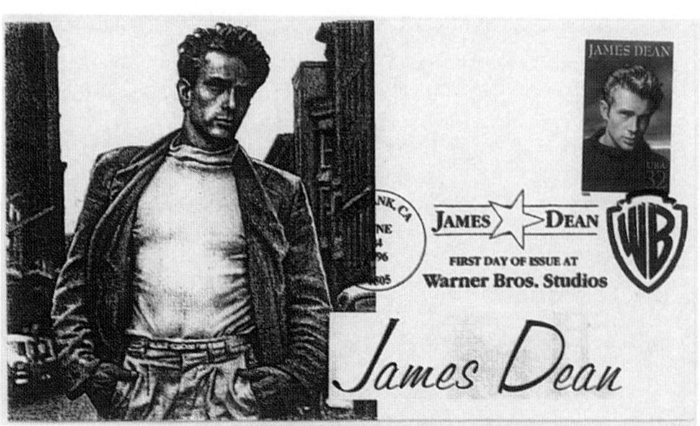

A selection of 8 different examples of First Day Covers. There are over 140 different styles that have been made.
USA - June 1996

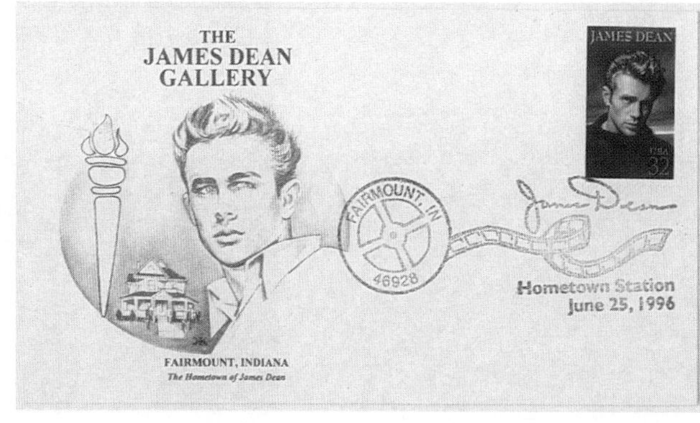

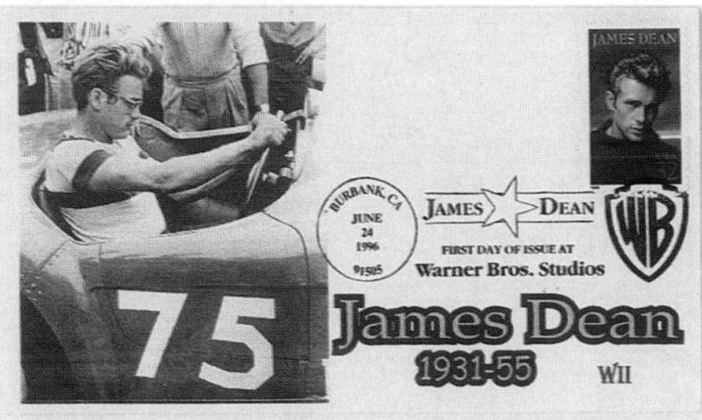

A selection of 8 different examples of First Day Covers. There are over 140 different styles that have been made.
USA - June 1996

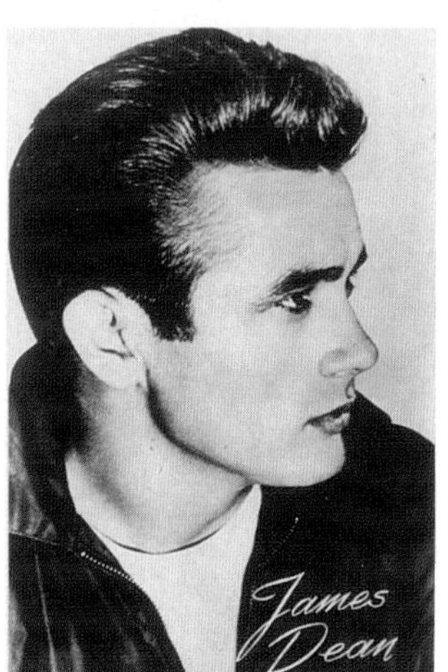

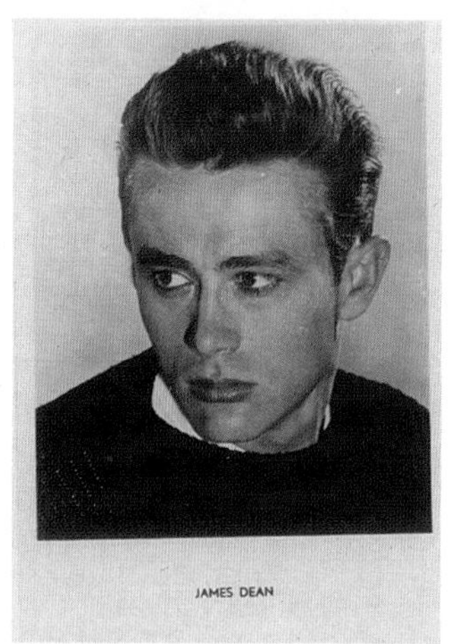

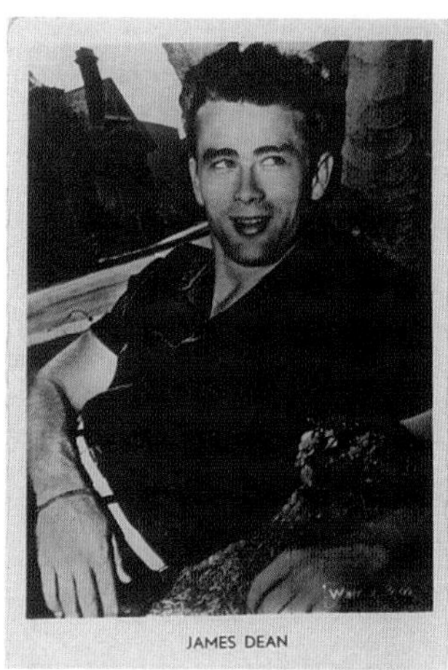

These are examples of Postcards produced in the mid to late 1950s in Germany, Belguim, and France.

Oversize Postcard Prints of Kenneth Kendall Paintings - 1980-1988 - USA

There have been several hundred commercially available postcards produced since the mid 1970s. These are examples of just a few.

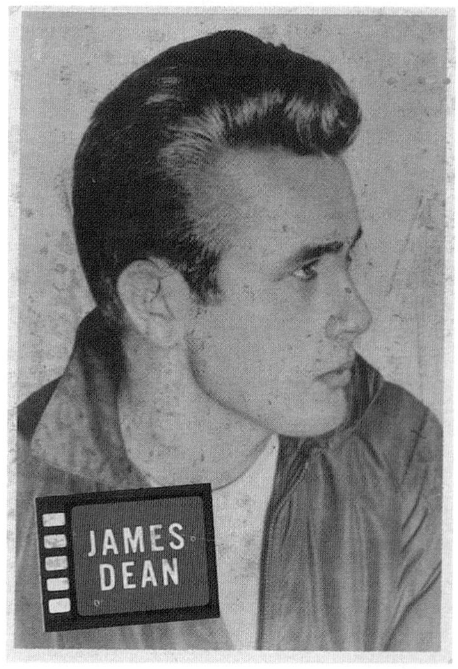

Hit Stars Gum Cards were a series of movie star trading cards.
There were four James Dean Cards in the set.
#65, #71, #66 and #63.
USA - 1957

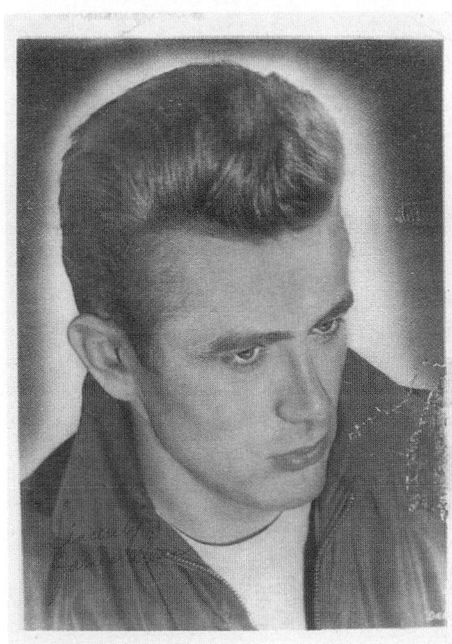

USA - 1956

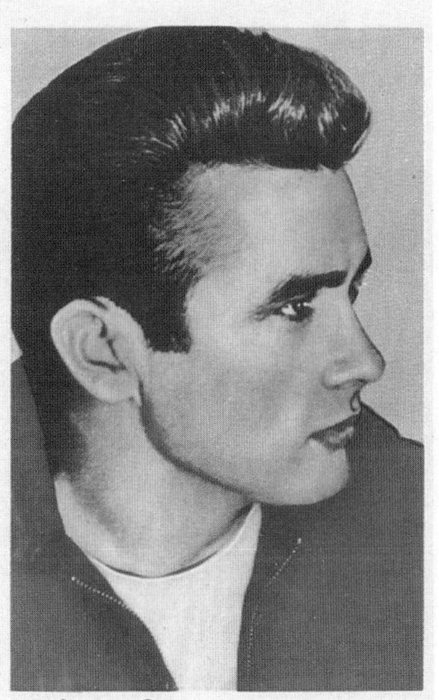

Maple Leaf, Ltd.
Holland - 1958

Boxed Set of 50 Cards
Active Marketing
USA - 1992

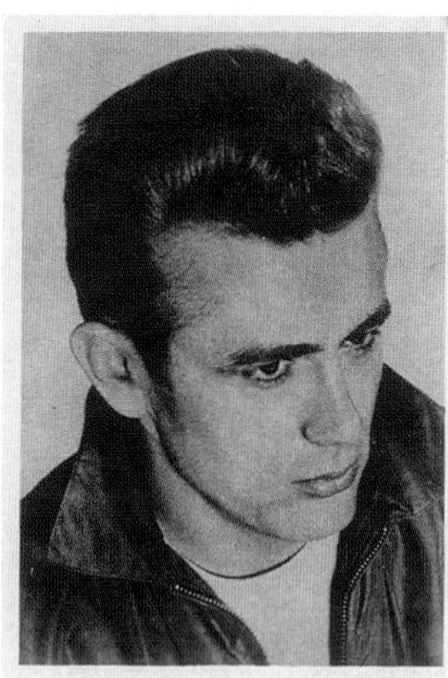

No Date - No Info Available

Starline, Inc.
#24 in a series of
movie star cards.
USA - 1991

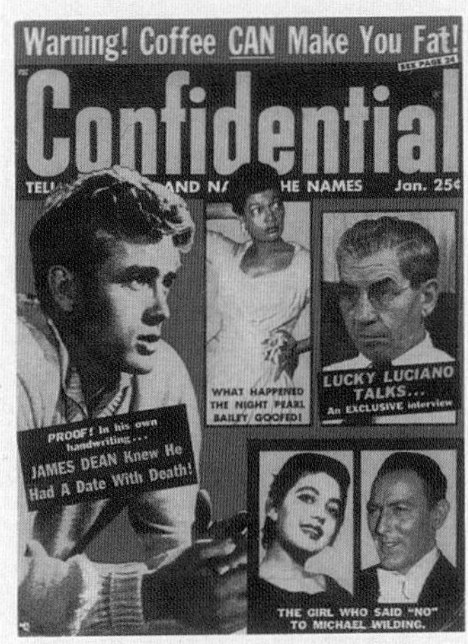

Confidential Magazine
Cover Trading Cards
#25 in a boxed set series of 36
Kitchen Ink Press
USA - 1993

Hollywood Legends
Hologram Trading Card
Vision Graphics
USA - 1992

A number of these prototype cards were produced but never marketed.

Legends of Hollywood
#11 in a Series of 20
Victoria Gallery
England - 1991

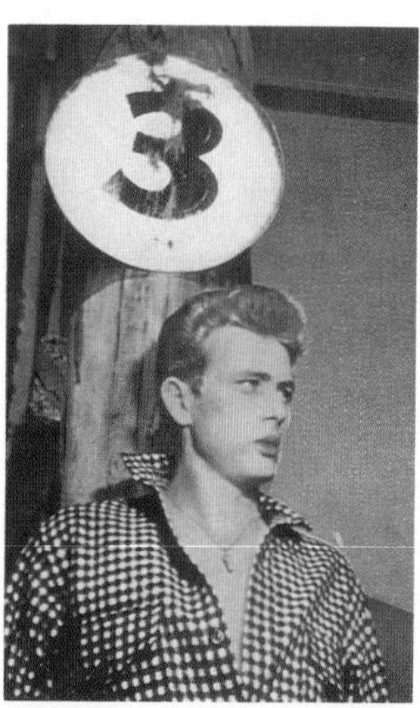

Schall - Film
E Tablissement
Germany - 1956

This trading card was one in a series given away free in movie theaters with the purchase of a box of popcorn Canada - 1958

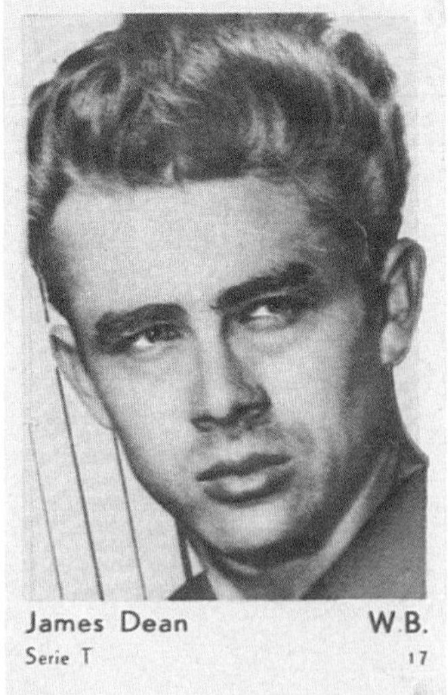

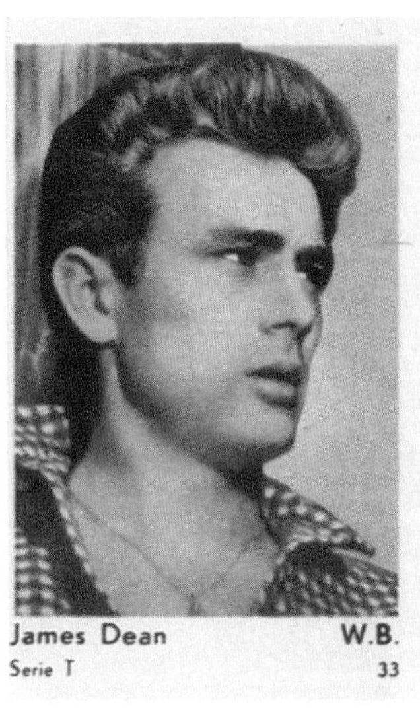

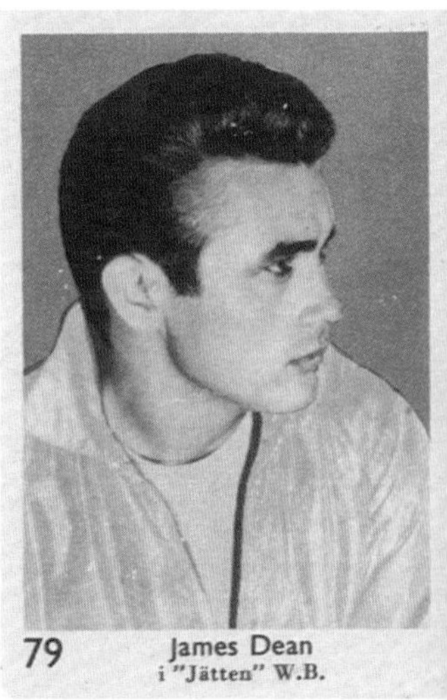

Twelve cards in a series of movie star cards from Canada in 1957.
The number of James Dean Cards in the series is unknown.

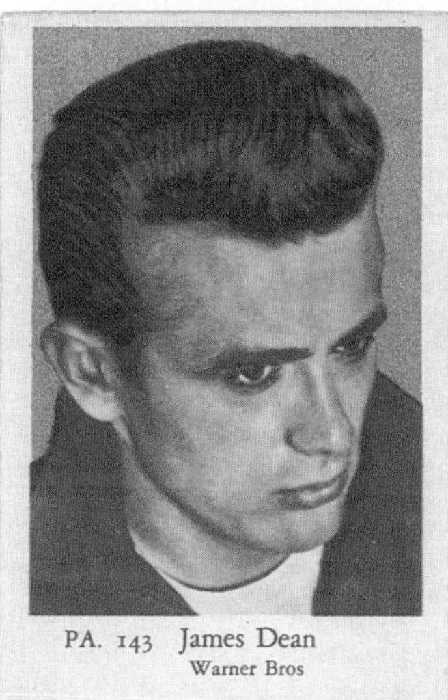

PA. 210 James Dean - Sal Mineo
Warner Bros

PA. 250
Elizabeth Taylor - James Dean
Warner Bros

Twelve cards in a series of movie star cards from Canada in 1957.
The number of James Dean Cards in the series is unknown.

There have been hundreds of commercially available calendars produced in various countries beginning in the early 1980s. These are examples of just a few.

Pomegranate
USA - 1989

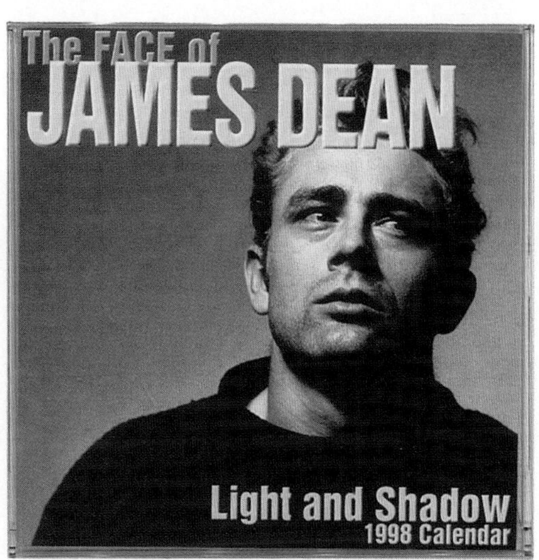

Desk Top Calendar
Japan - 1998

Culture Shock
United Kingdom - 1989

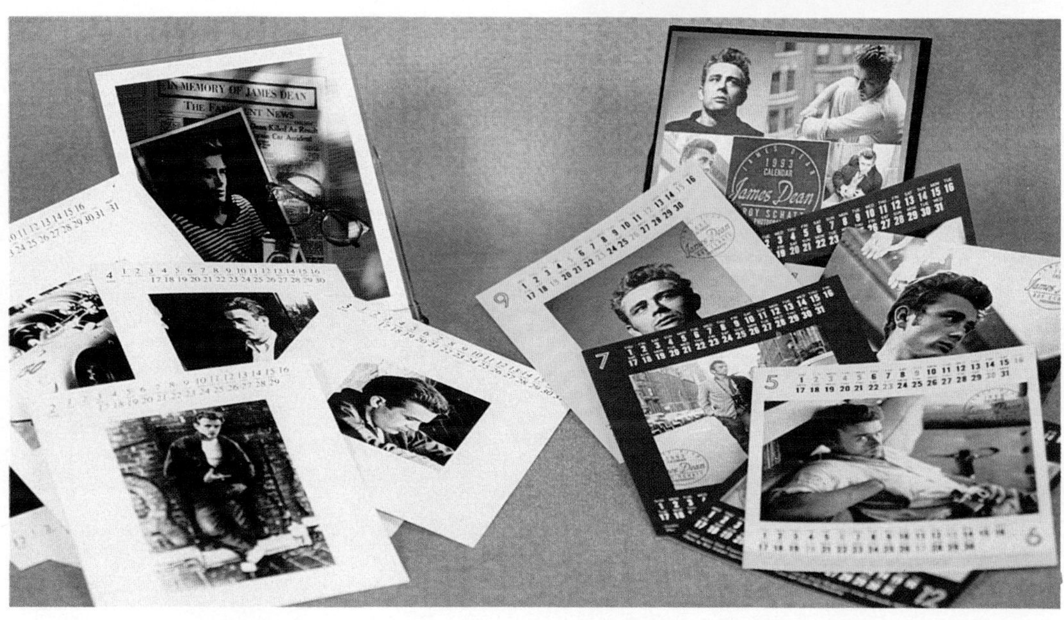

Desk Top Calendars

Left:
Wing - Japan - 1992

Right:
Orion Press - 1993

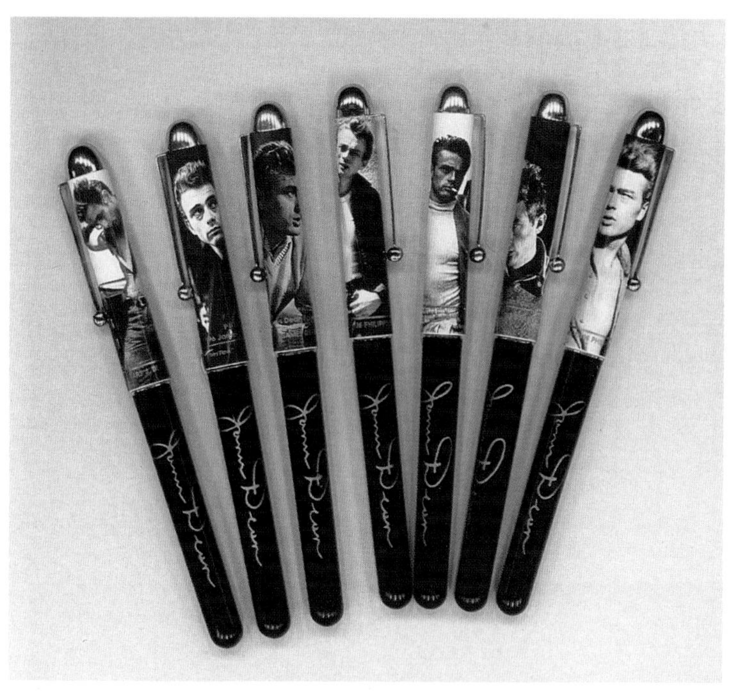

Culture Shock
United Kingdom - 1989

Left to Right:
James Dean Collection, Japan, 1989.
James Dean Pencil - HB Japan
James Dean Pencil, Leadworks, Inc., USA, 1992
James Dean Pencil, USA, 1986
James Dean Pencil, HB Japan, 1987

Paperweights from the 1980s.

Paperweight
Toney's Art Glass
Frankton - USA - 1996

Pencil Holders
Left one is from Japan, 1986
Right one is from France, 1982

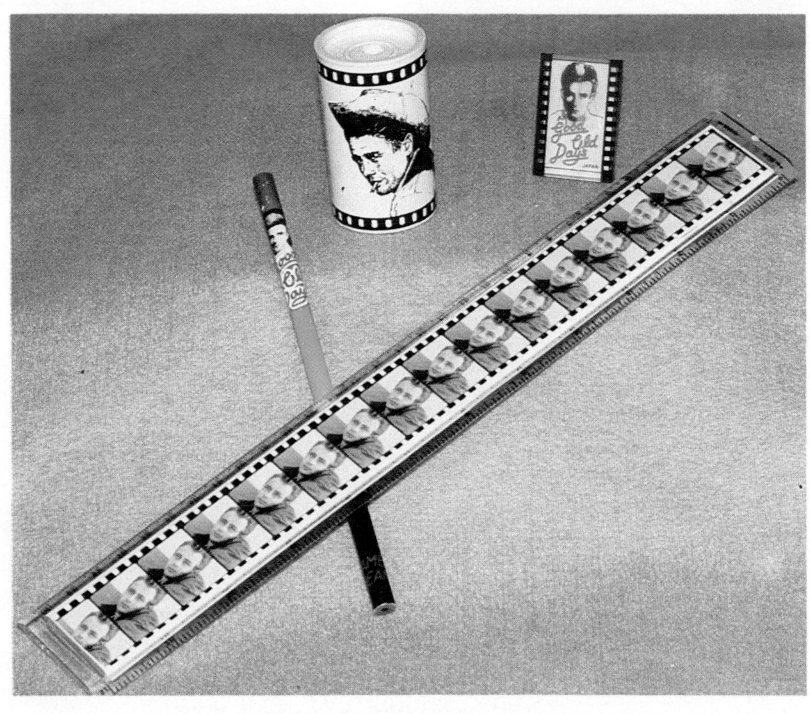

Front is a James Dean Ruler
Back Left is a Pencil Sharpener, Trevu, Italy, 1979
Back Right is an Eraser, Japan, 1986

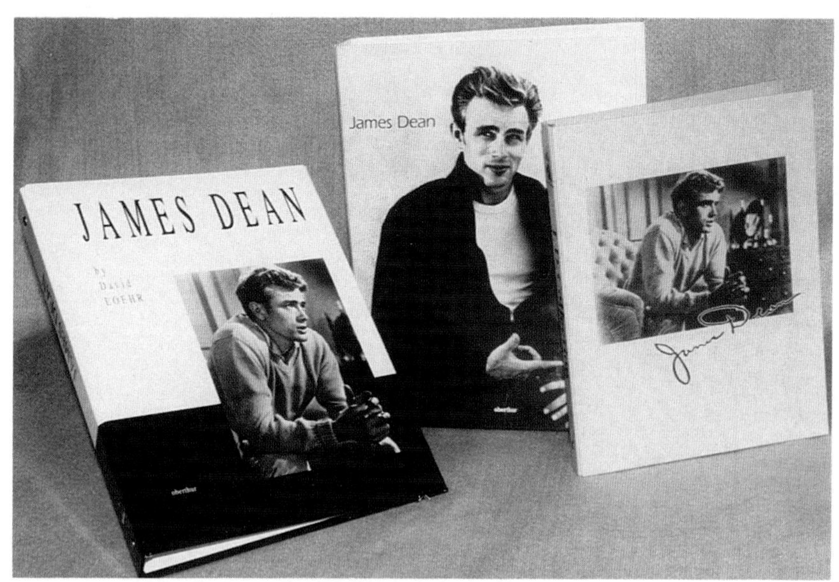

Ring Binders - Left to Right:
Oberthur, France, 1995
USA 1996
James Dean Collection, Japan, 1989

Ring Binders
DCC AG, Switzerland, 1991

Rubber Stamps - Left to Right
USA - (no information available)
Stamp Happy, Sherman Oaks, California

Book Mark
OSP Publishing
USA - 1990

Book Marks
Quality Artworks
Hatfield, PA - 1989

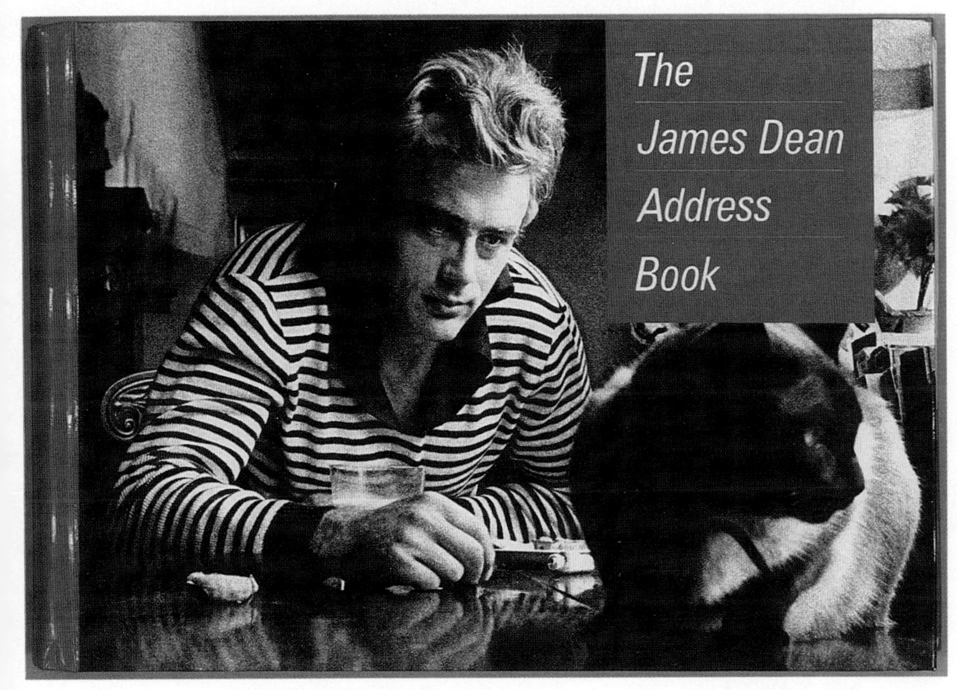

Pomegranate
USA - 1986

Pocket Size
Address Book
vinyl cover.

Pocket Size
Phone Index
metal on front and back
with accordian type pages
Japan - 1984

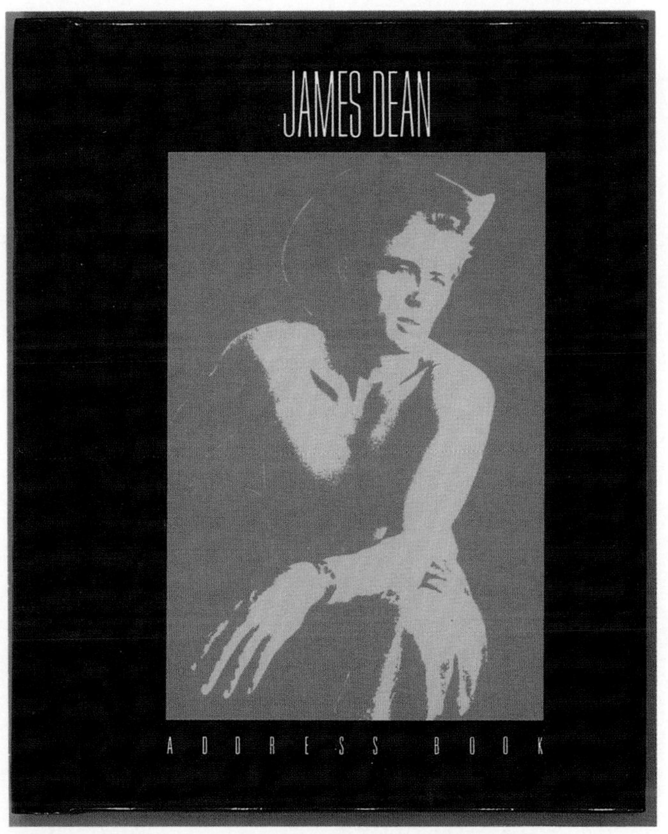

Pomegranate
Address Book
USA - 1988

Address and Telephone Books - (Check Book Covers), vinyl covers
Reed Productions, 1988.

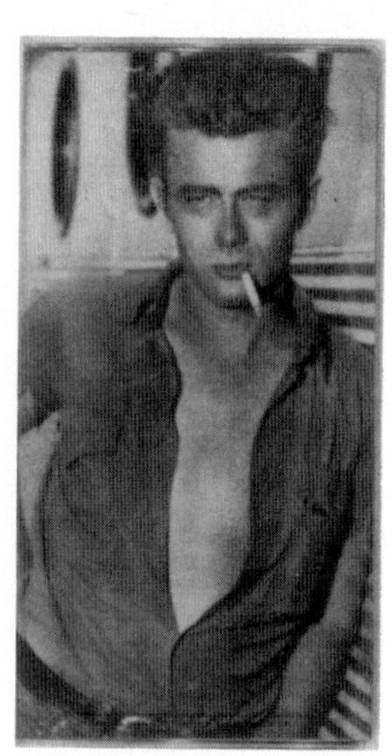

"He died at just the right time. If he had lived, he'd never be able to live up to his own publicity."
- - Humphrey Bogart

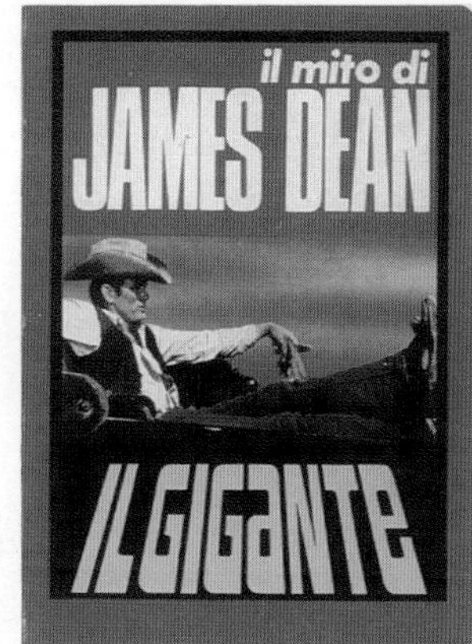

Note Book
Pic Distribution
Italy - 1990

Note Book
by Pigna
Italy - 1990

Note Book #390501
Japan Craft Co. - 1990

Note Book #390101
Japan Craft Co. - 1989

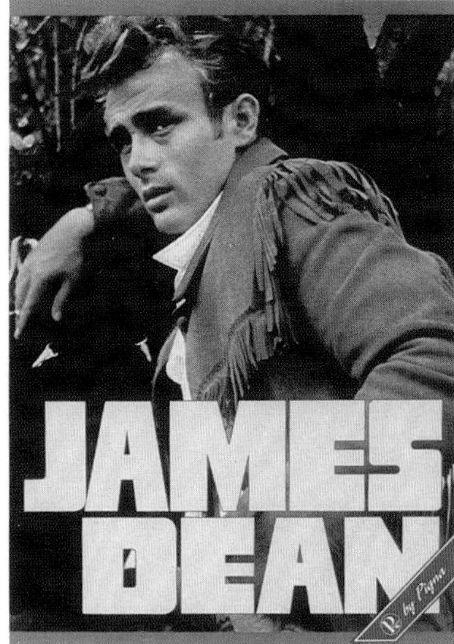

Note Book
by Pigna
Italy - 1990

Note Book
by Herakles
France - 1986

Note Book
by Herakles
France - 1986

Note Book
Edition F. Nugeron
Paris - 1982

Spiral Note Book
Paper Moon Graphics, Inc.
Los Angeles, Ca. - USA - 1982 SB 45

Spiral Note Book
Reed Productions
USA - 1982 SP 163

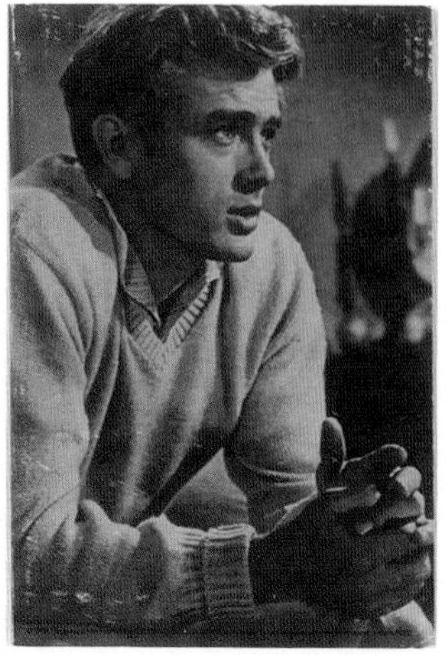

Note Book - Reed Productions- USA - 1988
NB - 195 NB - 173

Warner Brothers Expressions
15 Sheets - 10- Envelopes Stationary - 1992

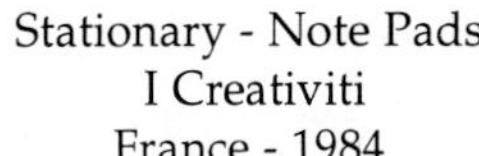

Stationary - Note Pads
I Creativiti
France - 1984

Stationary - 1986
World Creative Products
Japan - 1986
Delta Products - France #L-10

Damar Products, Inc.
made by Kettlesprings Kilns
in Alliance, Ohio
USA - 1956

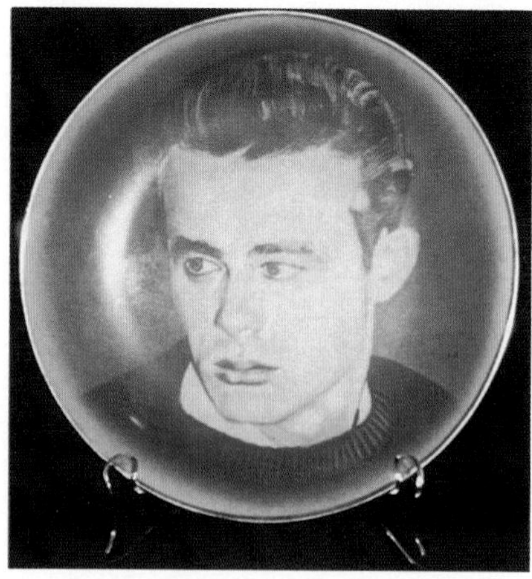

"We Will Remember"
by Charles Lee Todd
Numbered Edition of 5000
Character Plates - USA - 1956

Souvenir Plate From
Fairmount, Indiana
No Date

Plastic Plate
No Date

The James Dean Gallery
Art by Kenneth Kendall
Numbered Edition of 500
USA - 1988

"Jim Dean and Elvis were the spokesmen for an entire generation. When I was in acting school in New York, years ago, there was a saying that if Marlon Brando changed the way people acted, James Dean changed the way people lived. He was the greatest actor who ever lived. He was simply a genius."

- - Martin Sheen

"No one came before (Dean), and there hasn't been anyone since."

- - Martin Sheen

Series of Plates
made by Betty Green
in Fairmount, Indiana.
Artwork by Carol Redus
USA - 1985-86

"One of the deepest drives of human nature is the desire to be appreciated, the longing to be liked, to be held in esteem, to be a sought-after person."

Set of 4 Plates
Nostalgia Collectibles
USA - 1985

"James Dean - America's Rebel"
by William Jacobson
Numbered Edition of 25,000
Nostalgia Collectibles
USA - 1985

"James Dean"
by Thomas Blackshear
Numbered Edition of 25,000
The Hamilton Collection
USA - 1991

"Unforgotten Rebel"
by Morgan
Numbered Edition
The Hamilton Collection
USA - 1992

"James Dean American Legend"
by Gadino - The Franklin Mint
Numbered Edition - USA - 1994

#1 Hollywood Rebel

#2 Restless One

#3 Hollywood Cool

#4 Hollywood Giant

Series of 4 Plates by The Bradford Exchange
Numbered Editions - USA - 1996

Two different sets of Mugs
by Betty Green, Fairmount, Indiana.
Artwork by Carol Redus - 1985-86

The James Dean Gallery Souvenir Mugs
Left: Edition of 500 with imprinted bottom 1988
Right: 1997 - No bottom printing

Fairmount Historical Museum Souvenir
Glass and Mug Art by Carol Redus
No date available

Adeline Nall and James Dean Mug
by Mary Smithson
Fairmount, Indiana - USA - 1997

Series of 4 Mugs
Nostalgia Collectibles
USA - 1985

James Dean Sculpted Mug #1703
Clayart - USA - 1996

Clayart
USA - 1990

Mug with 3 different pictures on it
Centric Corporation - USA - 1993

Left to Right:
Graffics, No Date available
Fairmount Historical Museum, No Date available
No Date available on this mug

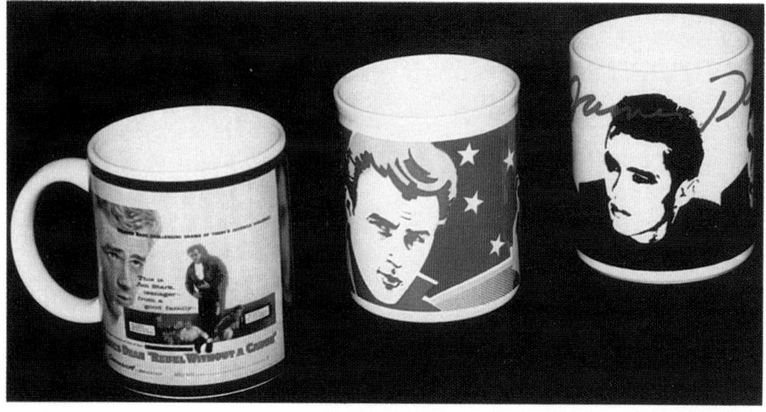

Left to Right:
Warner Brothers Stores, USA, 1993
Kiln Craft, England, 1979
Warner Brothers Stores, USA, 1993

Left to Right:
Warner Brothers Store, USA, 1996
Japan, no date available

Fairmount Historical Museum
USA - 1980-81

Shot Glasses (Left to Right)
Fairmount Historical Museum - 1985
James Dean Memorial Gallery - 1998

American Hero
Japan - No Date available

"The Young Giant"
by Susie Morton
The Ernst Corporation
USA - 1990

Jack's Ranch Cafe
Cholame, CA
USA - 1990

Left to Right:
Memories Diner, Fairmount, IN - USA - 1993
Lions Club, Fairmount, IN - USA - 1992
(2 cups at right) Fairmount, IN - no dates available

Among the first generation of Dean collectibles, the medallions advertised in *Modern Screen* magazine in the late-50s are one of the premiere novelty items. At the time, they sold for 25 cents each, a value that has appreciated many times over in the years since. Demand for the medallions proved so strong over the years that they were reproduced in 1985. There are several slight variations between the two issues, the most obvious being that the newer version is slightly larger. The 1985 medallions are now nearly as scarce as the originals, and their value has increased accordingly.

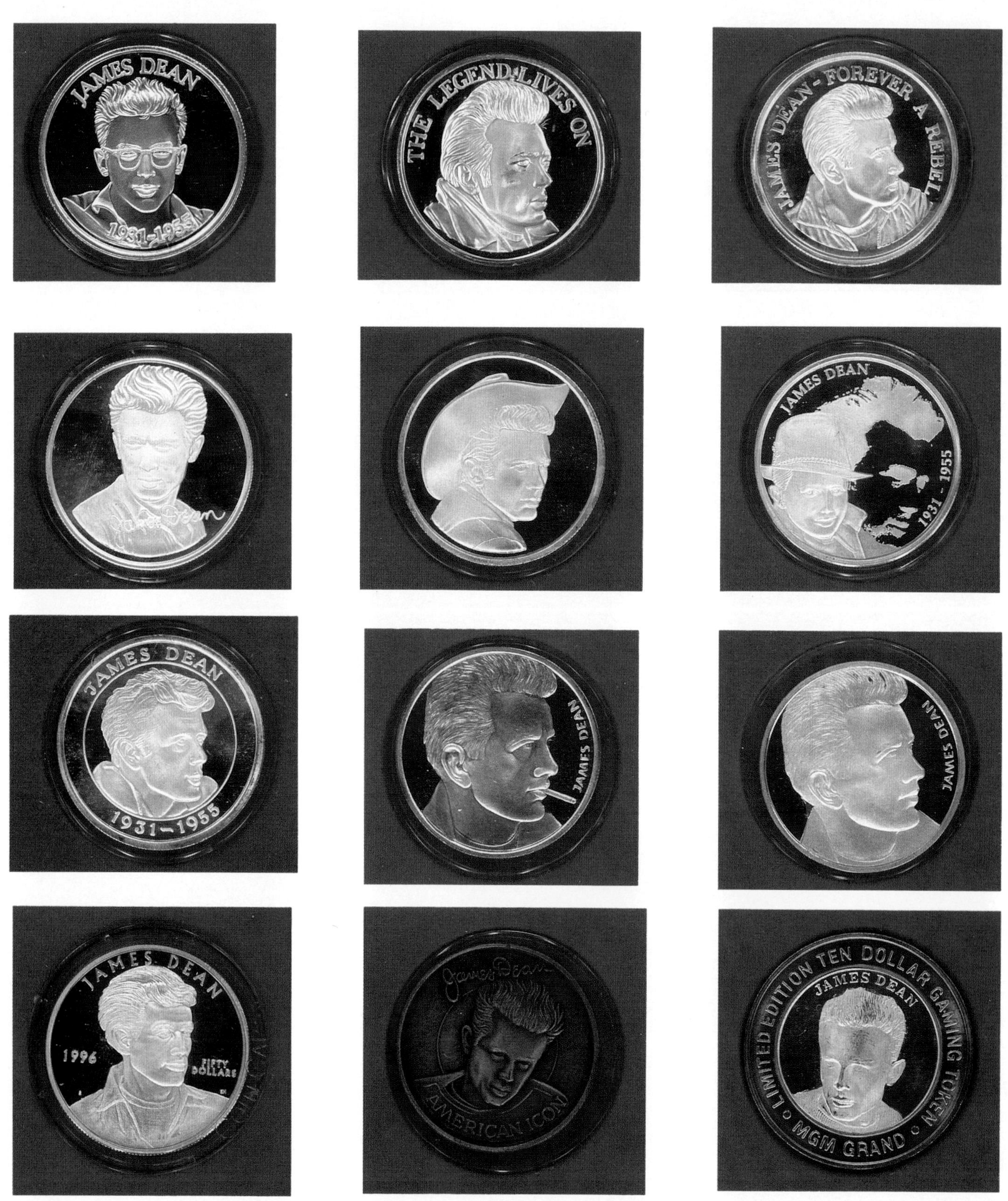

Examples of silver and bronze coins, keepsake medallions, AMC, MGM Grand - USA - Fifty Dollar Coin

Souvenir Coins,
Medallions and large plaque, 12" tall
made by Joe Payne in Fairmount, Indiana
USA - 1956

PLEASE SEND ME________
how many
JAMES DEAN MEMORIAL MEDALLION(S)
AT TWENTY-FIVE CENTS EACH TO COVER
THE COST OF MAILING AND HANDLING.
I AM ENCLOSING________AND A
amount
SELF-ADDRESSED ENVELOPE.
MAIL TO: MODERN SCREEN, Dept. D
10 WEST 33rd STREET, NEW YORK 1, N. Y.

Advertisements from "Modern Screen Magazine" and Bronze Medallions - 1956 - USA

Reproduction of "Modern Screen Medallion" These are slightly thicker than the originals and are less detailed and made of a lower-grade metal - 1985 - USA

Bronze Medallion by AMC
1987 - USA

Silver Medallion by Kenneth Kendall - 1985 - USA
Less than 20 produced

Souvenir of the Fairmount Historical Museum- No Date - USA

Pewter Medallion by Springsteen/Van Hook only 25 produced - 1988 -USA

Marion Fussgangers
Souvenir Medals
1988 - 1998
USA

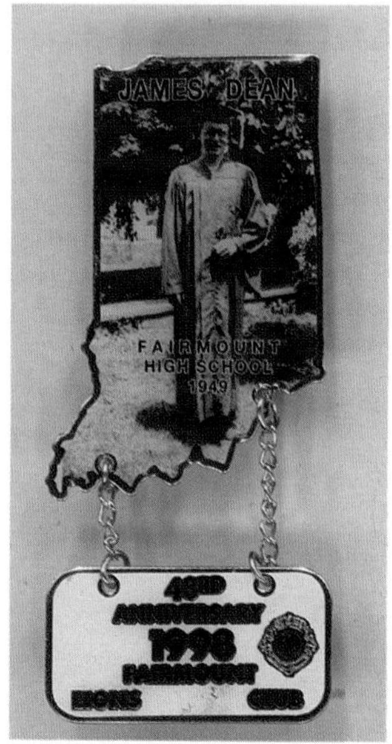

Fairmount Lions Club Souvenir Pins
Numbered Editions
USA - 1990 - 1998

Buttons and pins from 1956 to present. The two large yellow buttons are the oldest, 1956.

Assorted Enamel Pins
USA

Photo is compliments of the Wisconsin Center for Film and Theater Research

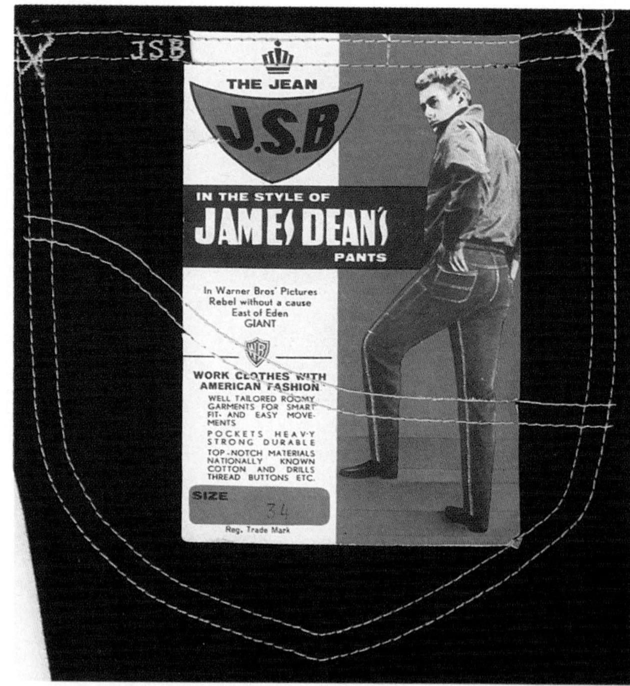

James Dean Jeans
Belgium - 1958

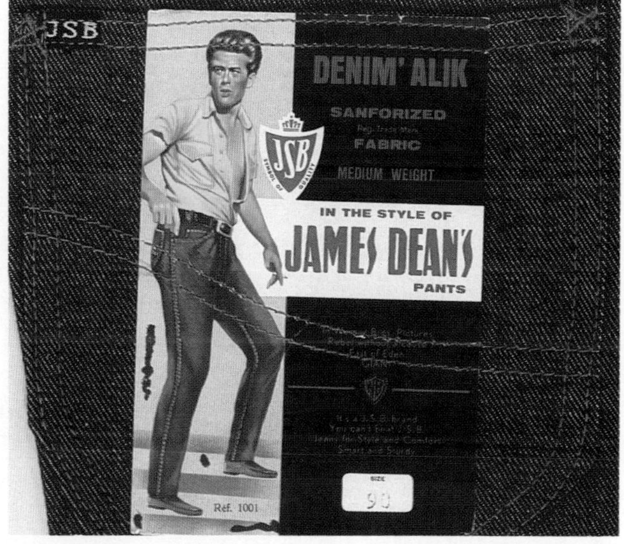

James Dean Jeans
Belgium - 1958

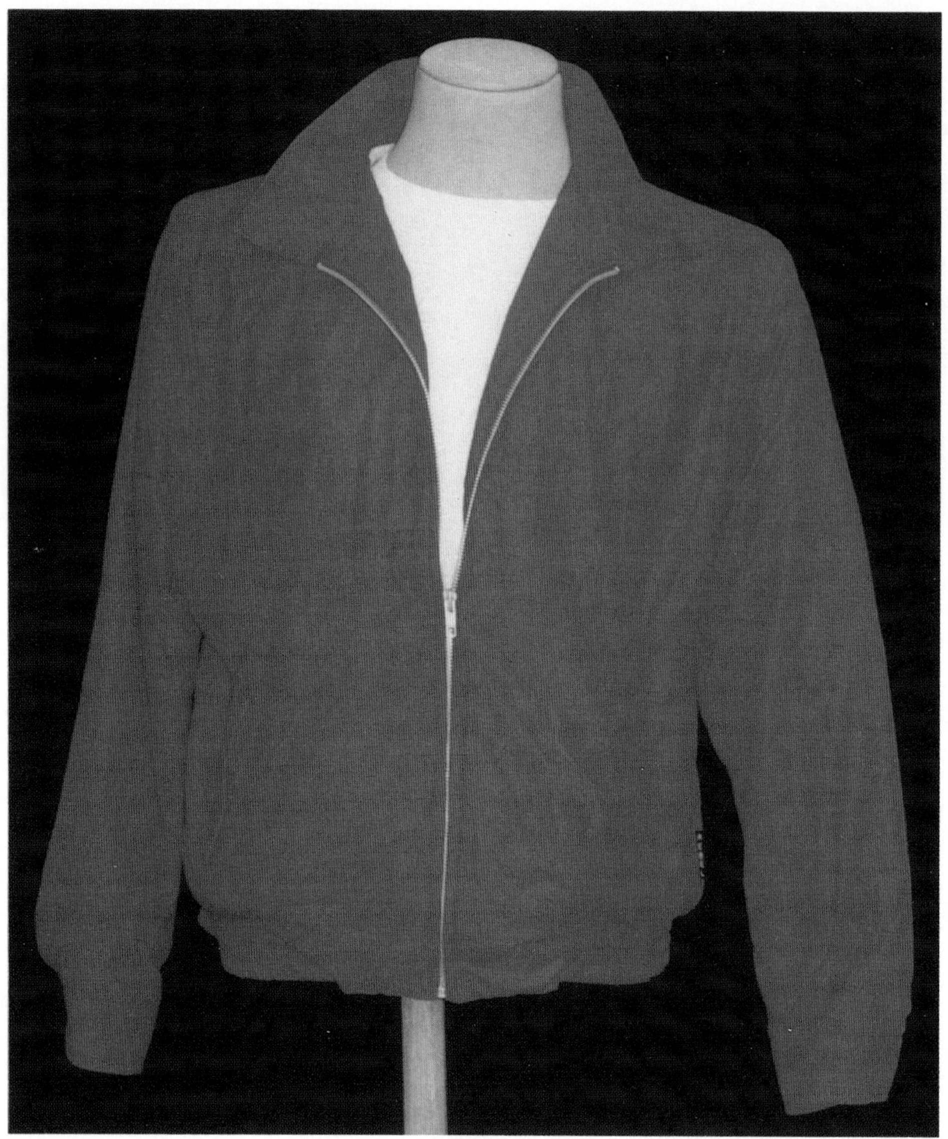

Pacific Trails - USA - 1985

Label and hang tag

Hang tag

Label

Two in a series of James Dean leather jackets
produced by Schott Bros. Inc.
USA - 1985

Sunworld Ltd.
Japan - 1989

French Connection
France - 1982

Levi's T-shirts
Japan - 1990

Sunworld Ltd.
Japan - 1990

Boxer Shorts
Nazook Pakistah - 1991
Painted Lady - USA - 1990

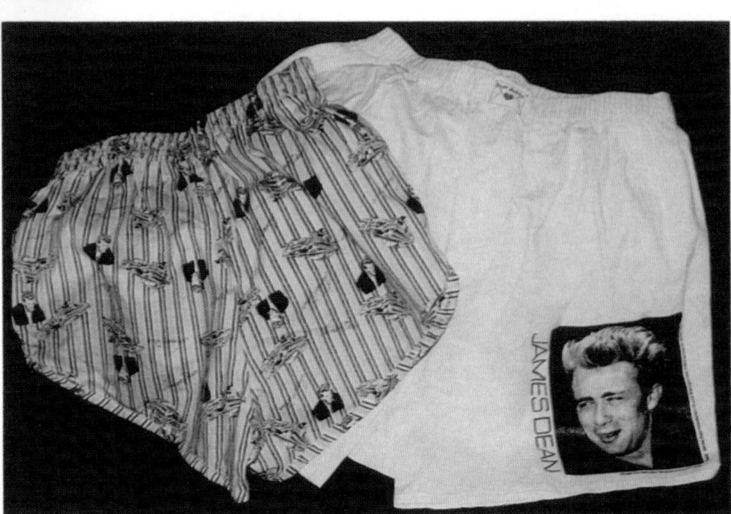

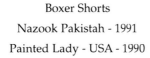

No! - France - 1989

Modern Culture
USA - 1986

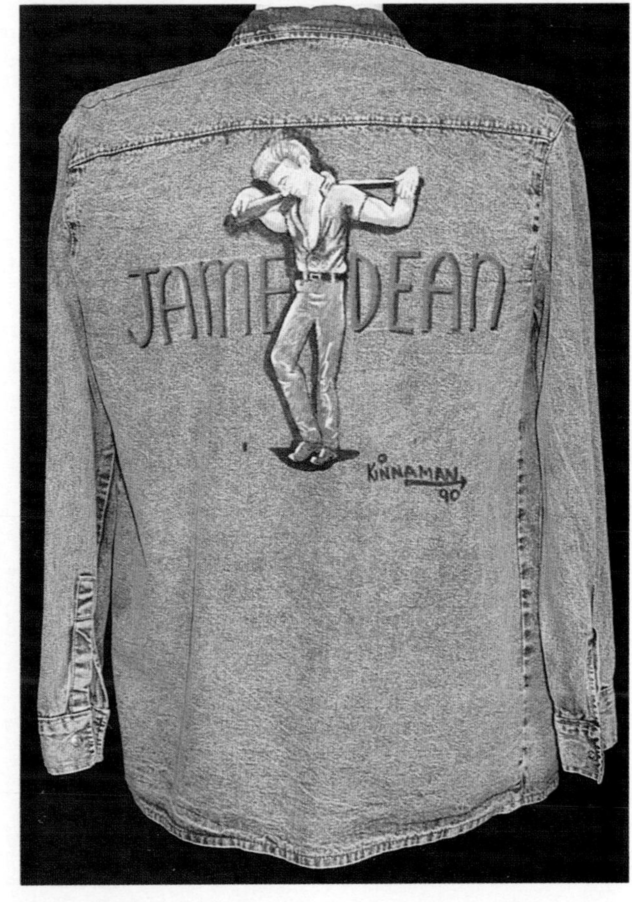

Hand painted jacket by Mark Kinnaman
USA - 1990

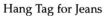

Hang Tag for Jeans

Sweaters, scarves and hats
by Ann Stinnett
Fairmount, Indiana
USA - 1990

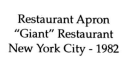

Restaurant Apron
"Giant" Restaurant
New York City - 1982

Detail of label inside the Stetson Hat

Two in a series of Reproduction Hats - Stetson USA - 1985

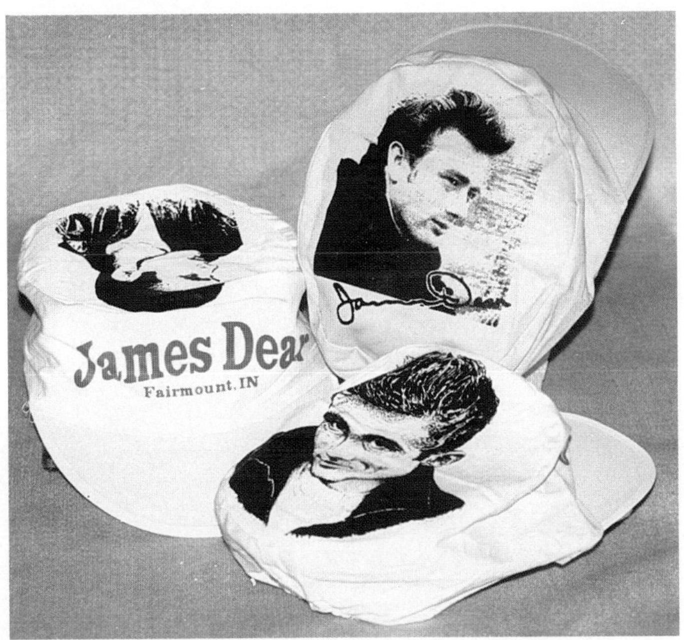

Souvenir Painter Style Hats - USA - 1986

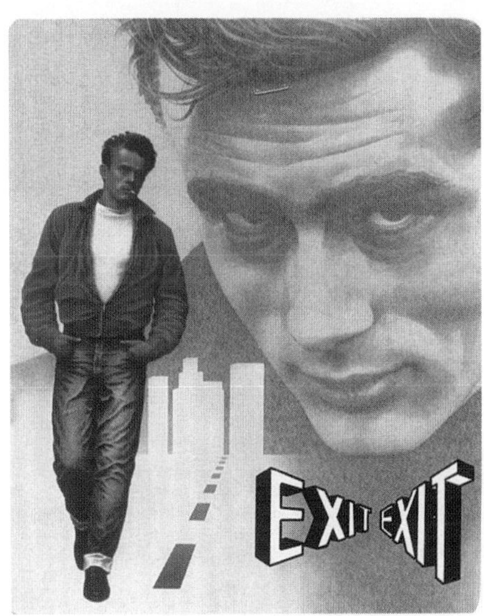

Hang Tag for Jeans

Left: James Dean Hat, black - USA - 1987
Middle: Fairmount Lions Club hat - USA - 1998
Right: James Dean Hat, white with black bill - USA - 1982

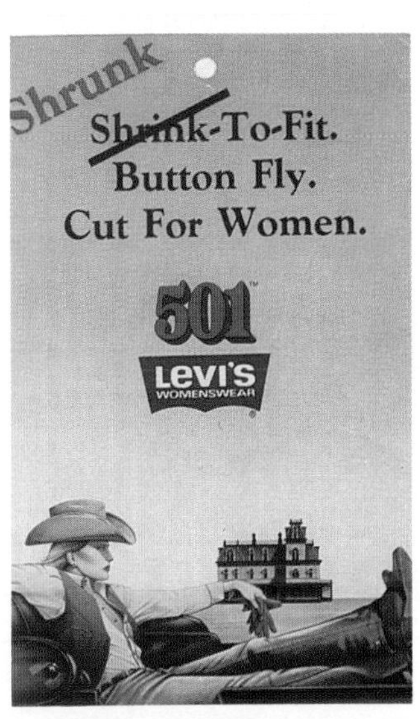

Hang Tag for Levi's
USA - 1982

ALGENE-CAROLL ACCESSORIES, INC.
LADIES' NOVELTY NECKWEAR AND HEADWEAR

40 WEST 37TH ST.

NEW YORK 18, N. Y.

TELEPHONE
BRYANT 9-4985-6-7

Dear James Dean Fan:

This offer has been authorized by the James Dean Memorial Foundation at Fairmont, Indiana.

We would like to offer you the colorful silk James Dean Memorial Scarf pictured above. The scarf, beautiful for wearing, will also be a tribute for a beloved actor because from each scarf sold the James Dean Foundation receives a royalty. Their work aids young actors and actresses in their careers and keeps alive the memory of James Dean.

Price is $1.00 (one dollar).

You can earn money for yourself and give other James Dean fans an opportunity to purchase this scarf by selling it for us. For each scarf sold, you will receive $.10 (ten cents); sell 20 scarfs, receive $2.00 (10% commission). Just have your friend send us $1.00 (or you send it for them) with their names and addresses and include your name. They will receive the scarf by return mail and you will receive your commission.

Send $1.00 for your beautiful James Dean Memorial Scarf, now! And let your friends in on it.

Thank you,

GC/hk

Gene Colman
ALGENE CAROLL ACCESSORIES INC.

PLEASE SEND TO: NAME ________

ADDRESS ________

CITY & STATE ________

________ JAMES DEAN MEMORIAL SCARVES AT $1.00 TOTAL ________

Algene Carroll Accessories Inc.
New York City - USA - 1956

England - 1957

Left to Right:
1. France - 1980
2. Japan - 1986
3. USA - 1982

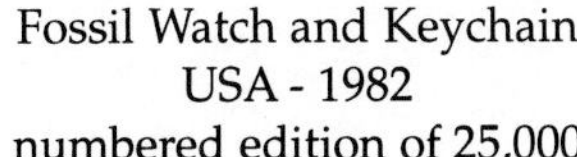
Fossil Watch and Keychain
USA - 1982
numbered edition of 25,000

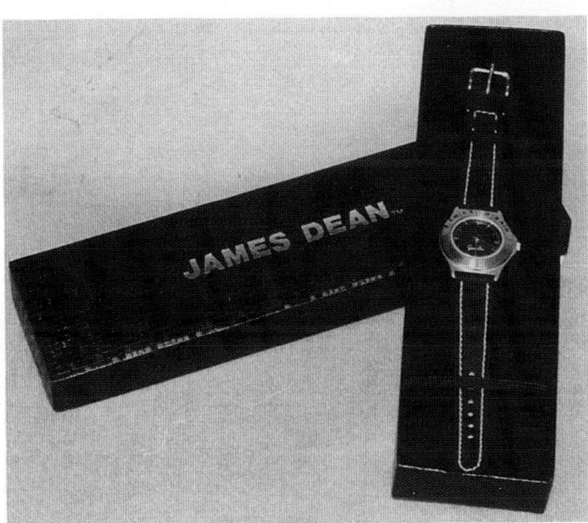

Japan - 1991

Memories by HBL
USA - 1987

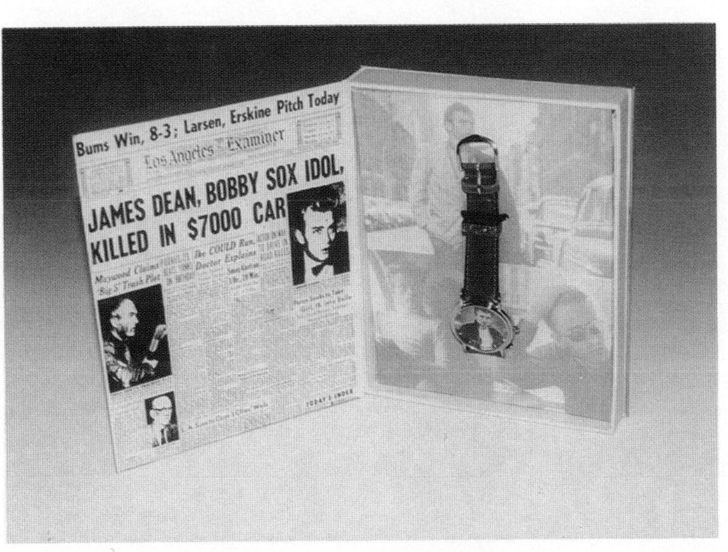

Japan 1995

2. 1987 - HBL - United Kingdom
3. 1989 - France
5. Centric Corp. - USA - 1991

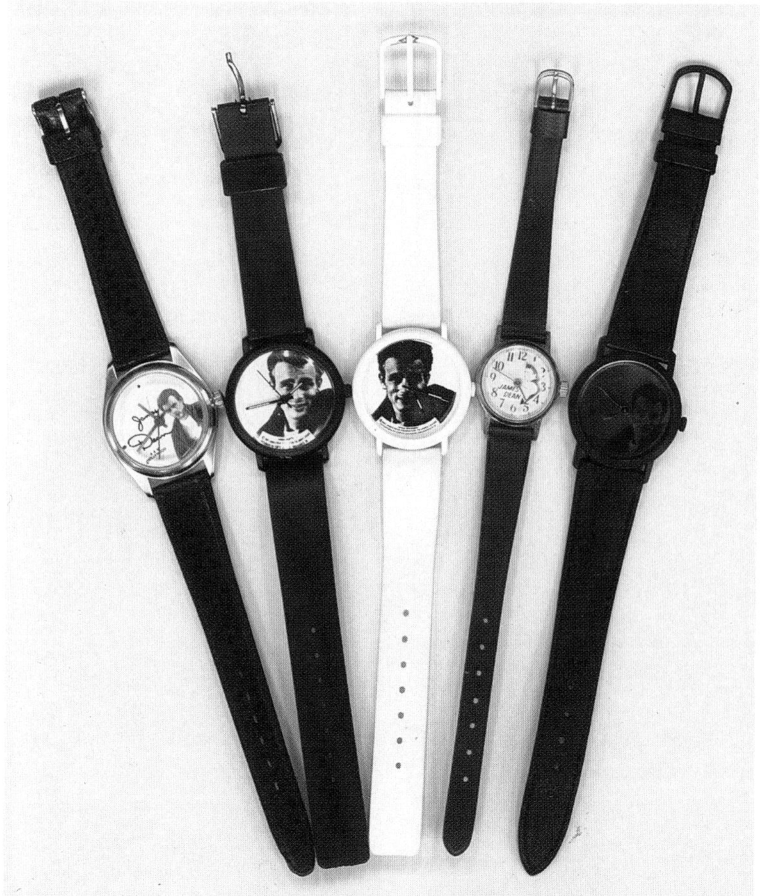

1. 1987 - HBL - United Kingdom
2. 1984
3. 1987 - HBL - USA
4. 1987 - HBL - USA
5. 1985 - A & M - USA

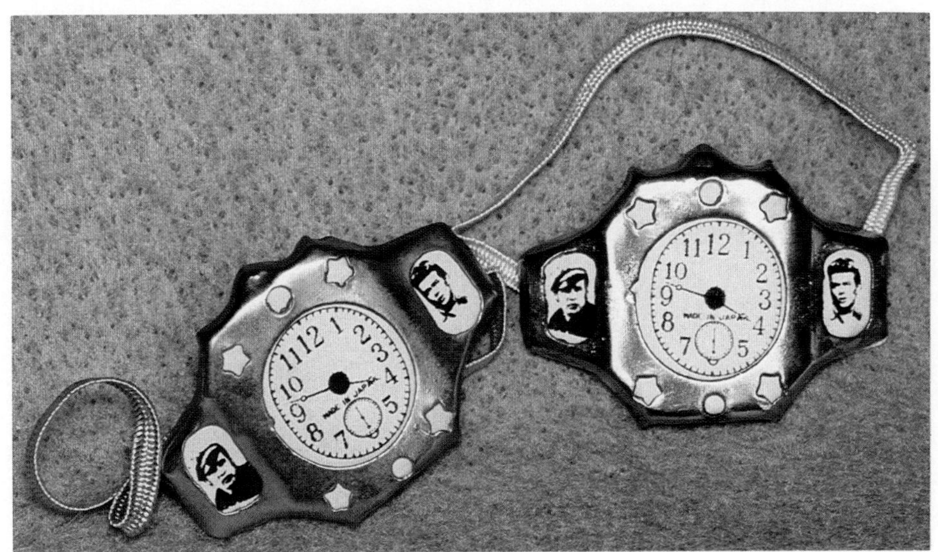

Toy Watch
Japan - 1950s

All are HBL - 1987
except the one on the far right - no info available

No information available

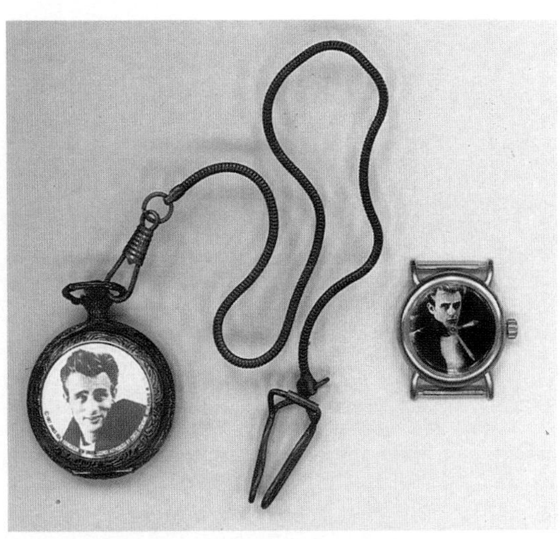

No information available

Shady Character Eyewear
and Counter Top Stand-up
USA - 1988

Japan - 1990

Sunworld Ltd. Eyewear Catalog
Japan - 1991

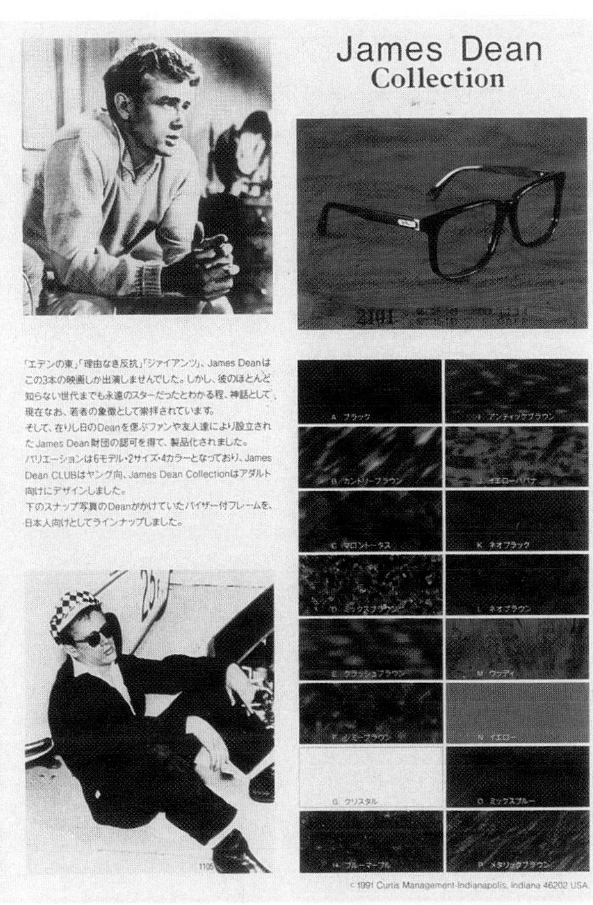

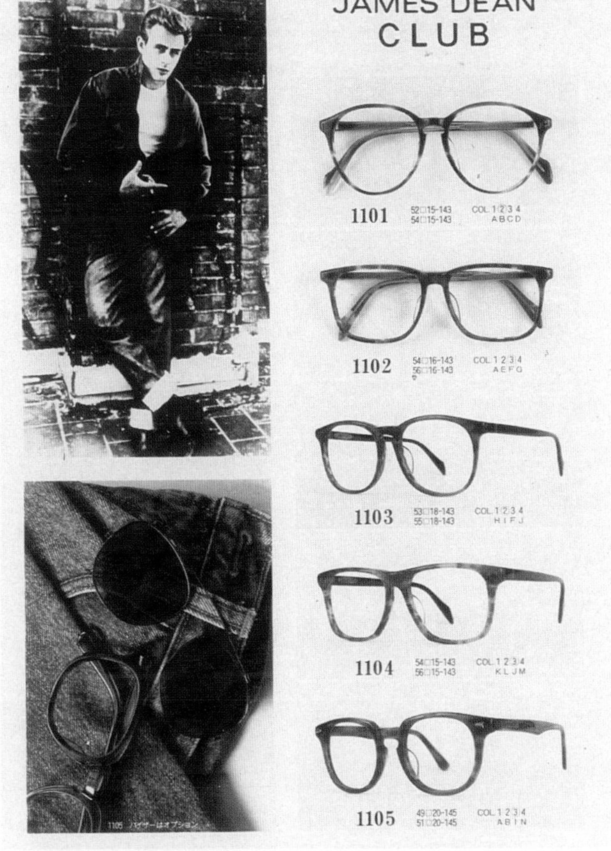

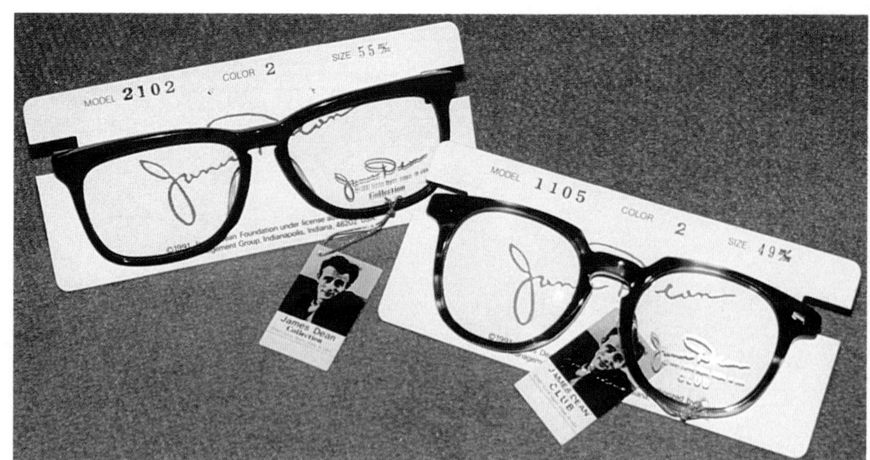

Sunworld Ltd.
Japan - 1991

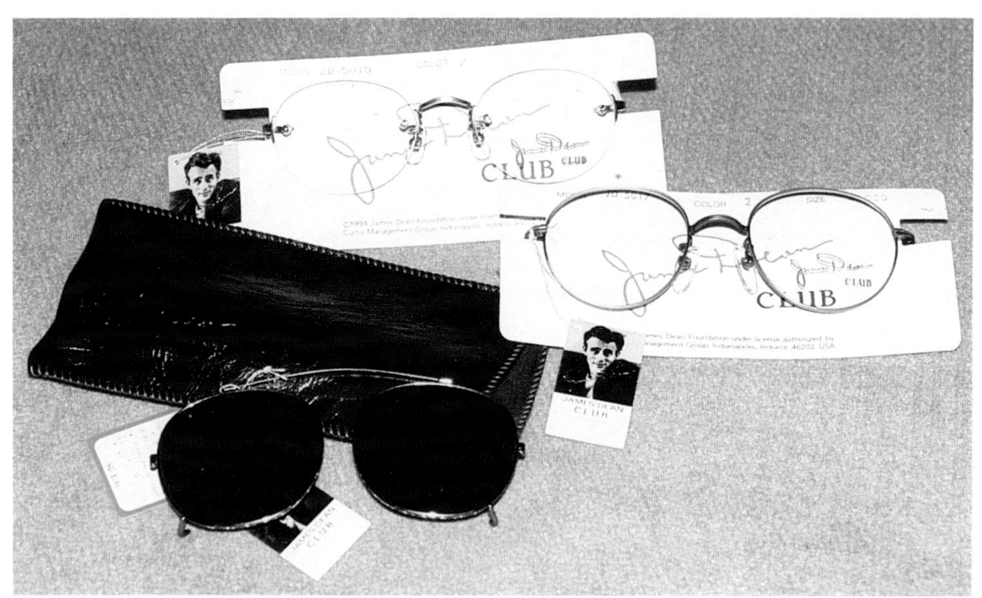

Sunworld Ltd.
Japan - 1991

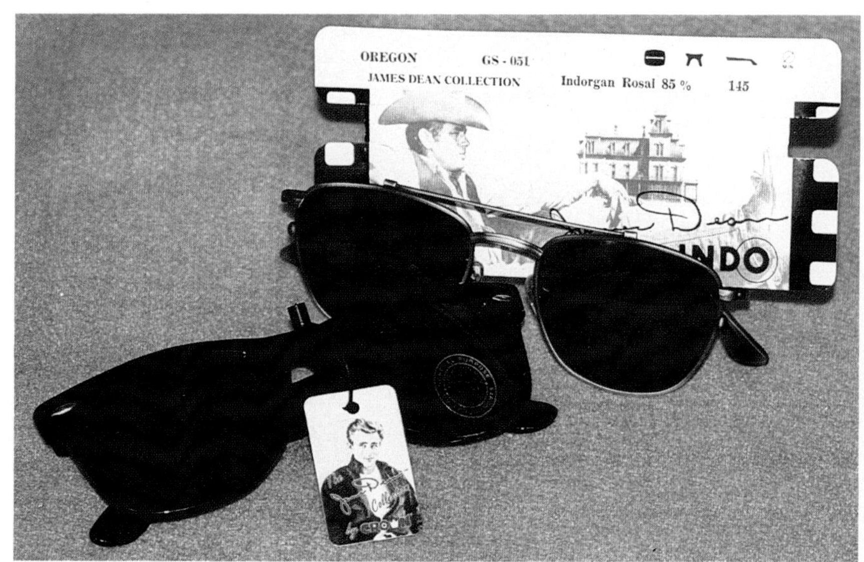

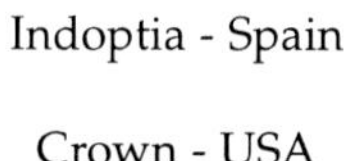

Indoptia - Spain

Crown - USA

Sunworld Ltd.
Japan - 1995

Sunworld Ltd.
Japan - 1995

Wallet
Japan - 1992

Bronze Belt Buckle
Sculpted and Cast by
Kenneth Kendall
USA - 1985

Less than 100 produced

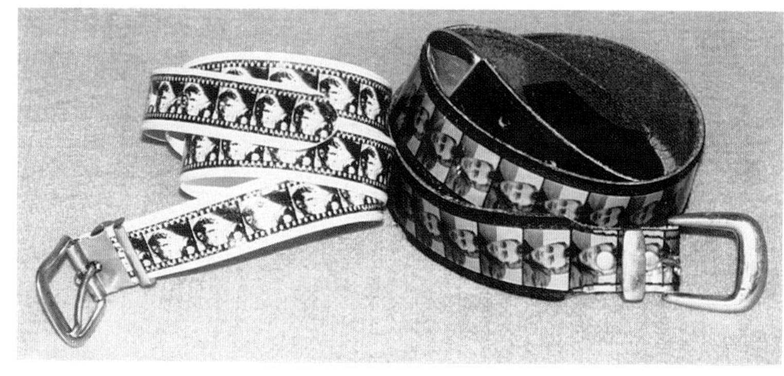

Plastic Belts

Left: Germany - 1983

Right: USA - 1995

Assortment of Leather Belts
Sunworld Ltd.
Japan - 1995

Cruising International - USA - 1998
American Legends - USA - 1991

USA
1985 - 1990

USA - 1990

Socks
France - 1990

Shoe Tote Bag & Shoes
Sunworld Ltd.
Japan - 1991

Umbrella
Gremo, Holland - 1990

Sunworld Ltd.
Japan - 1997

Sunworld Ltd.
Japan - 1997

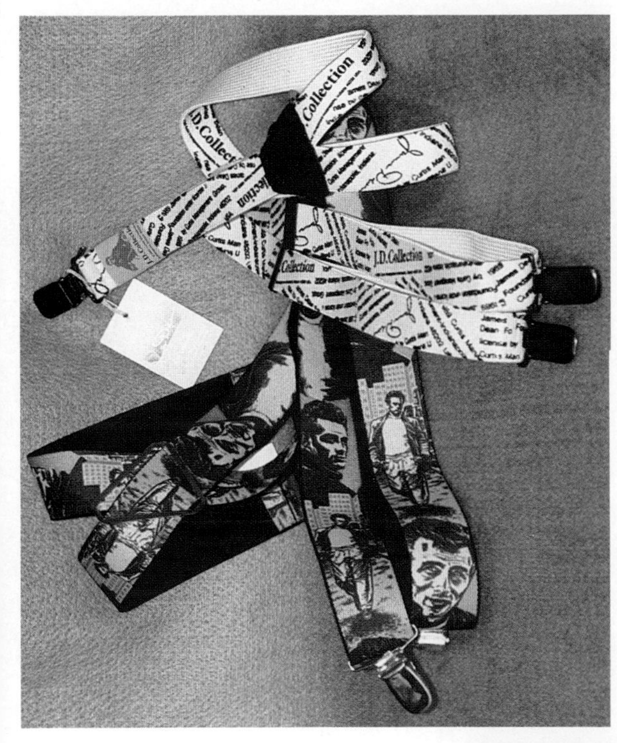

Top pair of Suspenders
Sunworld Ltd. - Japan - 1989

Bottom Pair of Suspenders
B & G - USA - 1994

Scarves
England - 1993
Japan - 1992

Sweatbands
USA - 1982

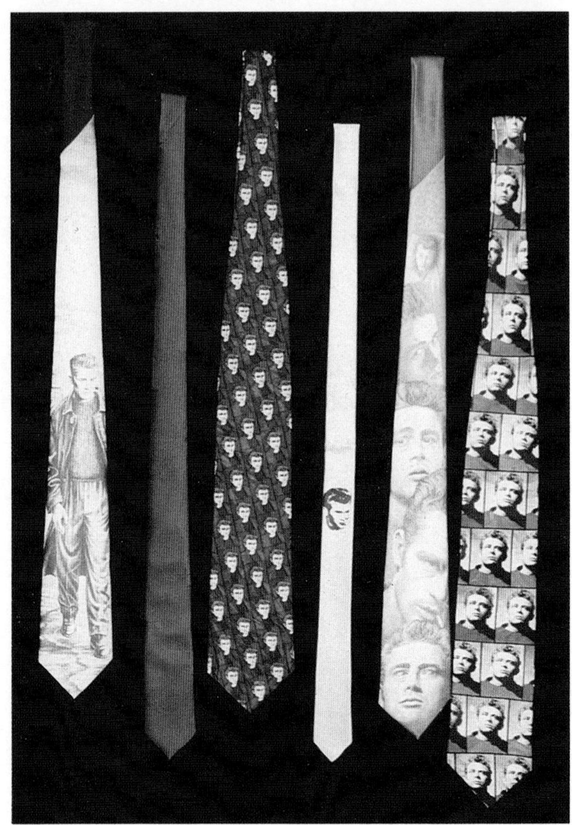

Assorted Neckties
Ralph Manlin - USA - 1994
Havana Fashions - England - 1990

Handmade Earrings By Betty Dixon
USA - 1988

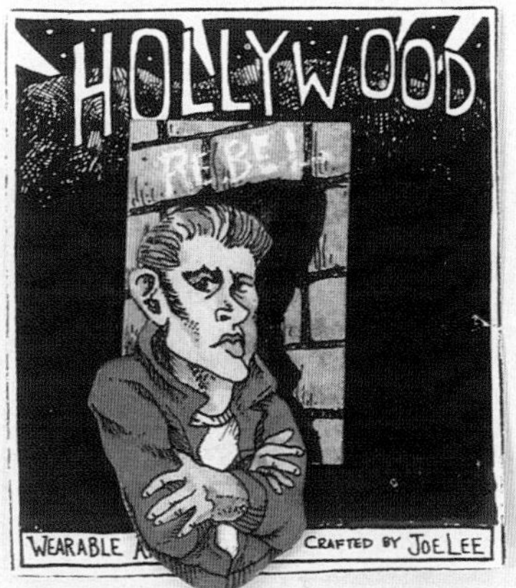

Wearable Art Pin
by Joe Lee
USA - 1990

Film Clip Earrings
USA - 1990

Handmade Pins by René
USA - 1998

Rings - Japan - no date available

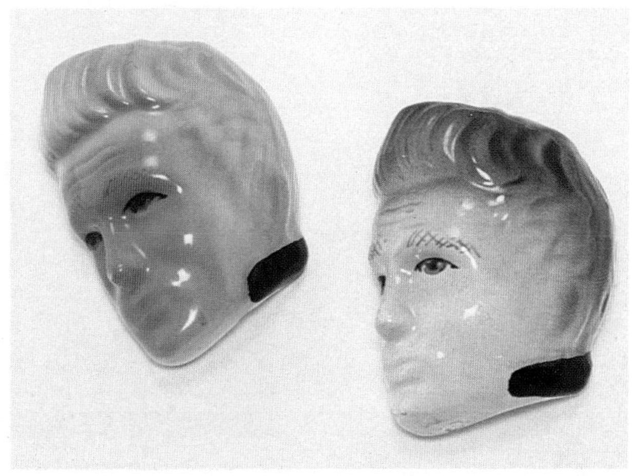

Ceramic Pins
Korea - 1986

"I think there's only one true form of greatness for a man. If a man can bridge the gap between life and death... I mean, if he can live on after he's died, then maybe he was a great man."
James Dean
JAMES DEAN
JAMES DEAN
CINEMASCOPE
BLACKWELL'S CORNER
130
HIGHWAY 46 & 33
LOST HILLS, CALIFORNIA
JAMES DEAN
james dean
EAST OF EDEN
DEAN
1931-1955
JAMES DEAN

T-Shirts

There have been hundreds of different James Dean T-Shirts produced, beginning in the 1970s. These are a few examples.

Hairbrush - Germany - 1989

Combs - USA - 1992

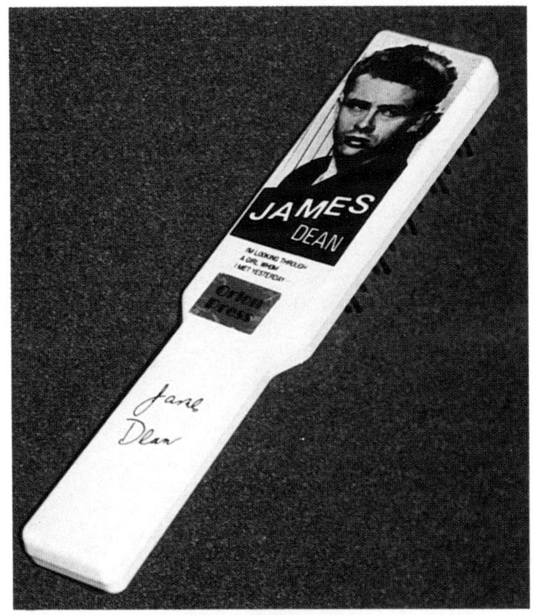

Hairbrush - Orion Press - Japan - 1990

Collector Spoon - USA - 1982

Thimble - USA - 1985

Left to Right:
Pocket Mirrors
Japan - 1992
USA - 1985

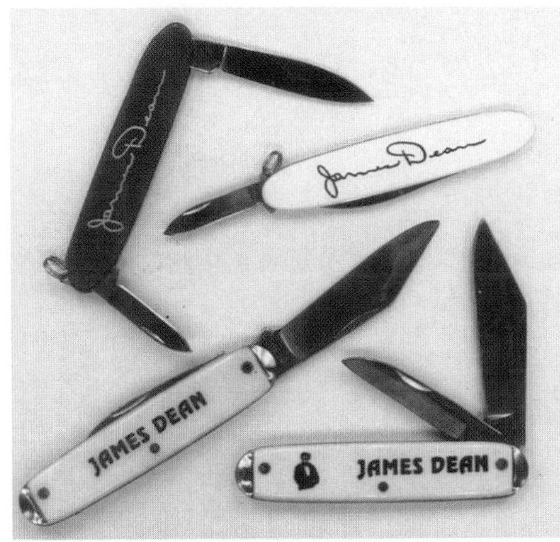

Jacknives - USA - 1992-94

Bottle Cap Opener
Koziol, Germany - 1982

Tall table lamp - Gerard Lamy
France - 1984

Globe lamp - James Dean Club - Japan

Triangle lamp - Japan - 1985

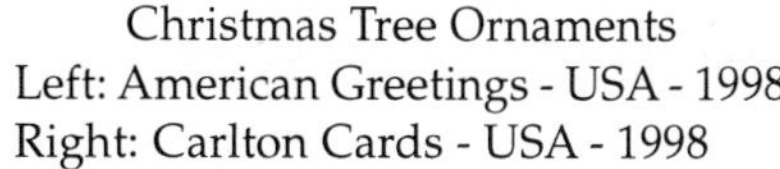

Christmas Tree Ornaments
Left: American Greetings - USA - 1998
Right: Carlton Cards - USA - 1998

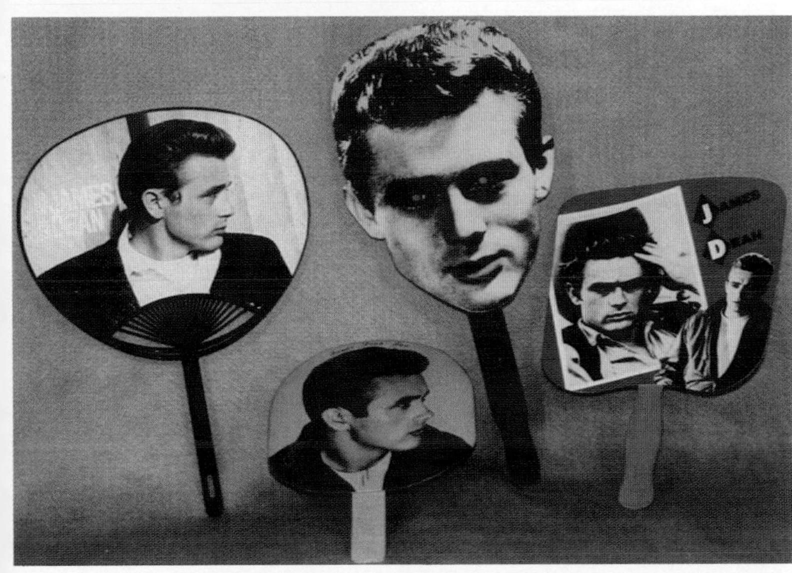

Fans - Japan - no dates available

Party Favor Edition F. Nugeron
France - 1987

Balloons - 1985

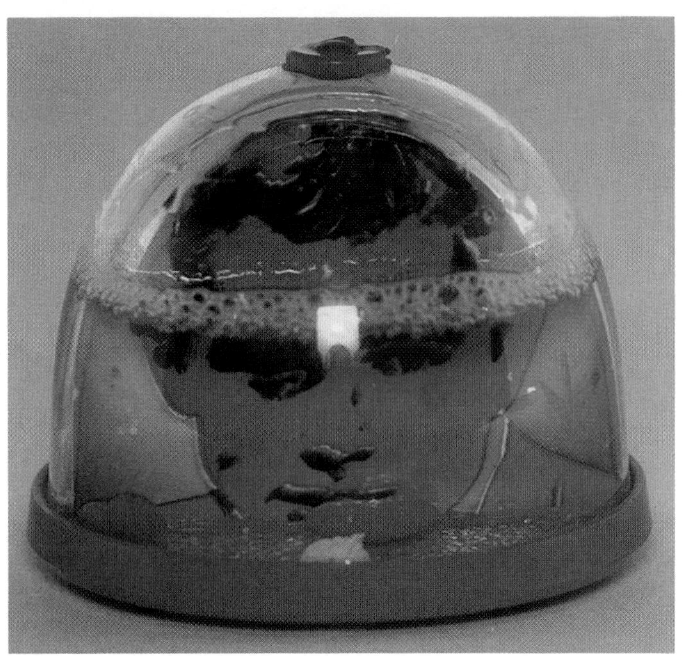

Snow Dome - Koziol, Germany - 1982

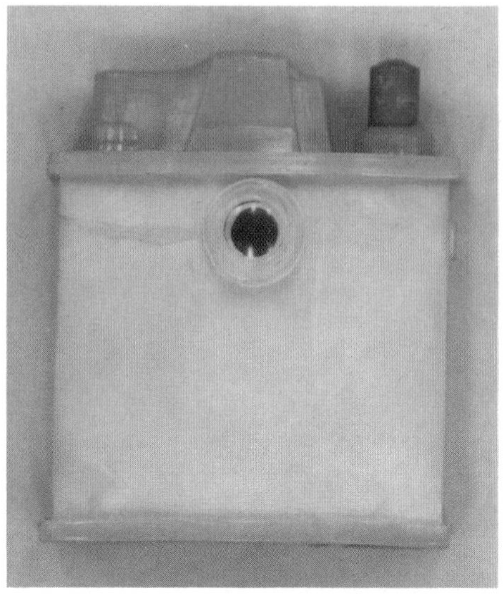

Plastic Viewer, made to resemble a cigarette lighter. By looking through the lens and clicking the blue button, you can see twelve images of James Dean.
Japan - 1957

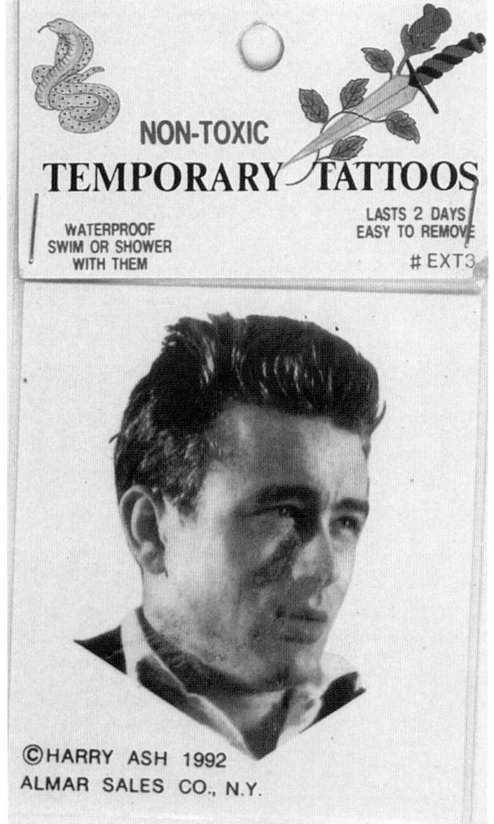

Temporary Tattos
Almar Sales Co. Ltd.
USA - 1992

Novelty Card
Maiden Jest, Inc. - USA - 1983

Placemat
USA - 1980

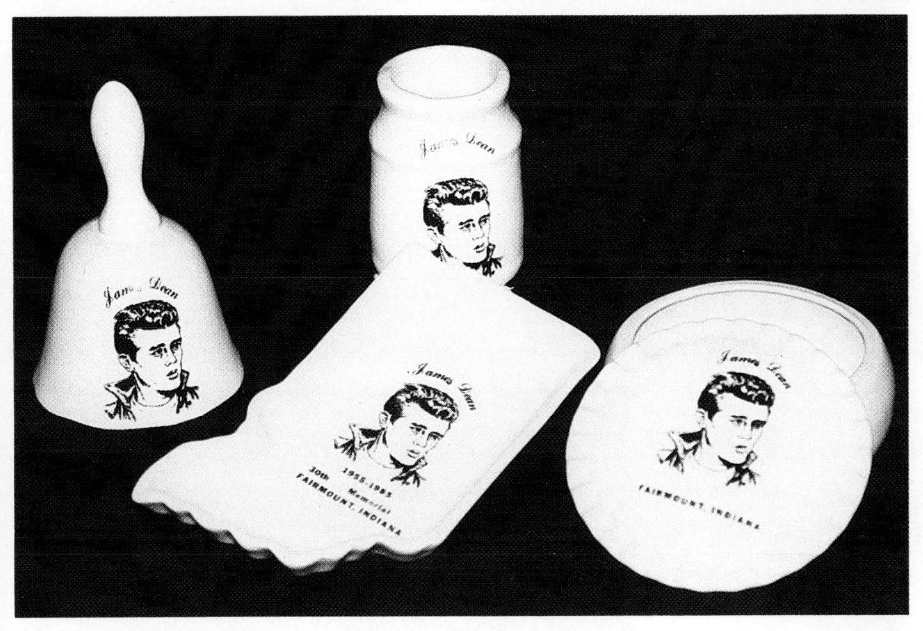

Ceramic Bell and three different containers.
No dates

Clay Art

USA - 1996

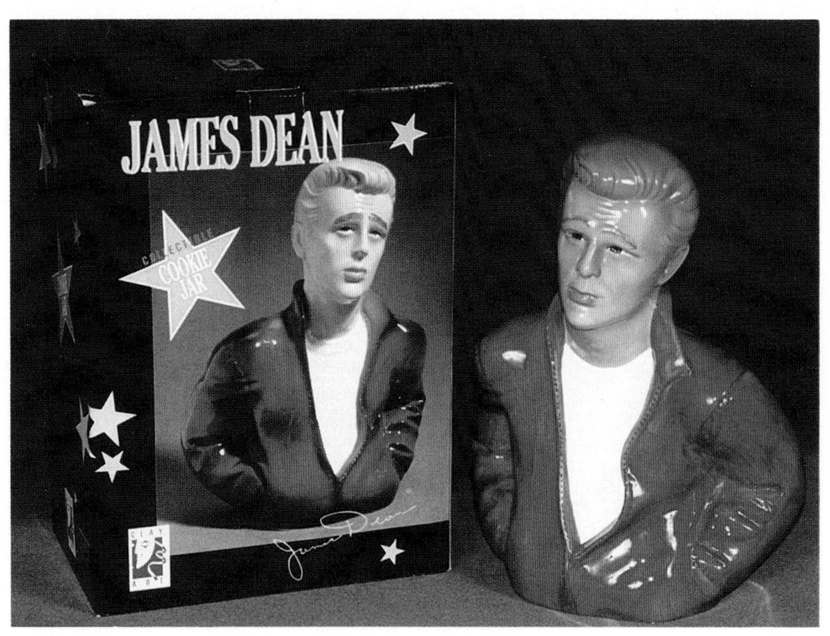

Cookie Jar - Clay Art
USA - 1996

Cookie Jars - Happy Memories Collectibles - USA - 1994
Numbered editions of 500

Ceramic Bobbing Head Doll
9″ tall - Sam Inc. - USA - 1995
Numbered edition of 10,000

Hinged Ceramic Box - 3″ tall
Kurt S. Adler - USA - 1998

Nostalgia Collectibles - 71/2″ tall
USA - 1985
Number edition of 10,000

Left to Right:
Clay Art - 1987
Small statue - Japan - 1965
Statue with red jacket - Esco Products - USA - 1982
The Image Company - USA - 1993
Diana Young - USA - 1997

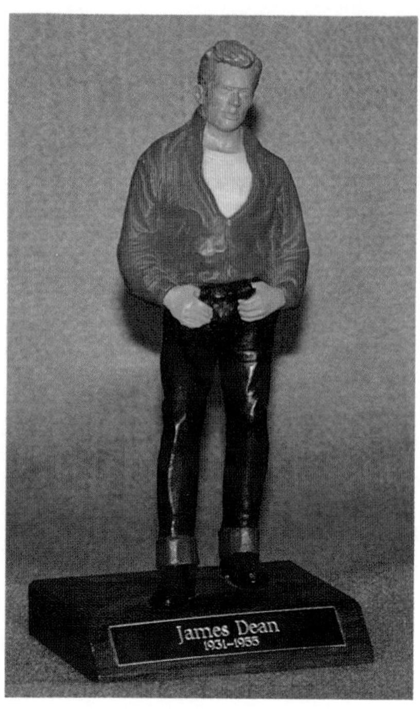

Statue - Spittin Image
8″ tall - USA - 1992

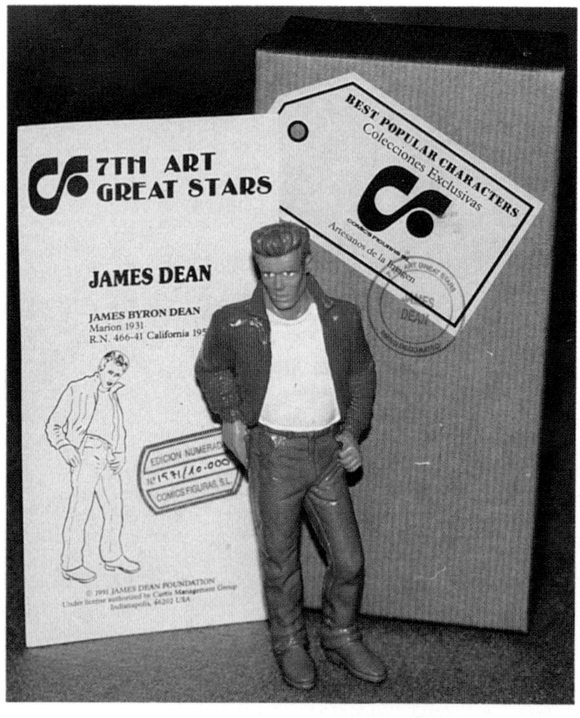

Figure by 7th Art Great Stars
5″ tall - Spain - 1991
Numbered edition of 10,000

Hot Properties, Inc.
Action Figure - 6″ tall - USA - 1993

Figures by Devirsified Specialists Inc.
12″ tall - USA - 1994

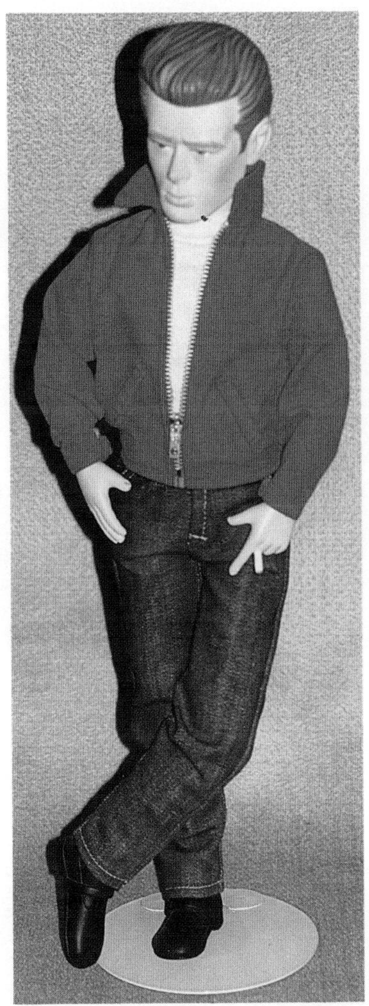

Figure by Dakin Doll Co.
18″ tall - USA - 1984

Star Sacks by Collecting Concepts
10″ tall - USA - 1998

Figures - Exclusive Toy Products
10″ tall - USA - 1998

Ashtrays - Japan and France - no dates available

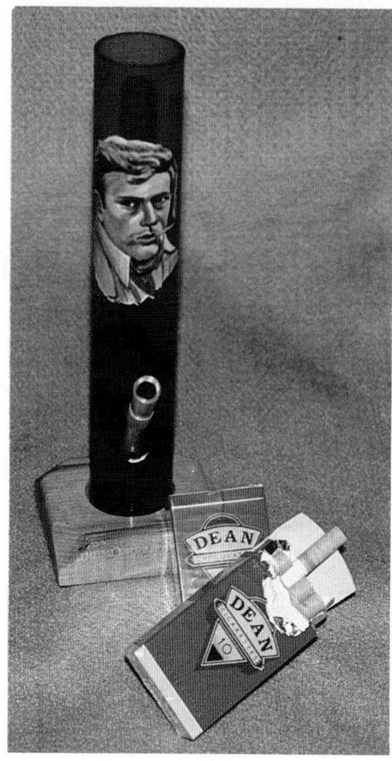

Smoking Pipe - USA - 1984
Dean Cigarettes - Japan - 1989

Cigarette Cases from Japan and France
no dates available

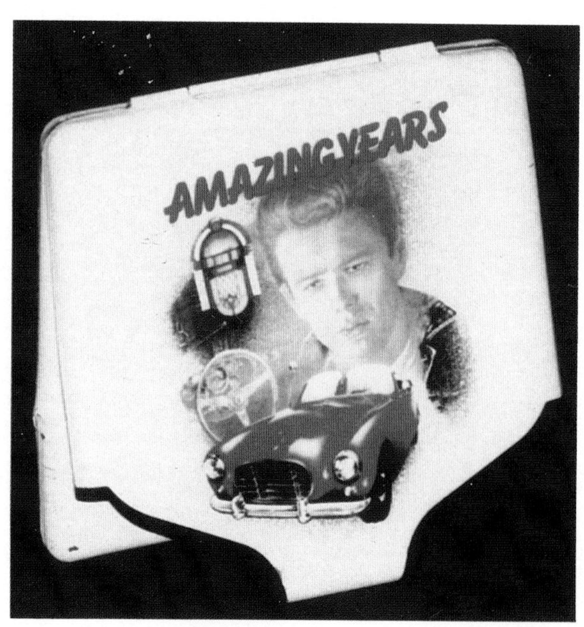

Cigarette Case
No information available

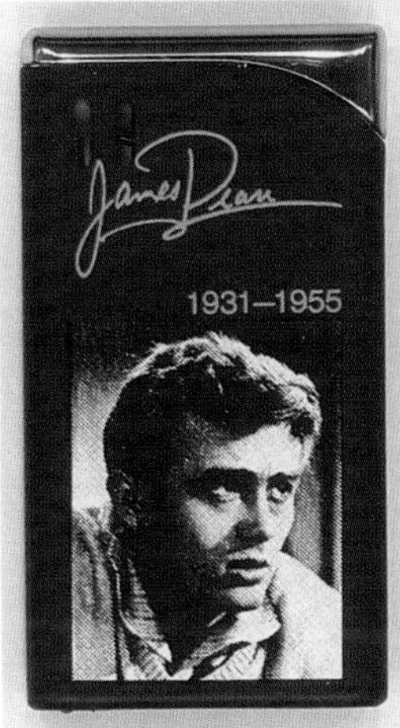

Butane Lighter
Modern Vista - Japan - 1995

The two silver lighters are zippos from 1989.
The others are inexpensive replicas.

Disposable Lighters - no information available

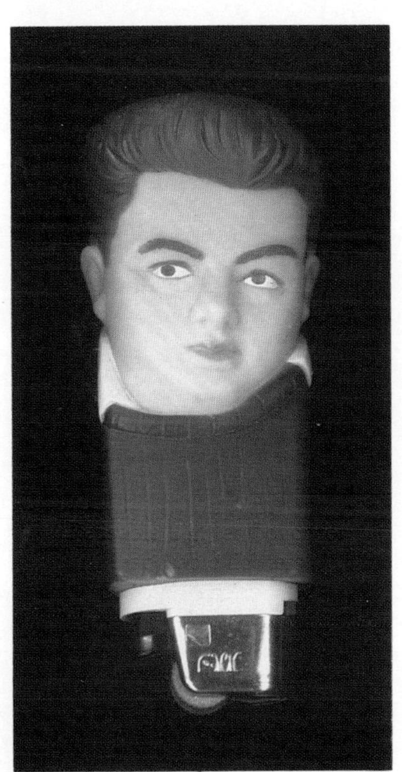

Reusable Lighter Cover for
disposable lighters
D.O.A. - Japan - 1992

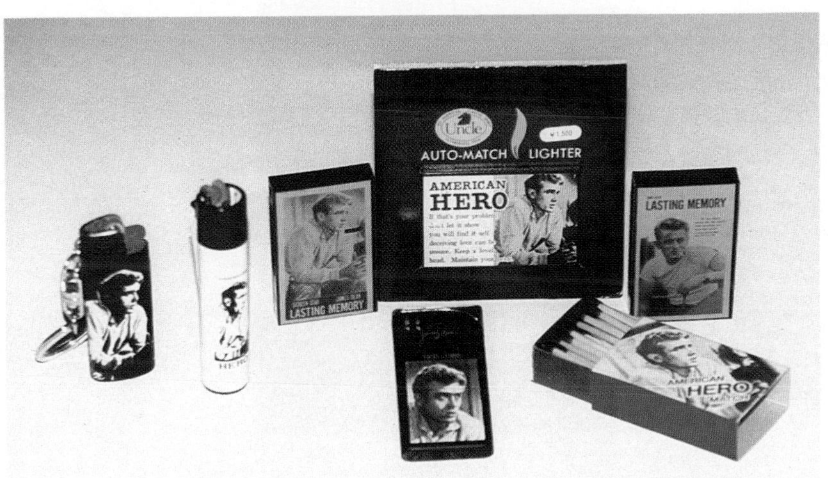

Butane Lighters and Matches
Japan - 1990-96

Tin Boxes - Japan

Selection Bernard Carant - Paris - 1986

Tin Boxes Left to Right:
James Dean Collection - Japan - no date available
F. Nugeron - France - no date available
Bernard Carant - France - no date available

Tin Boxes - Ellon - Japan - 1987

Tin Trays - Japan - no information available

Tin Boxes
Balvi - no information
Edition F. Nugeron France
Hollywood Stars - no information

Top:
Selection Bernard Carant, France - 1986

Bottom:
Lyric - Japan - 1986

Japan - no information

Puzzle Greeting Card
Puzzling Pieces - USA - 1998

Puzzle Post Card
Fairmount, Indiana - 1991

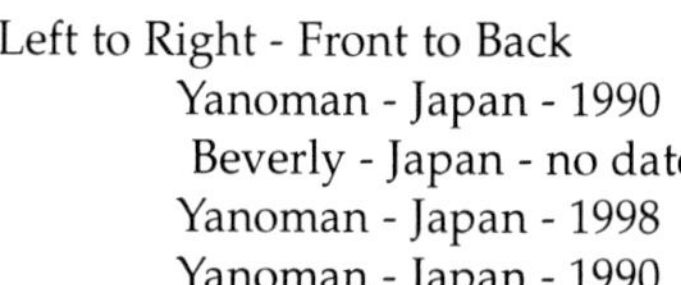

Left to Right - Front to Back
Yanoman - Japan - 1990
Beverly - Japan - no date
Yanoman - Japan - 1998
Yanoman - Japan - 1990

Front: Japan - no information
Left: Oh'Share Art - Japan - 1990
Right: Orion Press - Japan - 1992

Multi-Piece Magnet
Greeting Card
by Stinkers

Left: Coup de coeur - France - 1996

Right: Fink & Co. - USA - 1995

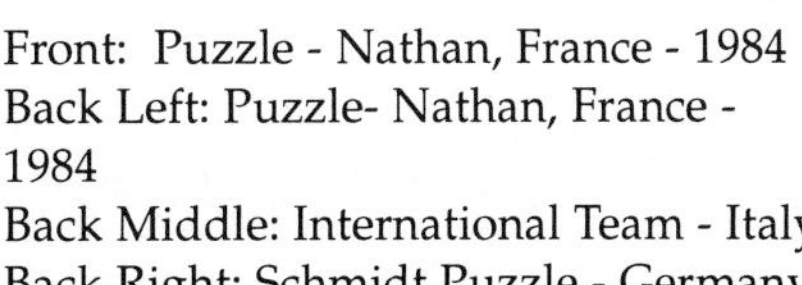
Front: Puzzle - Nathan, France - 1984
Back Left: Puzzle- Nathan, France - 1984
Back Middle: International Team - Italy
Back Right: Schmidt Puzzle - Germany

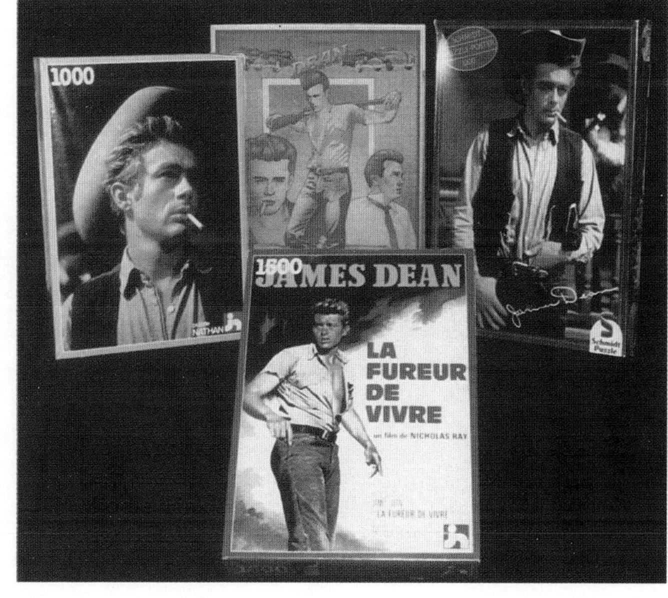

Front Middle: Missing Link Trading Co. - UK - 1987
Left: Golden Spotlight Puzzle - USA - 1991
Middle: Fink & Co. - USA
Right: Hallmark Cards Inc. - USA - 1985

Porche Spyder
Tootsie Toy - USA
no date available

Porche Spyder
Maisto International
USA - 1997

Front Left: Spec Cast - USA - 1995
Back Middle: Collector Cars Solido, France - 1994
Right: Solido, France - 1994

Porche Spyder
Solitair Model Cars
CMC exclusive numbered edition
Germany - 1998

Porche Spyder
Brumm - Italy - 1996

Porche Speedster
Brumm - Italy - 1996

Porche Spyder
Solido - France - 1995

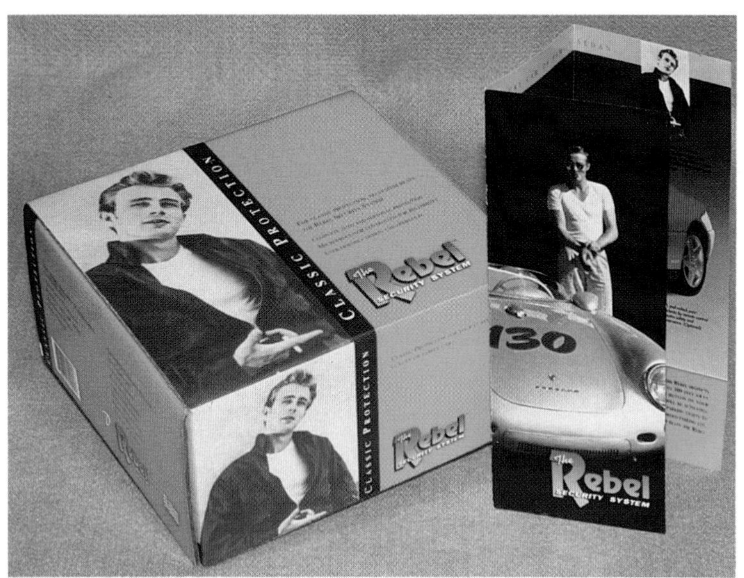

Rebel Car Security System
Accele, Inc. - USA - 1993

Disposable Breath Tester and Alcohol
Level Reducer S. O. B. A.
South Africia - 1998

Steering Wheel Knobs
no information

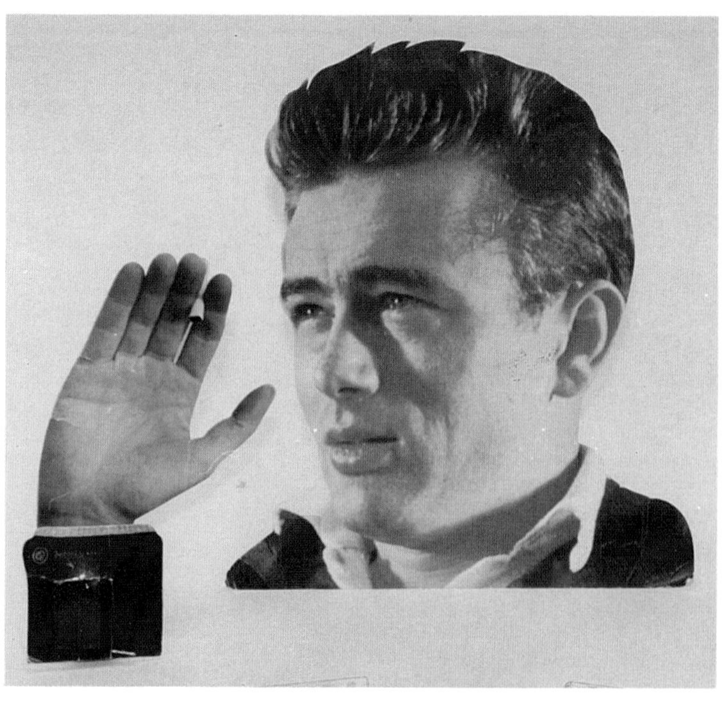

Car Window Waver - 1984

The face and the hand would stick to a car window. There is a spring between the hand and the cuff and the hand waves.

Car Assortment - Made in China
no date available

Automobile Sun Shade
Celebrity Shade - USA - 1986

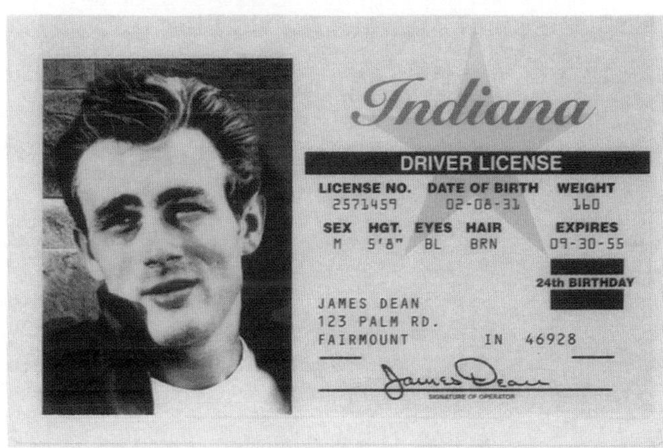

Novelty Drivers License
Mid South Products - USA - 1997

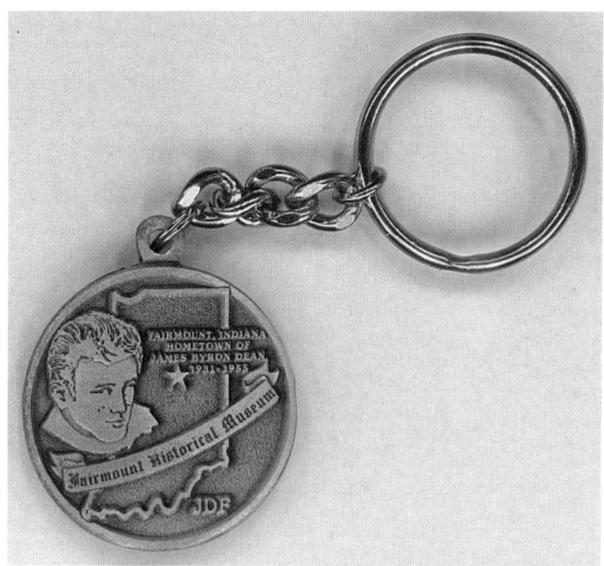

Souvenir of the Fairmount Historical Museum
Fairmount, Indiana - 1990

The March Company - USA - 1996

AMC - USA - 1997

Lights, Camera Action
USA - 1994

There have been several dozen different James Dean
Key Chains over the years. These are a few examples.

Examples of James Dean License Plates. Fans vanity plates, commemorative plates, and commercially available plates with various dates - USA

Rebel Deodorant and Cologne
South Africa - 1988

Shoe Cream
Japan - 1985

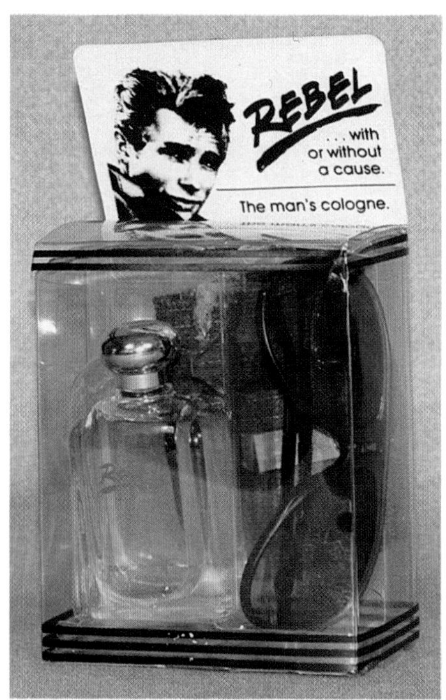

Rebel Cologne
USA - 1988

Aftershave and Stick Deodorant
By Bonnie Bell - Canada - 1990

Aftershave Cream
Spain - 1988

Aftershave, Shampoo and Perfume
Spain - 1988

Salle' Intnl.
USA - 1997

Krizia Uomo - USA - 1987

Andy Warhol prints - Neues Publishing Co.
11″ x 14″ - USA - 1990

Pomegranate - eight prints - 11″ x 14″
USA - 1990

Twelve prints individually signed by photographer Dennis Stock
11 3/4" x 15 3/4" - Japan - 1974

Six reproduction prints - Warner Brothers, Inc.
11" x 14" - USA - 1991

All the phone cards
measure approx. 2 1/8" x 3 3/8"

EZ Comm Prepaid Telephone Card
Issued 9-27-95 - USA

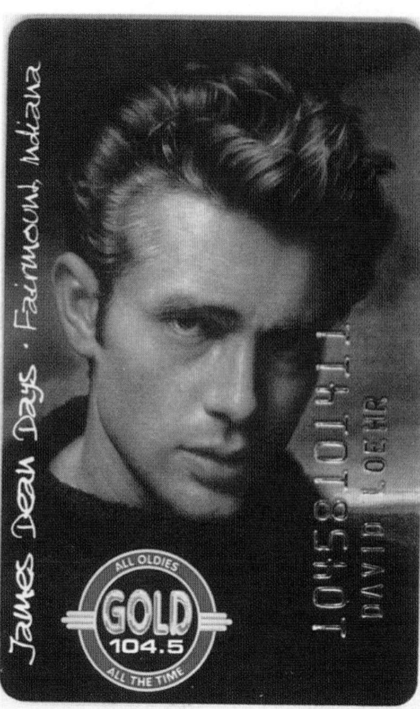

Gold 104.5 Membership and
Phone Card - 1998 - USA

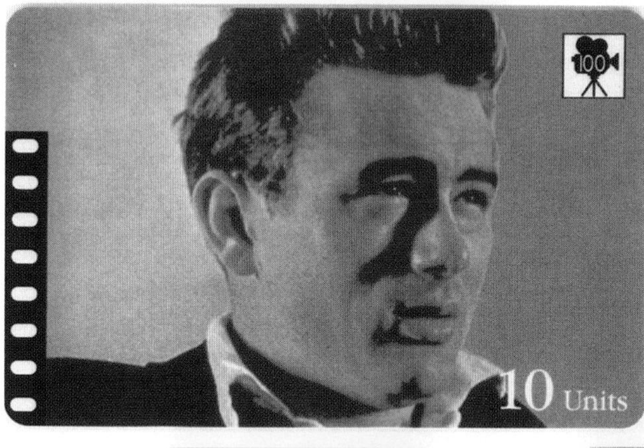

Sport Communicative Co.
USA - 1993

HT Technologies - USA - 1992

Strategic Telecom Systems - USA - 1998

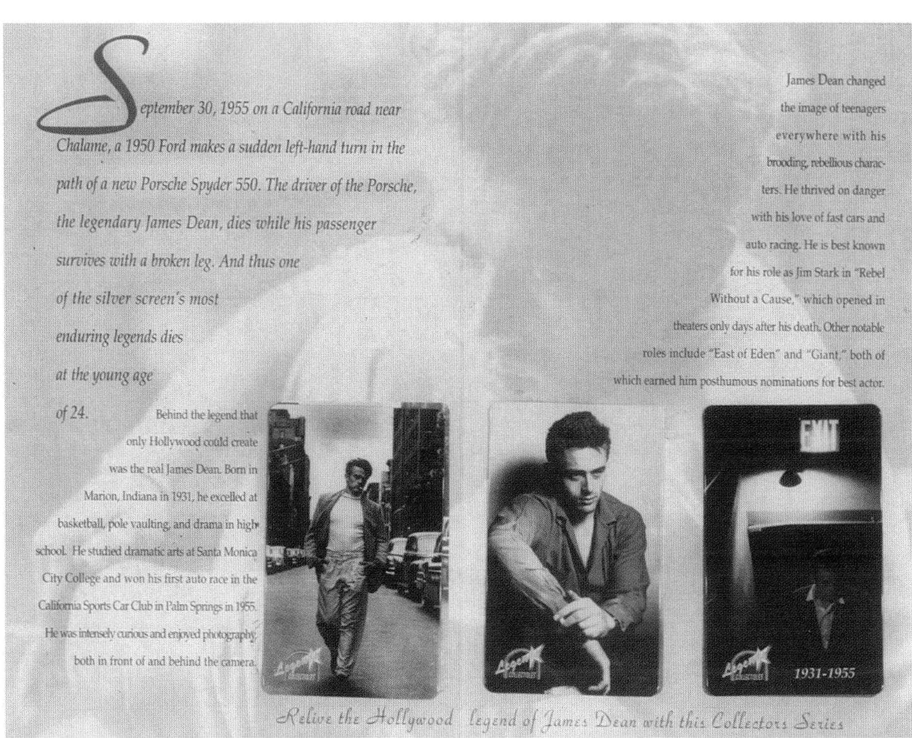

Phone Card Set - STS, Inc.
USA - 1996

Phone Card from K-Mart free with T-Shirt
USA - 1995

Centric - USA - 1996

No Information

1994 Centric USA

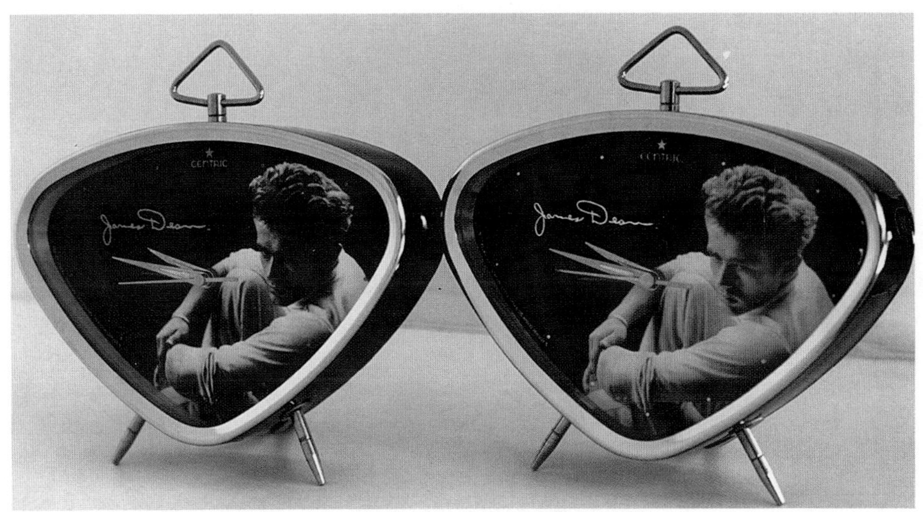

Centric - USA - 1996

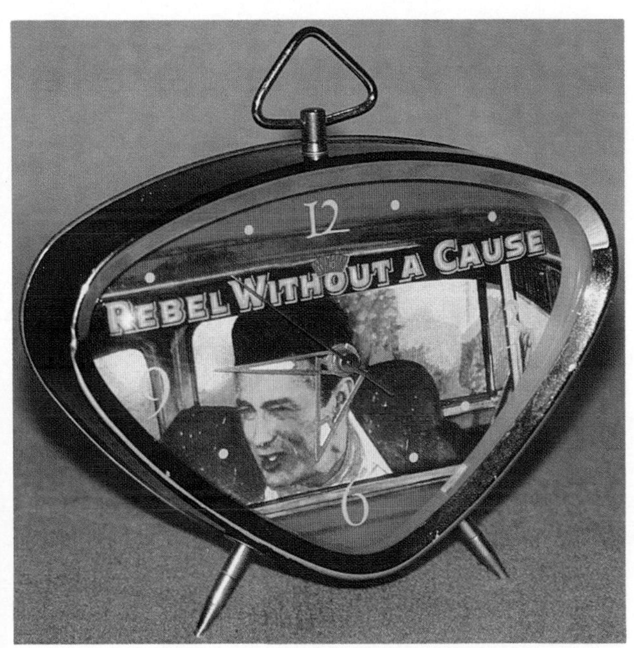

Warner Brothers - 1995 - USA

HBL - USA - 1987

Centric - USA - 1992

Left: No information Right: HBL - USA - 1987

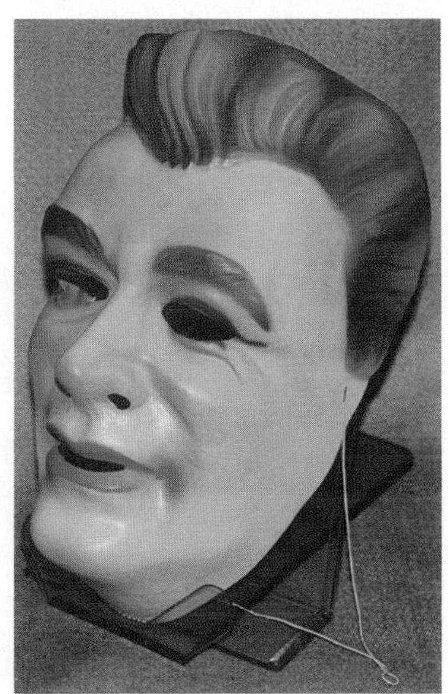

Halloween Mask
France - 1982

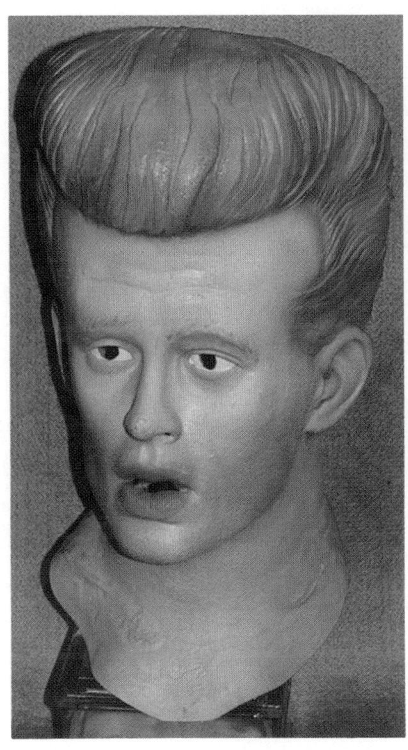

Halloween Mask
USA - 1994

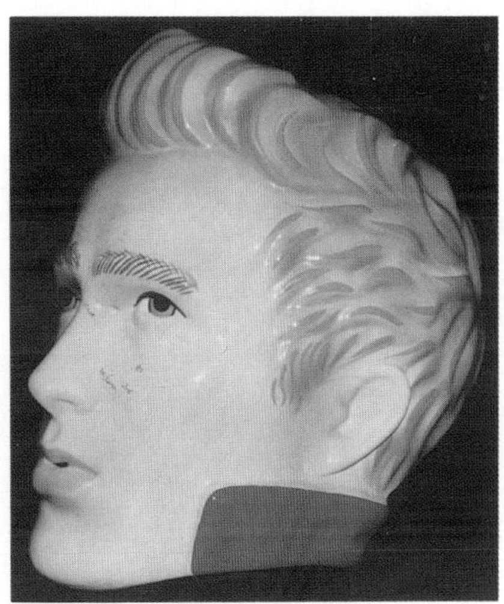

Ceramic Wall Mask
Clay Art - USA - 1986

Plastic Coat Hangers - USA - 1989

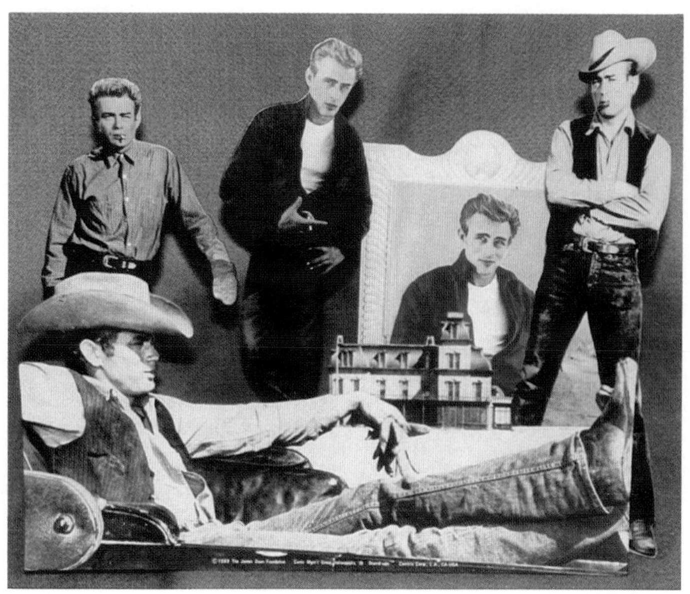

A & M Accessories
Triange Enterprises
USA - 1990-1993

A & M Accessories
Advanced Graphics
USA - 1982-1989

Advanced Graphics
USA - 1989

Advanced Graphics
USA - 1991

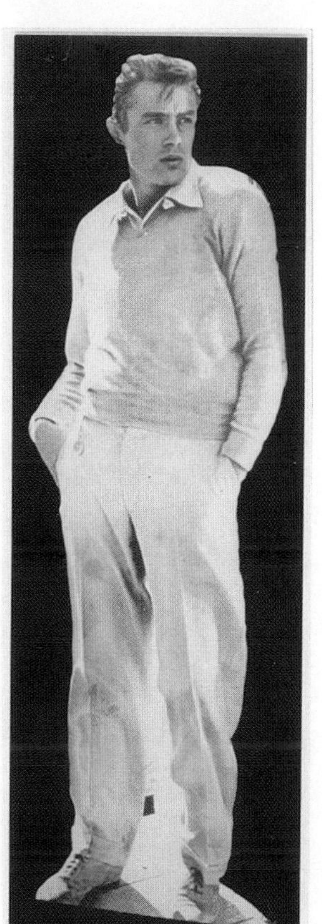

Advanced Graphics
USA - 1992

Advanced Graphics
USA - 1996

Assorted Cloth Wall Hangings
No Information

Nikry Co. - USA - 1987

Woven Afghan
USA - 1995

Nikry Co. - USA - 1987

American Flag - France - 1982

Rebel Flag - France - 1982

Beach Towel
Belgium - 1987

Beach Towel
Greco
USA - 1986

Beach Towel
No Information

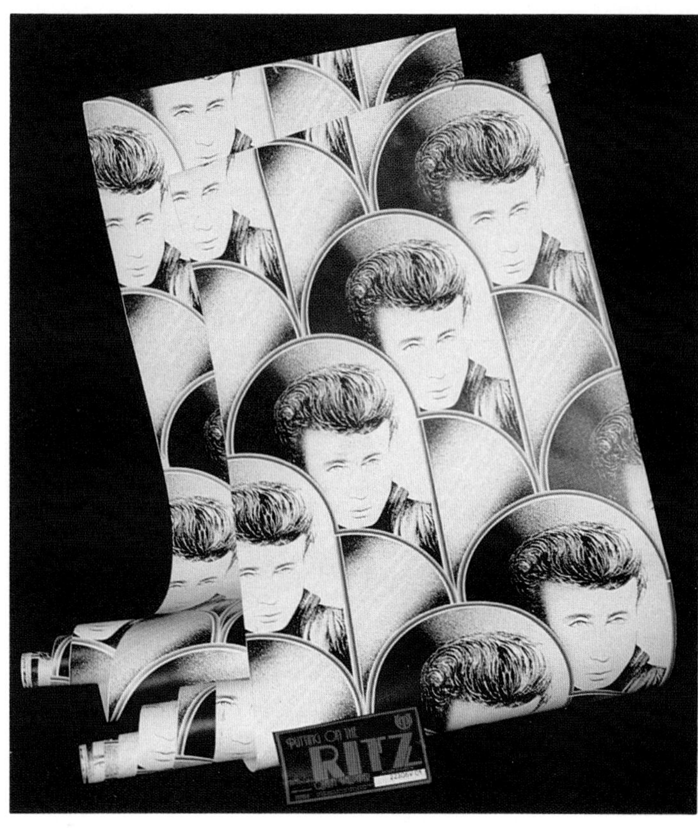

Wallpaper
Puttin On The Ritz
England - 1988

Roll Down Window Shade
Yamalon #R-142
Japan - 1989

Refrigerator Magnets
made by Ata-Boy, Polar Magnetics,
Clay Art and Reed Productions

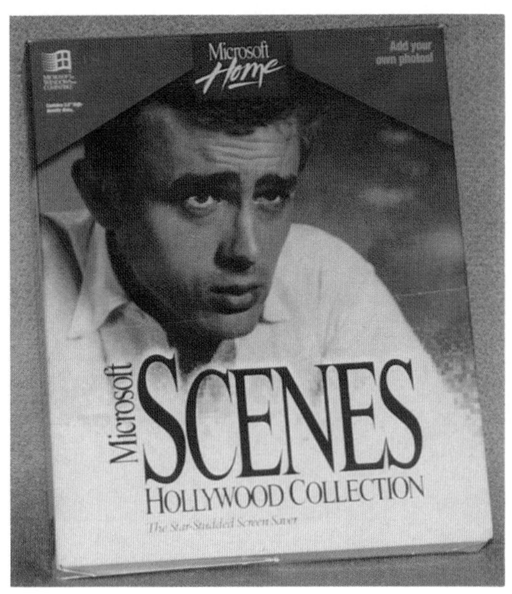

Hollywood Collection
Screen Saver - Microsoft
USA - 1994

Mouse Pads
American Covers
USA - 1997

Coaster Set
Clay Art
USA

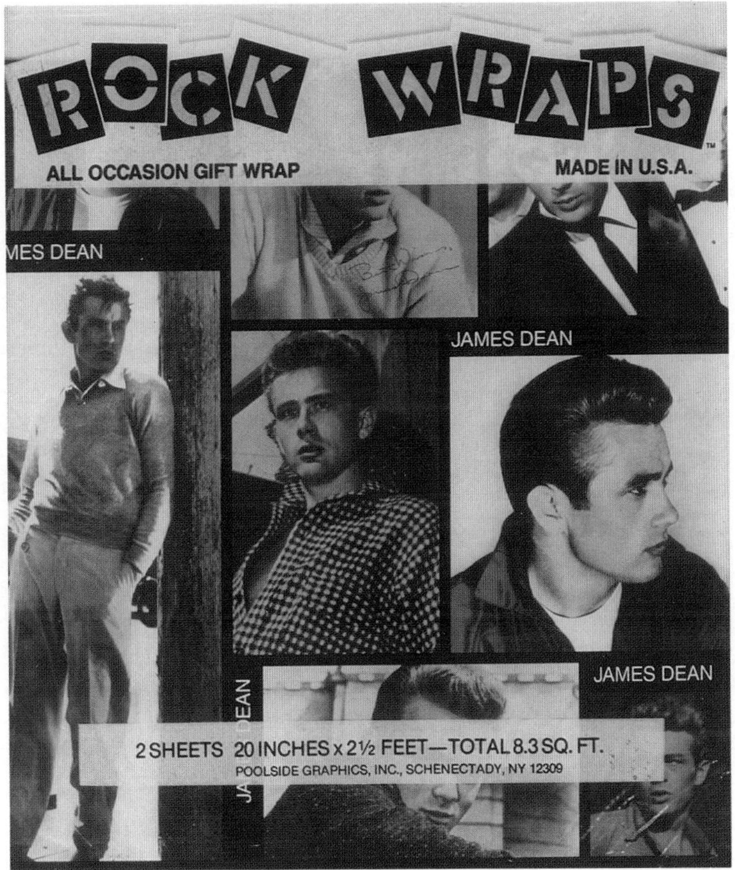

Gift Wrap
Poolside Graphics
USA - 1988

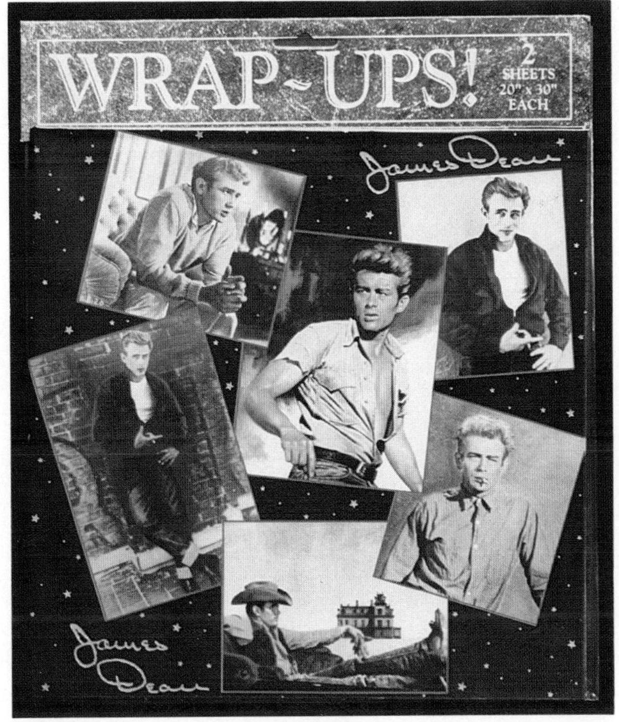

Gift Wrap
Triangle Entertainment
USA - 1992

Assorted Gift Bags
Triange Enterprises - USA - 1989
Portal - USA - 1989
Gideon - USA - 1988

Assorted Shopping Bags & Totes
Italy - 1985
Sari Fabrics Ltd. - France - 1984
Spain - 1986
Total Enterprise Co.

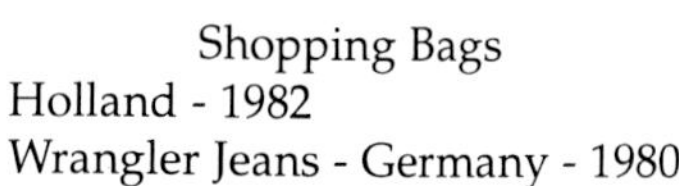
Shopping Bags
Holland - 1982
Wrangler Jeans - Germany - 1980

Pillowcases
Katy K - USA - 1986
HM Group - France - 1987
Associated Marxetin - USA - 1989

Pillows
USA - 1986
USA - 1987
Sunworld Ltd.
Japan - 1989

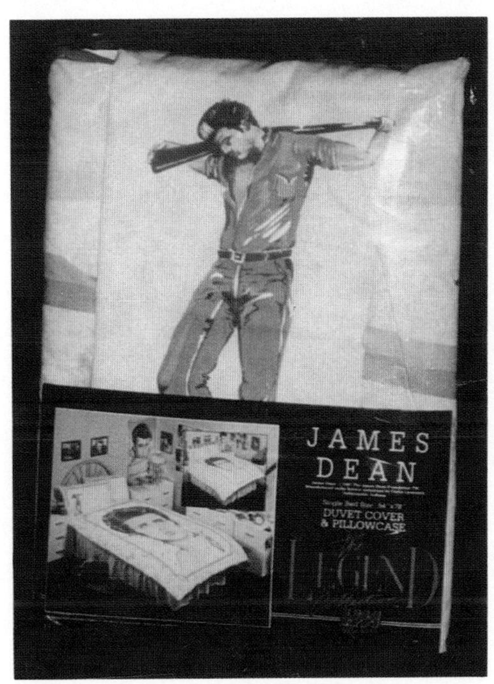

Comforter and Pillow Case Cover Set
HM Group - France - 1987

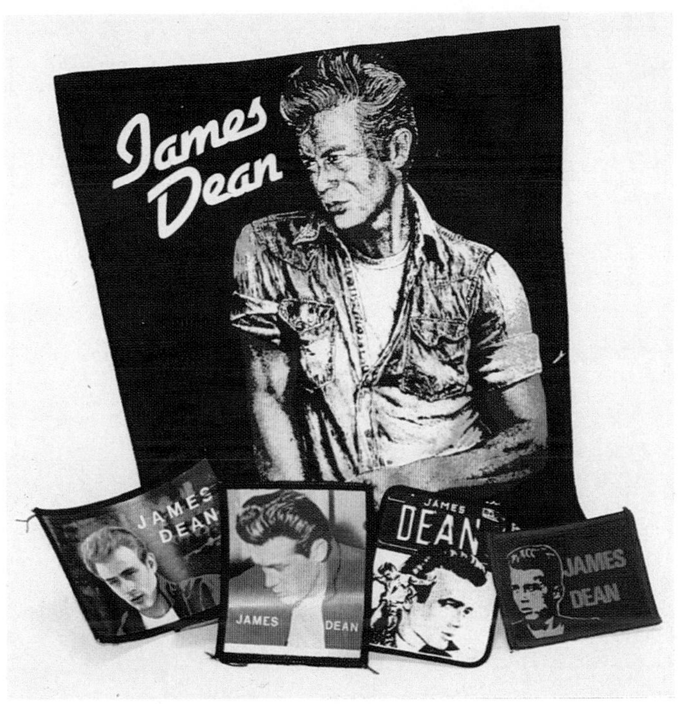

Assorted Sew-On Patches
No date available

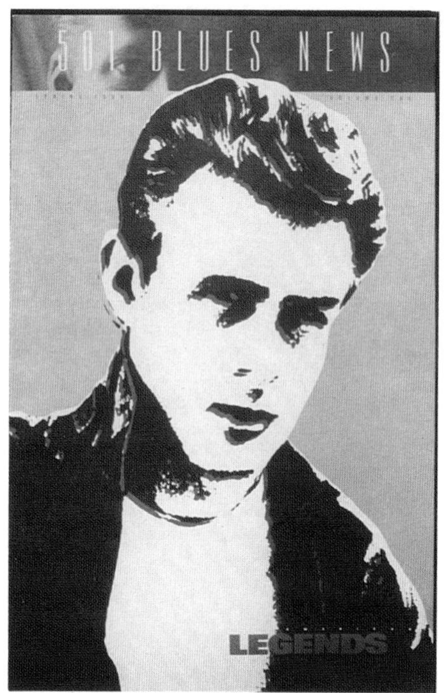

501 Blues News
Levi Strauss - USA - 1988

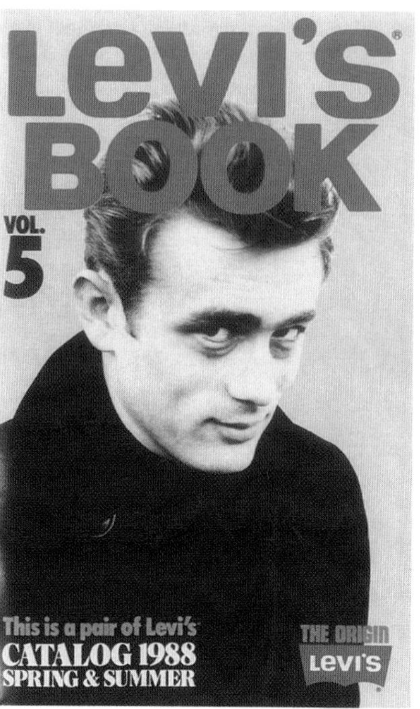

Levi's Book Vol. 5
Spring & Summer
Catalog 1988 - Japan

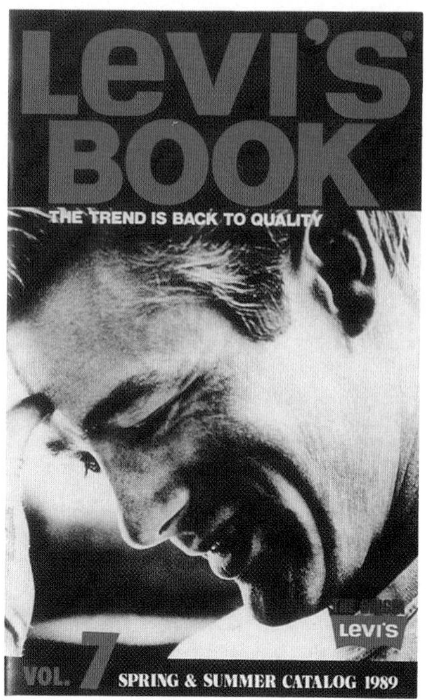

Levi's Book Vol. 7
Spring & Summer
Catalog 1989 - Japan

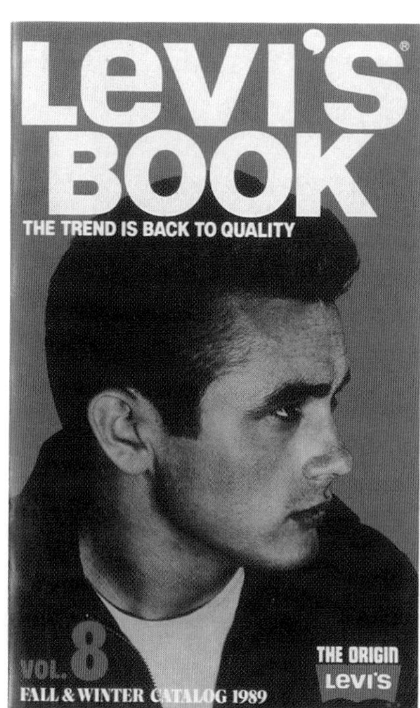

Levi's Book Vol. 8
Fall & Winter
Catalog 1989 - Japan

Levi's Book Vol. 10
Fall & Winter
Catalog 1990 - Japan

"I don't think people should be subservient to move idols . . . . I would like to be a star in my own sense. I mean to be a very consummate actor, to have more difficult roles and to fill them to my satisfaction. But not to be a star on the basis of gold plating. A real star carries its own illumination, an inward brightness."

--Dean to reporter Aline Mosley

Office Furniture Catalog
Corry Jamestown
USA - 1986

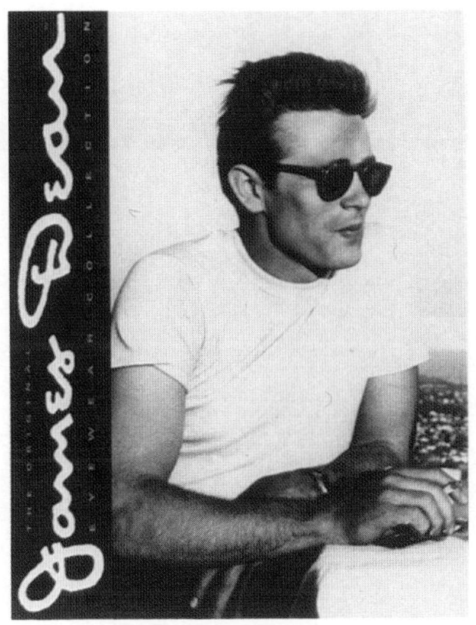

Eyewear Catalog
Shady Character
USA - 1989

Knife Catalog
The Edge Company
USA - 1989

Belt & Wallet Catalog
Sunworld Ltd.
Japan - 1995

Credit Card Advertisement
Japan - 1990

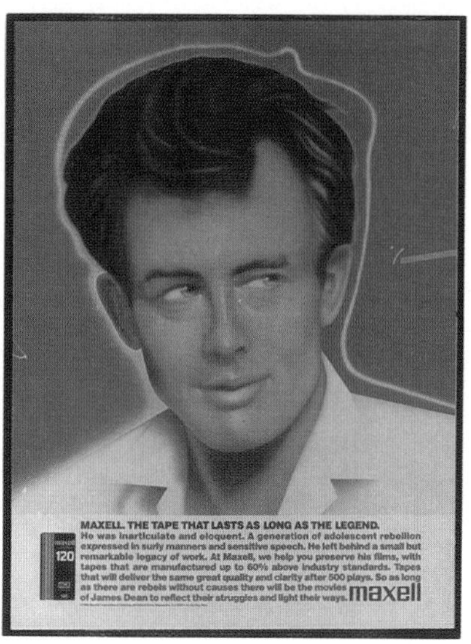

Maxell Tape Advertisement
USA - 1986

CD Player Advertisement
Japan - 1988

Laser Disc Advertisement
Japan - No date available

Casting Directory Listings

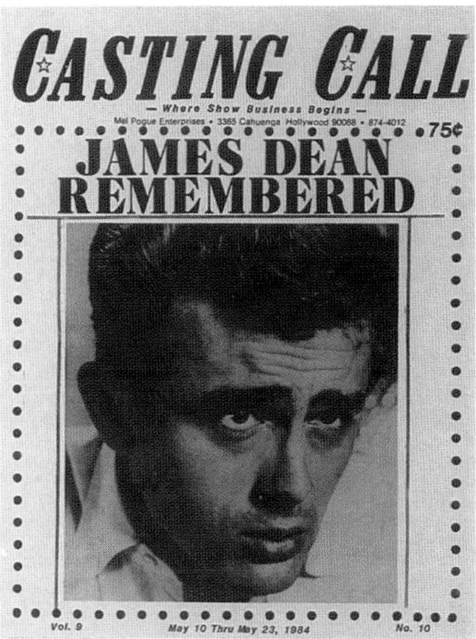

Casting Call Listings
May 10-23, 1994
USA

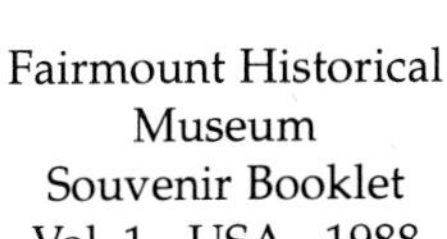

Fairmount Historical
Museum
Souvenir Booklet
Vol. 1 - USA - 1988

Program Brochure
Spain - 1996

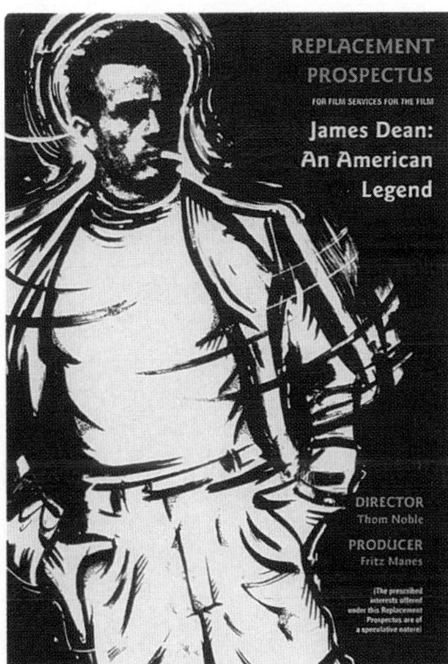

Prospectus for Potential
Film Investors
Australia - 1995

Atelier Michel Favre
Catalog of Art
France - 1988

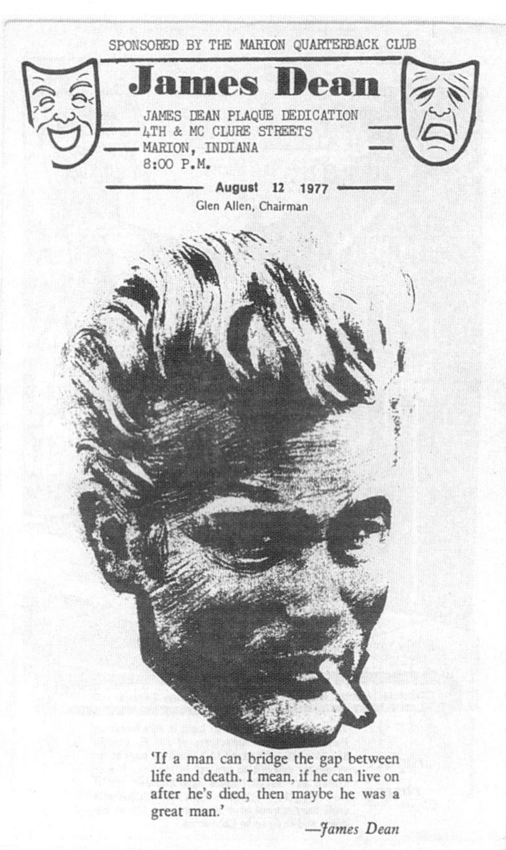

Program from James Dean Birthsite - Plaque and Dedication, Marion, Indiana USA - August 12, 1977

Souvenir Program from the 25th Memorial
Fairmount/Marion, Indiana
USA - September 27-30, 1980

Menu - Giant Restaurant - New York City
USA - 1981

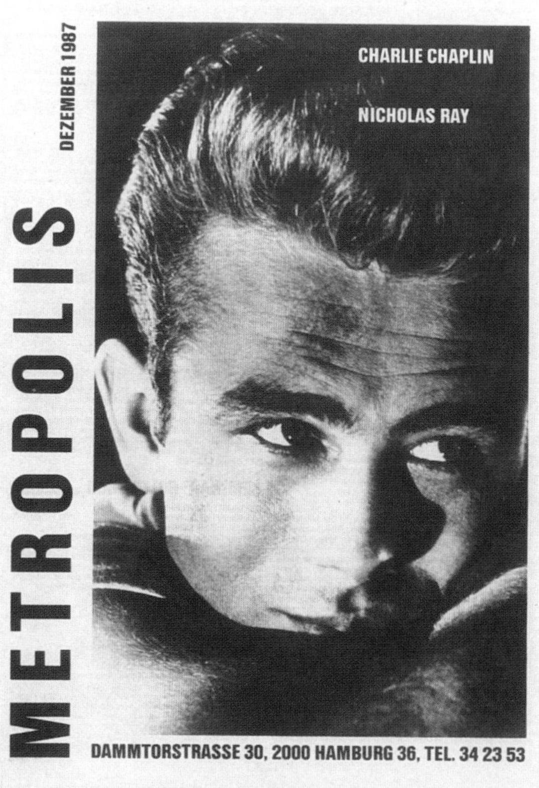

Metropolis Movie Theatre Film Schedule
Germany - December 1987

This photograph was taken by Roy Schatt in his studio at 149 East 33rd Street in New York City on December 29, 1954

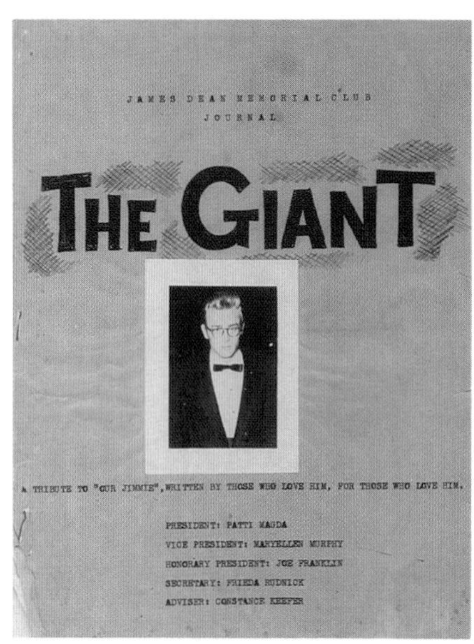

James Dean Memorial Club Journal
USA - 1956

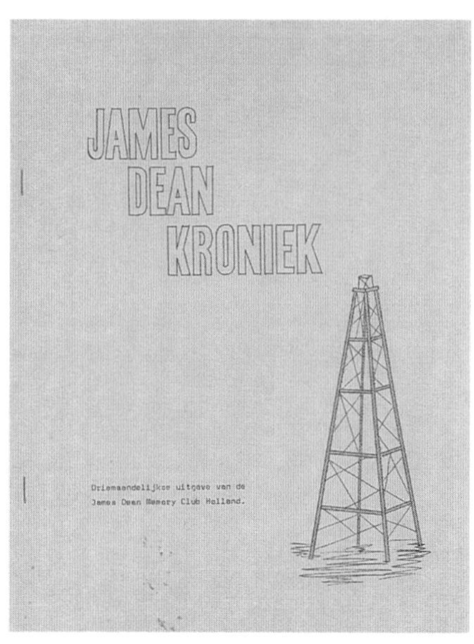

James Dean Kroniek
Holland #3 - 1967

LeBaladin #3
France - March 1959

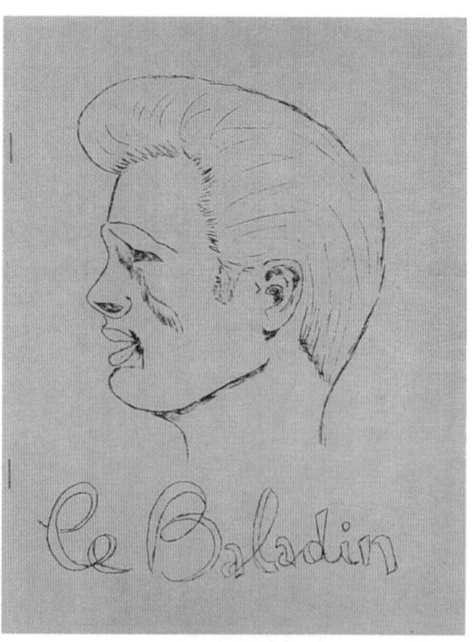

Le Baladin
France - May 1959

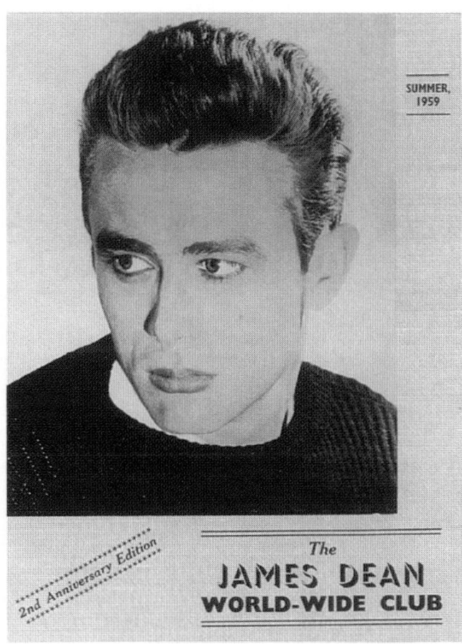

The James Dean World-Wide Club
England - Summer 1959

The James Dean World-Wide Club
England - Fall 1960

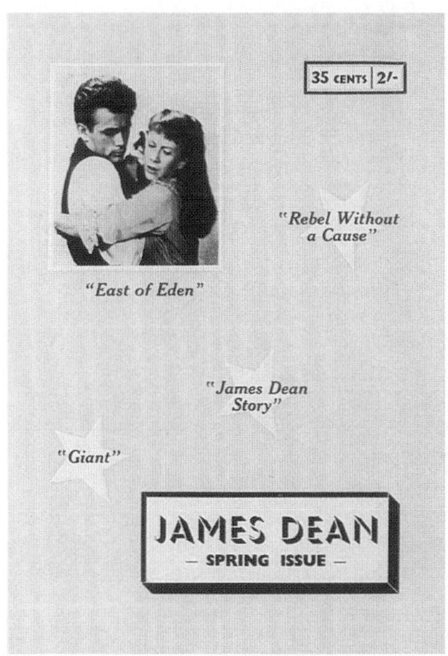

The James Dean World-Wide Club
England - Spring 1960

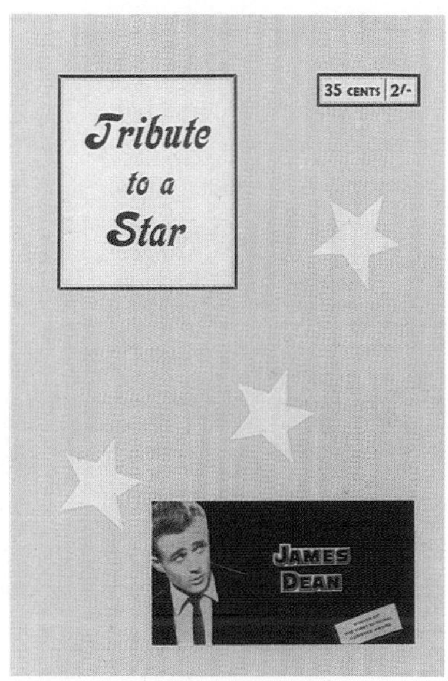

The James Dean World-Wide Club
England - Fall 1959

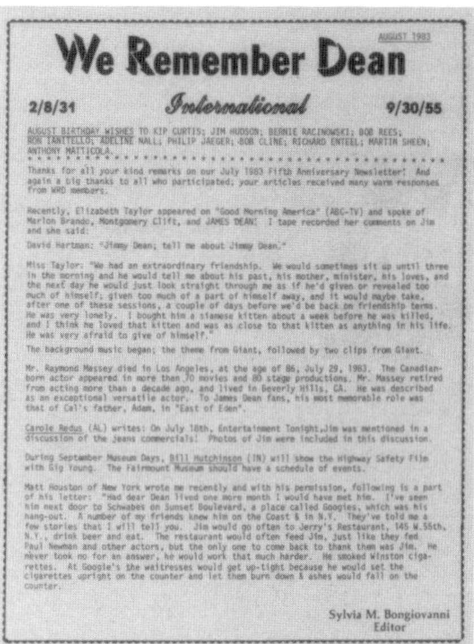

AUGUST 1983

We Remember Dean

2/8/31 International 9/30/55

AUGUST BIRTHDAY WISHES TO KIP CURTIS; JIM HUDSON; BERNIE RACINOWSKI; BOB REES; RON IANITELLO; ADELINE NALL; PHILIP JAEGER; BOB CLINE; RICHARD ENTEEL; MARTIN SHEEN; ANTHONY MATTICOLA.

* *

Thanks for all your kind remarks on our July 1983 Fifth Anniversary Newsletter! And again a big thanks to all who participated; your articles received many warm responses from WRD members.

Recently, Elizabeth Taylor appeared on "Good Morning America" (ABC-TV) and spoke of Marlon Brando, Montgomery Clift, and JAMES DEAN! I tape recorded her comments on Jim and she said:

David Hartman: "Jimmy Dean; tell me about Jimmy Dean."

Miss Taylor: "We had an extraordinary friendship. We would sometimes sit up until three in the morning and he would tell me about his past, his mother, minister, his loves, and the next day he would just look straight through me as if he'd given or revealed too much of himself; given too much of a part of himself away, and it would maybe take, after one of these sessions, a couple of days before we'd be back on friendship terms. He was very lonely. I bought him a siamese kitten about a week before he was killed, and I think he loved that kitten and was as close to that kitten as anything in his life. He was very afraid to give of himself."

The background music began; the theme from Giant, followed by two clips from Giant.

Mr. Raymond Massey died in Los Angeles, at the age of 86, July 29, 1983. The Canadian-born actor appeared in more than 70 movies and 80 stage productions. Mr. Massey retired from acting more than a decade ago, and lived in Beverly Hills, CA. He was described as an exceptional versatile actor. To James Dean fans, his most memorable role was that of Cal's father, Adam, in "East of Eden".

Carole Redus (AL) writes: On July 18th, Entertainment Tonight,Jim was mentioned in a discussion of the jeans commercials! Photos of Jim were included in this discussion.

During September Museum Days, Bill Hutchinson (IN) will show the Highway Safety Film with Gig Young. The Fairmount Museum should have a schedule of events.

Matt Houston of New York wrote me recently and with his permission, following is a part of his letter: "Had dear Dean lived one more month I would have met him. I've seen him next door to Schwabes on Sunset Boulevard, a place called Googies, which was his hang-out. A number of my friends knew him on the Coast & in N.Y. They've told me a few stories that I will tell you. Jim would go often to Jerry's Restaurant, 145 W.55th, N.Y., drink beer and eat. The restaurant would often feed Jim, just like they fed Paul Newman and other actors, but the only one to come back to thank them was Jim. He never took no for an answer, he would work that much harder. He smoked Winston cigarettes. At Googie's the waitresses would get up-tight because he would set the cigarettes upright on the counter and let them burn down & ashes would fall on the counter.

Sylvia M. Bongiovanni
Editor

We Remember Dean
International Newsletter
USA - August 1983

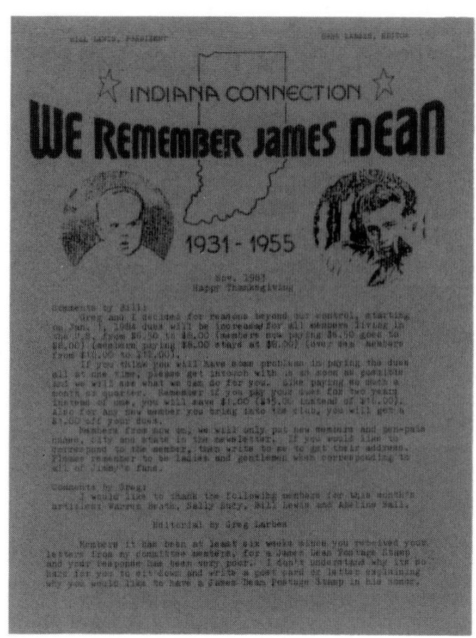

INDIANA CONNECTION

WE REMEMBER JAMES DEAN

1931 - 1955

Nov. 1983
Happy Thanksgiving

Comments by Bill:
Greg and I decided for reasons beyond our control, starting on Jan. 1, 1984 dues will be increased for all members living in the U.S. [illegible]

[illegible]

Comments by Greg:
I would like to thank the following members for this month's articles: [illegible]

Editorial by Greg Larbes

[illegible]

Indiana Connection Newsletter
We Remember James Dean
USA - November 1983

APRIL-MAY 1991

2/8/31 9/30/55

WE REMEMBER DEAN INTERNATIONAL

Thanks to Norman Patterson of South Africa for our new Newsletter design! What a great job Norman did - hope you all like it! Over the years, our Newsletters have been designed by Norman and Sherry Mauser of California. I'll use both designs.

Norman Patterson recently wrote that on February 26, 27 & 28th the major TV station in South Africa showed Jimmy's 3 movies. Norman designed a logo of Jimmy that appeared on the screen before each movie was shown! Norman must have been very proud to see his work on TV relating to Jimmy! Great work Norman!

This is a picture of the JAMES DEAN MEMORIAL AT GRIFFITH OBSERVATORY. Dedicated in October of 1988 by the artist KENNETH KENDALL it has been viewed by thousands of people visiting Griffith Observatory. If you are planning a trip to California, make sure you visit the Observatory and see this wonderful tribute to James Dean!

Copyright 1991 by WRDI.
All Rights Reserved.

We Remember Dean
International Newsletter
USA - April-May 1991

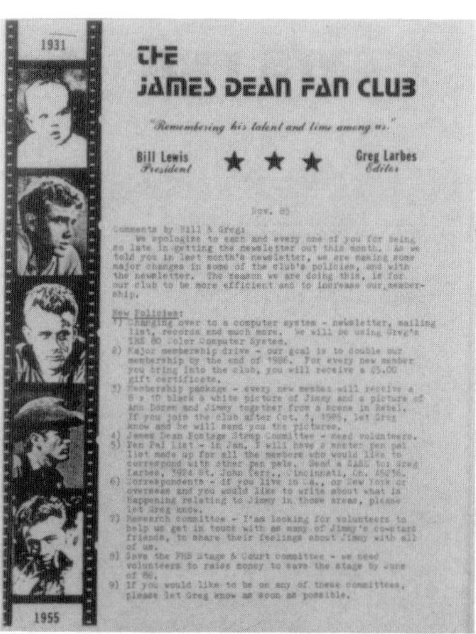

1931

THE
JAMES DEAN FAN CLUB

"Remembering his talent and time among us."

Bill Lewis
President

Greg Larbes
Editor

Nov. 85

Comments by Bill & Greg:
We apologize to each and every one of you for being so late in getting the newsletter out this month. As we told you in last month's newsletter, we are making some major changes in some of the club's policies, and with the newsletter. The reason we are doing this, is for our club to be more efficient and to increase our membership.

New Policies:
1) Changing over to a computer system - newsletter, mailing list, records and much more. We will be using Greg's TRS 80 Color Computer System.
2) Major membership drive - our goal is to double our membership by the end of 1986. For every new member you bring into the club, you will receive a $5.00 gift certificate.
3) Membership package - every new member will receive a 8 x 10 black & white picture of Jimmy and a picture of Ann Doran and Jimmy together from a scene in Rebel. If you join the club after Oct. 1, 1985, let Greg know and he will send you the pictures.
4) James Dean Postage Stamp Committee - need volunteers.
5) Pen Pal List - in Jan. I will have a master pen pal list made up for all the members who would like to correspond with other pen pals. Send a SASE to: Greg Larbes, 3924 St. John Terr., Cincinnati, Oh. 45236.
6) Correspondents - if you live in L.A., or New York or overseas and you would like to write about what is happening relating to Jimmy in those areas, please let Greg know.
7) Research committee - I'am looking for volunteers to help me get in touch with as many of Jimmy's co-stars friends, to share their feelings about Jimmy with all of us.
8) Save the FHS Stage & Court committee - we need volunteers to raise money to save the stage by June of 86.
9) If you would like to be on any of these committees, please let Greg know as soon as possible.

1955

The James Dean Fan Club Newsletter
USA - November 1985

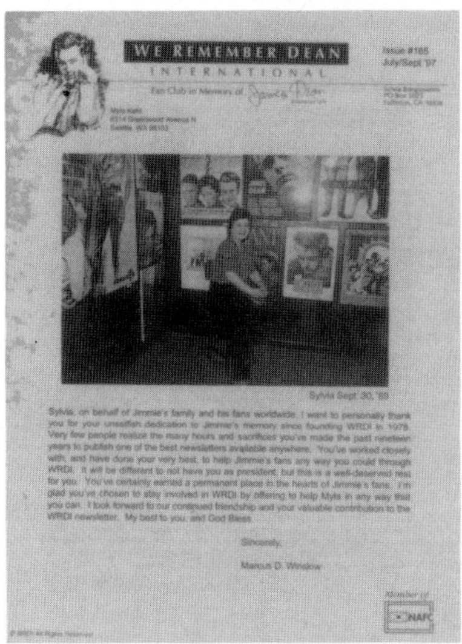
WE REMEMBER DEAN
INTERNATIONAL
Fan Club in Memory of James Dean

Issue #165
July/Sept '97

Sylvia Sept 30, '89

Sylvia, on behalf of Jimmie's family and his fans worldwide, I want to personally thank you for your unselfish dedication to Jimmie's memory since founding WRDI in 1978. Very few people realize the many hours and sacrifices you've made the past nineteen years to publish one of the best newsletters available anywhere. You've worked closely with, and have done your very best, to help Jimmie's fans any way you could through WRDI. It will be different to not have you as president, but this is a well-deserved rest for you. You've certainly earned a permanent place in the hearts of Jimmie's fans. I'm glad you've chosen to stay involved in WRDI by offering to help Myla in any way that you can. I look forward to our continued friendship and your valuable contribution to the WRDI newsletter. My best to you, and God Bless.

Sincerely,

Marcus D. Winslow

Member of NAFC

We Remember Dean
International Newsletter
USA - July/Sept. 1997

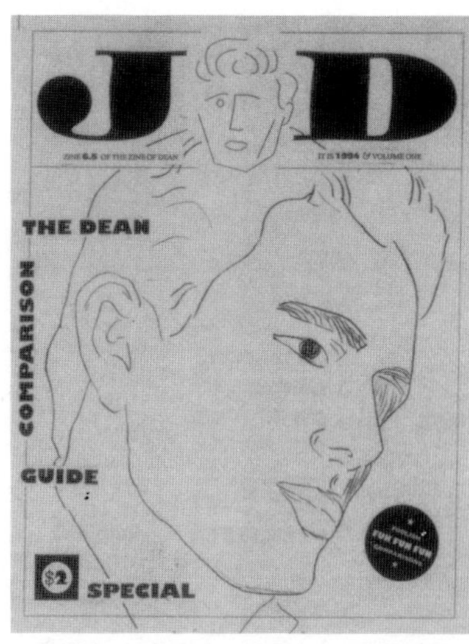

The James Dean Zine Vol. 1
USA - 1994

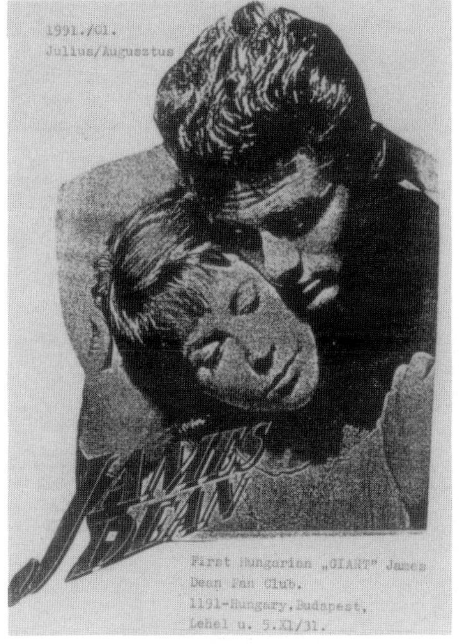

First Hungarian "Giant"
James Dean Fan Club Newsletter
Hungary - 1991

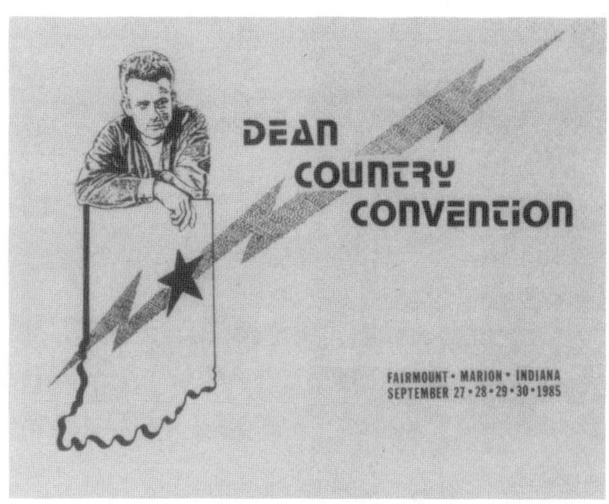

Souvenir Program Book for the Dean Country
Convention in Fairmount/Marion, Indiana
USA - Sept. 27-30, 1985

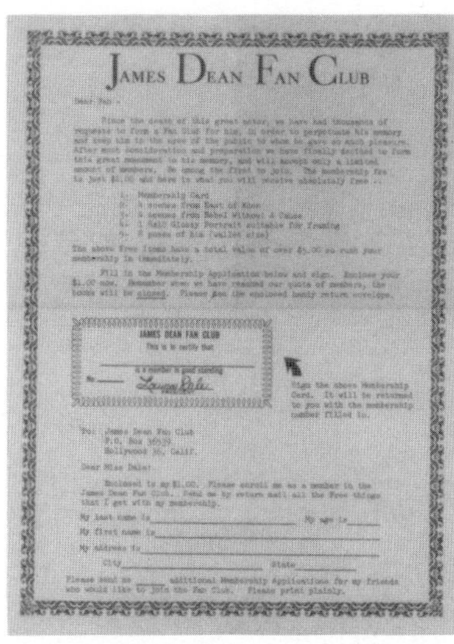
JAMES DEAN FAN CLUB

JAMES DEAN FAN CLUB
This is to certify that

Letters from
The James Dean Fan Club
USA - 1956

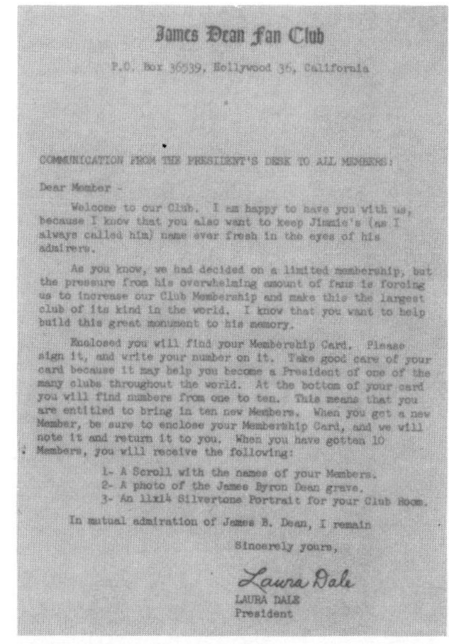
James Dean Fan Club

P.O. Box 36539, Hollywood 36, California

COMMUNICATION FROM THE PRESIDENT'S DESK TO ALL MEMBERS:

Dear Member -

Welcome to our Club. I am happy to have you with us, because I know that you also want to keep Jimmie's (as I always called him) name ever fresh in the eyes of his admirers.

As you know, we had decided on a limited membership, but the pressure from his overwhelming amount of fans is forcing us to increase our Club Membership and make this the largest club of its kind in the world. I know that you want to help build this great monument to his memory.

Enclosed you will find your Membership Card. Please sign it, and write your number on it. Take good care of your card because it may help you become a President of one of the many clubs throughout the world. At the bottom of your card you will find numbers from one to ten. This means that you are entitled to bring in ten new Members. When you get a new Member, be sure to enclose your Membership Card, and we will note it and return it to you. When you have gotten 10 Members, you will receive the following:

1- A Scroll with the names of your Members.
2- A photo of the James Byron Dean grave.
3- An 11x14 Silvertone Portrait for your Club Room.

In mutual admiration of James B. Dean, I remain

Sincerely yours,

Laura Dale
LAURA DALE
President

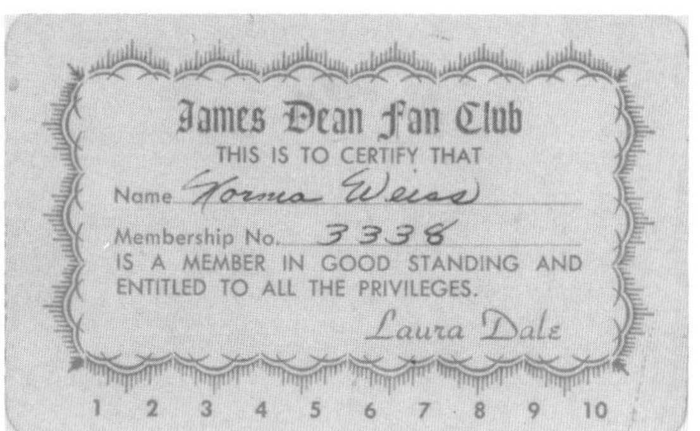

James Dean Fan Club Membership Cards

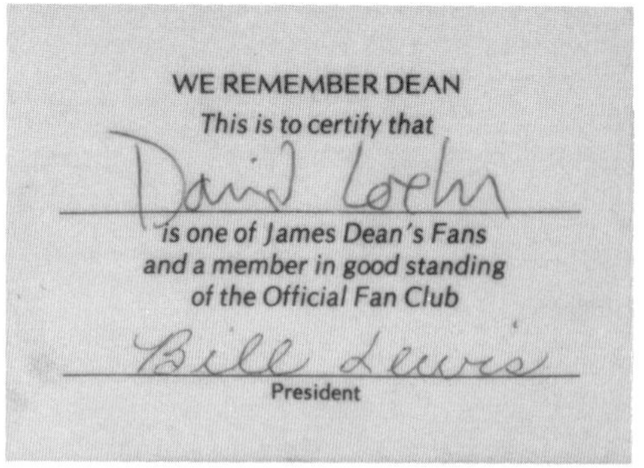

James Dean Fan Club Membership Cards

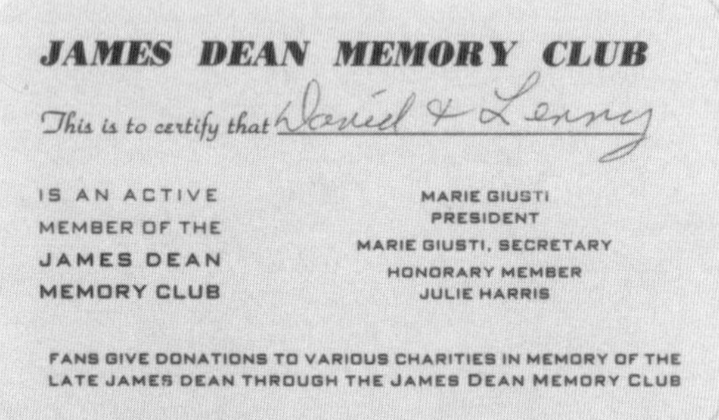

James Dean Memory Club Membership Cards

We Remember James Dean Card

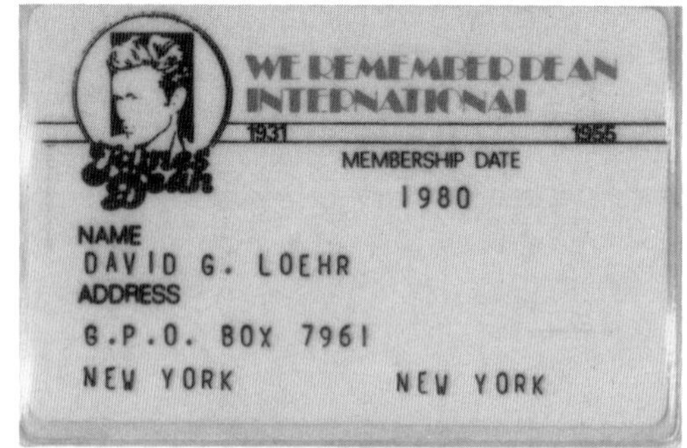

We Remember James Dean International

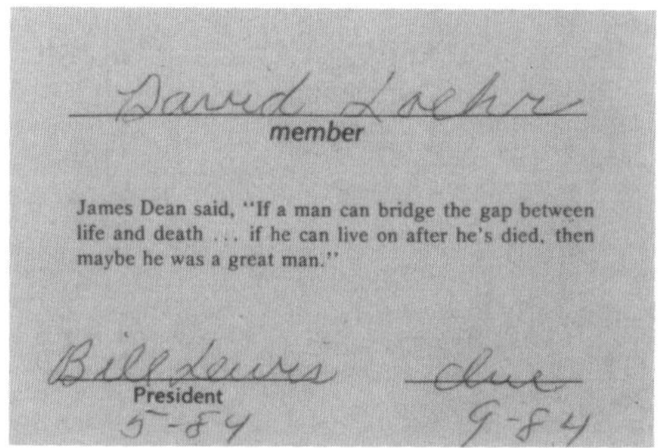

We Remember James Dean Card

We Remember James Dean Card

The James Dean
Memory Ring
USA - 1956

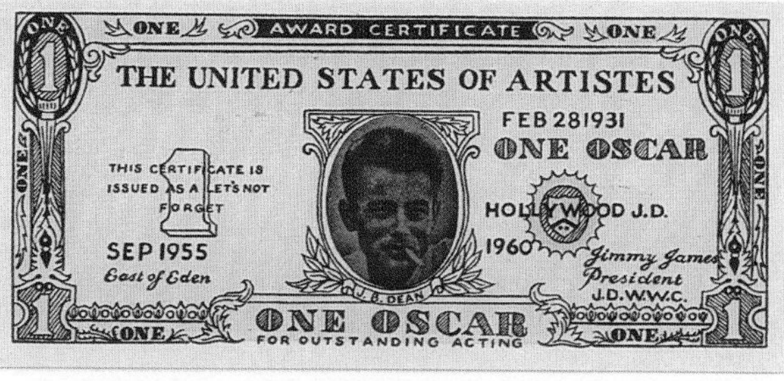

James Dean Worldwide Club
England - 1960

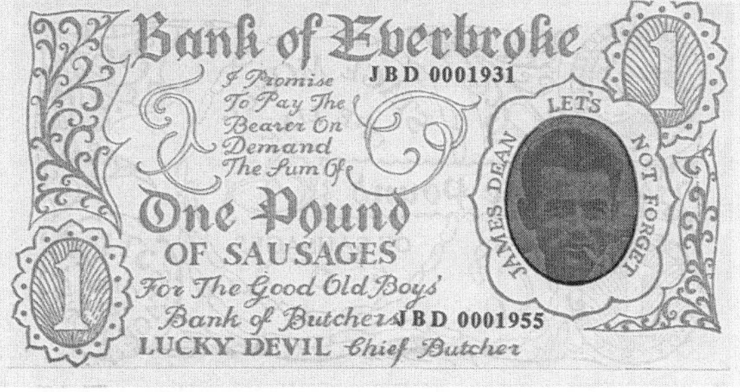

Bank of Everbroke Stage Money
England - 1959

Fan Club Button
USA - 1985

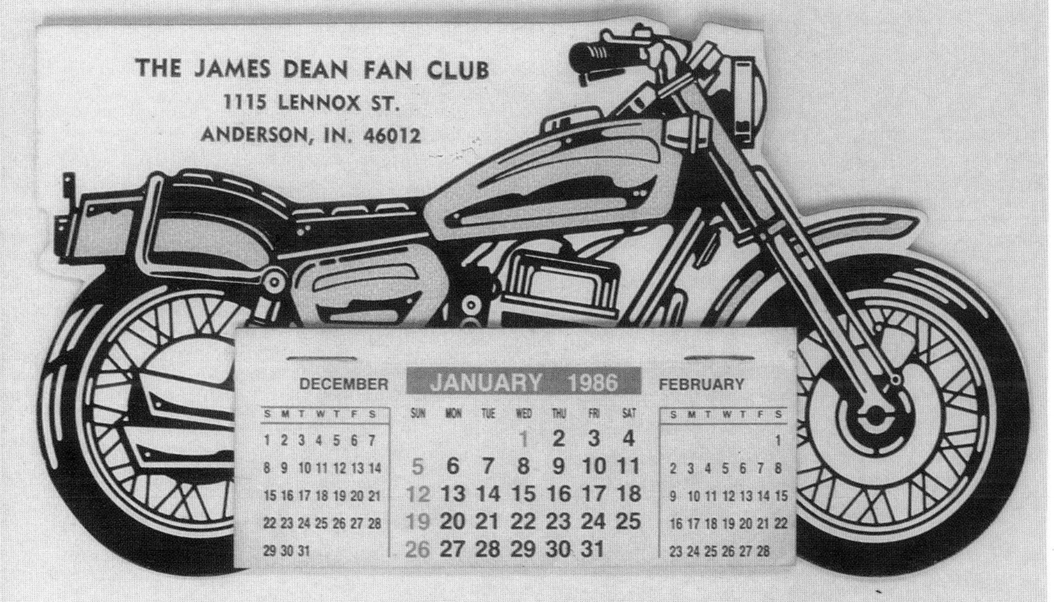

Motorcycle Calendar
USA - 1986

Posters

Although film was the media that made James Dean a star, the still image has played a tremendous role in his development as an icon. The emotional intensity that held movie audiences spellbound loses little of its power when captured in two-dimensional form.

The first Dean posters were those that accompanied his films. Of the three, *Rebel Without a Cause* had the smallest promotional budget, and the fewest posters printed. It has become the role for which Dean is best remembered, and, predictably enough, the posters are hard to find and very valuable. The bigger publicity push for Dean's debut film, *East of Eden,* makes those posters somewhat easier to come by at a reasonable price. The final installment of the Dean trilogy, *Giant,* created an extraordinary media frenzy. Dean's ascension as a cult idol combined with the popularity of director George Stevens and costars Rock Hudson and Liz Taylor to make the film one of the highest grossing pictures of its time. It was heavily promoted extravaganza, and remains the easiest of the three to collect.

Reissues, Reproductions and Foreign Releases

One method by which collectors with limited funds can build a poster collection is by focusing on reissues. In the years before video tape, it was common practice for popular films to be periodically re-released. These theatrical second comings were usually accompanied by reissues of the movie posters. Reissues offer collectors a chance at honest-to-goodness theatrical release posters, usually at a fraction of the price of the first run. While they will never be as valuable as originals, reissues generally appreciate at a similar rate. Each of Dean's movies has been re-released several times, with a variety of accompanying posters. Most of these reissues can be easily identified by the dates printed in tiny type along their bottom edge.

In addition to the re-releases in the United States, Dean's films have been shown in almost every country in the world. Many of these showings have also inspired creative new poster art. Foreign movie posters range widely in style and desirability, but add a great deal of diversity to a Dean collection.

Many foreign and domestic Dean posters have been reproduced since their original issue. If a poster is undated, distinguishing reissues and reproductions from originals can be very difficult. Reproductions are usually smaller, frequently printed on heavier stock, and sometimes exhibit color variations. But without an original for purpose of comparison, these points are difficult to detect.

Advertising

James Dean posters have been used to sell a lot more than just his movies. In the years since his death, Dean has "endorsed" Converse sneakers, K-Mart t-shirts, and Champion Spark Plugs, among others. As time goes by, Dean's popularity as a silent pitchman continues to grow, although his connection to the products he promotes is often tenuous. He has been featured on a series of Levis catalog covers, but not one shows him wearing the product. Winston cigarettes thought him the perfect embodiment of their "Taste America, Light a Winston" campaign, even if he preferred Chesterfields.

Champion and Converse are among the very few companies that have utilized images of the young actor actually *using* their wares. While other companies have bent reality a bit in order to associate themselves with Dean, at least one has played on the idea that Dean didn't use their services, but should have. In the weeks before his death, Dean drafted (but never signed) a will and had taken out his first insurance policy. But he didn't have a living trust. Austin Living Trust turned Dean's omission in their own favor with ads that featured Dean's photo, and the caption, "A Living Trust Would Have Saved His Family $11,062.27 in Probate Costs."

Just James Dean

Although they are slow to appreciate in value, some of the most popular James Dean posters are those featuring candid or studio shots by photographers like Sanford Roth, Frank Worth, Phil Stern, Roy Schatt or Dennis Stock. Many of these photographs feature Dean in private, introspective moments at home or at work. With a star whose look plays such an important role in his legacy, it is not surprising that many fans have a favorite Dean photograph. Hundreds of shots have been turned into posters, and a few more are added to the list each year.

Without a doubt, more new fans are introduced to James Dean through posters than through any other media, including film. His popularity as a wall hanging is largely responsible for the phenomenon that keeps Dean among the most recognizable images in the world.

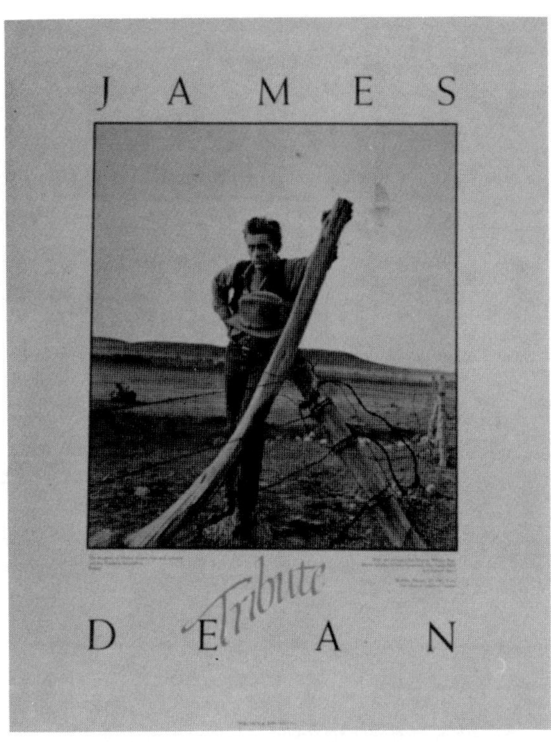

Academy of Motion Picture Arts and Sciences
September 14, 1981 - USA

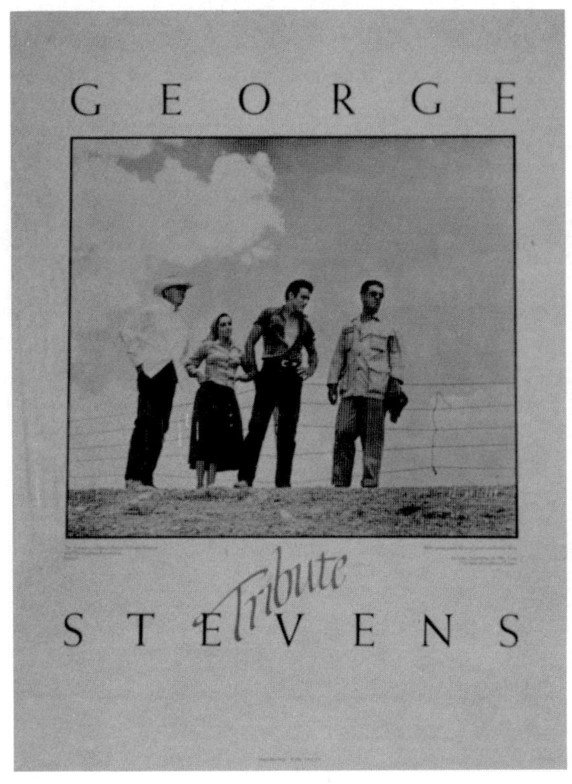

Academy of Motion Picture Arts and Sciences
January 24, 1983 - USA

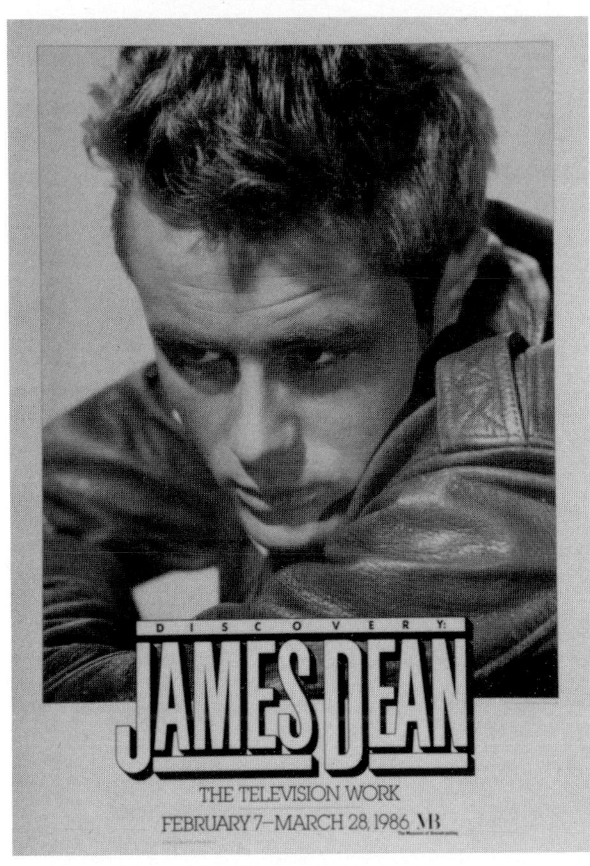

The Museum of Broadcasting N.Y.C.
20" x 28" - USA

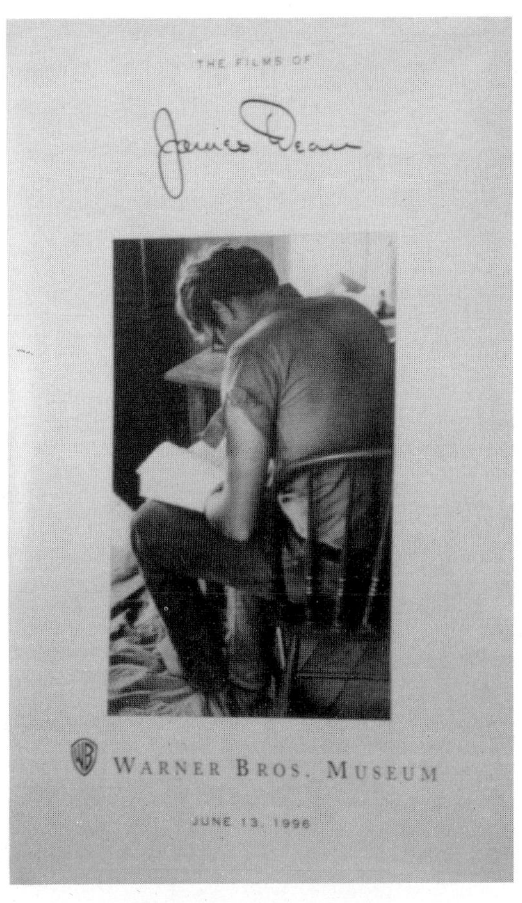

Warner Brothers Museum
20 x 30 - June 13, 1996

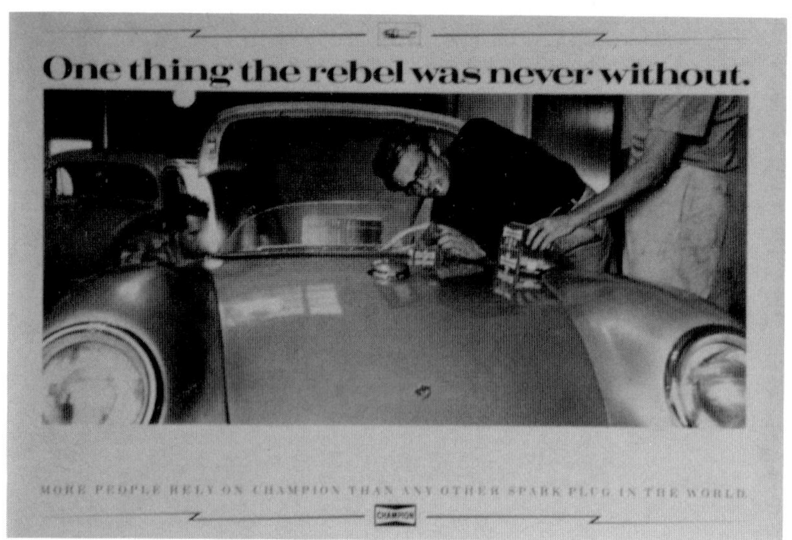

Champion Sparkplug Promotional Poster
18″ x 28″ - USA - 1988

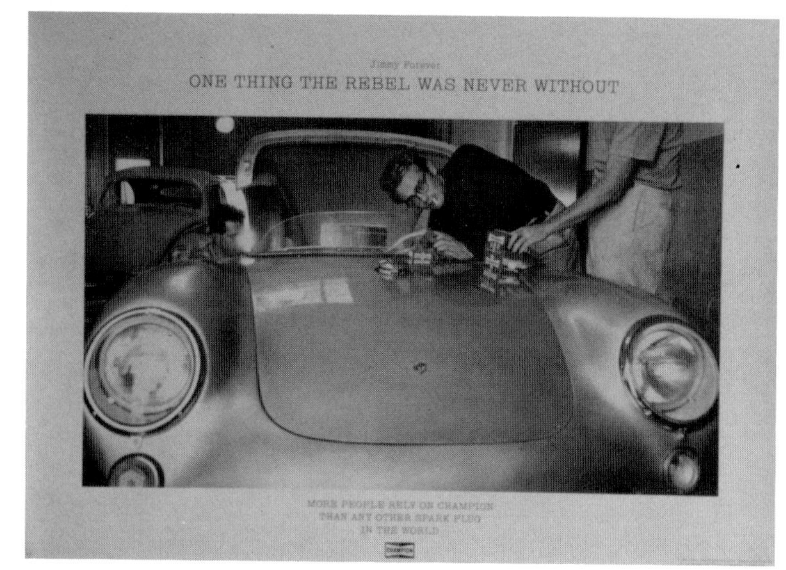

Champion Sparkplug Promotional Poster
23″ x 33″ - Japan - 1990

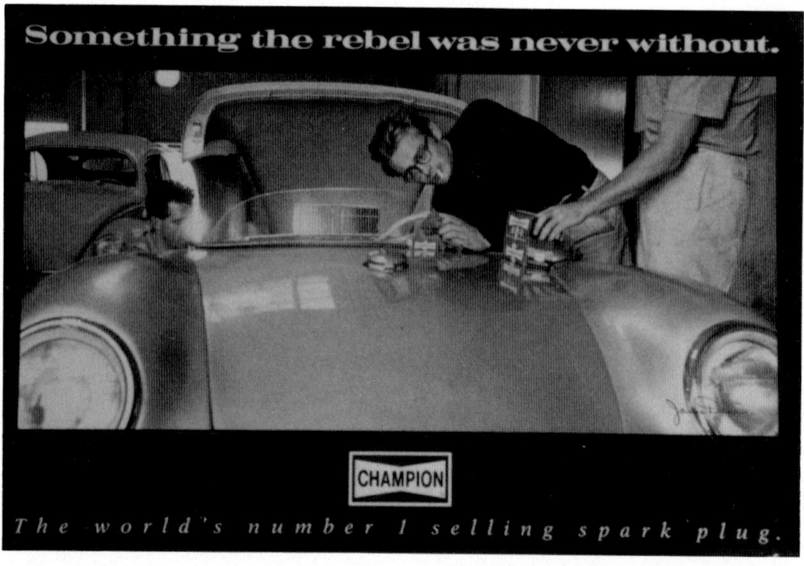

Champion Sparkplug Promotional Poster
18″ x 28″ - USA - 1991

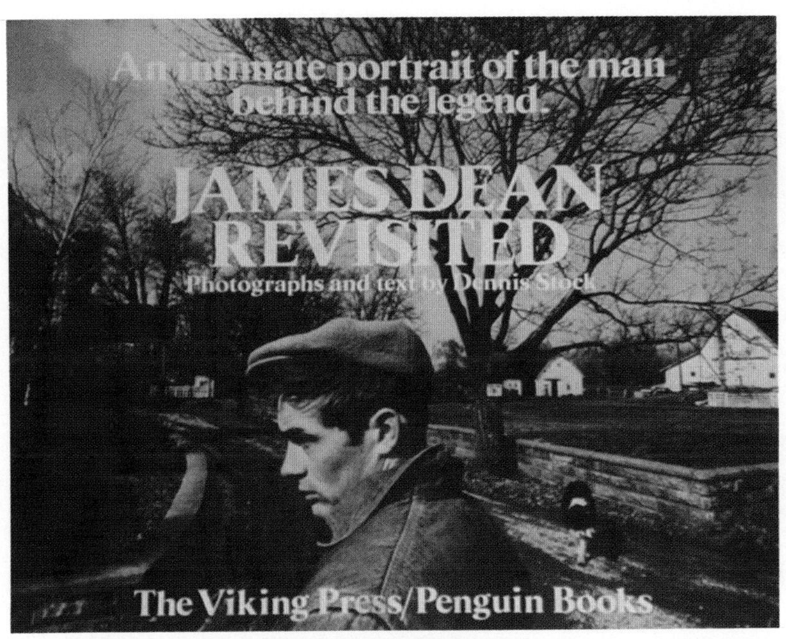

James Dean Revisited
16″ x 20″ - USA

James Dean The Mutant King
18″ x 28″ - 1974

Ellas con Estrellas
29″ x 43″ - Argentina

The Last James Dean Book
14″ x 17″ - USA

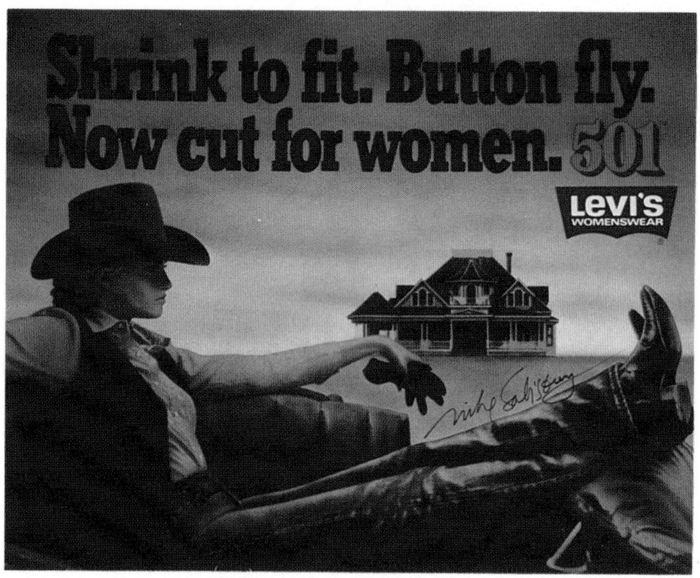

Levi's 501 Womanwear Poster
signed by artist Mike Salisbury
24" x 30" - 1982

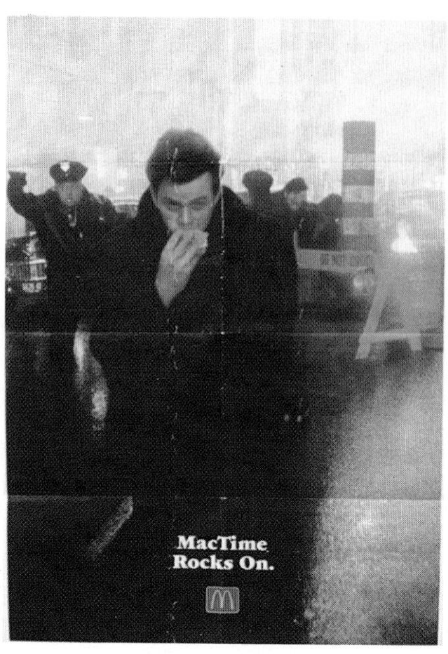

McDonald's
24" x 33" - Australia - 1994

Dr. Pepper - Cardboard, two sided
11" x 18" - USA - 1985

K-Mart Promotional Poster, two sided
11" x 14" - USA - 1995

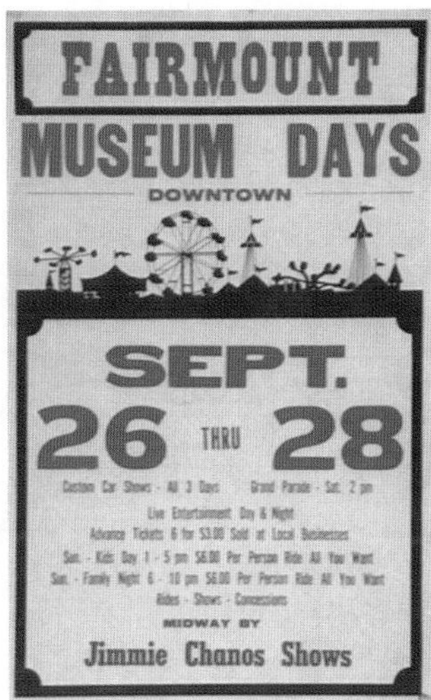

Fairmount Museum Days
Promotional Poster
14″ x 22″

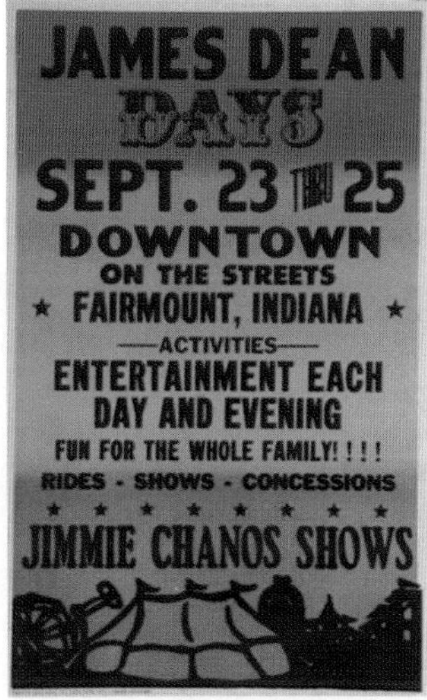

James Dean Days
Promotional Poster
14″ x 22″

Fairmount Museum Days
Promotional Poster
14″ x 22″ - 1989

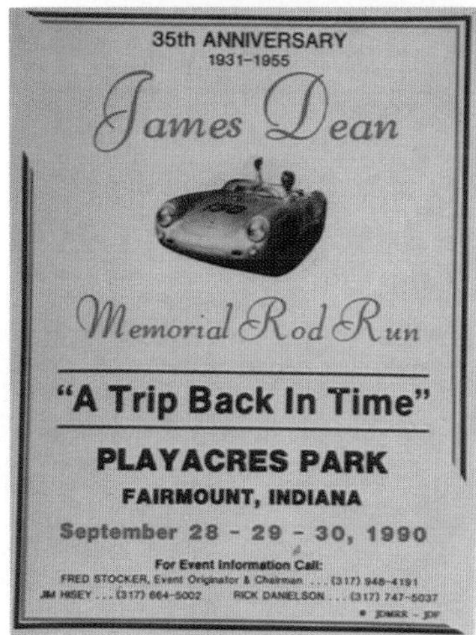

James Dean Memorial Rod Run
Promotional Poster
16″ x 21″ - 1990

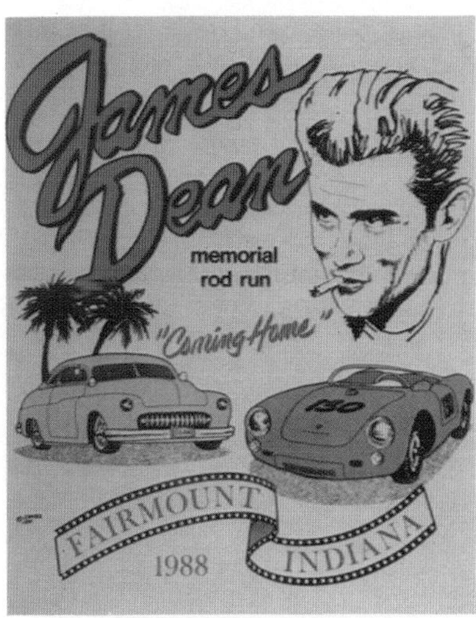

James Dean Memorial Rod Run
Promotional Poster
14″ x 22″ - 1988

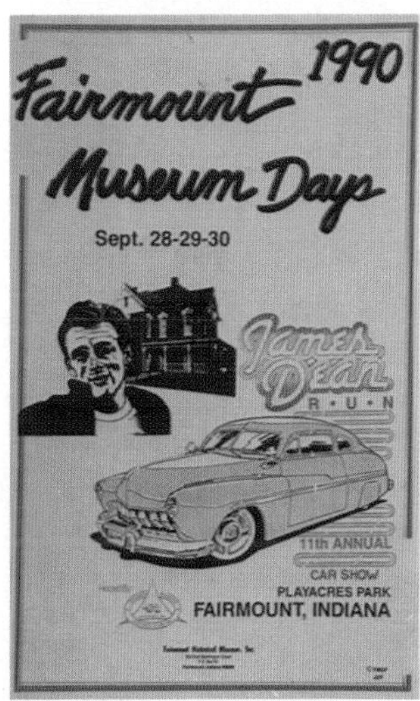

Fairmount Museum Days
Promotional Poster
14″ x 22″ - 1990

Come Back to the 5 & Dime Jimmy Dean
Christ Church Cathedral, Hartford, Connecticut
13″ x 16″ - USA - 1992

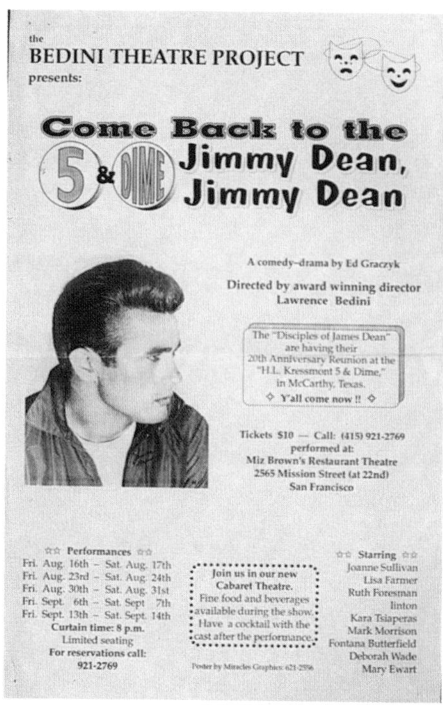

Bedini Theatre Project
Promotional Poster
San Francisco, California
11″ x 17″ - USA - 1991

Come Back to the 5 & Dime Jimmy Dean,
Jimmy Dean - 14″ x 22″ - France - 1992

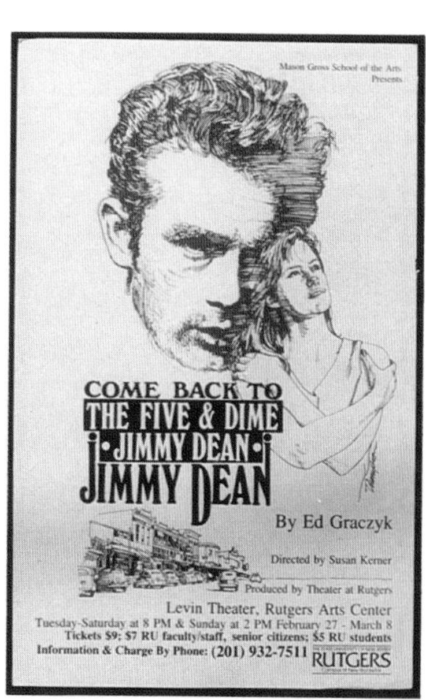

Come Back to the 5 & Dime Jimmy Dean
Rutgers University, Princeton, New Jersey
11″ x 17″ - USA - 1990

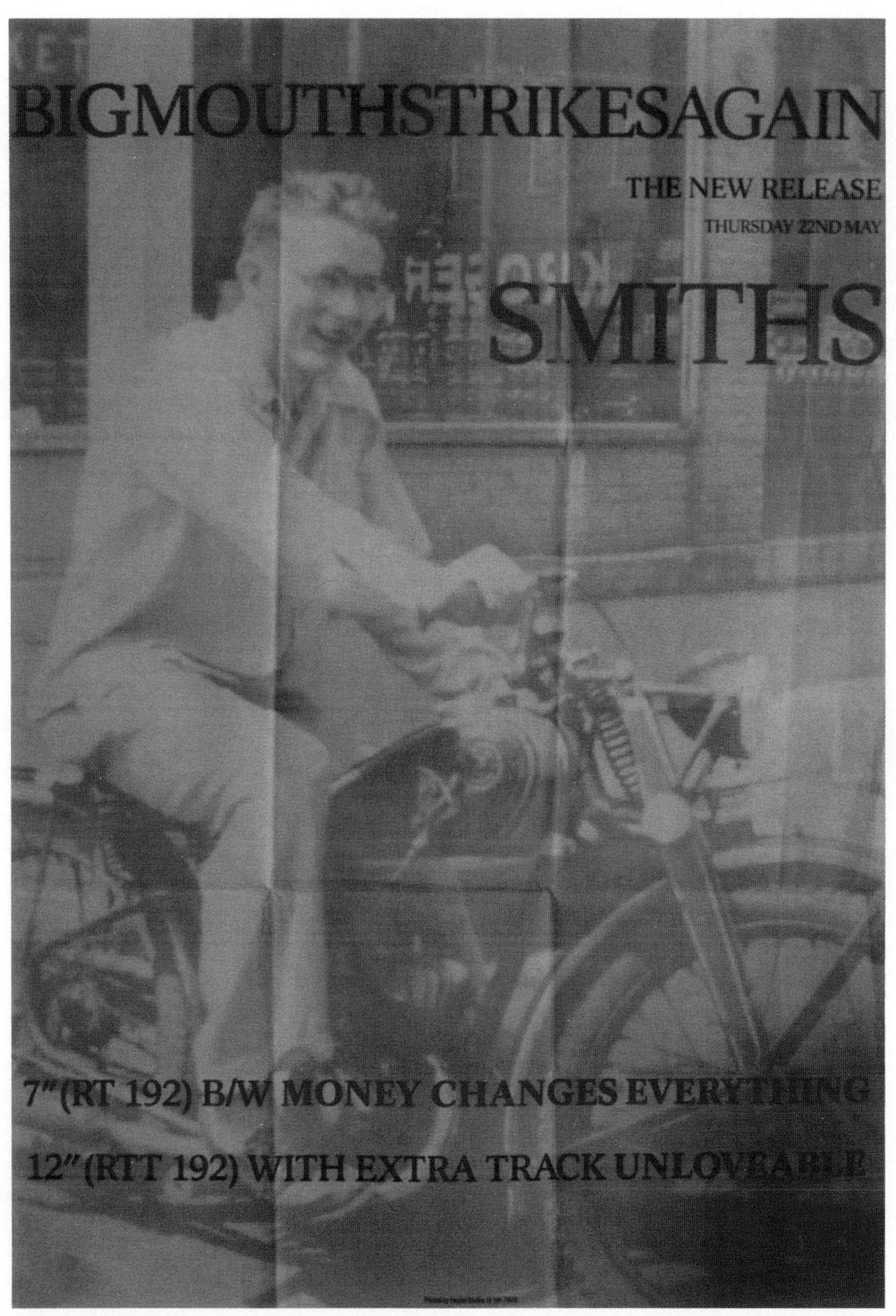

Promotional Poster
The Smiths
40″ x 56″ - England

Koss Headphones
Promotional Poster
16″ x 32″ - 1987

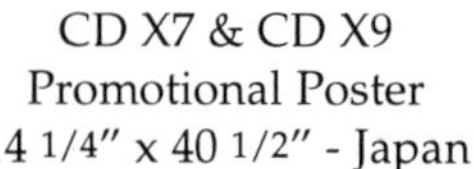
CD X7 & CD X9
Promotional Poster
14 1/4″ x 40 1/2″ - Japan

Dean Legacy - Warner Home Video
Promotional Poster
20″ x 30″ - 1985

Giant - Warner Home Video
Promotional Poster
20″ x 30″ - 1985

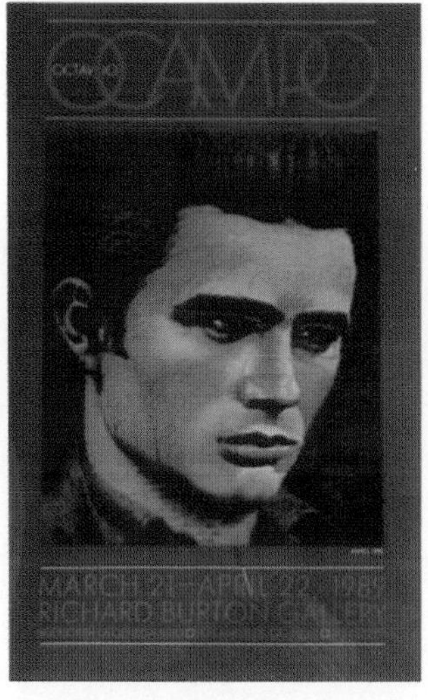

Ocampo
Promotional Poster
23″ x 36″ - USA - 1989

Crazy About The Movies
Cinemax Promotional Poster
27″ x 40″ - 1987

James Dean Special
Promotional Poster
29″ x 40″ - Japan - 1991

Dean Promotional Poster
20″ x 30″ - England - 1974

Promotional Poster
16″ x 23″ - France
September 22, 1990

Promotional Poster
16″ x 24″ - France
November 10, 1988

Roseland Ballroom, New York City
Cardboard Poster - 25″ x 29″
February 27, 1987

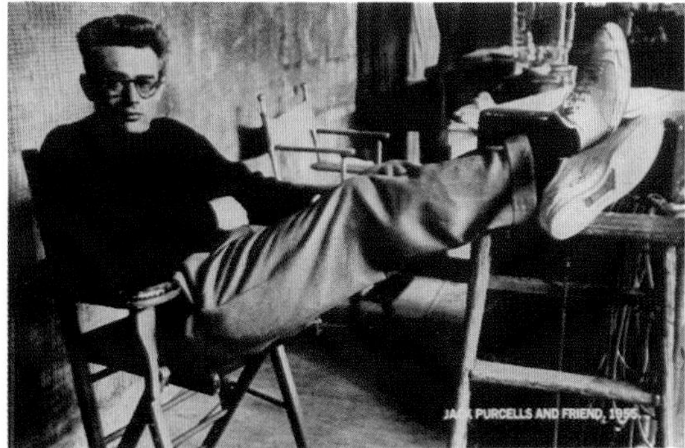

Converse - Promotional Poster
17″ x 23″ - USA - 1988

Shady Character Eyewear
Promotional Poster
24″ x 36″ - USA - 1988

The Atomics CD Advertisement
Count Orlok Music
18″ x 23″ - Netherlands - 1993

DC One Jeans
19″ x 26″ - France - 1982

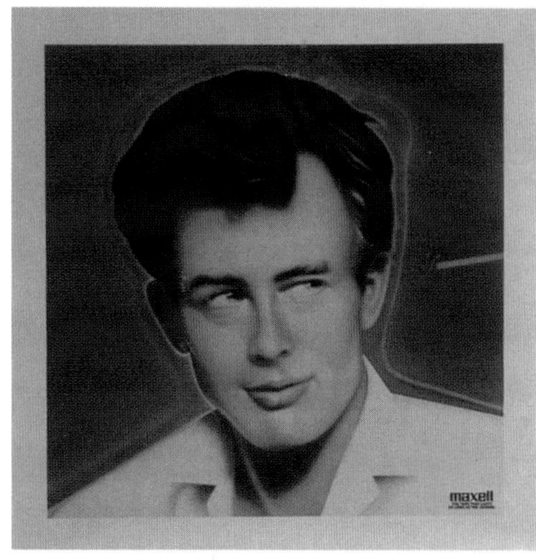

Maxwell Promotional Poster
28″ x 28″ - USA - 1986

Cause, The Personal Programmer
Promotional Poster - 18″ x 21″

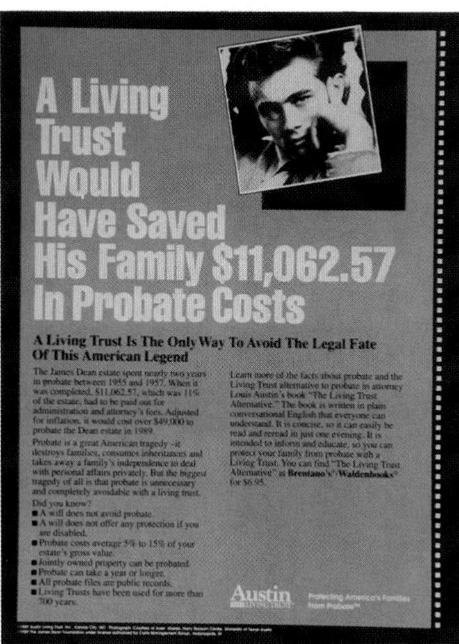

Austin Living Trust Promotional Poster
17″ x 22″ - 1989

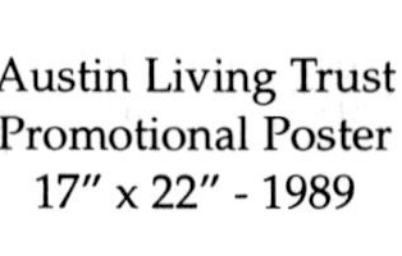
Austin Living Trust
Promotional Poster
17″ x 22″ - 1989

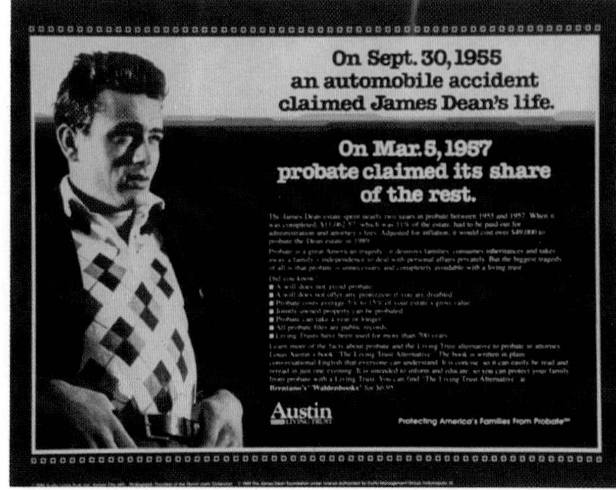

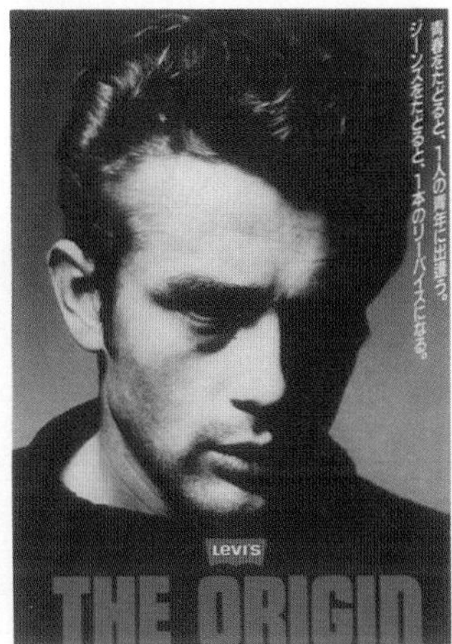

Levi's
Promotional Poster
20"x 28 1/2" - Japan

Levi's Promotional Poster
28 1/2" x 40 1/2" - Japan - 1990s

Levi's Promotional Poster
20" x 29" - Japan - 1990s

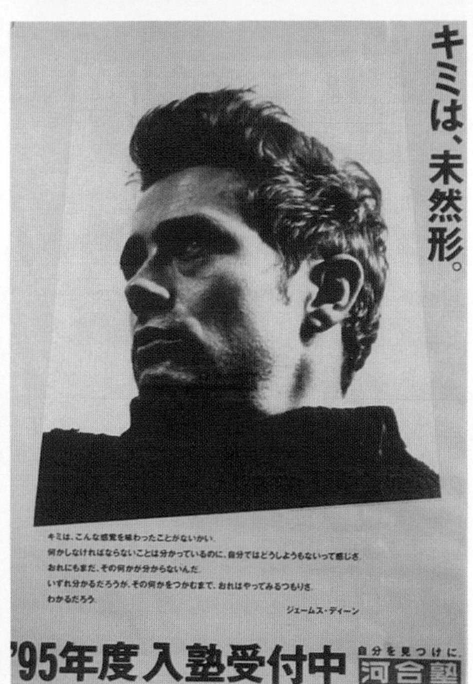

Promotional Poster
29" x 40" - Japan - 1995

Promotional Poster
29" x 40" - Japan - 1995

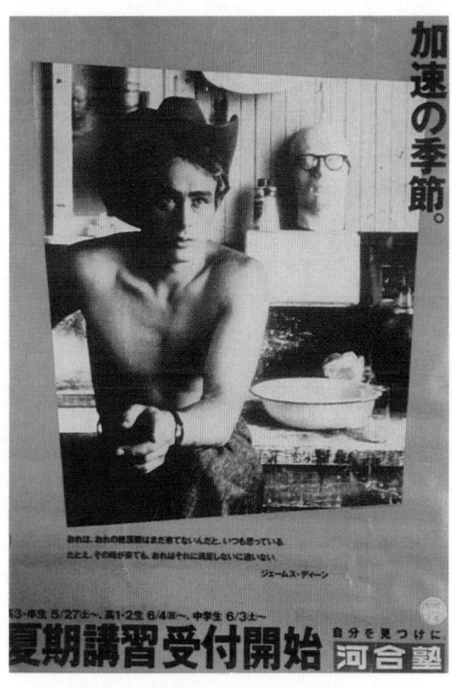

Promotional Poster
29" x 40" - Japan - 1995

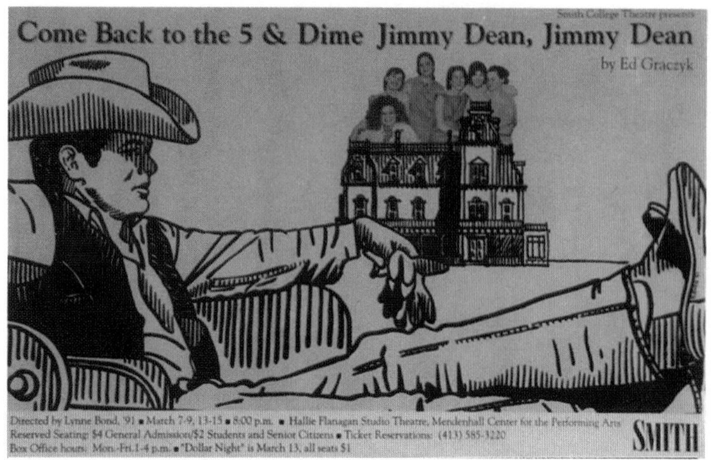

Come Back to the 5 & Dime Jimmy Dean - Promotional Poster
Smith College Theatre, North Hampton, Massachusetts
14″ x 22″ - 1991

SALES BY ASSOCIATION

Sneaker manufacturer Converse resurrected plummeting sales in 1980 with a James Dean ad campaign. By the late 1970s, the popularity of leather athletic shoes had drawn customers away from Converse's canvas classics. Sales had dropped from an all-time high of 750,000 pairs each year in the middle part of the decade to just over 50,000 by decade's end. The James Dean/Converse connection happened accidentally. Out for a walk in Cambridge, Massachusetts, a marketing manager for the company spotted a photo of Dean in a store window. The actor sat slouched in a chair with his Converse-clad feet propped on a desk. Within a year, that shot was the centerpiece of a $500,000 advertising blitz that coincided with the introduction of vibrant new colors into the Converse lineup. Young buyers returned in droves, and Converse sneakers quickly became one of the most important teen fashion accessories of the 1980s.

Come Back to the 5 & Dime Jimmy Dean
Theatre Off Broadway
Frankfort, Kentucky
11″ x 14″ - USA - 1991

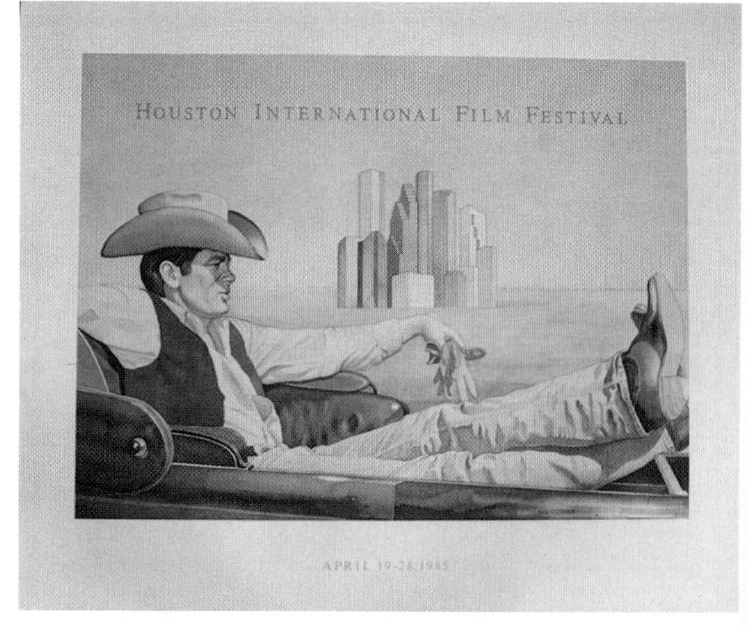

Houston International Film Festival
April 19-28, 1985
19″ x 23″

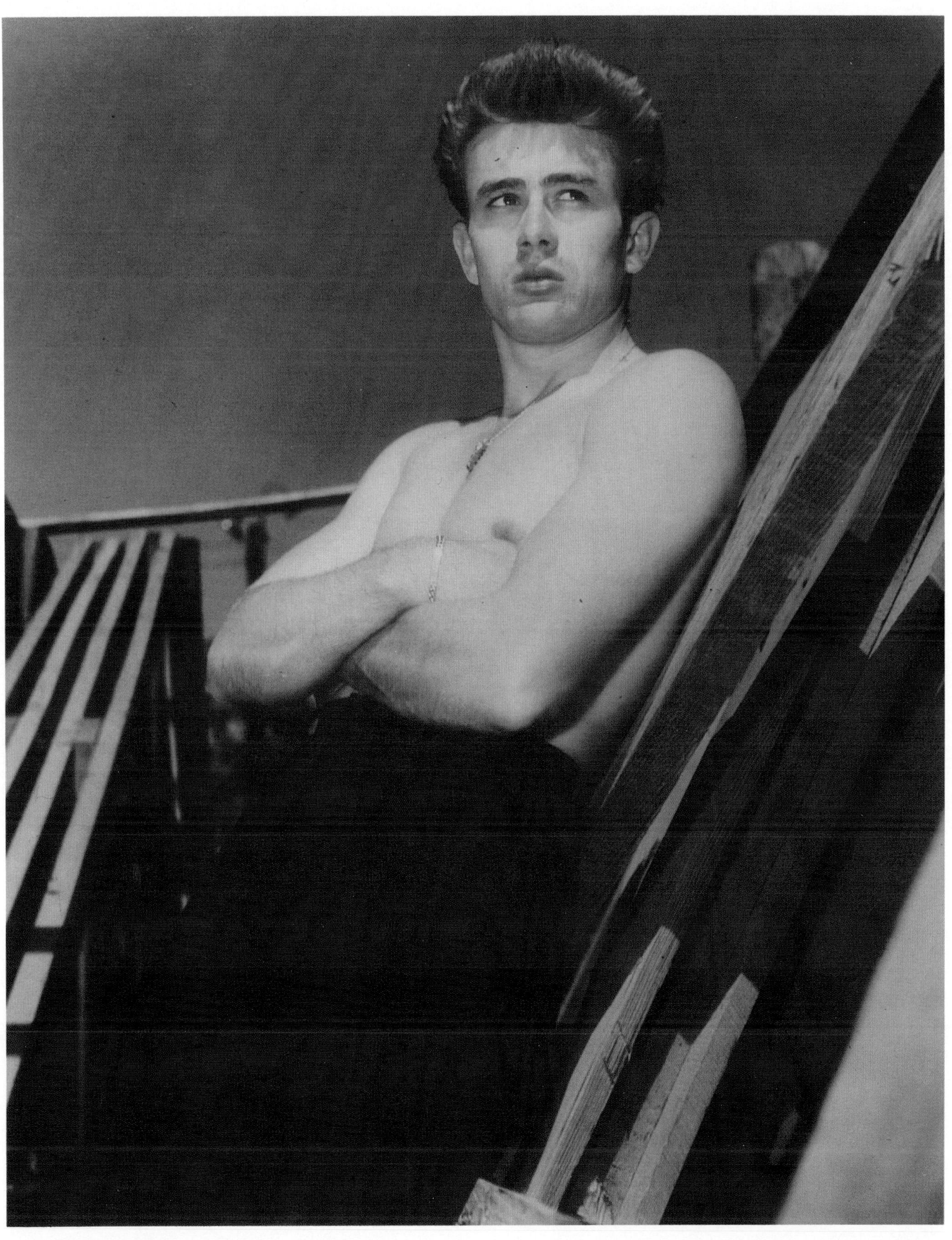

Premier December 3, 1952
James Dean as Wally Wilkens
in *"See the Jaguar"*
The Playbill for the Cort Theatre

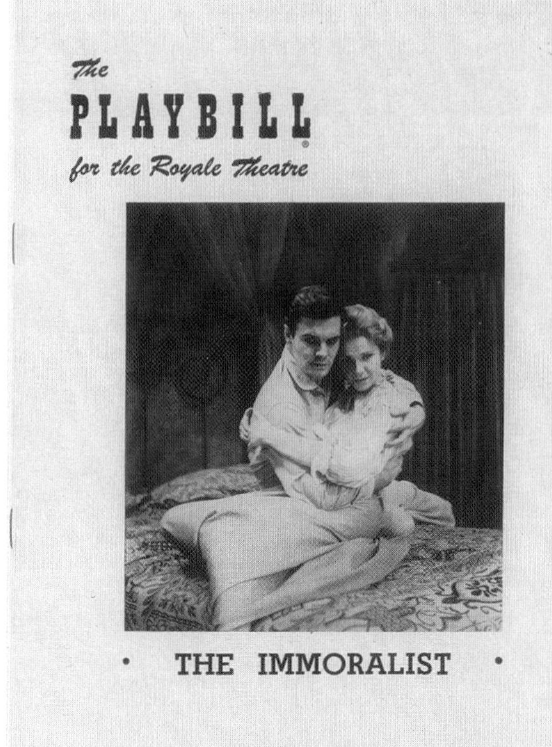

Premier
James Dean as Bacchir in *"The Immoralist"*
The Playbill for the Royale Theatre

East of Eden Souvenir Program from 1955

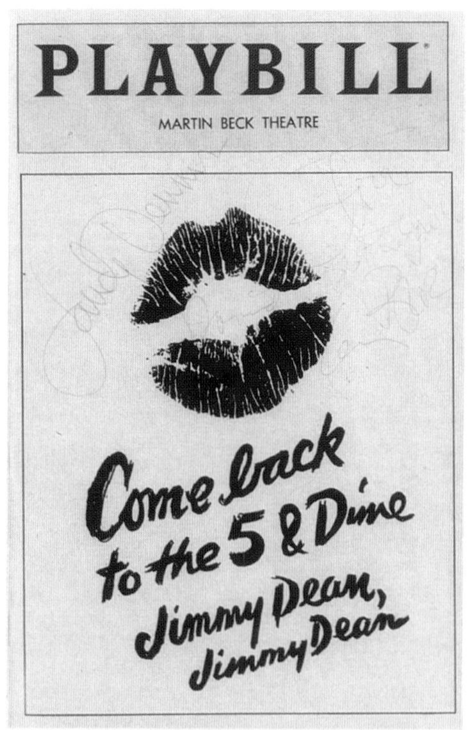

Playbill from Martin Beck Theatre
from February 1982 - USA
"Come Back to the 5 & Dime Jimmy Dean"
Signed by Cher, Sandy Dennis,
Karen Black and Robert Altman

1956 Program for Giant, USA

Ticket to the Premier of Giant at Grauman's Chinese Theatre Hollywood
October 17, 1956 - size 6" x 11"

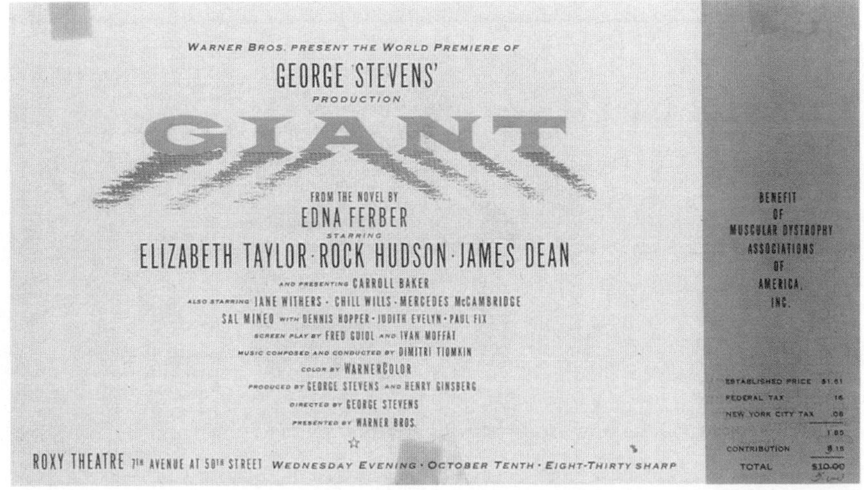

Ticket to the New York Premier of Giant at The Roxy Theatre
October 10, 1956 - size 6" x 11"

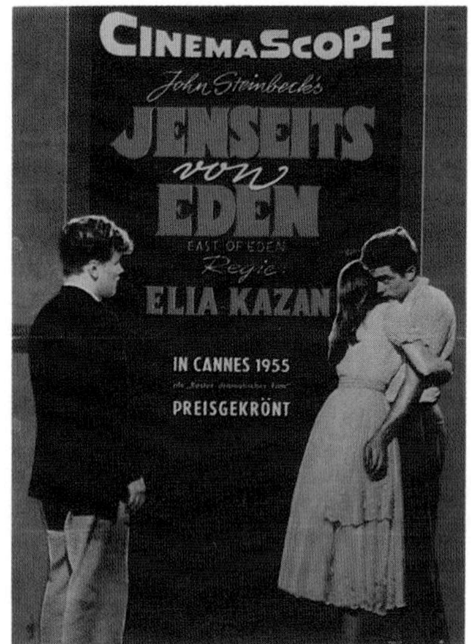

Jenseits von Eden
Austria - 1955

Tenseits von Eden
Illustriete Film-Buhne
#2828 - Germany - 1955

A L'est D'Eden
Mon Film - France
September 21, 1955

. . . denn sie wissen nicht, was sie tun
Illustriete Film-Buhne #3211
Germany - 1956

James Dean Ein Kurzes Leben Für den Film
Germany - 1957

. . . denn sie wissen nicht, was sie tun
Das Neve Film Programm
Germany - 1957

La Fureur De Vivre - Mon Film
France - May 30, 1956

Giganten - Germany -1956

Giganten - Germany - 1956

Giant
Japan - 1959

James Dean
1st American Teenager
Japan - 1977

East of Eden
Japan - 1958

East of Eden
Japan - 1964

East of Eden
Japan - 1980

Giant
Japan - 1964

Giant
Japan - 1972

Giant
Japan - 1991

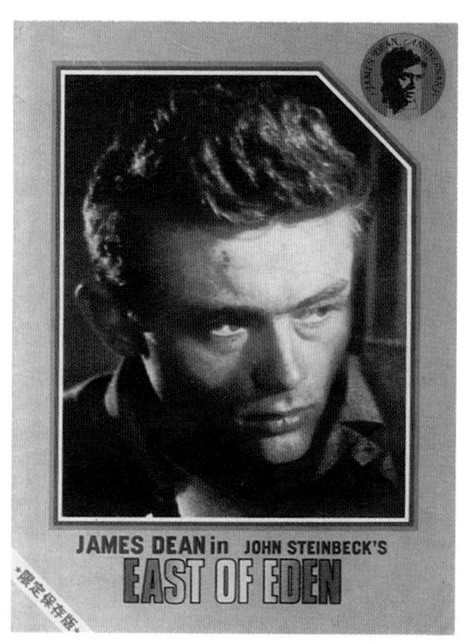

East of Eden
Japan - 1980

James Dean The First
American Teenager
Japan - 1980

The James Dean Story
Japan - 1962

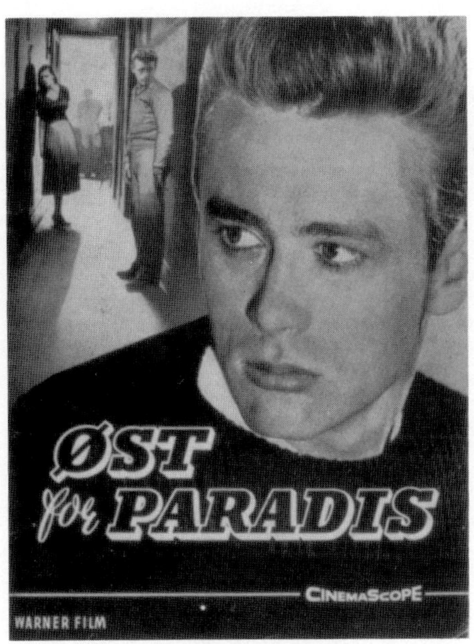

Øst for Paradis
(East of Eden)
Denmark - late 1950s

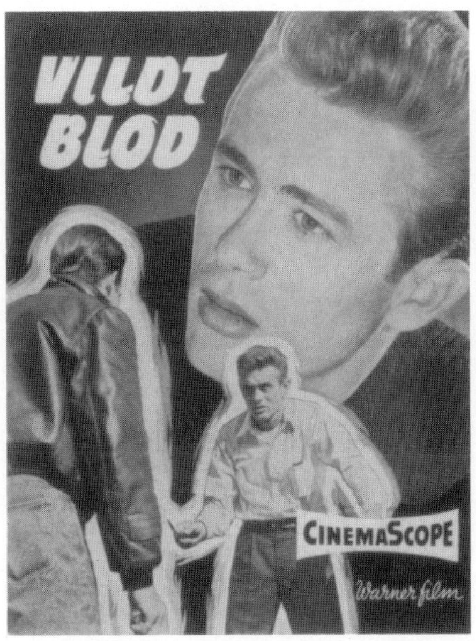

Vildt Blod
(Rebel Without A Cause)
Denmark - late 1950s

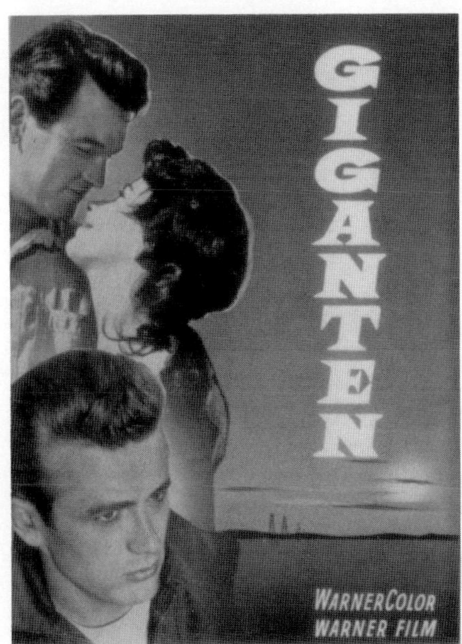

Giganten (Giant)
Denmark - Late 1950s

o Gigante (Giant)
Cine Romance #12 Vol. 9
Portugal - April 16, 1957

Programs and Stage Play Flyers

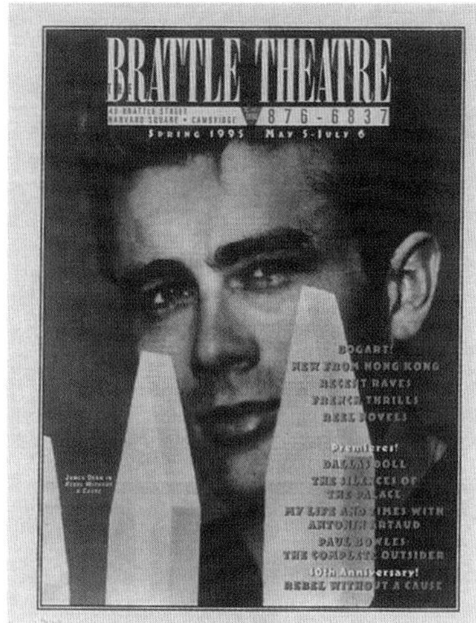

Brattle Theatre Movie Listings
Spring 1995
May 5 thru July 6 - USA

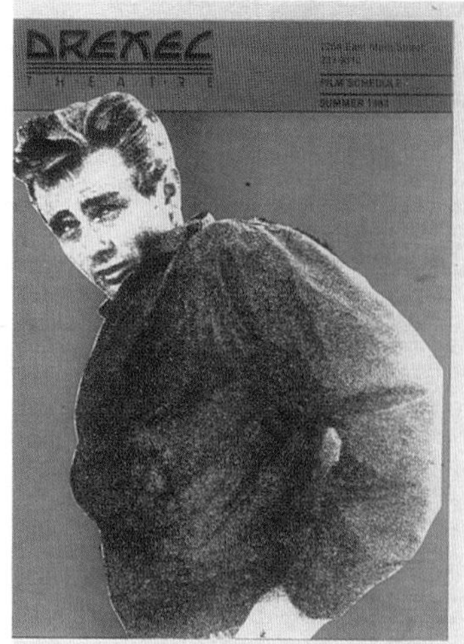

Drexel Theatre
Film Schedule
Summer 1983

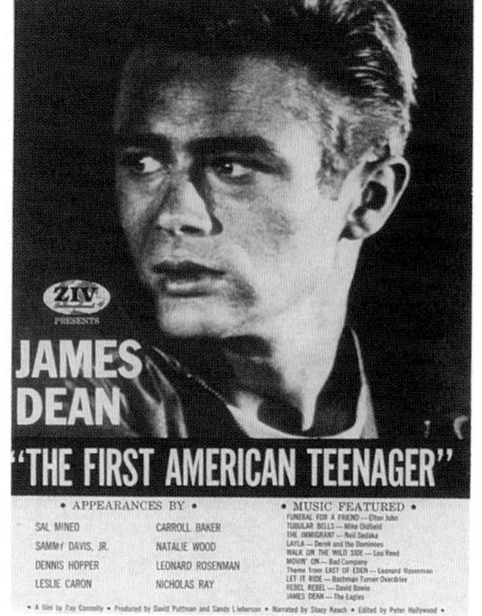

James Dean Program
"The First American Teenager"
Westwood, California - 1975

Flyer for the
Stage Play "Dean"
England, August 1977

LA County Museum of Art
Rebel Film Series Program
June 3 - July 1, 1975

Advertising Flyer for "Will The Real
James Dean Please Stand Up"
England - 1995

Program for James Dean
A Dress Rehearsal
USA - 1992

Program for "Rebel
Without A Cause"
Fairmount, IN - 1989

Program for "Come Back
to the 5 & Dime Jimmy
Dean, Jimmy Dean"
Canada - March 1988

Movie Ads that were run in
The Chronicle Tribune
Marion, Indiana
April 1955

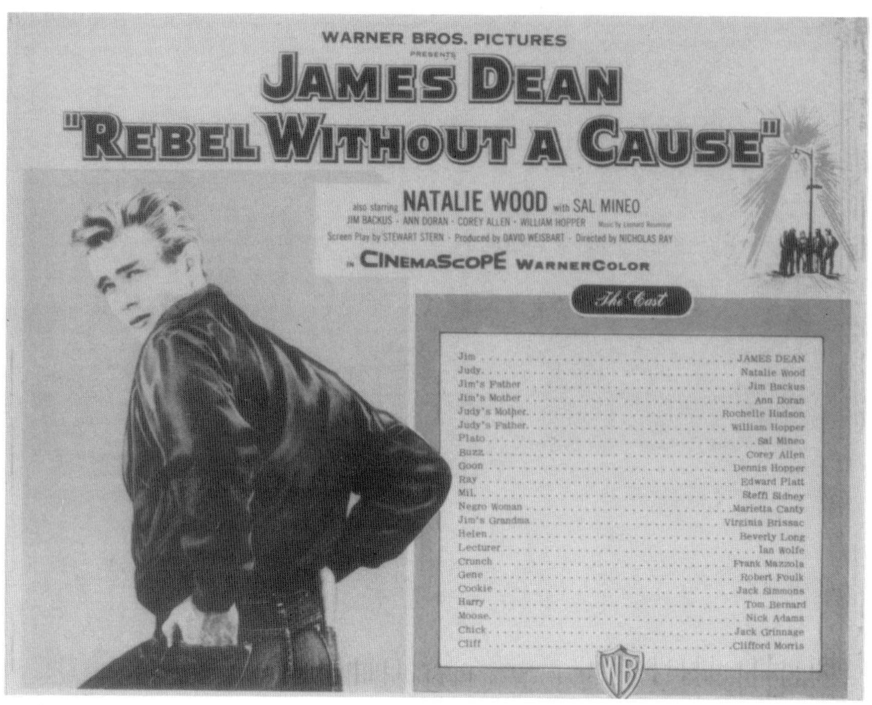

Two Sided Movie Flyer
USA - 1955

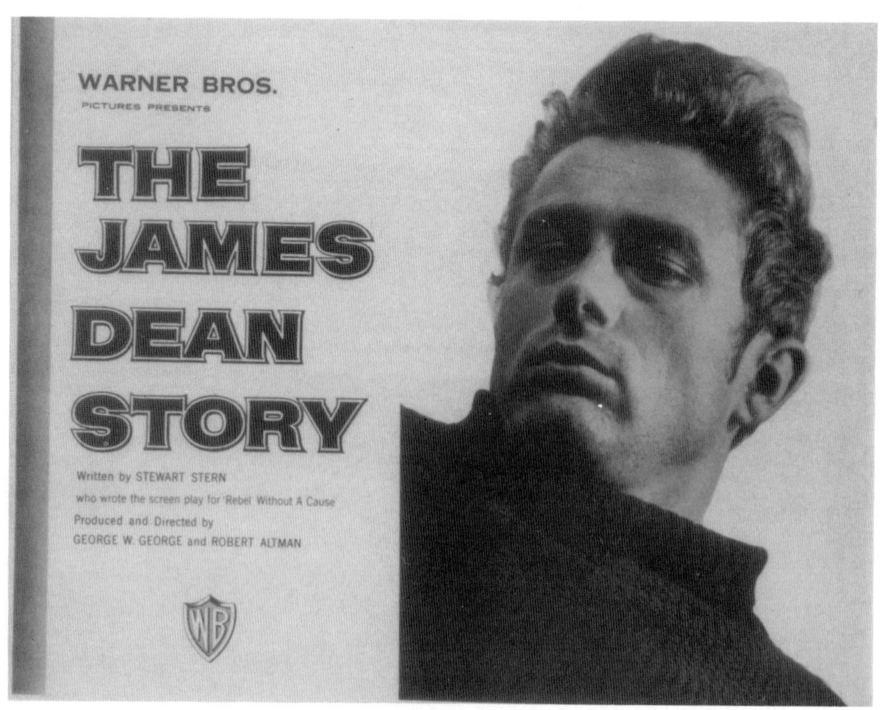

Two Sided Movie Flyer
USA - 1957

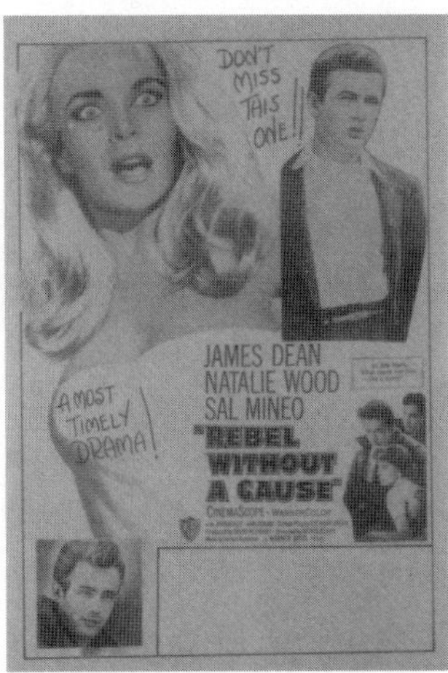

Movie Ad
Theatre Flyer
USA - No Date Available

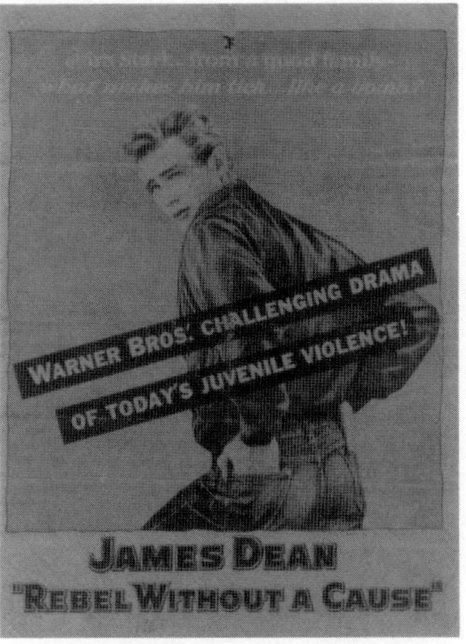

Movie Theatre Program - 4 pgs.
from the Akron Theatre
USA - Sept. 19-20 (year not avail.)

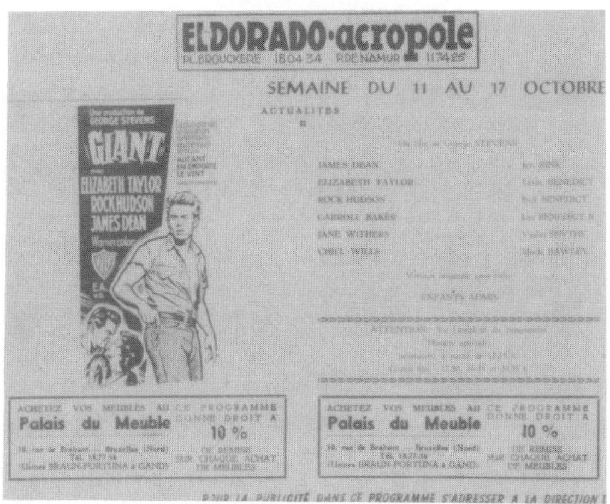

Movie Theatre Flyer for Giant
Belguim - 1957

Advertising Flyer for
"Giant" from the
Liberty Theatre in
Libertyville, Illinois - March 1956

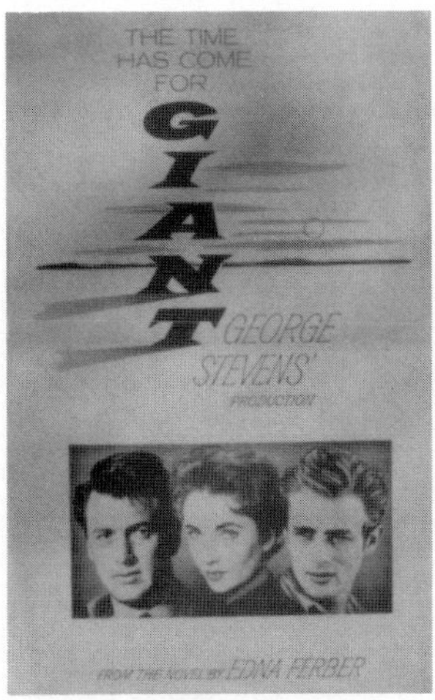

Movie Theatre Herald
(4 pages)
USA - 1956

Niota Theatre
Thurs. Aug. 9 (no year avail.)

Movie Ad for Giant
Japan - 1958

Movie Ad for Giant
Japan - 1960

Movie Ad for East of Eden
Japan - (no date available)

Movie Ad for Giant
Japan - 1991

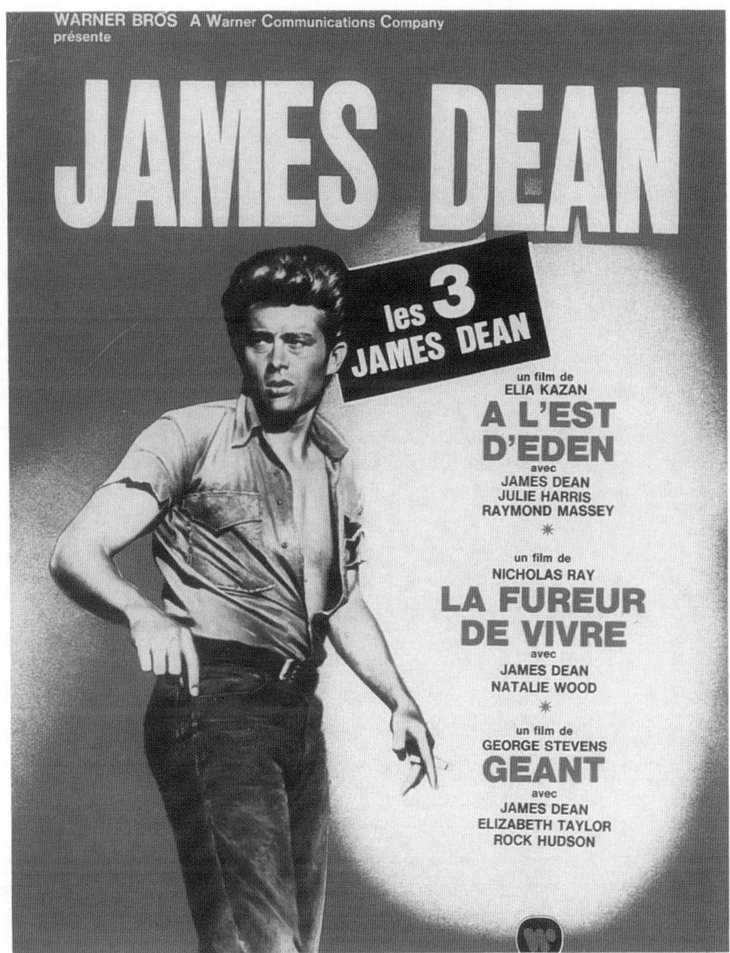

Two sided Movie Flyer - France - 1985

Two sided Movie Flyer - France - (No date available)

USA - 1955

USA - 1955

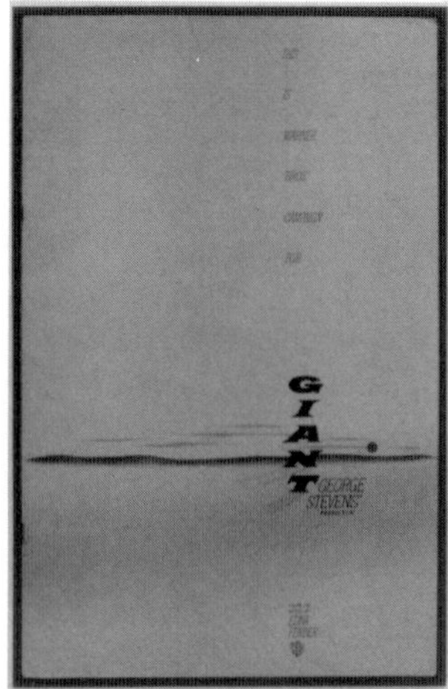

USA - 1956

USA - 1956

USA - 1957

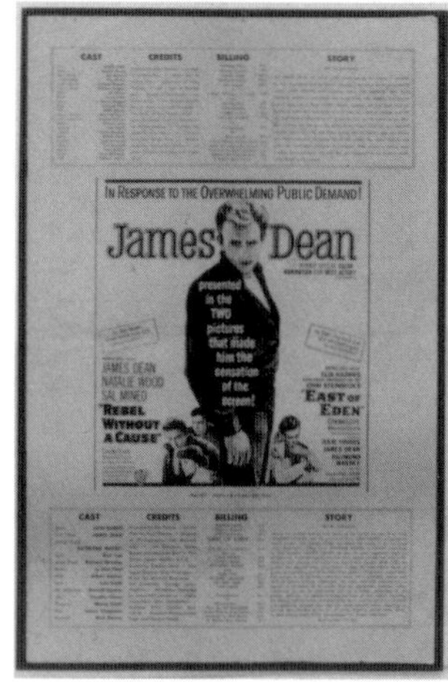

USA - 1957

USA - 1963/66

USA - 1970

USA - 1977

Pressbooks were sent to movie theatres when they would schedule a film to be shown. The pressbooks included ads and reviews that would be used in newspapers. The different sizes and types of movie posters, lobby cards and other promotional materials that were available were also pictured. Pressbooks can range anywhere from four to fifty pages.

Pressbook for
Rebel Without A Cause
Spain - 1956

Pressbook for
The James Dean Story
Spain - 1957

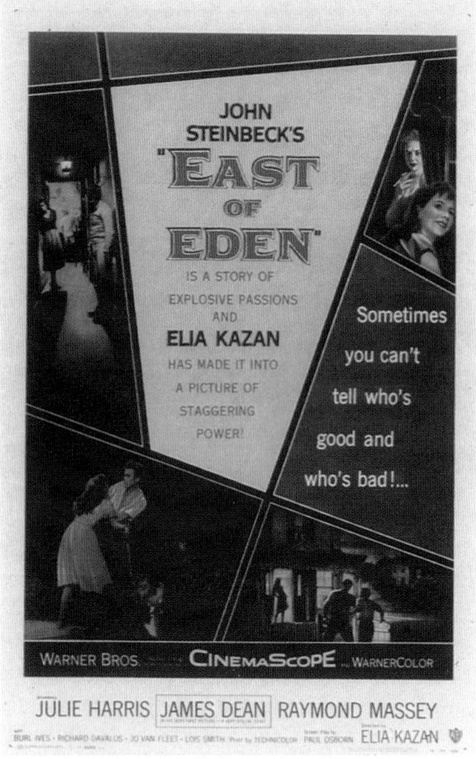

"East of Eden" Movie Poster in sizes of 27" x 41" and 40" x 60"
USA - 1955

"East of Eden" Movie Poster
Silk Screened - Cardboard
24" x 82" - USA - 1955

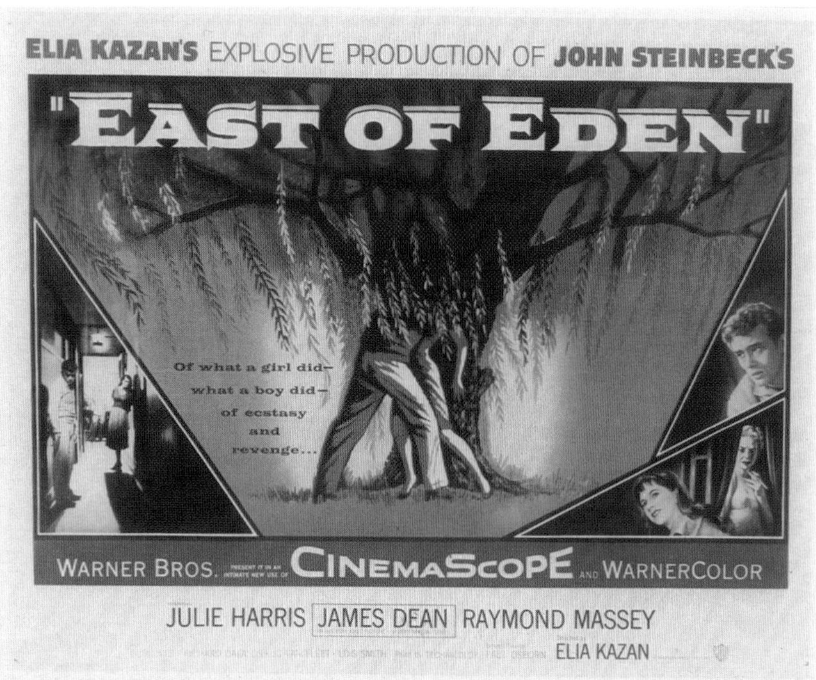

"East of Eden" Movie Poster
22" x 28" - USA - 1955

"East of Eden" Movie Poster
41" x 78" - USA - 1955

"East of Eden" Movie Poster
22" x 28" - USA - 1957

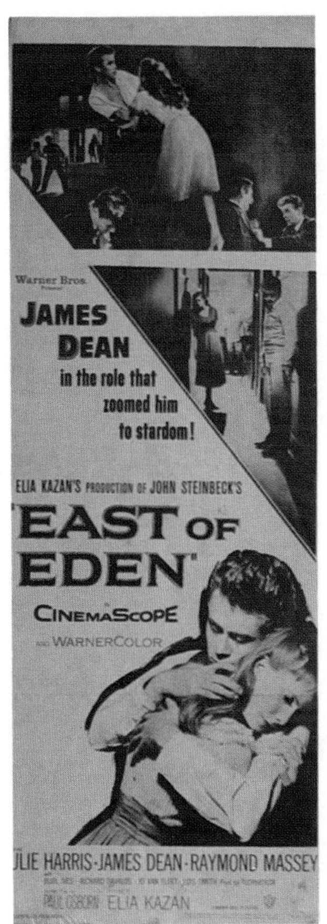

"East of Eden" Movie Poster
14" x 36" - USA - 1957

"East of Eden" Movie Poster
27" x 41" - USA - 1957

"Rebel Without A Cause" Movie Poster
27" x 41" - USA - 1955

AN ABBREVIATED HISTORY OF MOVIE POSTERS

In the early days of Hollywood, theater owners were required by law to return posters to the studio or distributor. Returned poster were stored in warehouses pending re-release of the films. World War II paper drives wiped out many of these warehouses, making posters from the first half of the decade especially rare. In postwar years, fewer and fewer theaters returned their posters, and with neither time nor desire to push the issue, most of the larger companies gave in and dropped the demand entirely. By 1980, Disney was the only major Hollywood studio persisting with the return requirement.

In the 70s and 80s, poster shops and other retail outlets supported an increased consumer demand for movie art, and the entire industry adjusted. Posters had always been printed in limited quantities, based on an estimation of the number of venues in which a movie would be shown. To extend shelf life and facilitate retail sales, printers now utilize a heavier stock of paper and have adopted a process that allows for essentially unlimited print runs. The one-sheet, always produced in the largest quantity, has become the only poster for many films. As with baseball cards, comic books and other mass-produced collectibles, overwhelming quantity limits the value of modern posters. With few exceptions, supply will overwhelm demand for the foreseeable future.

"Rebel Without A Cause" Movie Poster
22" x 28" - USA - 1955

"Rebel Without A Cause" Movie Poster
78″ x 78″ - USA - 1955

"Rebel Without A Cause"
Movie Poster
14″ x 41″ - USA - 1955

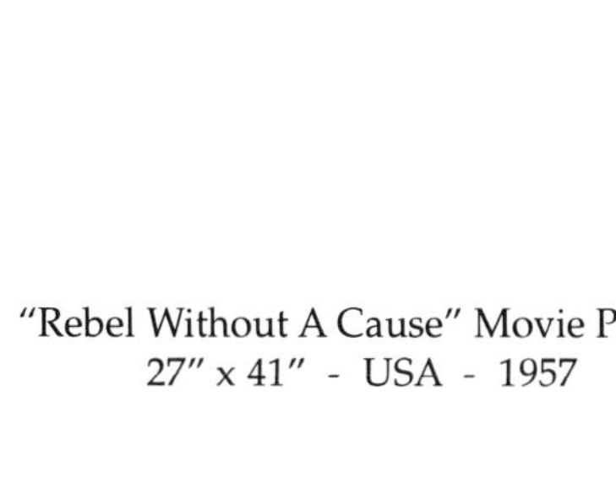

"Rebel Without A Cause" Movie Poster
27″ x 41″ - USA - 1957

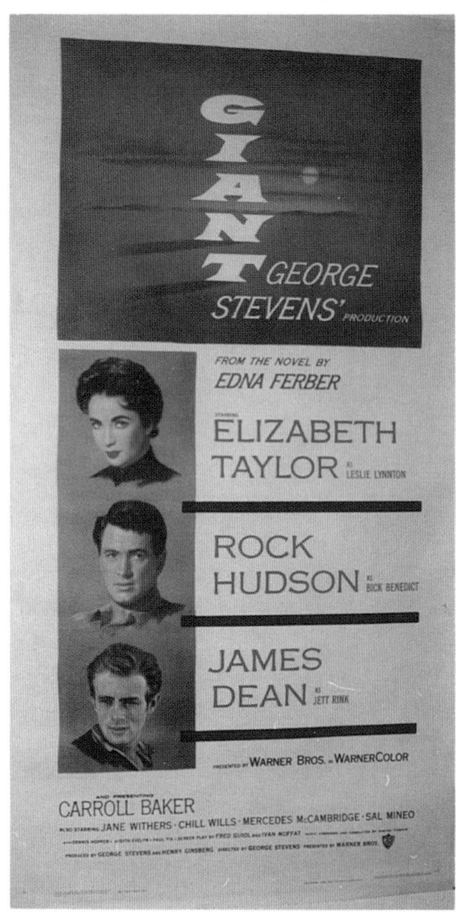

"Giant" Movie Poster
41" x 78" - USA - 1956

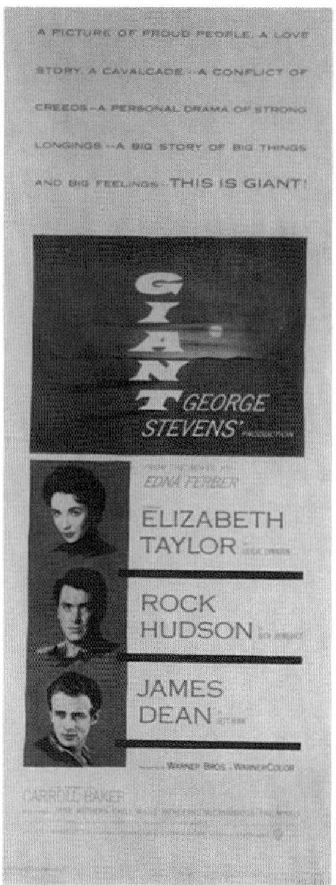

"Giant" Movie Poster
14" x 41" - USA - 1956

"Giant" Movie Poster
14" x 22" - USA - 1956

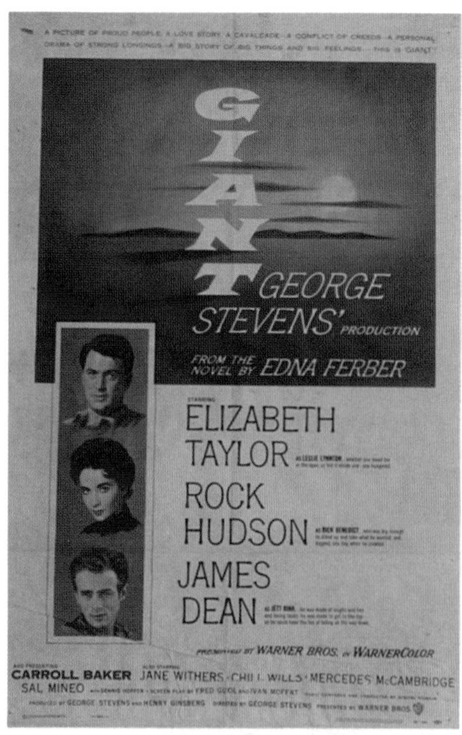

"Giant" Movie Poster
27" x 41" - USA - 1956

GRADING POSTERS

Mint - *To be mint, a poster should be new, unused and rolled never folded.*

Near Mint - *An otherwise mint folded poster or a rolled poster with slight wrinkles, crinkled edges, minor fold wear, light stains or a small tear in the border. In a near mint poster, no more than one of these defects should exist, and the problem should not affect the image.*

Excellent - *An excellent poster may exhibit small separations in a fold line, light staining in a non-critical area, clean pin holes in the borders or minor wrinkling. A poster of this grade can be displayed without restoration.*

Very Good - *In very good condition, a poster may be missing small pieces of paper from the border. While it may be displayable without restoration, linen backing would be recommended on a poster with enough value to justify the expense.*

Good - *Same as very good, but in definite need of restoration if intended for display.*

Poor - *A poor poster is in rough enough shape that restoration will be necessary regardless of whether it is intended for display.*

Movie Poster from "Giant"
40" x 60" - USA - 1956

Movie Poster from "Giant"
22" x 28" - USA - 1956

Movie Poster from"Giant"
in sizes 27″ x 41″ and 40″ x 60″
USA - 1963 and 1966

Movie Poster
from"Giant" - 14″ x 41″
USA - 1963 and 1966

Movie Poster from"Giant"
27″ x 41″ USA - 1963 and 1966

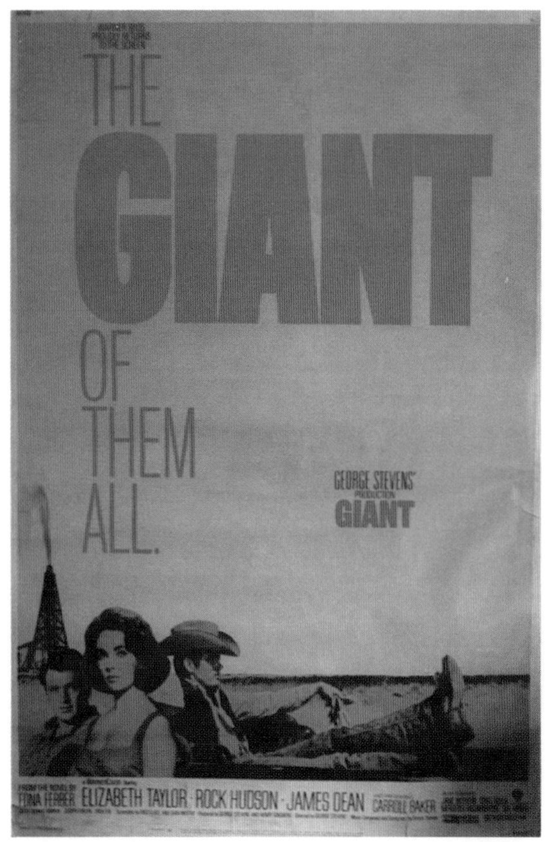

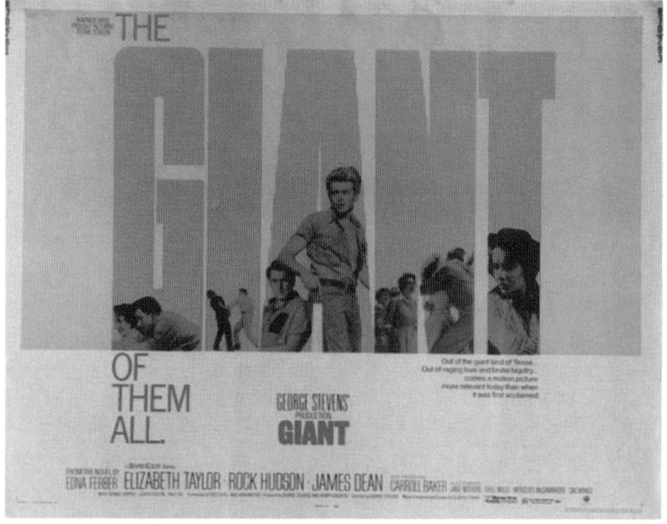

Movie Poster from"Giant"
22″ x 28″ USA - 1970

Movie Poster from"Giant"
in sizes from
40″ x 60″ - 27″ x 41″ - 41″ x 78″
USA - 1970

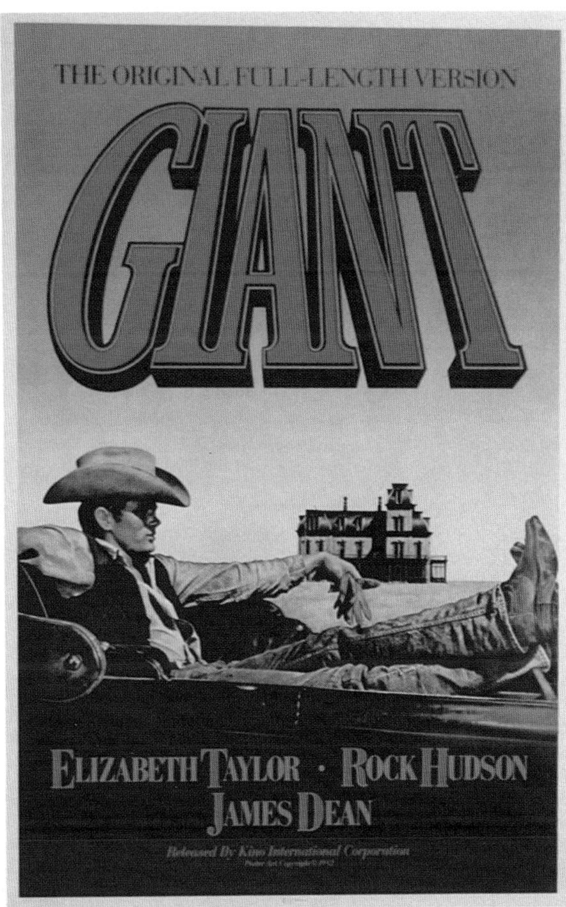

Movie Poster from "Giant"
27" x 41" USA - 1982

STANDARD HOLLYWOOD MOVIE POSTER SIZES

One-Sheet (27" x 41")
The most popular size for movie posters, printed on paper stock. The only poster for many contemporary films.

Half-Sheet (22" x 28")
Card stock posters.

Insert (14" x 36")
Also printed on card stock.

Window Card (14" x 22")
Printed on card stock, often used for promotion away from the theater.

Three-Sheet (41" x 78")
Three times the size of a one-sheet, printed on paper stock.

Six-Sheet (78" x 78")
Huge paper stock posters that could only be displayed by select theaters, six-sheets are relatively rare.

Lobby Cards (11" x 14" or 14" x 17")
Available in sets of 8, each featuring a scene from the movie. On card stock.

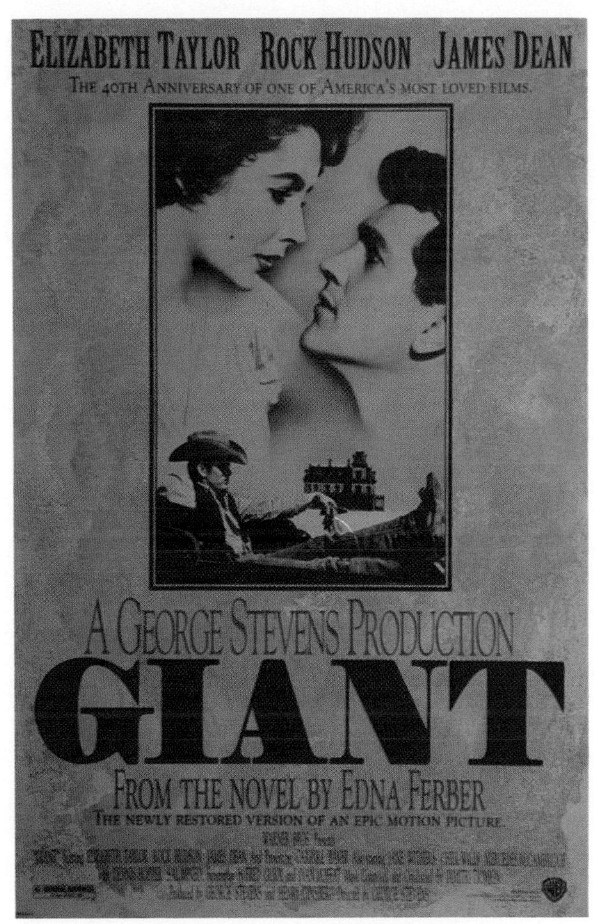

Movie Poster from "Giant"
27" x 41" USA - 1996

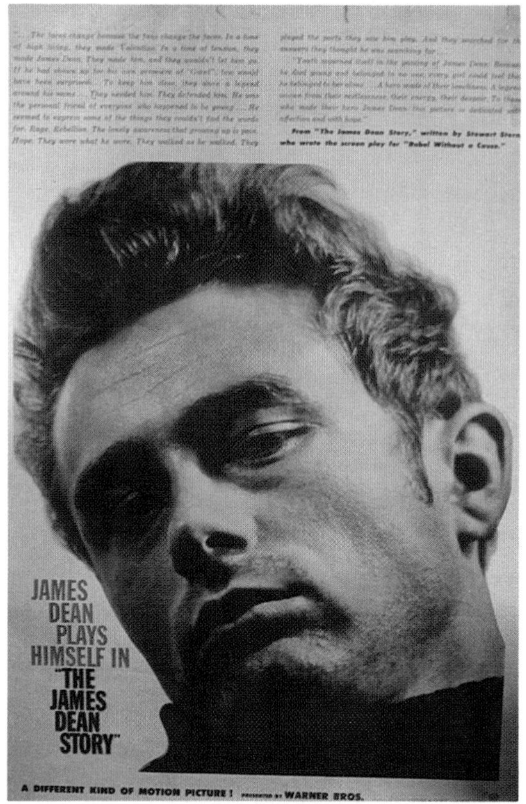

Movie Poster from"The James Dean Story"
40″ x 60″ USA - 1957

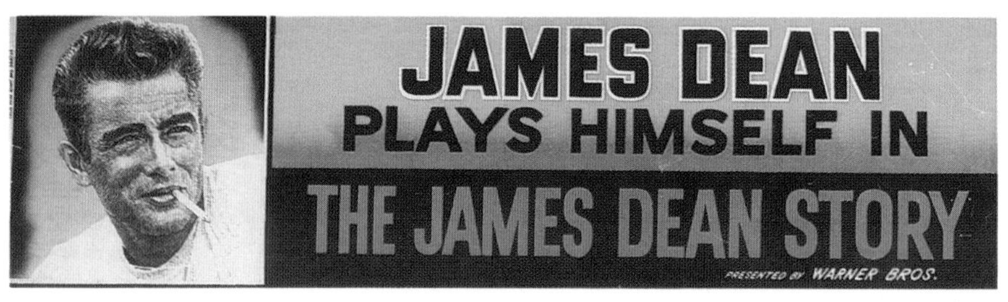

Movie Poster from"The James Dean Story"
24″ x 82″ USA - 1957

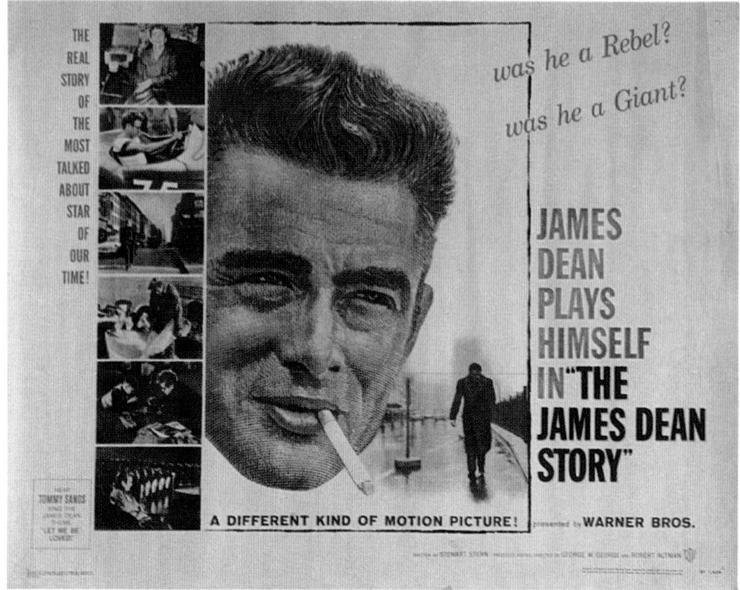

Movie Poster from"The James Dean Story"
22″ x 28″ USA - 1957

Movie Poster from
"The James Dean Story"
in sizes from 14" x 22" and 27" x 41"
USA - 1957

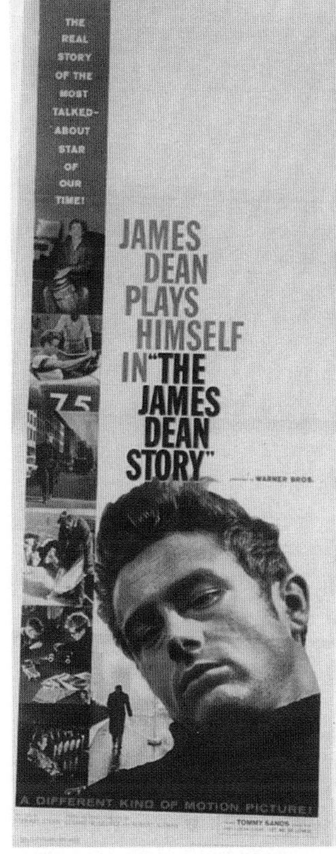

Movie Poster from
"The James Dean Story"
14" x 41" USA - 1957

Movie Poster from "James Dean:
The First American Teenager"
27" x 41" USA - 1976

Movie Poster from
"The James Dean Story"
41" x 78" USA - 1957

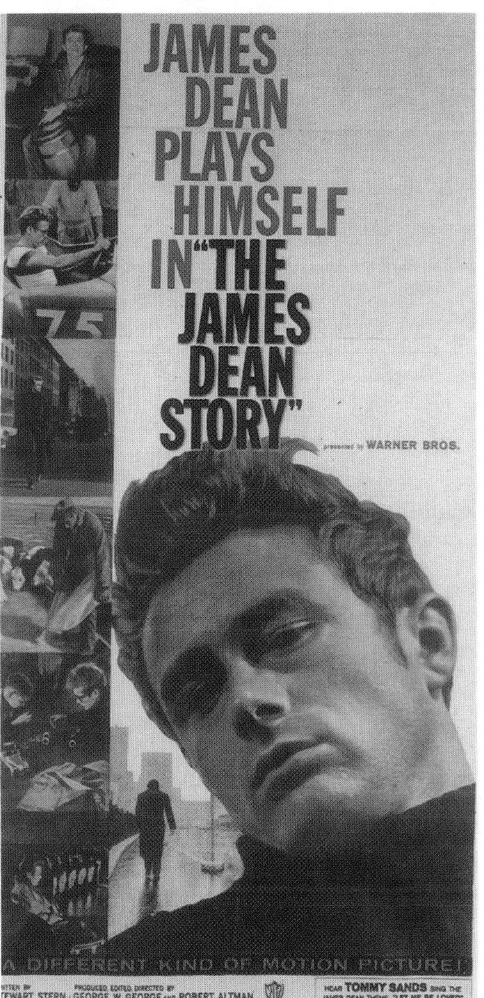

Movie Posters from"Giant"
18" x 26" - Italy - 1957

Movie Posters from "Giant"
18" x 26" - Italy - 1957

Movie Poster from "Rebel Without A Cause"
18" x 26" - Italy - 1956

Movie Poster from "Rebel Without A Cause" - 18" x 26" - Italy - 1956

Movie Poster from "Rebel Without A Cause" - 18" x 26" - Italy - 1956

Movie Poster from "Rebel Without A Cause"
27" x 41" - Italy - 1958

Movie Poster from "Rebel Without A Cause" - 18" x 26" - Italy - 1980s

Movie Poster from
"The James Dean Story"
18" x 26" - Italy - 1958

Movie Poster from
"The James Dean Story"
18" x 26" - Italy - 1958

Movie Poster from "Giant"
18" x 26" - Italy - 1980s

Movie Poster from "Giant"
27" x 41" - Italy - 1958

Movie Poster from "The James Dean Story"
18" x 26" - Italy - 1958

Movie Poster from "East of Eden"
39" x 55" - Italy - 1955

Movie Poster from "East of Eden"
Cannes Film Festival
France - August 1955

Movie Poster from "East of Eden"
30" x 40" - England

Movie Poster
11" x 16" - Czechoslovakia

Movie Poster from "Rebel Without A Cause"
19" x 25" - England - 1980s

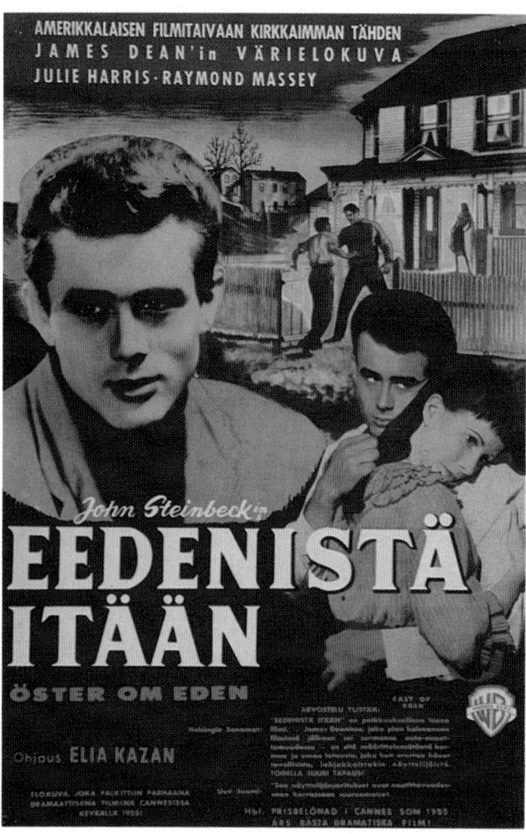

Movie Poster from "East of Eden"
15" x 23" - Finland - 1955

Movie Poster from "East of Eden"
17" x 24" - Finland - 1980

Movie Poster from "Giant"
15" x 23" - Finland - 1980

Movie Poster from "Rebel Without A Cause"
27" x 39" - Belgium - 1958

Movie Poster from "East of Eden"
24" x 33" - Denmark - 1958

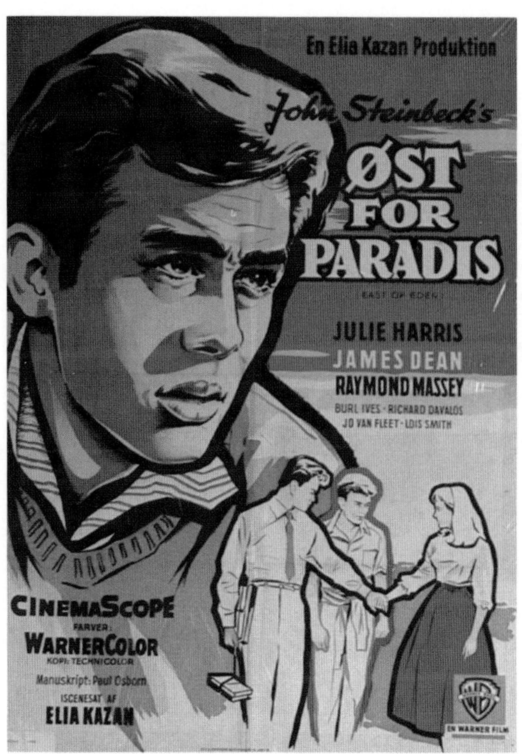

Movie Poster from "Giant"
24" x 33" - Denmark - 1955

Movie Poster
20" x 28" - Israel - March 29, 1978

Movie Poster from "East of Eden"
24" x 33" - Denmark - 1980

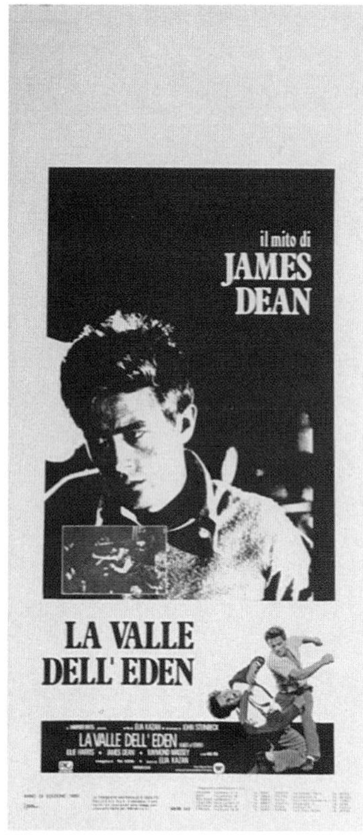

Movie Poster from
"East of Eden" in sizes
13" x 28" and 40" x 56"
Italy - 1980s

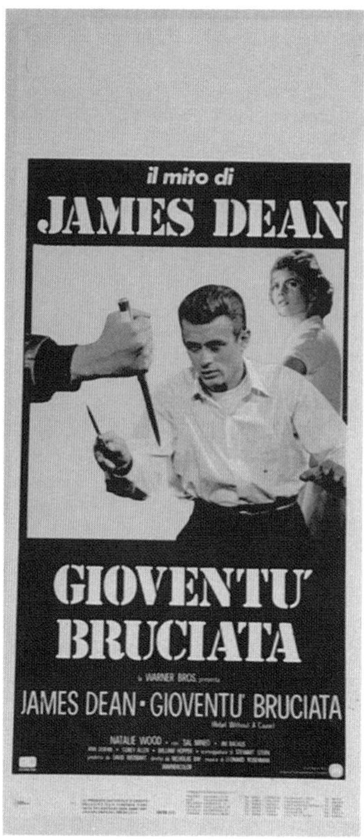

Movie Poster from
"Rebel Without A Cause" in
sizes 13" x 28" and 40" x 56"
Italy - 1980s

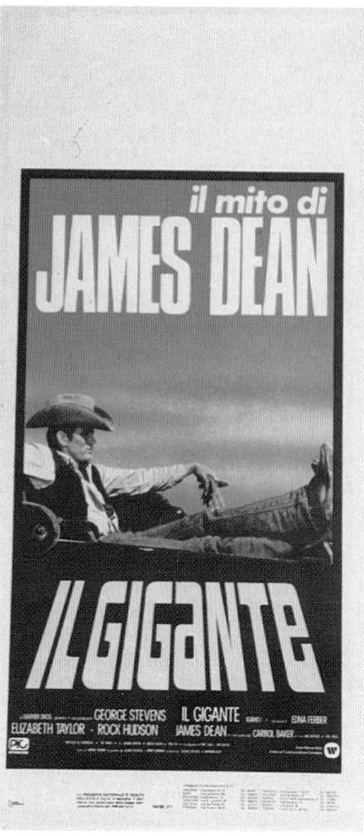

Movie Poster from "Giant" in
sizes 13" x 28" and 40" x 56"
Italy - 1980s

Movie Poster from
"Rebel Without A Cause"
23" x 33" - Poland - 1958

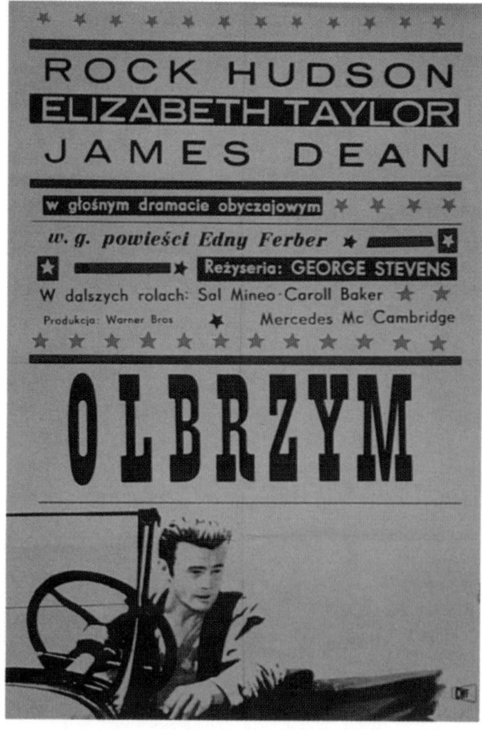

Movie Poster from "Giant"
23" x 33" - Poland - 1958

Movie Poster from "East of Eden"
43" x 58" - Argentina - 1955

Movie Poster from "East of Eden"
29" x 43" - Argentina - 1957

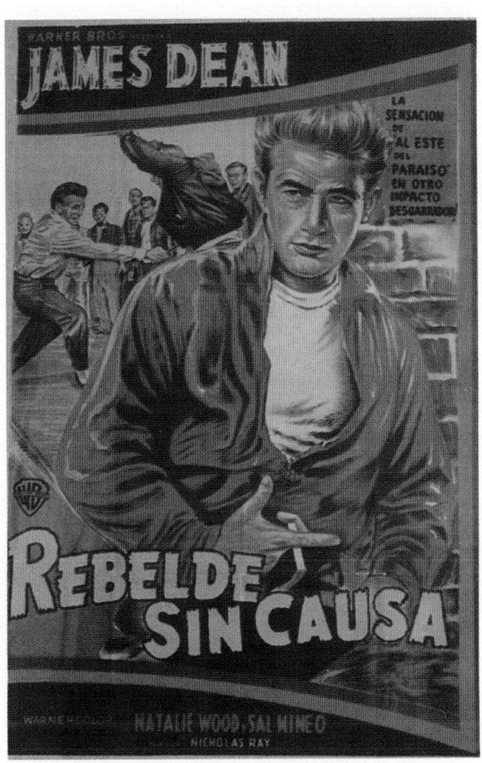

Movie Poster from
"Rebel Without A Cause"
29" x 43" - Argentina - 1955

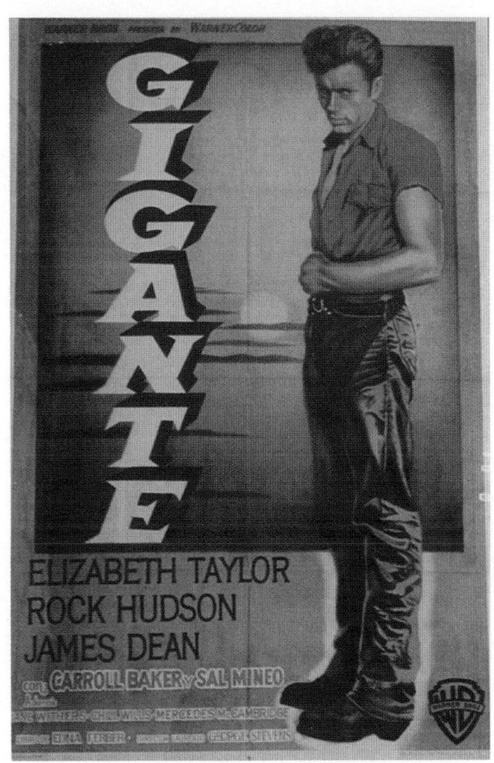

Movie Poster from "Giant"
29" x 43" - Argentina - 1956

Movie Poster from "East of Eden"
20" x 28" - Japan - 1980

Movie Poster from "Rebel Without A Cause"
20" x 28" - Japan - 1980

Movie Poster from "Giant"
20" x 28" - Japan - 1980

Movie Poster from "James Dean
The First American Teenager"
20" x 28" - Japan - 1980

Movie Poster from "Giant"
20" x 28" - Japan

Movie Poster from "Giant"
20" x 28" - Japan

Movie Poster from "Rebel Without A Cause"
28" x 40" - Italy - 1980

Movie Poster from "Rebel Without A Cause"
30" x 40" - England - 1975

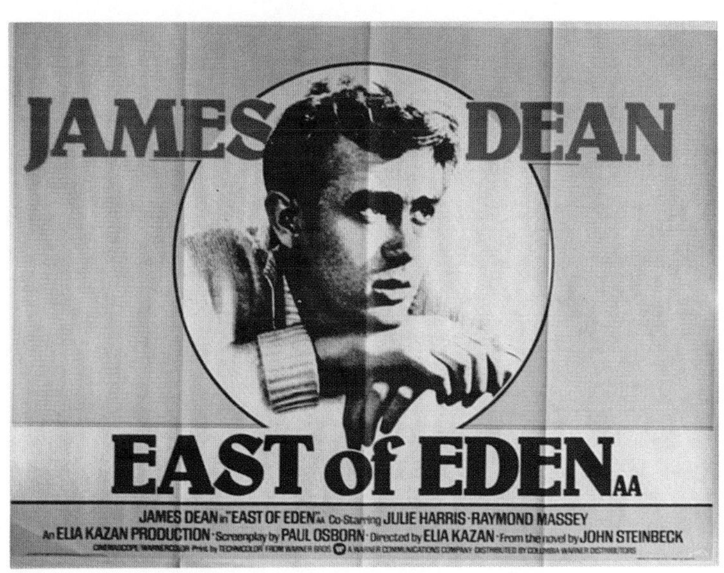

Movie Poster from "East of Eden"
30" x 40" - England - 1980s

Movie Poster
19" x 27" - Italy - 1995

Movie Poster from
"Rebel Without A Cause"
27" x 39" - Spain - 1964

Movie Poster from
"Rebel Without A Cause"
27" x 37" - Spain - 1980

Movie Poster from "Giant"
27" x 39" - Spain - 1970

Movie Poster from "Giant"
27" x 39" - Spain - 1959

Movie Poster from
"Rebel Without A Cause"
27" x 39" - Spain - 1964

Movie Poster from "East of Eden"
27" x 39" - Spain - 1969

Movie Poster from
"East of Eden"
27" x 39" - Spain - 1958

Movie Poster from
"Rebel Without A Cause"
27" x 39" - Spain - 1958

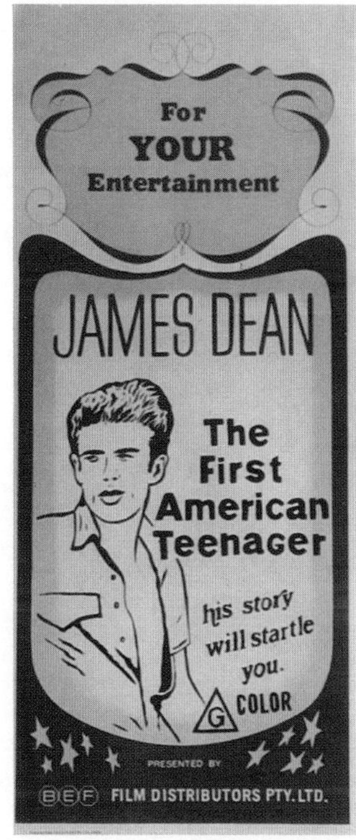

Movie Poster from "The
First American Teenager"
13" x 30"- Australia - 1978

Movie Poster from "East of Eden"
31" x 47" - France - 1955

Movie Poster from "East of Eden"
in sizes of 47" x 63" and 24" x 32"
France - 1985

Movie Poster from "East of Eden"
46" x 61" - France - 1955

Movie Poster from
"The James Dean Story"
46" x 63" - France - 1980

Movie Poster from
"Rebel Without A Cause"
46" x 63" - France - 1955

Movie Poster from
"Rebel Without A Cause"
46" x 63" - France - 1957

Movie Poster from
"Rebel Without A Cause"
46" x 63" - France - 1956

Movie Poster from "Rebel Without A Cause"
in sizes 22" x 30" and 47" x 63"
France - 1980

Movie Poster from "Giant"
46" x 63" - France - 1956

Movie Poster from "Giant"
in sizes 40" x 56" and 23" x 34"
France - 1985

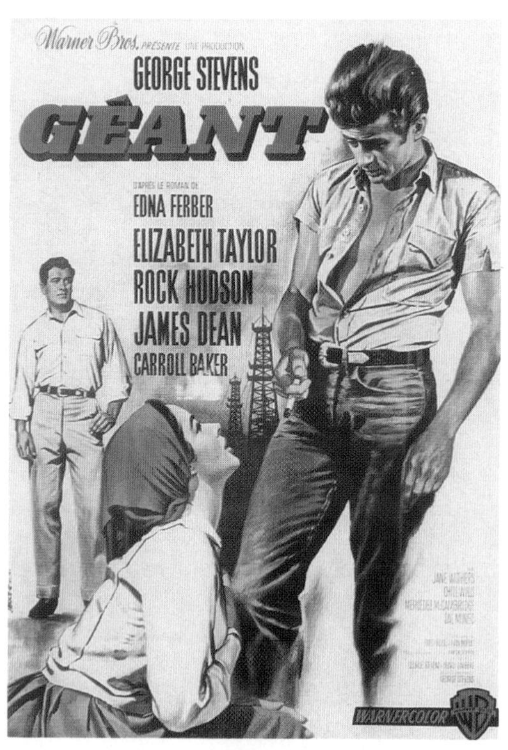

Movie Poster from "Giant"
46" x 63" - France - 1956

Movie Poster from "Giant"
20" x 25" - France - 1982

Movie Poster from "East of Eden"
24" x 34" - Germany - 1980

Movie Poster from
"Rebel Without A Cause"
24" x 34" - Germany - 1956

Movie Poster from "Giant"
24" x 34" - Germany - 1956

Movie Poster
46" x 63" - France

Movie Poster from "Giant"
24" x 34" - Germany - 1958

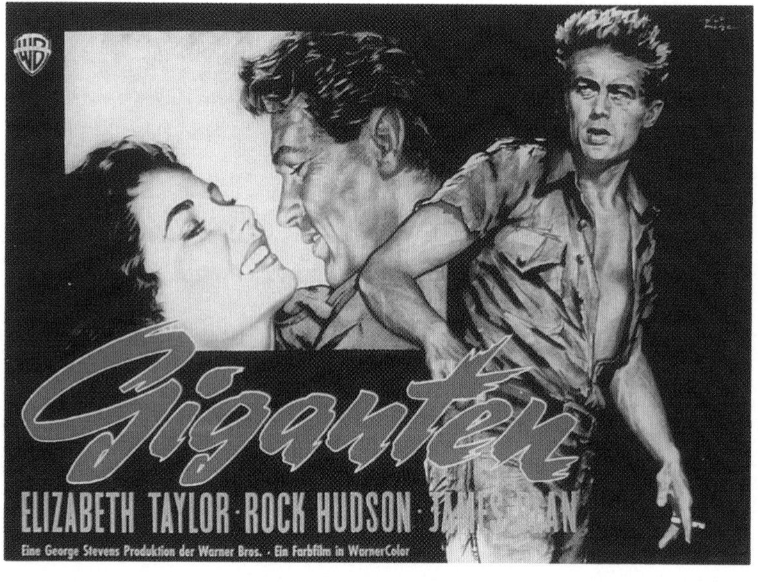

Movie Poster from "Giant"
26" x 38" - Germany - 1958

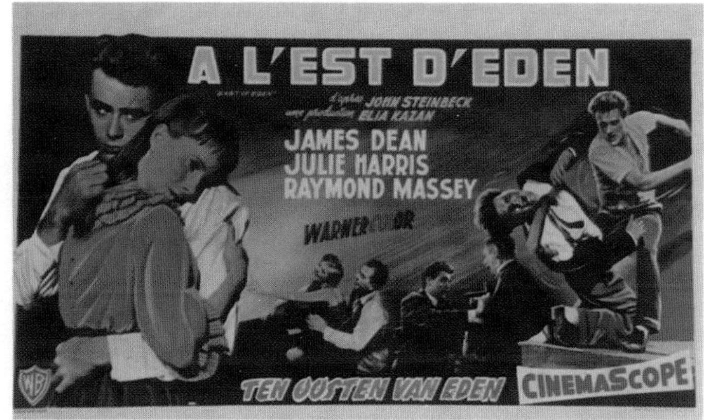

Movie Poster from "East of Eden"
15" x 21" - Belguim - 1955

Movie Poster from
"Rebel Without A Cause"
15" x 21" - Belguim - 1956

Movie Poster from "Giant"
15" x 21" - Belguim - 1957

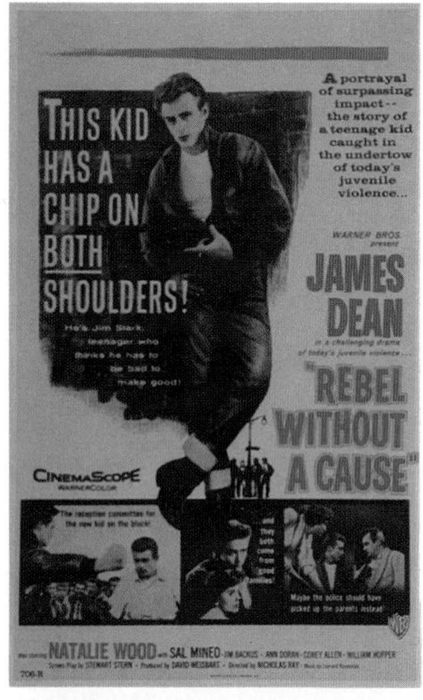

Movie Poster from
"Rebel Without A Cause"
14" x 22" - USA - 1970

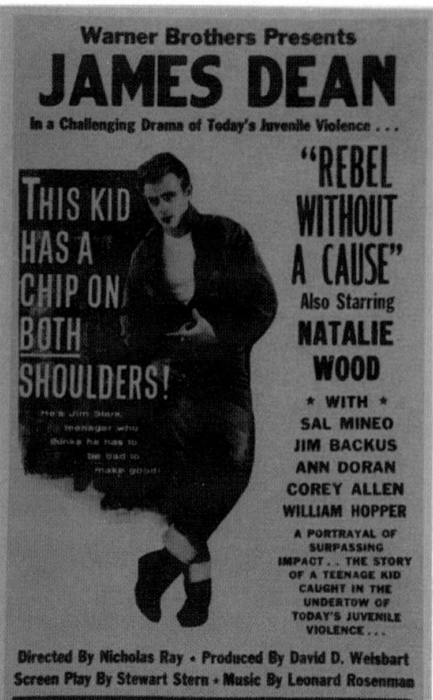

Movie Poster from
"Rebel Without A Cause"
14" x 22" - USA - 1996
Reproduction

Movie Poster from "9/30/55"
12" x 18" - USA - 1977

Movie Poster from
"Hollywood Graffiti"
45" x 62" - France - 1980

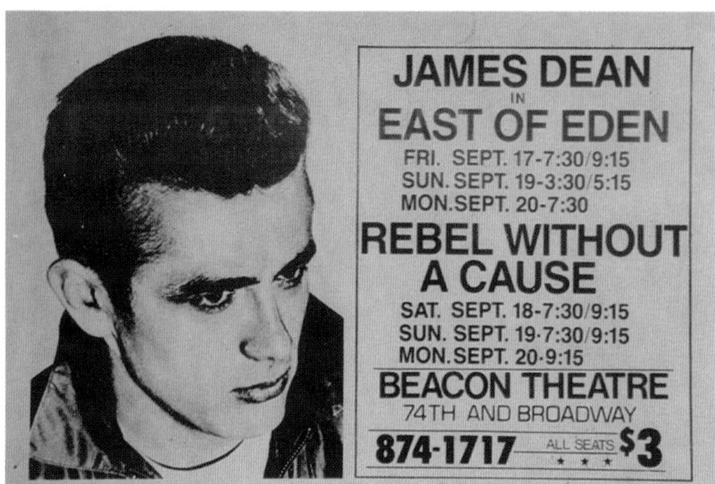

Movie Poster - 14" x 22" - NYC - Cardboard

Movie Poster from"The First American Teenager"
30" x 40" - England - 1977

Set of Lobby Cards from "East of Eden"
cards are 11" x 14" - USA - 1955

Each set of Lobby Cards contain 8 different cards

Set of Lobby Cards from "Rebel Without a Cause"
cards are 11" x 14" - USA - 1955

Each set of Lobby Cards contain 8 different cards

Set of Lobby Cards from "Giant"
cards are 11" x 14" - USA - 1956

Each set of Lobby Cards contain 8 different cards

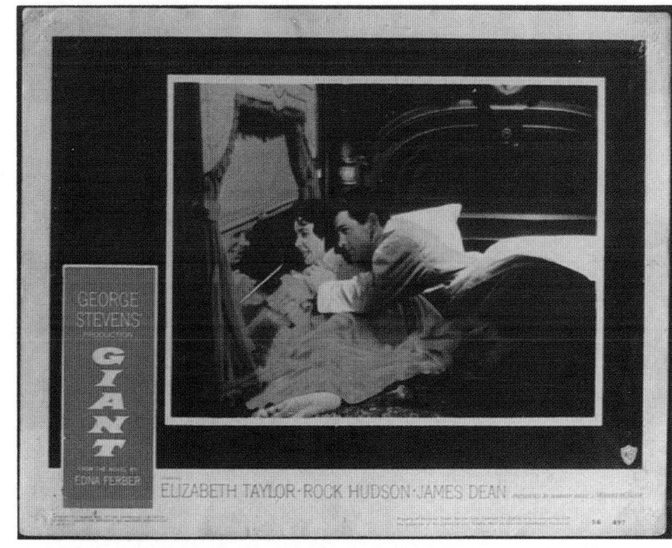

Set of Lobby Cards from "The James Dean Story"
cards are 11" x 14" - USA - 1957

Each set of Lobby Cards contain 8 different cards

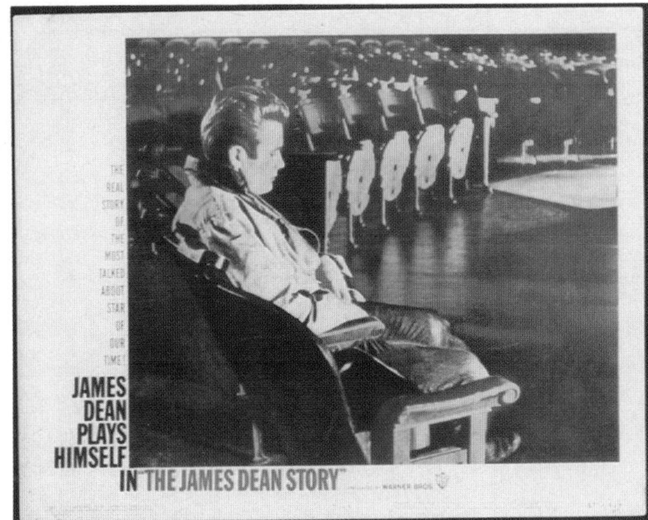

Set of Reissued Lobby Cards from "Giant"
cards are 11" x 14" - USA - 1970

Lobby Cards

Each set of Lobby Cards contain 8 different cards

Reissued Lobby Card from "East of Eden"
card is 11" x 14" - USA - 1957

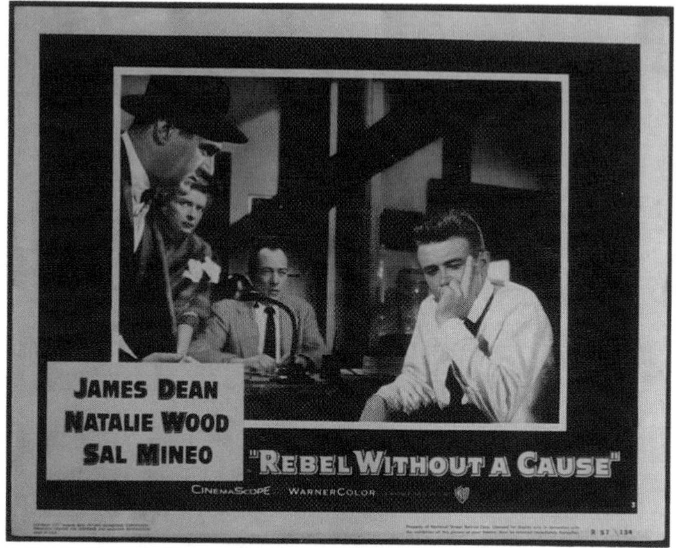

Reissued Lobby Card from "Rebel Without A Cause"
card is 11" x 14" - USA - 1957

Reissued Lobby Card from "Giant"
card is 11" x 14" - USA - 1963

Reissued Lobby Card from "Giant"
card is 11" x 14" - USA - 1966

First 6 in a Set of 12 Lobby Photos from "East of Eden"
8" x 10" - USA - 1955

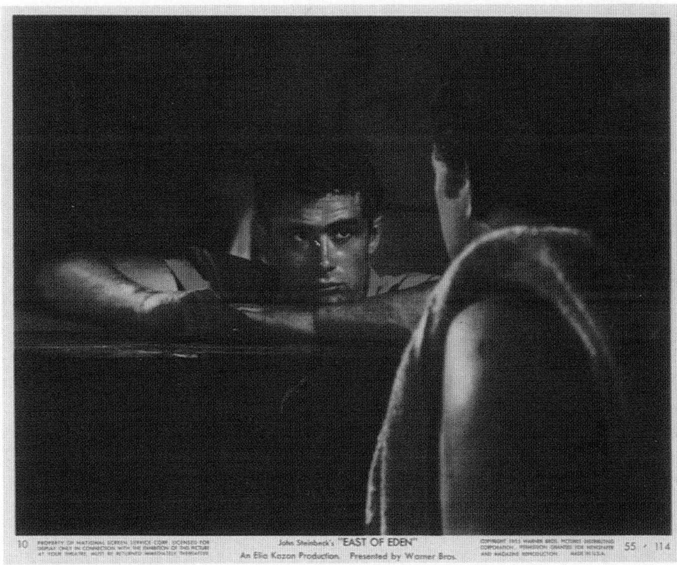

Second 6 in a Set of 12 Lobby Photos from "East of Eden"
8" x 10" - USA - 1955

First 6 in a Set of 12 Lobby Photos from "Rebel Without a Cause"
8" x 10" - USA - 1955

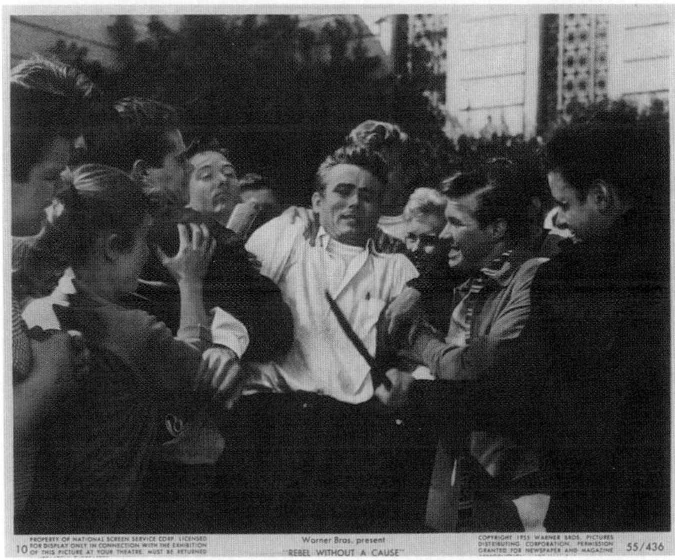

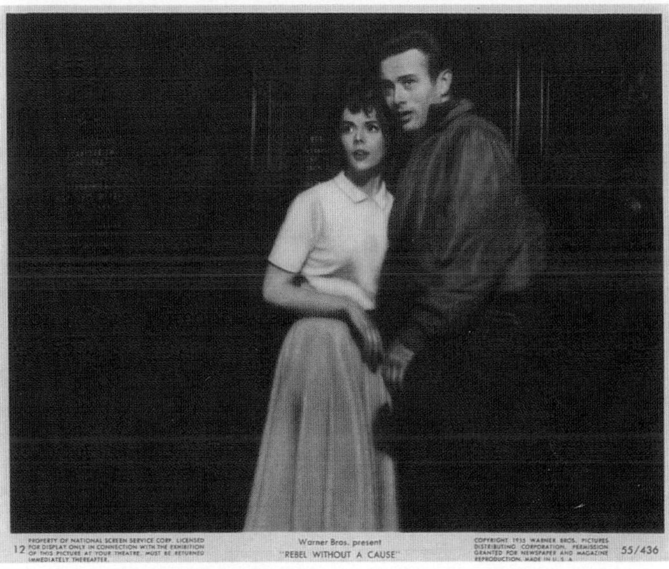

Second 6 in a Set of 12 Lobby Photos from "Rebel Without a Cause"
8" x 10" - USA - 1955

First 6 in a Set of 12 Lobby Photos from "Giant"
8" x 10" - USA - 1956

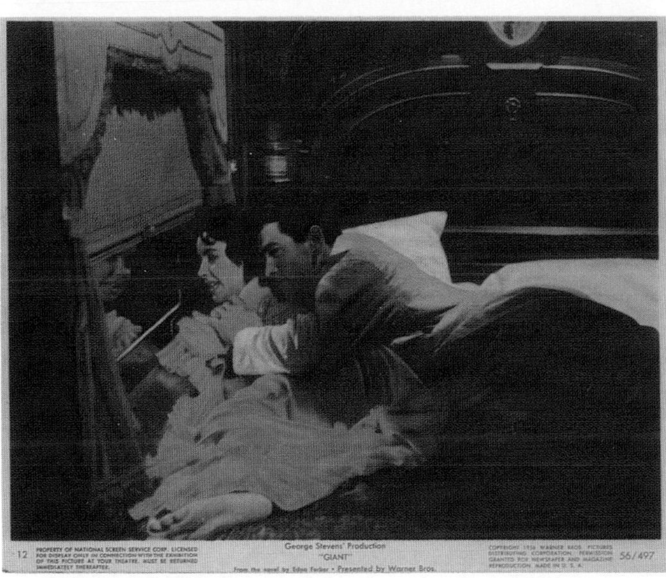

Second 6 in a Set of 12 Lobby Photos from "Giant"
8″ x 10″ - USA - 1956

First 6 in a Set of 12 Lobby Cards from "East of Eden"
9 1/4" x 11 1/2" - France

Second 6 in a Set of 12 Lobby Cards from "East of Eden"
9 1/4" x 11 1/2" - France

First 6 in a Set of 12 Lobby Cards from "Rebel Without A Cause"
9 1/4" x 11 1/2" - France

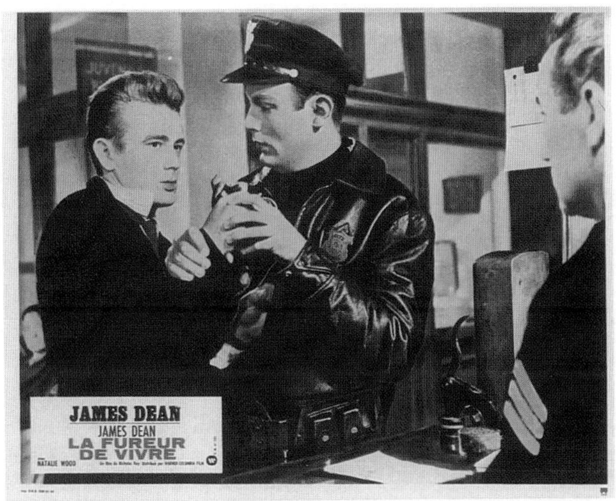

Second 6 in a Set of 12 Lobby Cards from "Rebel Without A Cause"
9 1/4" x 11 1/2" - France

Set of 12 Lobby Cards from "Giant"
9 1/4" x 11 1/2" - France

Set of 12 Lobby Cards from "Giant"
9 1/4" x 11 1/2" - France

Examples of Lobby Cards from "Rebel Without A Cause"
9 1/4" x 11 1/2" - France

Set of Lobby Cards from "East of Eden" - 12 1/2" x 16 1/4" - Mexico

Set of Lobby Cards from
"Rebel Without A Cause"
12 1/2" x 16 1/4"
Mexico

Set of Lobby Cards from
"Giant"
12 1/2" x 16 1/4"
Mexico

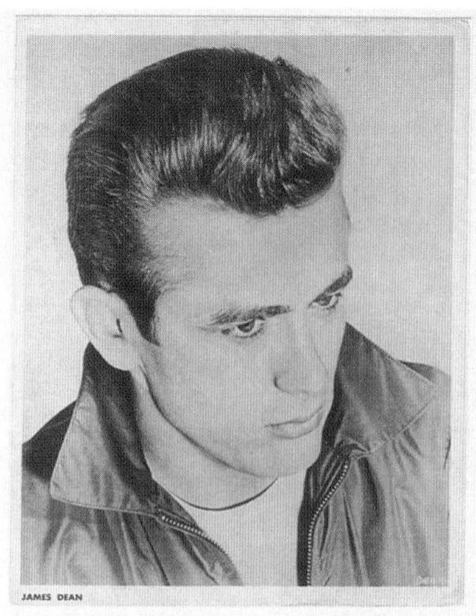

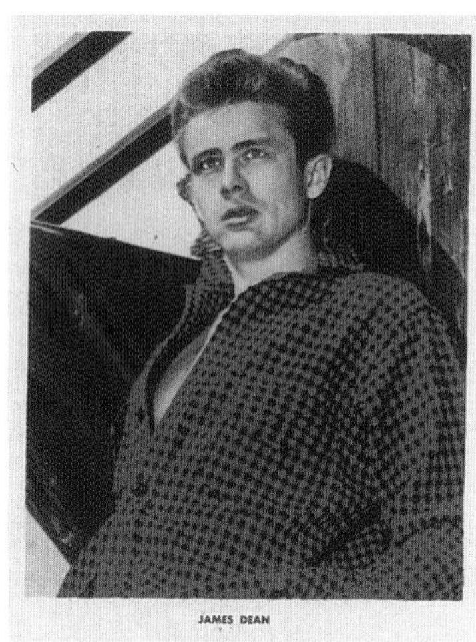

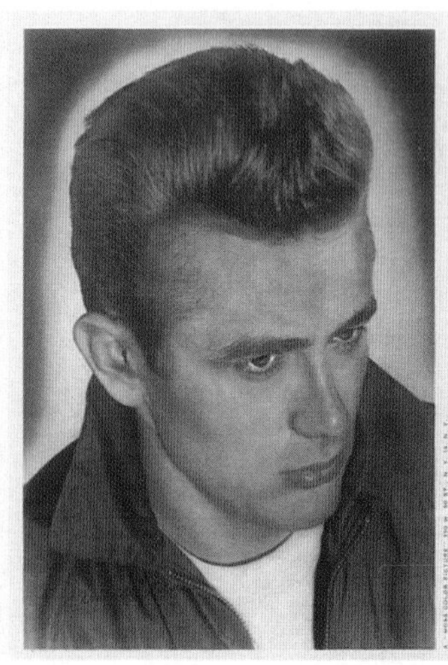

Promotional Photos printed on paper for give-aways at
Movie Theatres - USA - 1956

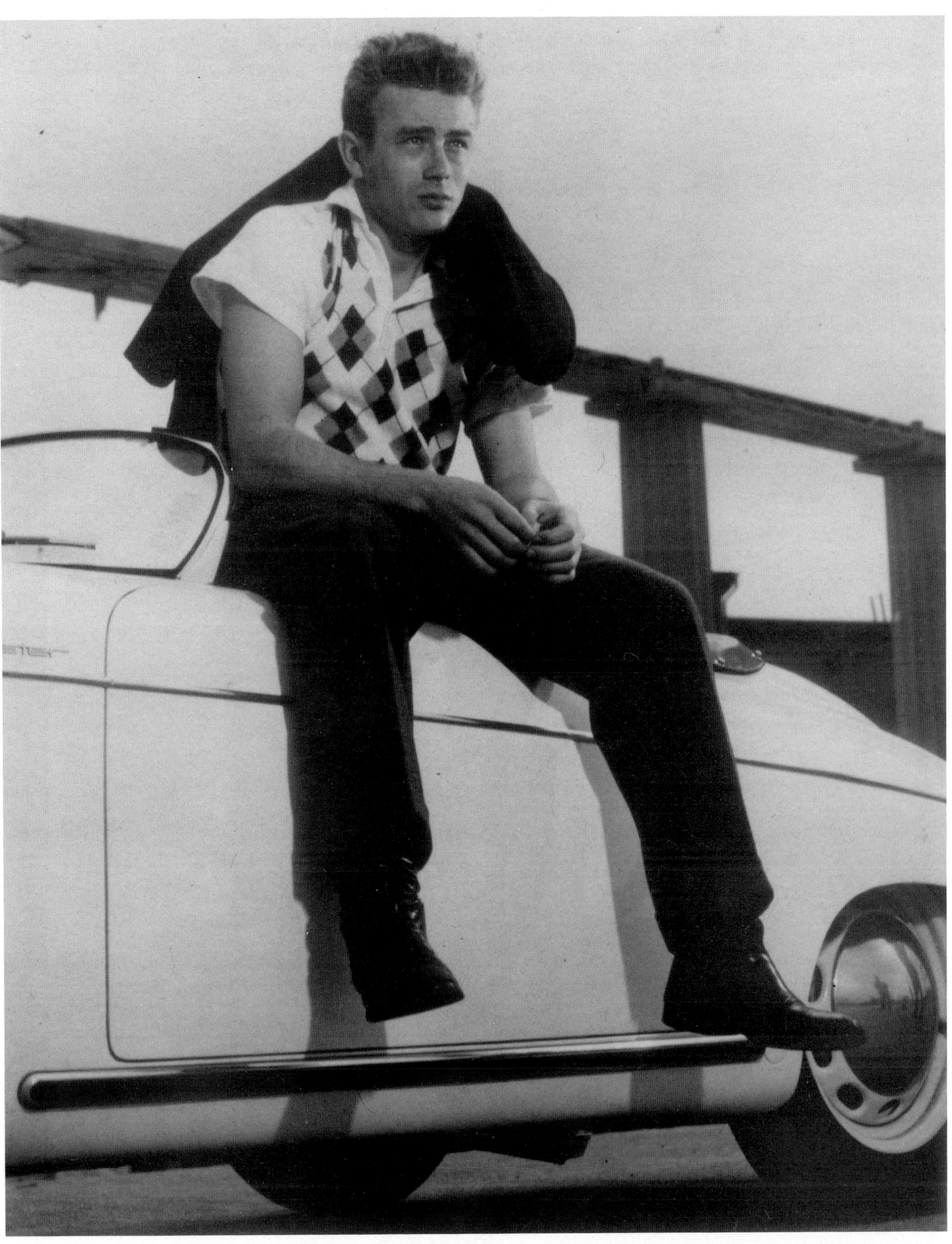

Rarities

Rarities are the Holy Grails of Dean collectors. Included in this category are one-of-a-kind items with special connection to Dean - autographs, movie props, personal possessions - as well as commemorative objects that are prohibitively expensive or particularly difficult to find.

Autographs

Condition, content and celebrity name are the three tenets of autograph collecting. For most celebrities, fame is fleeting. But James Dean is one of those rare stars who never go out of style. His enduring popularity and the scarcity of his signature keep Dean at the top of many philographers' most wanted lists.

Because Dean's autograph is notoriously rare, it has frequently been forged. Determination of autograph authenticity can be a challenge, since no two signatures are ever quite the same. An autograph hastily scribbled on a photograph while walking down the street will not be identical to one written on a napkin at a table in a restaurant. Even amongst twenty-five signatures penned in a single sitting, each will differ from the others at least slightly. In recent years, authentication has been further complicated by the advent of high-tech reproduction techniques. Autopens are capable of churning out thousands of identical signatures in a short time. Viewed individually, autopen autographs are difficult to distinguish. Collectively, their lack of variation can tip off an experienced eye. There is no sure-fire way to avoid phony signatures, but as a collector gains experience, the obvious fakes will start to stand out. Common sense and an eye for detail are the keys to autographing success, but even expert philographers will sometimes be fooled into thinking that a fake is real, or vice versa.

One common misconception of beginners is that an inscription lessens the value of an autopgraph. This is false on two counts. First, an inscription, especially to someone the signer knew personally, is often much easier to verify than a simple signature would be. Second - and this is increasingly true the older and more valuable the document - since it is the handwriting that gives the item its value, it stands to reason that more is better. When writing a passage of several lines, it is more likely that the writer will fall into his or her individual patterns of penmanship. The extra writing, therefore, makes it that much more difficult to pull off a convincing fake.

With autographs, condition is everything. Many dealers sell autographs framed or mounted, sometimes together with a photograph or some other collectible. These presentations can make attractive displays, but get certification of authenticity for each individual item before buying. Many times, reproduction objects are sold side by side with genuine artifacts or autographs.

Clothing and Props

Movie costumes will usually have studio tags that make them easily identifiable. Wardrobe items are seldom one-of-a-kind, more often assembled in matched sets of two or three. The tags will sometimes specify that a shirt is number one of three, for example, indicating that at the time of production, they had three identical shirts on hand. In the case of James Dean, the most famous article of clothing by far is the red windbreaker from *Rebel Without a Cause* (see sidebar in Novelties chapter). Personal clothing items are much more difficult to authenticate, making documentation all the more important.

Because Dean became a legend so soon after his "arrival" in Hollywood, props from his movie sets have always been treasured and many have been very well maintained. Pieces of the Reata mansion, cowboy gear, switchblades and the infamous toy monkey are among the most coveted items for well-bankrolled collectors. It sometimes seems that everything Dean saw or touched has been made available for sale. Although undoubtedly one of the most exciting categories of collecting, props and personal belongings of the stars often have questionable provenance, encouraging scams and trickery. As with any high-ticket items, props are best purchased from established, reputable dealers.

Although he did not have much time to practice and develop, James Dean was a talented visual artist. Naturally, the cartoons, photographs, sculptures and paintings Dean created hold great appeal to fans and collectors. His works vary widely - some amateurish, others amazingly polished - but all demonstrate his underlying gift for visual expression. Among Dean's artistic subjects were bullfighters, his friends (especially actor/musician Bill Gunn), and self-portraits, often with a surreal twist.

In the years since his death, hundreds of artists working in every conceivable medium have been inspired by James Dean, and have produced works of tribute to him. These individual interpretations of Dean's resonance range from realistic portraiture to explorational fantasy, making original artwork one of the categories of collectible that best captures tangibly the range of the actor's influence.

One of the most interesting aspects of a rarities collection is that the items themselves are so specific to their subject. Among James Dean treasures, objects like high school and college yearbooks, the lease to his home, the eulogy that was read at his funeral and even pages (complete with doodles) from his elementary school notebooks have been sought out by collectors. Some zealots, sadly, take things too far. Several letters have been pried from the monument marking the fatal crash site in Cholame, California. Dean's gravesite has been vandalized and his headstone stolen on several occasions. Such selfish acts are violent crimes not only against Dean's fans and family, but against his very memory. Collectors who buy items of dubious lineage encourage such crimes.

Established of authenticity is of primary importace with rarities. A collector must never be afraid to ask questions or to insist that purchases be documented in detail and authenticity guaranteed. Be suspicious of sellers who balk at such basic requirements. Over time, most collectors will find particular dealers whom they can trust. Stick by those honest professionals, rewarding them with your repeat business.

JAMES DEAN MEMORIAL FOUNDATION

The James Dean Foundation is a name that will turn up frequently during a collector's pursuit of Dean memorabila. In various incarnations, James Dean Foundations have produced, sold and licensed items for many years. Knowledge of the evolution of these groups can be helpful in determining the provenance of items associated with them.

Incorporated in May of 1956, the first James Dean Memorial Foundation was established to perpetuate Dean's memory, primarily through a scholarship program that would "Encourage Talent, Recogize Achievement and Reward Genius" in the hopes of developing "future James Deans." The group got off to a good start, as founders Lewis Crist and Kent Williams arranged for such dignitaries as Ed Sullivan, Leonard Bernstein, Steve Allen and Geraldine Paige to hold honorary advisory positions. The Foundation funded a production of Thornton Wilder's play "Our Town," with Dean's young cousin Markie Winslow featured in the east. The group soon lost momentum, and before long, lack of funds led the Foundation to disband.

Bill Dakota resurrected a version of the James Dean Memorial Foundation in 1984, with the aim of financing a monument to Dean in Los Angeles. In 1987, Dakota opened a Dean memorabilia shop in L.A., but licensing concerns closed him down the following year.

Currently overseeing Dean's estate and the licensing of his image is the James Dean Foundation, which is run by the actor's family and is in no way affiliated with either version of the James Dean Memorial Foundation. Virtually all licensed items since the mid-1980s will bear the mark of the Foundation or its agent, Curtis Management Group.

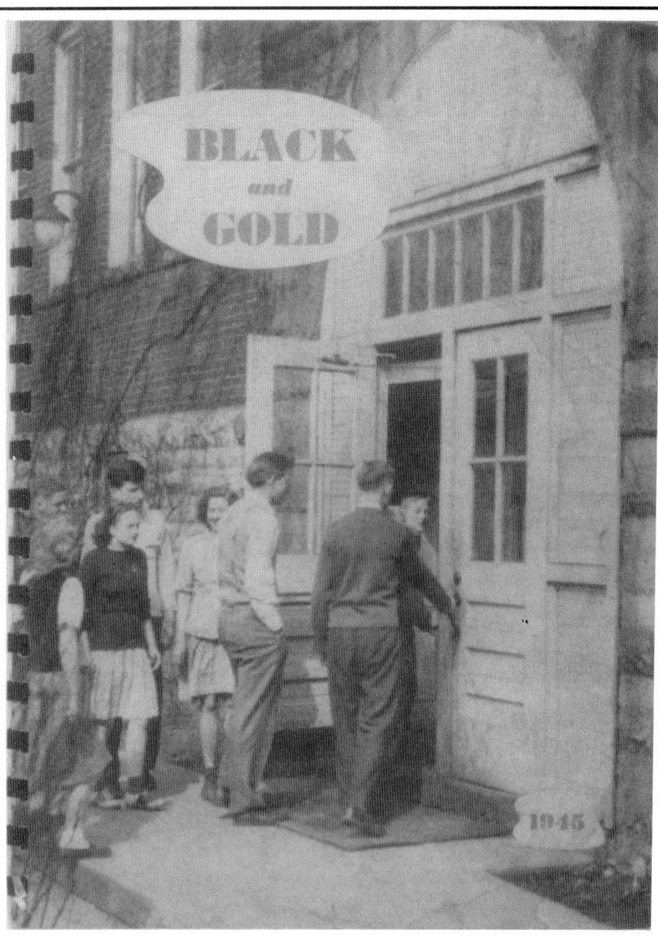

1945 Fairmount High School Yearbook

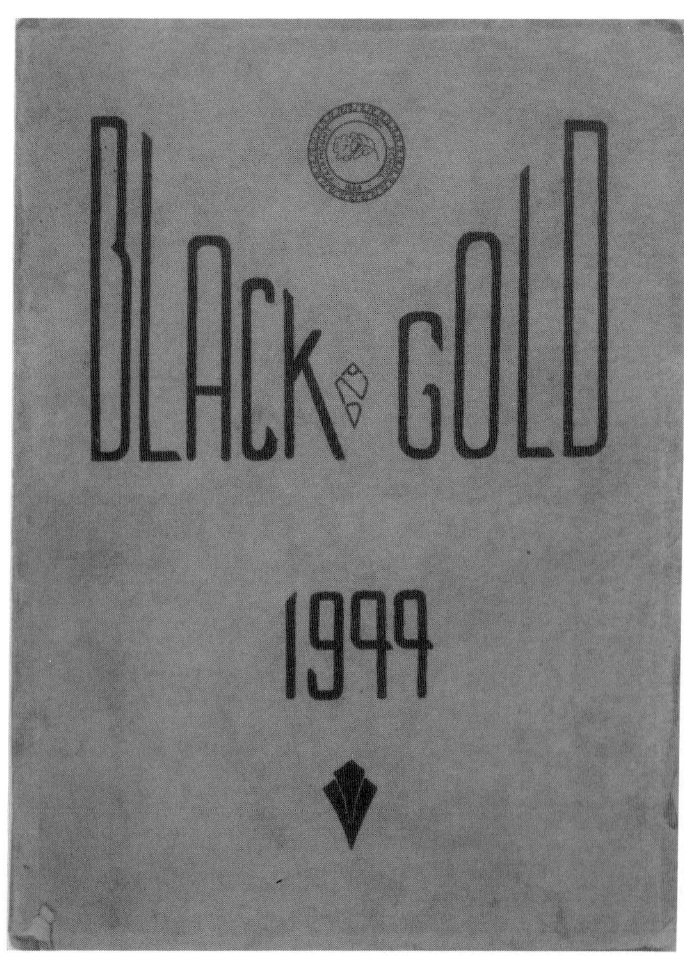

1944 Fairmount High School Yearbook

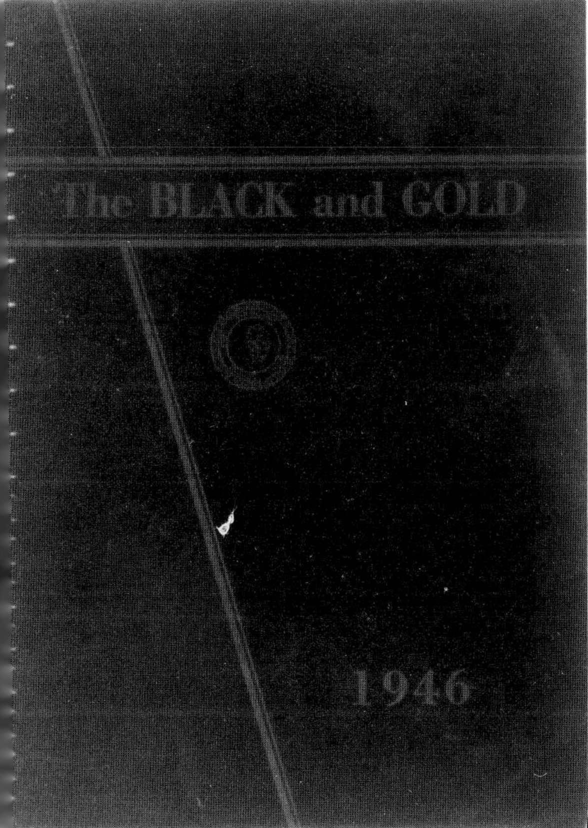

1946 Fairmount High School Yearbook

Band Photo
James Dean is seated in front row at the far right.

Track Photo
James Dean is seated in the front row far left.

1947 Fairmount High School Yearbook

Basketball Photo
James Dean is second from the left.

1948 Fairmount High School Yearbook

Junior Class Play Photo
James Dean is on the top row third from the right.

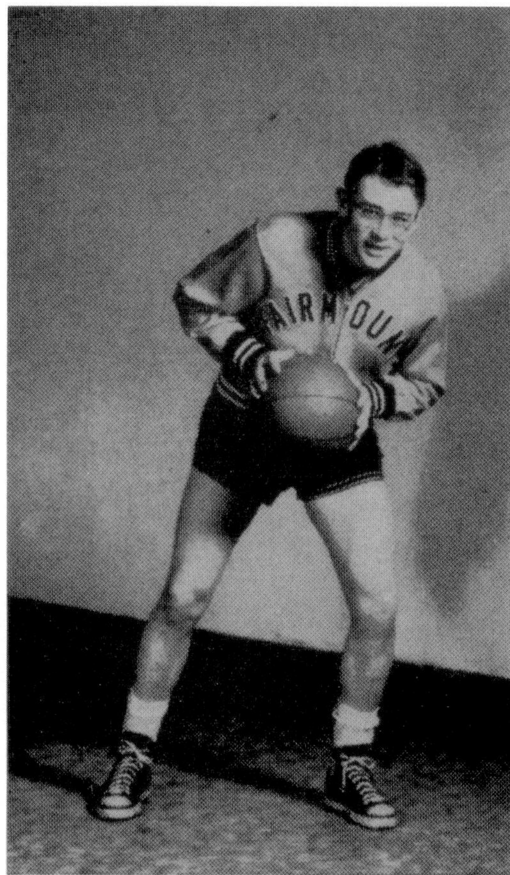

1949 Fairmount High School Yearbook

Thespians Photo: James Dean is seated in front row center.

Senior Class Photo

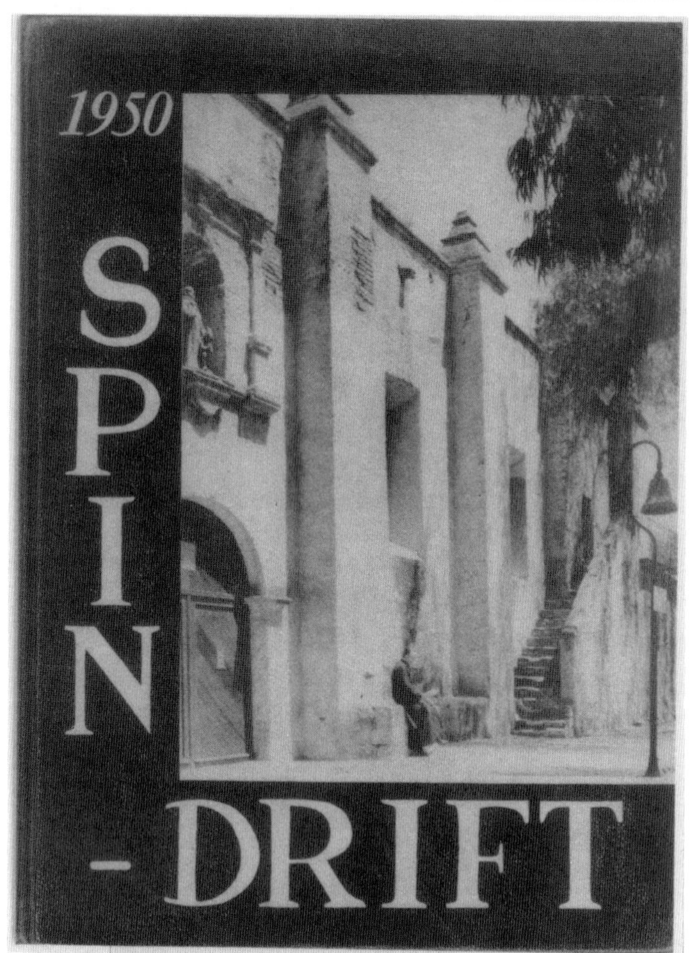

1950 Santa Monica Community College

To my mother
My inspiration
and idol I confess;
I can't think of a
darn thing to say except
that I'm hoping for equal
friendship next semester
James Byron Dean

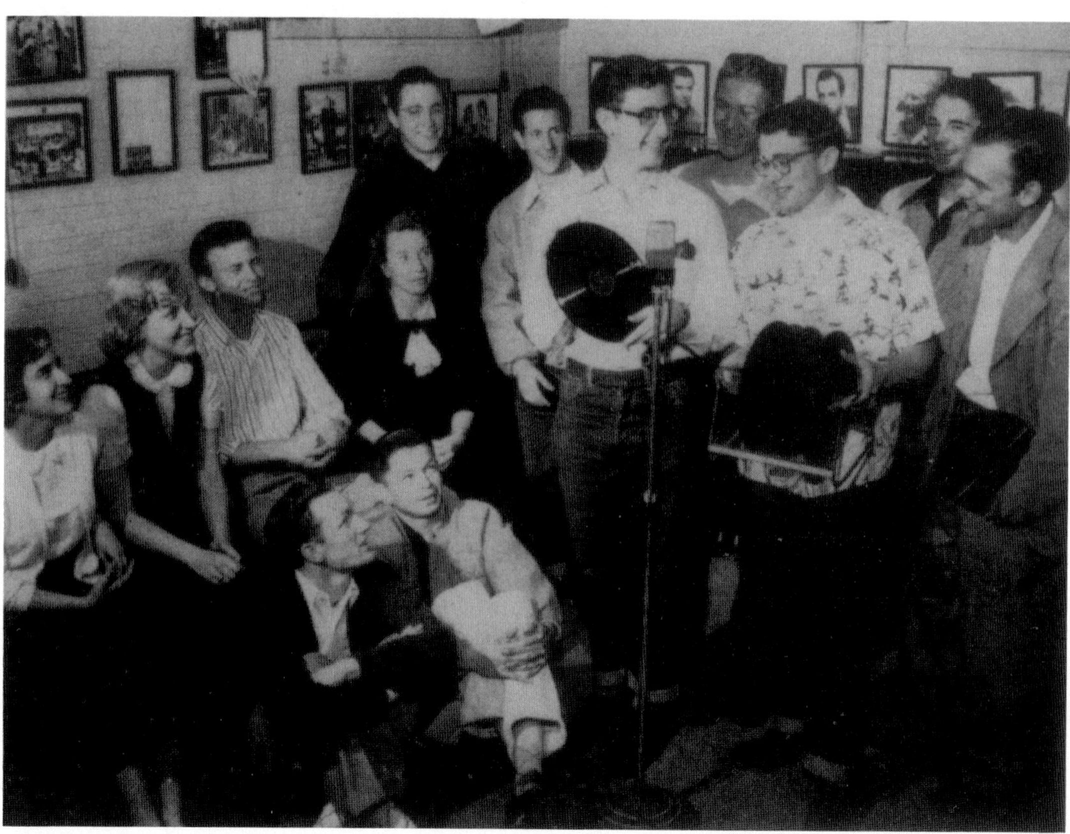

The Jazz Club

Basketball Team Photo at Santa Monica Community College

The Ophelos

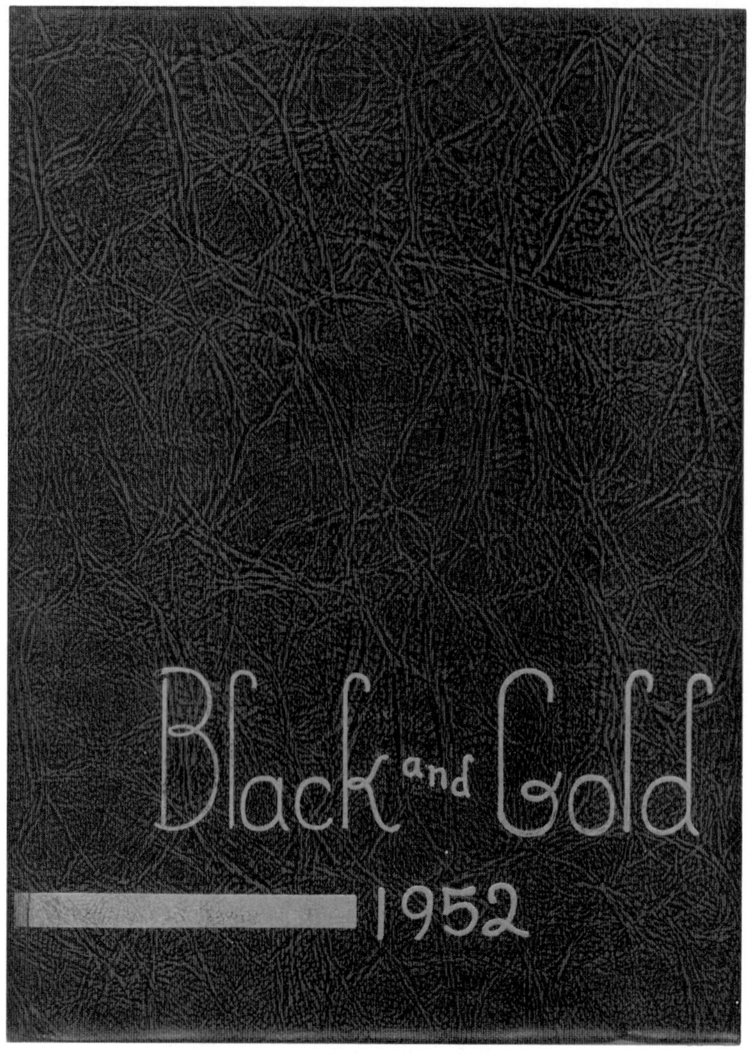

1952 Fairmount High School Yearbook
James Dean is shown here with Adeline Nall during a visit home.

The Cover of the 1955 Fairmount High School Yearbook is not shown because the cover is too worn and the photograph is totally black. The gold embossing is worn off of most copies.

Left:
James Dean is shown here at the "Sweetheart Ball" with photographer Dennis Stock during a visit home February 12, 1955.

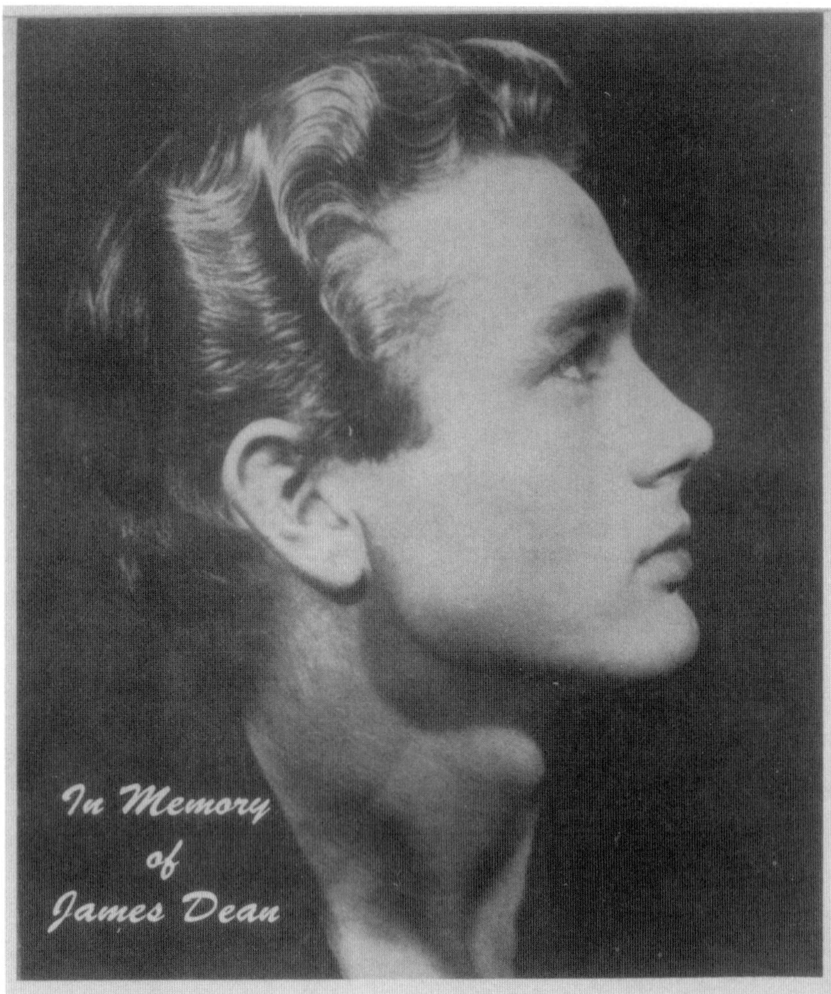

They tell me you are dead, yet I cannot
This night believe the unbelievable;
The restless beauty of your mind and heart
Will not be quenched within the shallow grave.
As beautiful as music to the soul;
The smile that probed the memory with pain
Your hands that moved caressing weightless things,
Of much remembered and of more foregone;
Your eyes that looked upon a mocking world,
Their laughter misted with uncertainty,
That could so love and hate and then forgive . . .
Beyond the barriers of time and space
Must have their measure in Eternity.
Your guileless grace will here no more be seen;
No tears can recreate the lifeless clay;
Yet if your body but a spark retained
That love could fan to flame, my years I'd give
That you might walk the lovely earth again,
The valiant and the free—The unacclaimed.
The wind will scatter golden coins of leaves
Across your grave. But where are you? Oh, where? —EVELYN HUNT

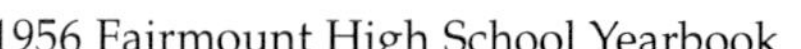

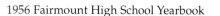

1956 Fairmount High School Yearbook

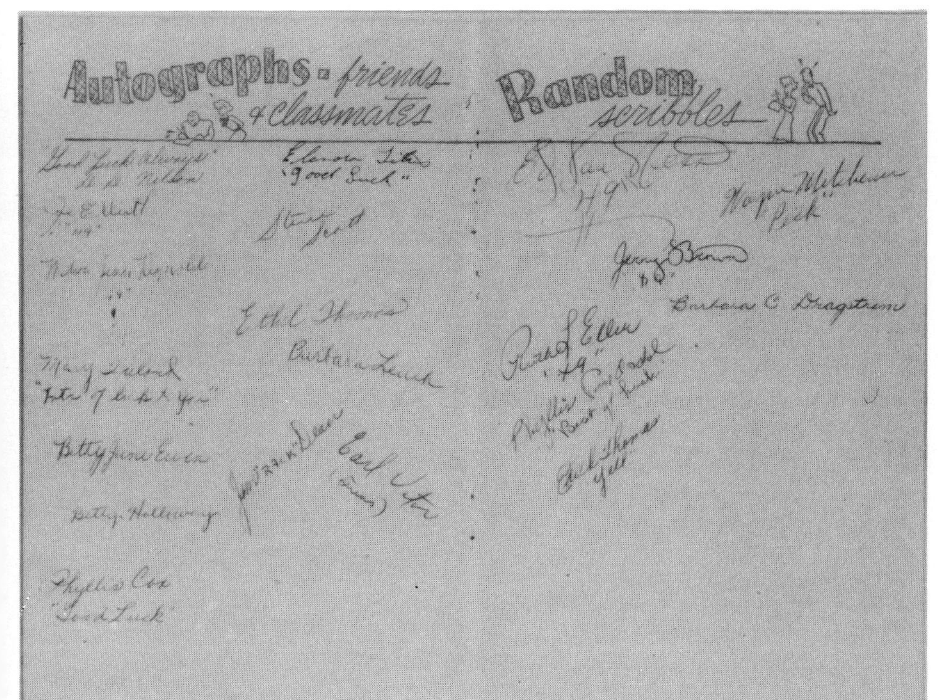

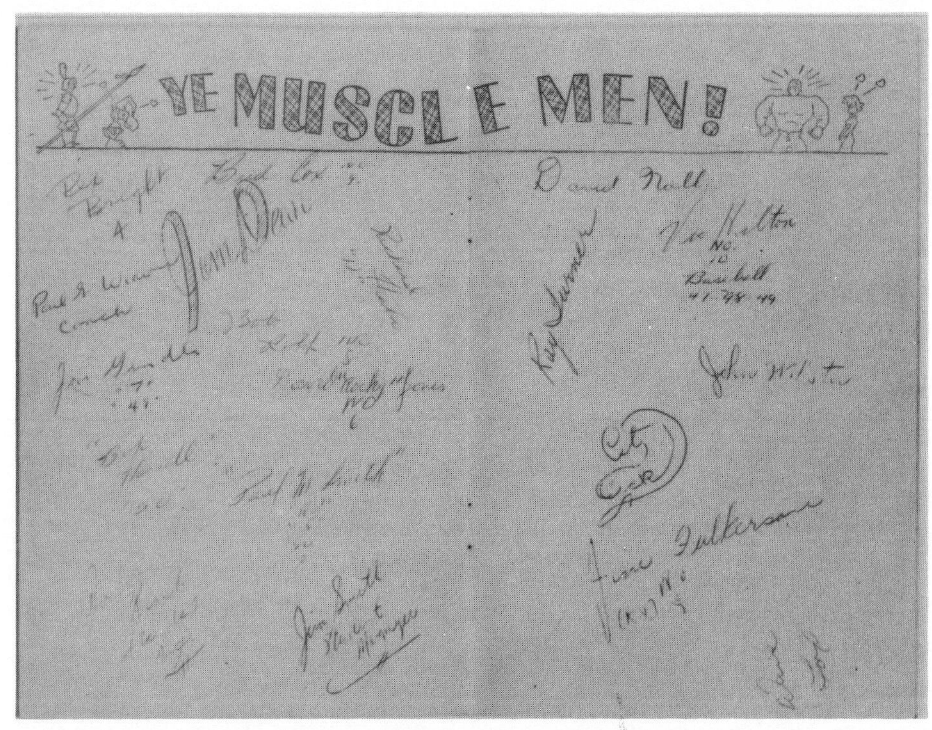

1949 Fairmount High School "Log of Memories" with one Jim "Rack" Dean signature and a very stylized Jim Dean signature.

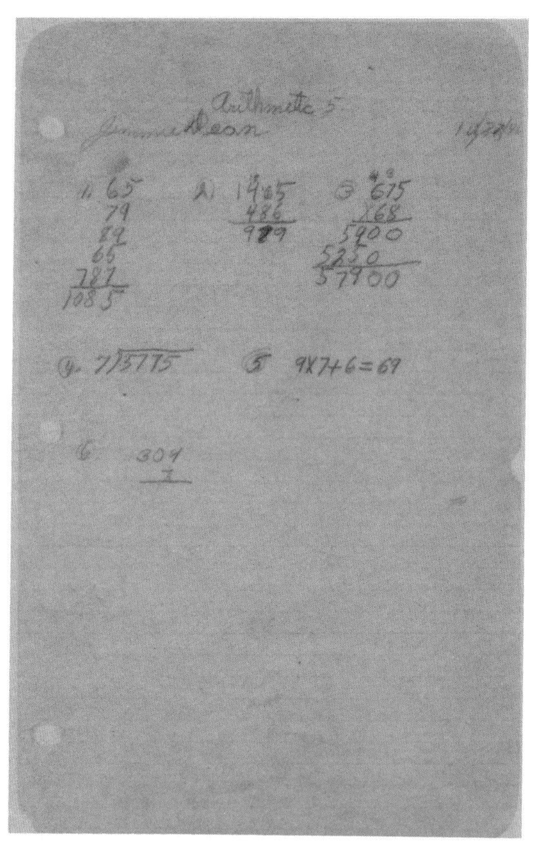

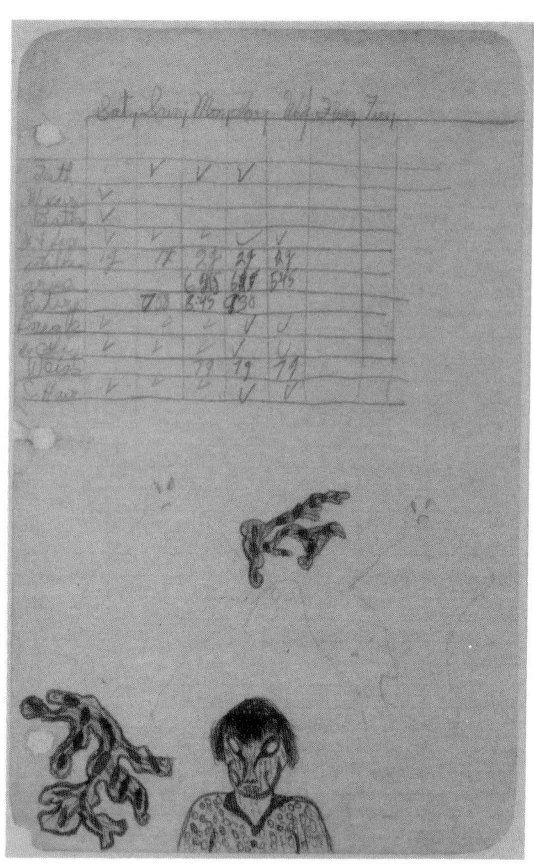

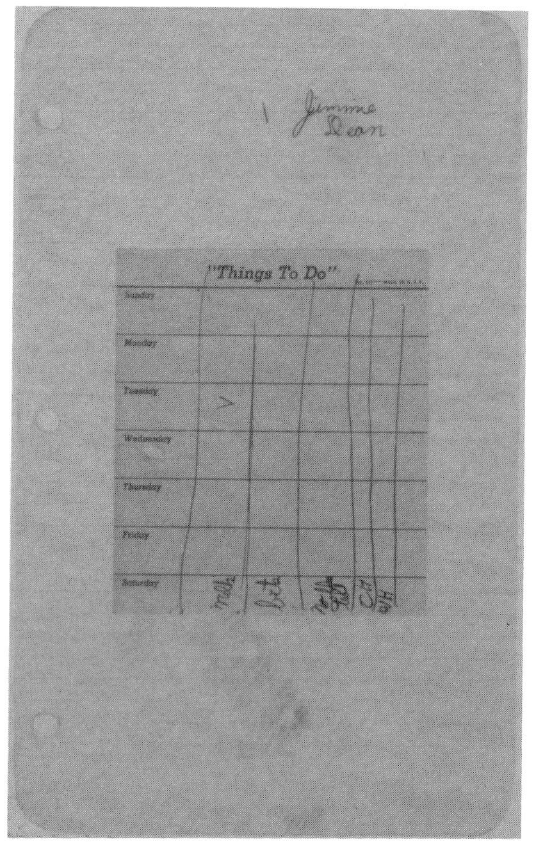

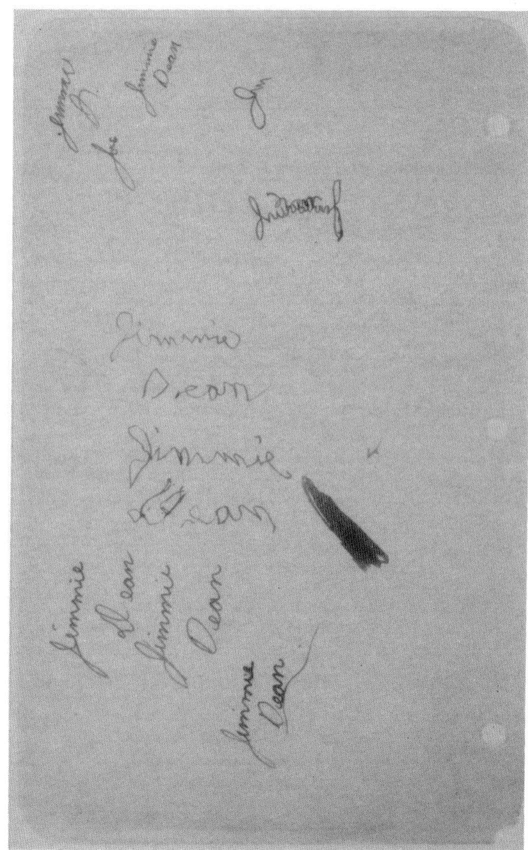

School work and doodles from Jimmie Dean's
1941 - 5th Grade Ring Binder

JUNIOR CLASS
OF
FAIRMOUNT HIGH SCHOOL
PRESENTS
"Our Hearts Were Young and Gay"

THREE ACT COMEDY
DIRECTED BY
ADELINE NALL BROOKSHIRE

High School Auditorium
Thursday and Friday, October 16 and 17

Program from the Fairmount High School production of
"Our Hearts Were Young and Gay"
October 16 & 17, 1948
Jimmy played the part of Otis Skinner.

THE SENIOR CLASS OF
Fairmount High School

— PRESENTS —

"You Can't Take It With You"

BY MOSS HART AND
GEORGE S. KAUFMAN

HIGH SCHOOL AUDITORIUM
8:00 P. M.
Wednesday and Thursday, April 6-7, 1949

Program from the Fairmount High School production of
"You Can't Take It With You"
April 6 & 7, 1949
Jimmy played the part of Boris Kolenkov and
was also stage manager and a member of the orchestra.

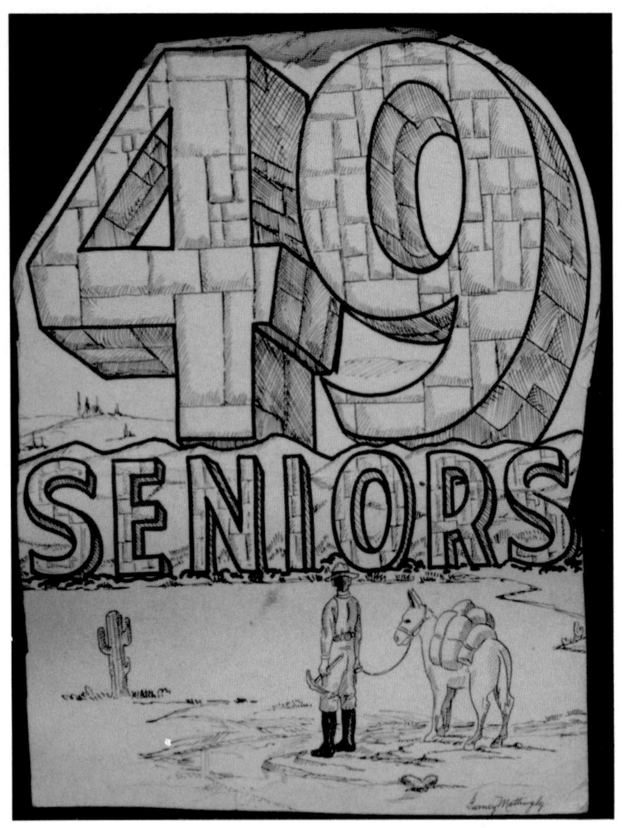

Original art by Fairmount High School art teacher Gurney Mattingly which was used as the opening page of the 1949 yearbook Seniors section.

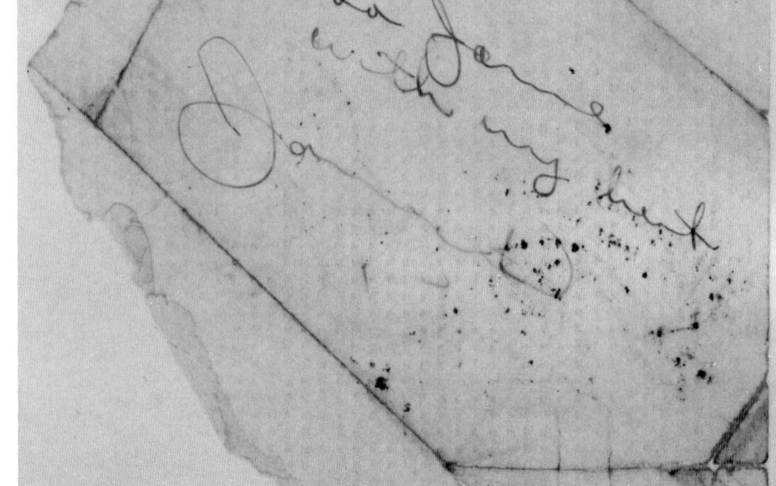

Signature obtained at "The Sweetheart Ball" Fairmount High School on February 12, 1955

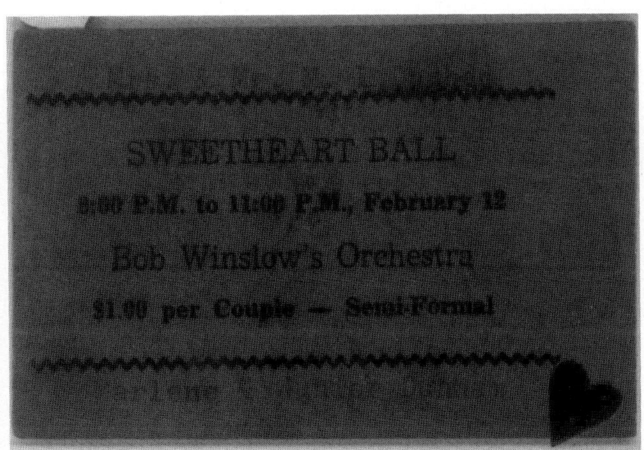

Sweetheart Ball Ticket
Signed on the back by James Dean

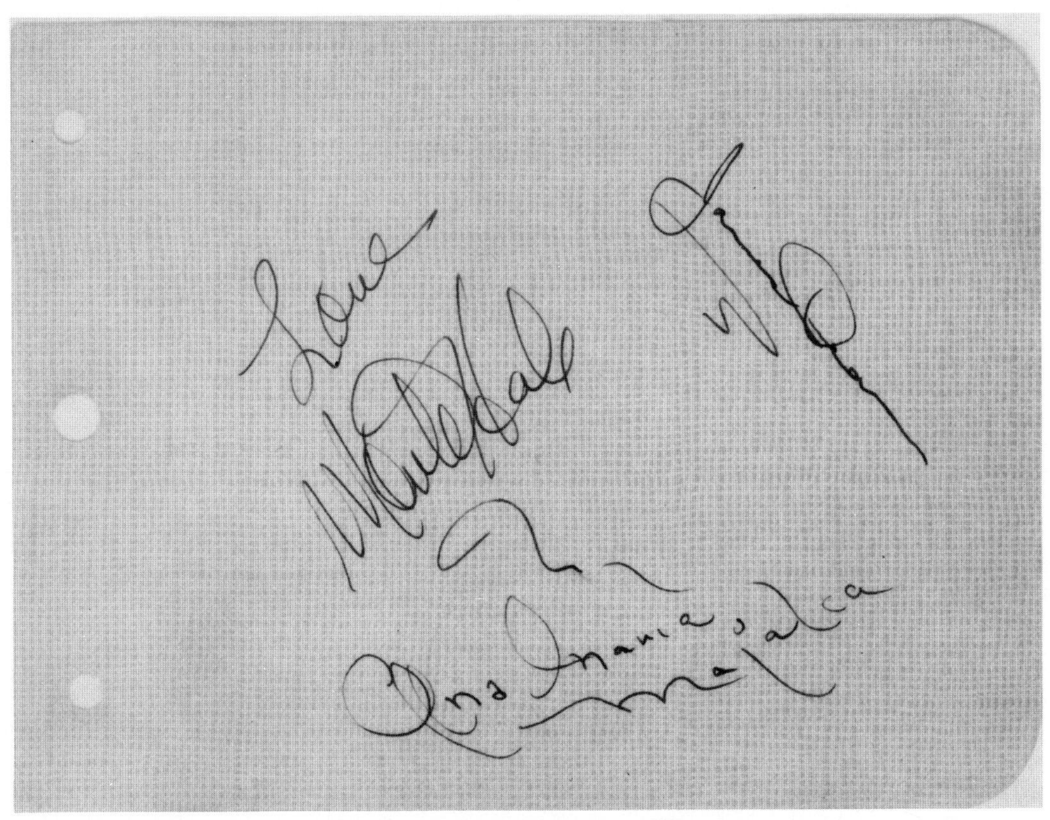

Autograph obtained on the set of "Giant"
in Marfa, Texas in 1955.

Signed 8 x 10 photo

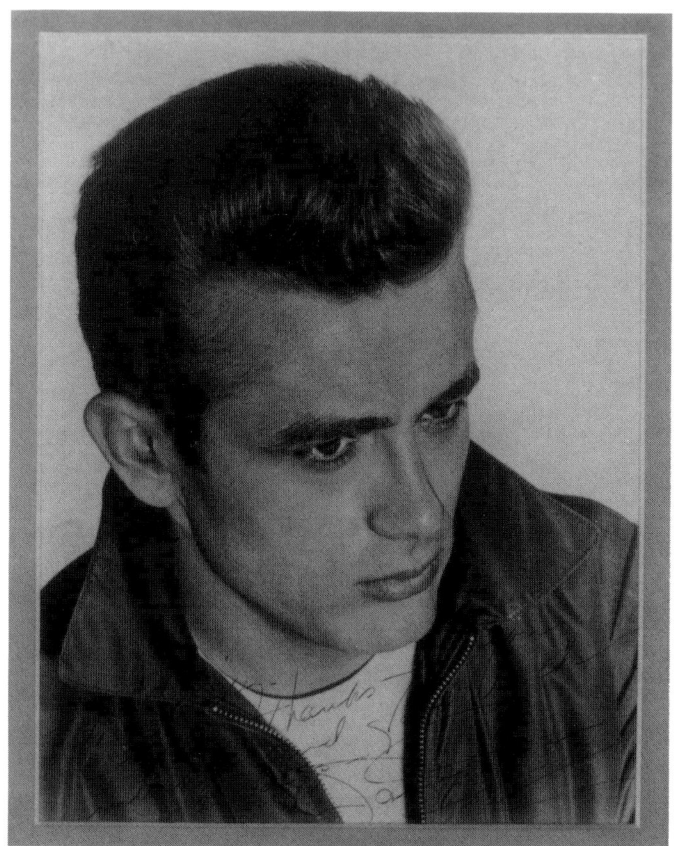

8 x 10 Photo inscribed:
To Shirley, many thanks for your intress *(sp)*
and good luck always, James Dean

House Lease

THIS INDENTURE, *made the* .... *day of* July, 1955

BETWEEN NICOLAS ROMANOS and GRACE ROMANOS, husband and wife,

, *Lessor (whether one or more)*;

AND JAMES DEAN

, *Lessee (whether one or more)*;

WITNESSETH: *That for and in consideration of the payments of the rents, and the performance of the covenants contained herein, on the part of the said Lessee, and in the manner hereinafter specified, said Lessor does hereby lease, demise and let, unto the said Lessee, that certain* furnished *dwelling house and its apurtenances situated at*

14611 Sutton Street
Sherman Oaks, California

Furnished according to attached Inventory to be approved by Lessor and Lessee,

for the term of One Year, *commencing on the* 1st *day of* August 19*55*, *and ending on the* 31st *day of* July 19*56*, *at the total rent or sum of* Three Thousand and no/100 ($3,000.00) *Dollars, payable* monthly *in advance on the* first *day of each and every calendar month of said term in equal* monthly *payments of* Two Hundred Fifty and no/100 ($250.00) *Dollars,*

Lessor acknowledges receipt of the sum of $250.00 as the first month's rent, and also the additional sum of $250.00 as a consideration for the Lessor entering into this lease. However, if the Lessee faithfully and promptly performs each and all of the terms and conditions hereof, and this lease is in full force and effect and Lessee is in possession at the beginning of the last month of the term hereof, Lessor will apply said $250.00 as rental for the last month of the term hereof.

AND *the said Lessee does hereby promise and agree to pay to the said Lessor the said rent, herein reserved in the manner herein specified.*

AND *not to let or sublet the whole or any part of said premises, nor to assign this lease, and not to make or suffer any alteration to be made therein without the written consent of the said lessor. And it is further agreed, that the said Lessor* ~~*shall not be called upon to make any improvements or repairs whatsoever upon the said premises, or any part thereof, but the said Lessee agrees to keep the same in good order and condition at own expense*~~ Lessor will make necessary repairs.

AND *it is agreed, that if any rent shall be due and unpaid, or if default shall be made in any of the covenants herein contained then it shall be lawful for the said Lessor to re-enter the said premises and to move all persons therefrom.*

LEASE – HOUSE – WOLCOTTS FORM 888

AND THAT *at the expiration of the said term or any sooner determination of this lease the said Lessee will quit and surrender the premises hereby demised, in as good order and condition as reasonable use and wear thereof will permit, damage by the elements excepted. And if the Lessee shall hold over the said term with the consent, expressed or implied, of the Lessor, such holding shall be construed to be a tenancy only from month to month, and said Lessee will pay the rent as above stated for such term as* Lessee *hold* s *the same.* Lessee *agrees to pay the water rate during the continuance of this lease,* as well as all other utility rates.

IN WITNESS WHEREOF: *the said parties have hereunto set their hands and seals the day and year first above written.*

Nicolas Romanos LESSOR

Grace Romanos LESSOR

James Dean LESSEE

No. ....

House Lease

NICOLAS ROMANOS and GRACE ROMANOS

Lessor

To

JAMES DEAN

Lessee

DATED JULY 19 55

Original Lease dated July 1955 signed and initialed by James Dean from 14611 Sutton Street in Sherman Oaks, California. This was his last place of residence.

Three original oil paintings
done by James Dean in 1954

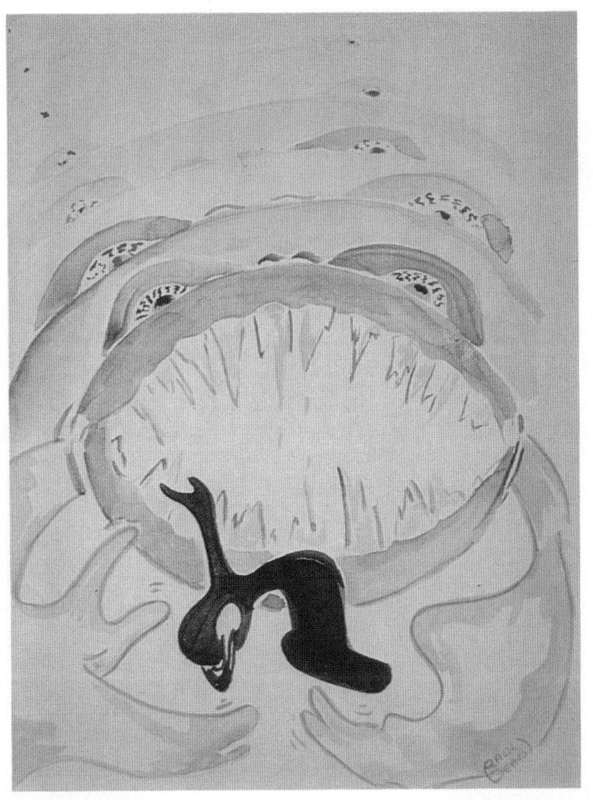

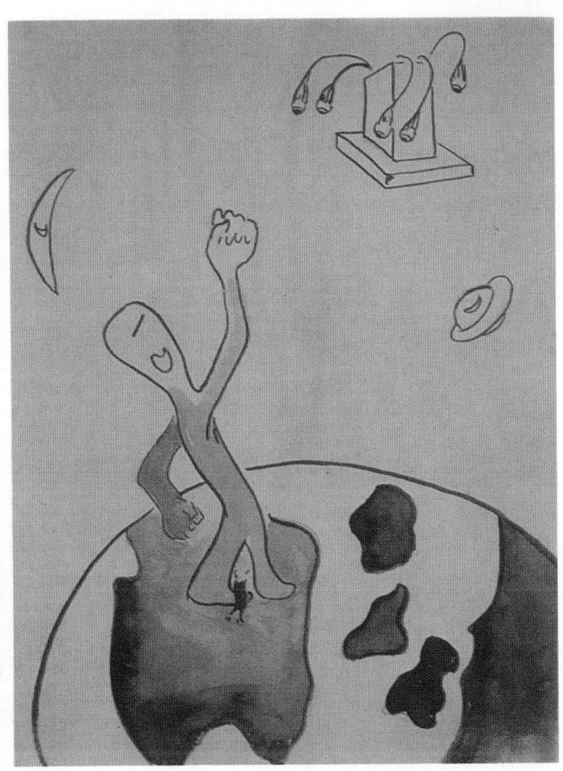

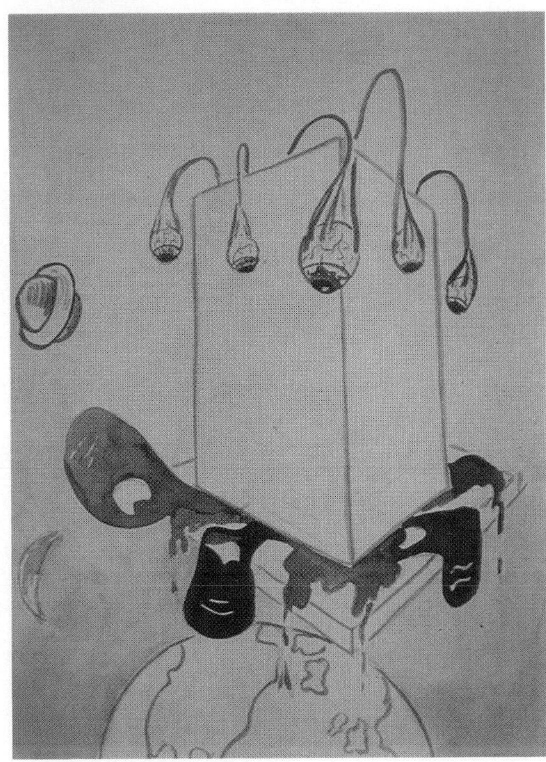

Watercolor paintings done by James Dean
in his Senior Year of High School, 1949.

Shirt, pants, belt, sport jacket and ties
worn by James Dean in East of Eden.

Plain white t-shirt owned by James Dean and the brown wool trousers that he wore in "Rebel Without A Cause."

Lee Riders
worn by James Dean
in "Giant".

WARNER BROS. STUDIOS
WARDROBE TEST
FOR
#403 GIANT
OF
JAMES DEAN
AS
JETT
(1924)
WARDROBE CHANGE#
WORN IN
SET INT. JETTS PLACE
EXT. JETTS PLACE
SCENE (LESLIES VISIT)
W-B
55
W-B

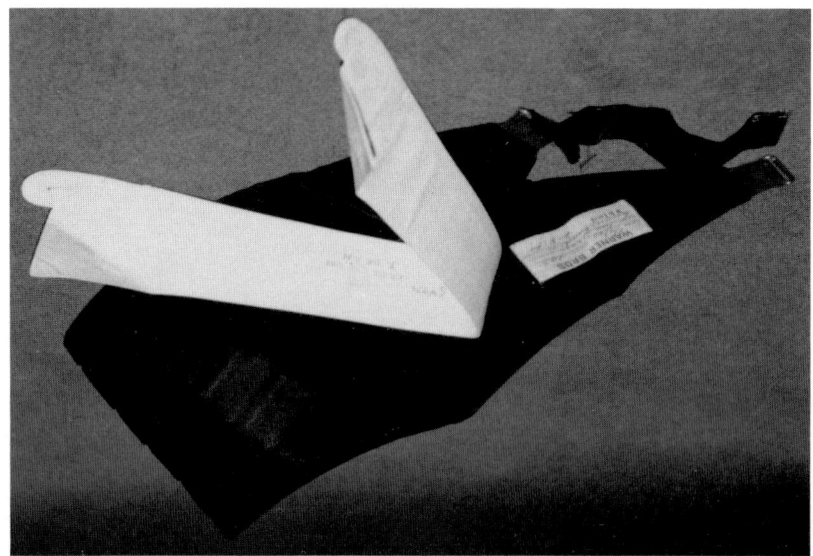

Stand-up Collar and Cummerbund
worn by James Dean in "Giant".

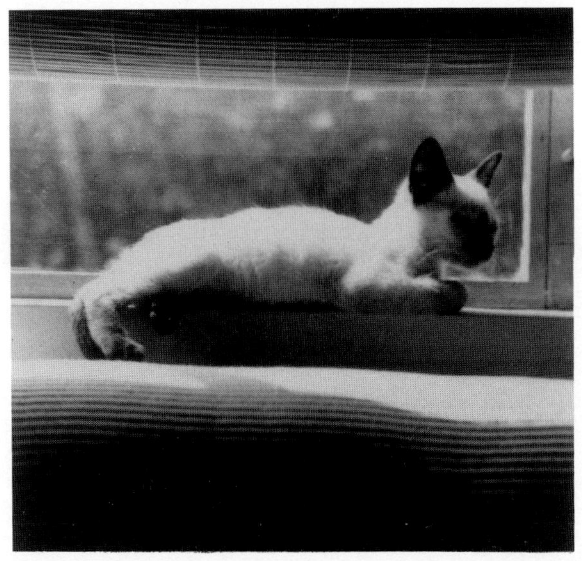

1 teaspoon White Karo

1 big can evaparated milk

equal part boiled water or
distilled water

1 egg yoke

mix and chill

Don't feed him meat or formula
cold.

1 drop vitamen solution per day

take Marcus to Dr. Cooper
on Melrose for shots
next week

James Dean wrote these feeding instructions for his cat, Marcus, around 9:30 pm September 29, 1955, the night before his fatal accident.

FINAL

THE JAMES DEAN STORY

Original script from
"The James Dean Story" 1957

FINAL

IMPORTANT - FILE COPY

WARNER BROS. PICTURES, INC.

BURBANK, CALIFORNIA

REBEL WITHOUT A CAUSE

March 25, 1955

THIS SCRIPT IS THE PROPERTY OF
WARNER BROS. PICTURES INC.
NO ONE IS AUTHORIZED TO DISPOSE OF SAME.
PLEASE DO NOT LOSE OR DESTROY THIS SCRIPT.
RETURN TO STENOGRAPHIC DEPARTMENT.

Original script from
"Rebel Without a Cause" 1955

Silver Flask owned by
James Dean

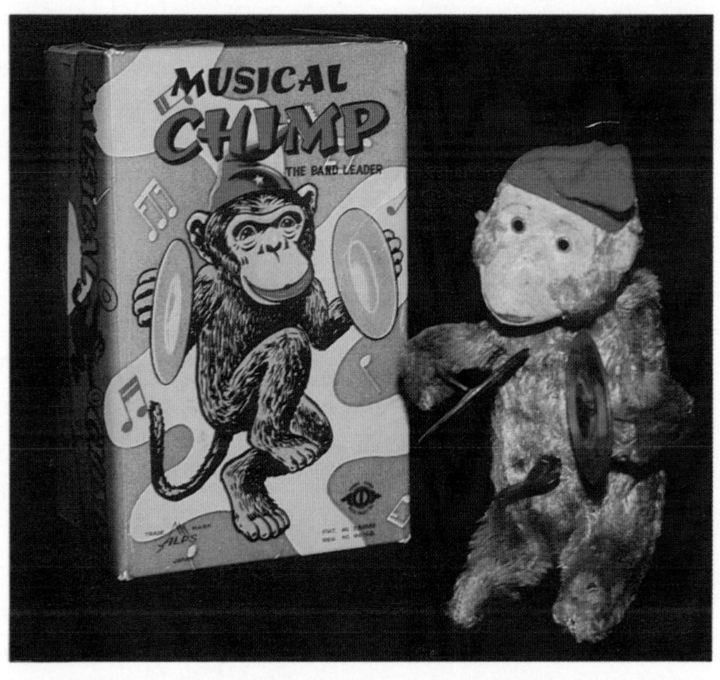

Wind-up Musical Chimp exactly like the one Dean used
in "Rebel Without A Cause."

The Life of James Dean - A Drama in Three Acts

I shall always remember the life of James Dean as a drama in 3 acts. Act I was his boyhood and youth. Act II represents the career that gained national prominence. And Act III is the new life into which he has just entered. Here in Fairmount, it was in the very first act of this drama that we learned to love James Dean. We loved him as a small boy in and out of town; we loved him when he was fast breaking with the basketball team; we loved him in the lean, hungry years of his career; and we loved him as he stood on the mountain peak of success.

We loved him so much, it is a bit difficult for us to be understanding with those who, in the emptyness of their lives, and the littleness of their spirits, have come only out of curiosity, to look and to stare. However, in contrast to this, we appreciate deeply all of you who have come because you, too, learned to love him along the way. We know you came to share our sorrow and we humbly thank you. Also, we find it hard to be charitable with publicity hungry, amateur psychologists, who have entertained themselves psychoanalyzing our boy. Because we knew him as a normal boy, who did the things normal boys do. He was part of a good solid home in the community where understanding people live. He was loved by the members of that home, and he loved them in turn. He was not brooding, or weird, or sullen, or even odd. He was fun loving and too busy living to sulk.

Though he was a normal boy, he had an extra measure of energy and talent. What energy he had! On the basketball court he didn't have the physical equipment to be a basketball star. But what he lacked in stature he made up in fighting spirit. He was one of the teams leading scorers just because of his great energy and drive.

With affection, we remember how he hustled that little English motorcycle around town in high school days. That motorcycle had a rough existence. When Jimmy was riding it, he was always in a hurry.

When we speak of his talent, we naturally think of the theater. But his talent was not limited to acting. He was interested in all the arts. Much has been said of his interest in bull fighting, but it is only right that you know he was a serious amateur sculptor. You know of the bongo drums, but you should know he was devoted to the best in classical music. He enjoyed also the best in fine literature and was a student of philosophy. He could discuss intelligently the great philosophers and their schools of thought, Wm. James pragmatism for example.

But for all of his interest in the other arts, the theater was his first love. James Dean was an actor. He was an actor in the noblest meaning attached to the term. He lived with the characters he portrayed. He was so sensitive he suffered when they suffered, brooded when they brooded, and rejoiced when they rejoiced. He was the master of his profession.

Like other masters of his art, he took the values of all good literature and multiplied them time upon time. To some he brought rest and relaxation and to others hope and challenge.

Just a word in regard to the worthiness of his profession. In days gone by when the church was all powerful politically, it would reach out with its long arm of censorship and ban the theater entirely. But the agency that always brought back the theater was the church. It was needed, not only to dramatize that scene that happened so long ago in Galilee, but to make vivid the lessons that the best of literature has to teach.

Original Eulogy written and read by
Reverand Xen Harvey at the Funeral of
James Dean on October 8, 1955

-2-

Now the curtain has fallen on Act II of James Dean's life. We can not help but feel that his activity here in time and space has ended far too soon. But for those of you who really loved him, will you remember you were far more fortunate to have had him as your friend and loved one for 24 years, than to have had some other for a normal life time? I am sure you would not trade the 24 years you have had Jimmy for 74, or 84 or even 94 years with another. You see it isn't how long we live that is so important, but how well. It is not how much time we have, but the use of time that really matters. And Jimmy had filled these years with accomplishment. In only a little over a score of years, he had soared to greater heights than most of us will reach in our full 3 score and 10. So when you think of his early departure, think not how short, but how full his life here was.

But we cannot go farther without thinking directly of the One who is the maker of us all. Now this One, who is the King of the Universe, and who we so tenderly call God, has a tremendous plan for all of us. It is a plan that will not be thwarted by the loss of our physical selves. Down through the ages, those who believe in the Christian message have said that man is far more than a physical body. Turning again to Jimmy's profession for a figure of speech, we believe the physical body is a stage property that we use in the drama of this world and this life. When our bodies either meet sudden injury or gradually decay, we lay them aside and go on without them. And it does not affect the existence of the person anymore than it affects an actor to lay aside one stage property used in one act of a play, and go on to another act where it is not needed.

We do not believe, as we have been hearing all week, that James Dean was returned from California to Fairmount. Nor, do we believe in any sense, that James Dean is lying in state before us. But it is only his body that was returned from California, and his body that is here before us. The real James Dean has moved on ahead of us into another world. We most certainly do not believe his life has ended! Nor, do we believe that his career has ended!

In the days ahead, we will think of a new career unfolding before him. We have spoken of his tremendous energy. We will picture God as helping him harness that energy and directing it to new levels of usefullness.

A few weeks ago Jimmy was quoted as saying this, "I've just been searching, investigating, trying to learn about me." In the days ahead God will help him find his true selfhood. He will groom him for stardom in new roles, on a larger stage, before vaster audiences.

To those of you who were closest to James Dean, remember that this God of whom we speak, is more than trustworthy and can be trusted with your loved one. The career of James Dean has not ended, it has just begun. And remember, God Himself is directing the production.

1956 - Free 8 x 10 Photo
with the purchase
of James Dean by William Bast

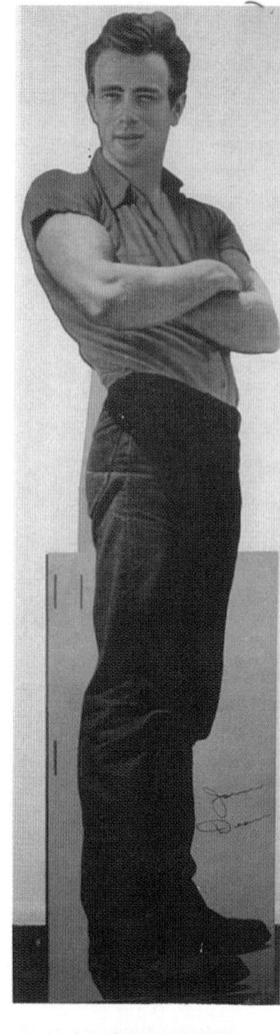

Six foot tall Cardboard Stand-up
displayed in Movie Theatres
for "Giant" - USA - 1956

Introduce New Star JAMES DEAN
-DESTINED FOR SCREEN GREATNESS-
With This Lapel Button Campaign!

EXHIBITORS: JAMES DEAN is being hailed everywhere as the-most-sure-to-be-talked-about acting find in years! LOOK Magazine predicts certain stardom for this dynamic young discovery. Capitalize on all the interest being generated by news-papers, fan magazines and nationally-known feature writers —pin one of these lapel buttons on every person who leaves your theatre. Use Style A in conjunction with the trailer or with Style B during the picture's run. Get your order in early as the supply is limited

STYLE A

$5.00 BUYS 500

Order in 500 lots only
specify Style A or B

Send payment with order to:

STYLE B

CAMPAIGN PLAN EDITOR, WARNER BROS. PICTURES, INC.
321 WEST 44TH STREET, NEW YORK, N. Y.

Page Nineteen

Lapel Button given away in
movie theatres for
"East of Eden" - USA - 1955

Cardboard Advertisement
4" x 11" - USA - 1955

Original 19" model which was made by Kenneth Kendall and presented as a proposal to the Griffith Observatory in Los Angeles in 1985.

The project was approved, and in November of 1988 the 8' tall concrete and bronze monument was dedicated.

On September 30, 1995 an identical monument was dedicated in Fairmount, Indiana.

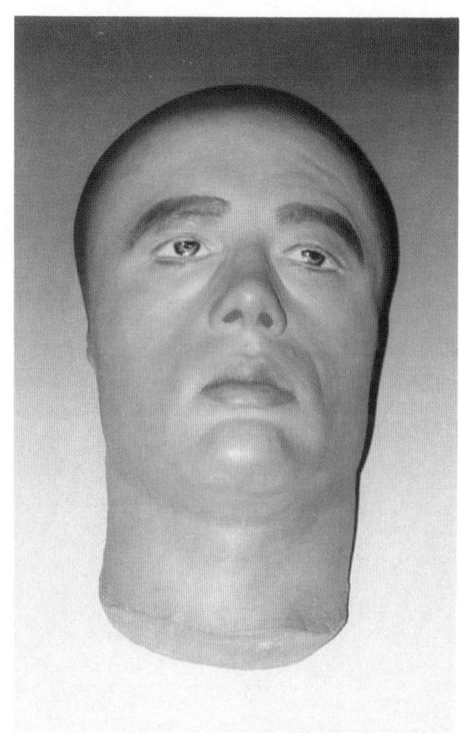

Life Mask Cast from Original that Warner Brothers Make-up Department made for Giant, painted by Kenneth Kendall.

16 mm Film

East of Eden Trailer, Highway Safety Interview, Steve Allen Tribute. Hill Number One, The Unlighted Road, The James Dean Story, Something for An Empty Briefcase.

37" Tall Bronze Statue of James Dean as Bacchir from The Broadway Play "The Immoralist" by Kenneth Kendall only two produced. - 1993

8″ tall Bronze
spittin′ image - USA - 1993

5½″ tall Pewter Statue
Australia - 1992

12″ tall Bronze Bust by
Kenneth Kendall - USA - 1993

8″ Tall Bronze Body Study by
Kenneth Kendall - 1993

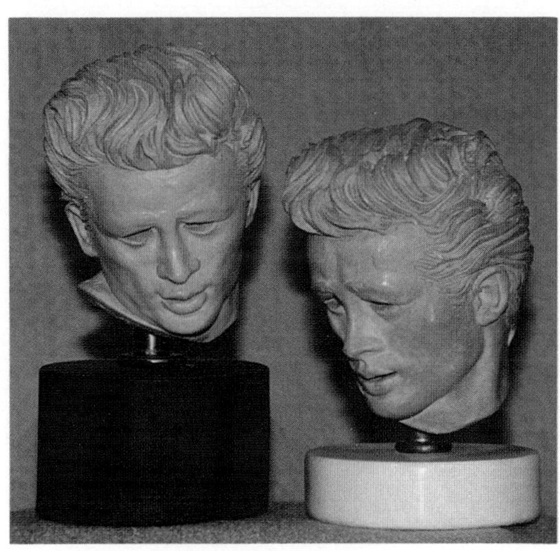

Small Hydrostone Busts
produced by Kenneth Kendall
1955 - 1990

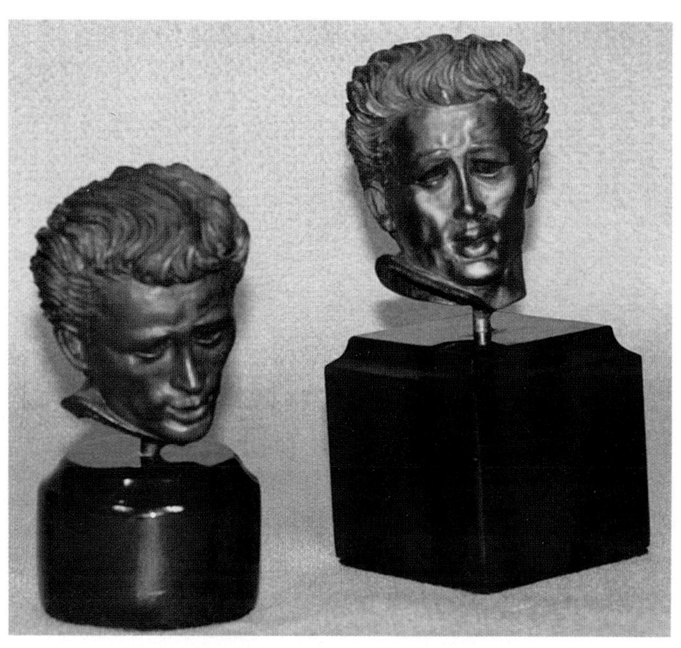

Small Bronze Busts produced by
Kenneth Kendall - 1991-1997

9″ Diameter Plaster Wall Medallion
produced by Kenneth Kendall - 1980

2″ Diameter Plaster Medallion
by Kenneth Kendall - 1985

Leading figures from the major educational institutions are conducting seminars with the officials of the Foundation to formulate an effective scholarship program. Dr. Thomas E. Jones, national authority on foundations, is heading up a group of distinguished experts which include Dr. Paul H. Davis of Stanford University who was formerly with Eisenhower at Columbia. With this kind of aid, THE JAMES DEAN MEMORIAL FOUNDATION expects to announce its scholarship program sometime prior to the beginning of the next fiscal school year.

It is Foundation policy that general contributions shall all go into the scholarship fund, while monies for any building or monument shall be a specific financial project of local origin. The current task of the Foundation is the building of accumulative funds sufficiently high to do an adequate and sustained job.

THE JAMES DEAN MEMORIAL FOUNDATION is most willing to accept both counsel and contributions from those who are seriously interested in helping worthy youngsters to create a new artistic heritage for the American Theater.

For further information write
JAMES DEAN MEMORIAL FOUNDATION
FAIRMOUNT, INDIANA

TOMORROW'S STAR?

OUR CREED

"Encourage Talent, Recognize Achievement, and Reward Genius"

The

Story

. . . his organization and yours.

IT BEGAN . . .

Foundation Trustees pictured with STEVE ALLEN.

. . . WITH AN IDEA . . . an idea that came from you . . . and you . . . and you . . . all over the world. Within days after James Byron Dean's tragic death, thousands of letters came to his home town of Fairmount, Indiana, asking that a memorial of some type be established. The first concept was local and tended toward an edifice of marble. In trying to interpret the wishes of his worldwide friends, Jimmy's fellow townsmen travelled across America to both coasts . . . conferring with the authorities in various fields and . . . with the average people . . . his average friends – legions of them . . . with his father, Winton, and with the Winslows who reared him as their own, after his mother's unfortunate death.

Two facts stood out. James Dean's memorial belonged to *all* the people and it must be *living*. THE JAMES DEAN MEMORIAL FOUNDATION was born.

On January 12, 1956, with representatives from over 40 state and national organizations present, that name was adopted. Four months later, May 14, 1956, articles of incorporation were filed and the FOUNDATION became a fact. The United States Treasury Department recognized this nonprofit corporation as a force of educational and charitable purposes conducive to the advancement of the dramatic, musical and literary arts.

The trustees are all personal friends of Jimmy . . . they knew him well . . . loved him very much. They are also all successful business men who, while working with a labor of love, have neither asked nor received anything for themselves.

They never will, for they have bound themselves accordingly. Their reward is in the fulfillment of a vision. A vision of future 'James Deans' being discovered, encouraged and pushed on to success, if success is theirs to have.

"Boy From Indiana"

From life, by Robert DeWayne Ormsby. Owned by the Winslows and loaned to the James Dean Memorial Foundation.

Visions are not always things of substance. A way must be found to implement this dream . . . the right way. Counsel was sought among the great names in the arts. To note only a few, such people as Stewart Stern, distinguished author of "Rebel Without a Cause", Dmitri Metripoplus, Leonard Bernstein, Ed Sullivan, Geraldine Page, and Steve Allen have accepted advisory posts.

From Left to Right: Foundation Headquarters, Fairmount, Indiana, home of James Dean.

The Executive Secretary, Les Johnston, and the office staff at work.

The distinguished Winslow Family in the Foundation reception lounge.

Original brochure from
"The James Dean Memorial Foundation"
in Fairmount, Indiana 1956

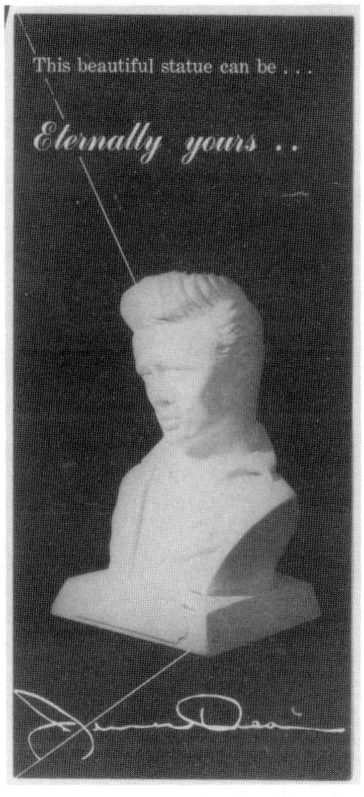

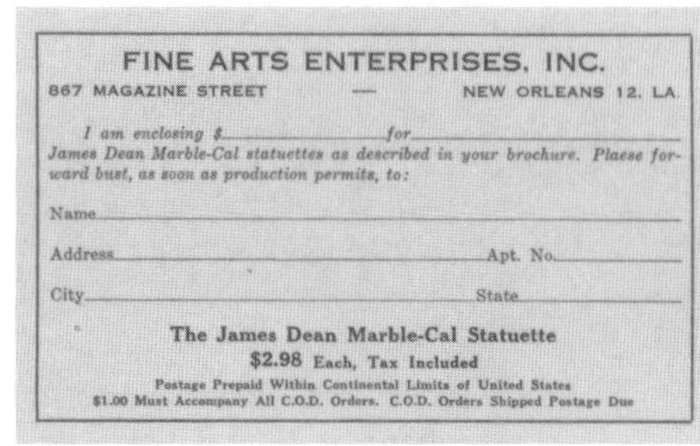

FINE ARTS ENTERPRISES, INC.

867 MAGAZINE STREET — NEW ORLEANS 12, LA.

I am enclosing $_______ for _______ James Dean Marble-Cal statuettes as described in your brochure. Please forward bust, as soon as production permits, to:

Name________________

Address________________ Apt. No.________

City________________ State________

The James Dean Marble-Cal Statuette

$2.98 Each, Tax Included

Postage Prepaid Within Continental Limits of United States
$1.00 Must Accompany All C.O.D. Orders. C.O.D. Orders Shipped Postage Due

Chalk Bust and Advertising Materials
made by Fine Arts Enterprises, Inc. in 1957.

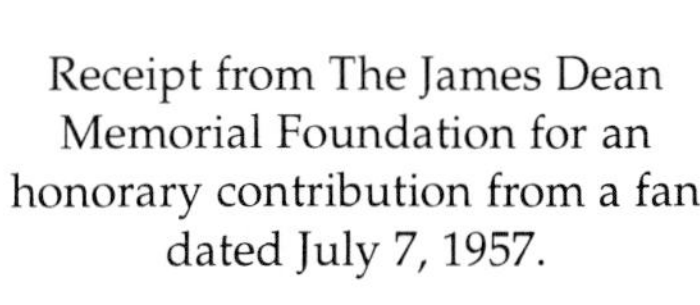

Receipt from The James Dean Memorial Foundation for an honorary contribution from a fan dated July 7, 1957.

Thanks

FOR THE MEMORY

Date 7-7-57

Received From Iva M. Merck Kuhn
R. #1
Tamiami Trail, Naples, Fla.

$ 2.00

JAMES DEAN MEMORIAL FOUNDATION
c/o 41 Drive Inn
Naples, Fla

Honorary Contribution

Louise Crist
SECRETARY

Paper coupon
USA - 1956

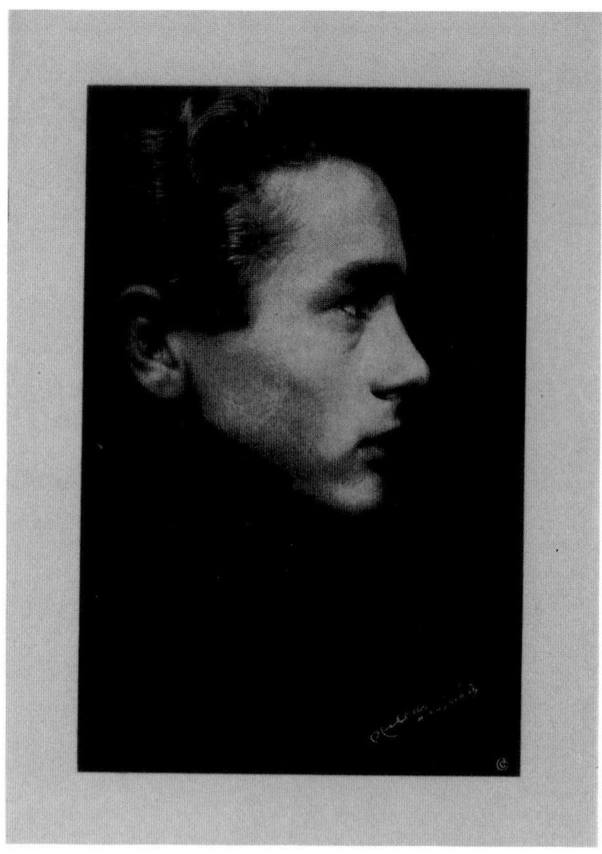

James Dean
Memorial Foundation

Presents

THORNTON WILDER'S

Our Town

WITH MUSIC

Fairmount, Indiana
Summer 1956

DIRECTED BY

Coy Bronson

Program for James Dean Memorial Foundation
presentation of "Our Town" Fairmount - 24 pages - 1956

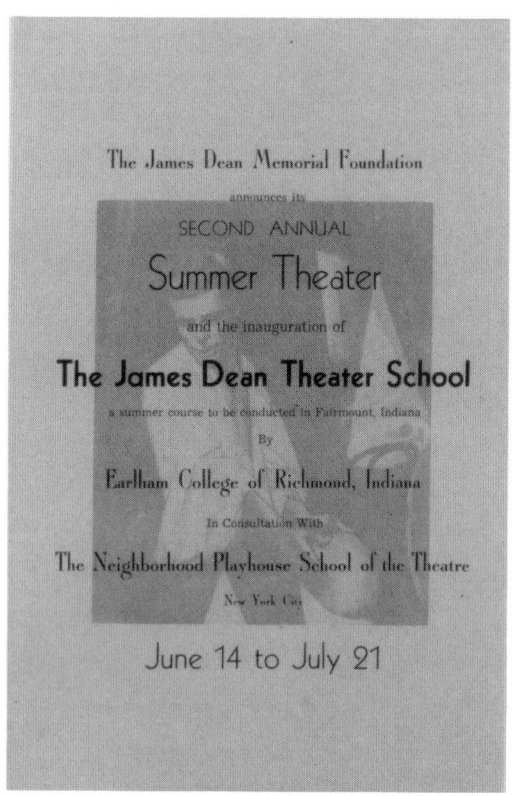

The James Dean Memorial Foundation
announces its
SECOND ANNUAL
Summer Theater
and the inauguration of
The James Dean Theater School
a summer course to be conducted in Fairmount, Indiana
By
Earlham College of Richmond, Indiana
In Consultation With
The Neighborhood Playhouse School of the Theatre
New York City

June 14 to July 21

James Dean Theatre School
Summer Program & Schedule 1957

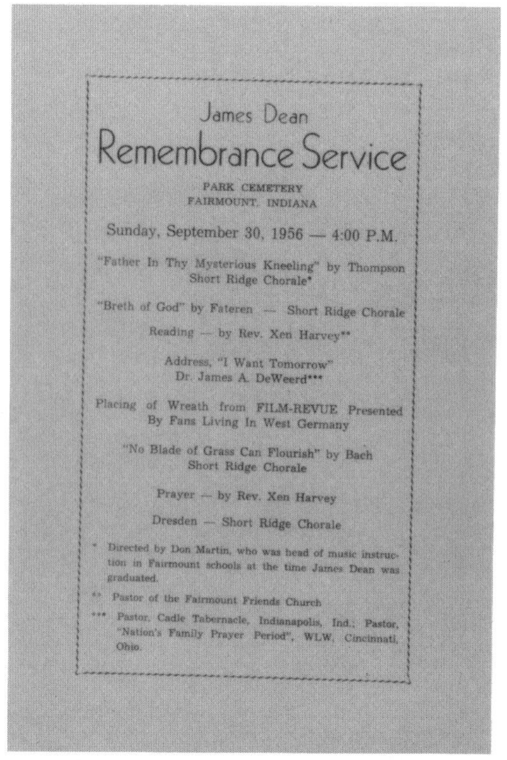

James Dean
Remembrance Service

PARK CEMETERY
FAIRMOUNT, INDIANA

Sunday, September 30, 1956 — 4:00 P.M.

"Father In Thy Mysterious Kneeling" by Thompson
Short Ridge Chorale*

"Breth of God" by Fateren — Short Ridge Chorale

Reading — by Rev. Xen Harvey**

Address, "I Want Tomorrow"
Dr. James A. DeWeerd***

Placing of Wreath from FILM-REVUE Presented
By Fans Living In West Germany

"No Blade of Grass Can Flourish" by Bach
Short Ridge Chorale

Prayer — by Rev. Xen Harvey

Dresden — Short Ridge Chorale

* Directed by Don Martin, who was head of music instruction in Fairmount schools at the time James Dean was graduated.

** Pastor of the Fairmount Friends Church

*** Pastor, Cadle Tabernacle, Indianapolis, Ind.; Pastor, "Nation's Family Prayer Period", WLW, Cincinnati, Ohio.

Program from The First Memorial Service
in Fairmount, Indiana - September 30, 1956

Program 1957 for "Our Town"
"Our Hearts Were Young &* Gay"

CHAMBER OF COMMERCE INVITES YOU TO

FAIRMOUNT

INDIANA

WELCOME

Chamber of Commerce
Information Booklet (12 pgs.) 1956

Lithograph of an original
water color painting by James Dean
16" x 20" - numbered edition of 500

Etching of an original ink sketch by
James Dean - 11 1/2" x 12"
numbered edition of 500

Serigraph of an original oil painting
by James Dean

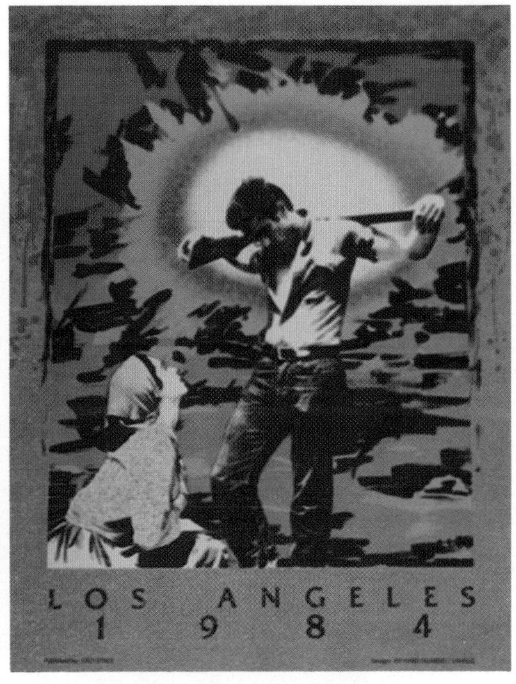

Silk Screen 22″ x 28″
by Richard Duardo - USA - 1984

Silk Screen 20″ x 26″
by John M. Smith - USA
numbered edition of 11

Air Brush Painting 81/2″ X 11″
By John Smith - USA - 1993

Lithograph 16″ x 20″
by William Jacobson - USA - 1985
numbered edition of 950

"The Drive Inn"
Signed A. Olsan
numbered edition of 700

Three hand made dolls - left to right
Maxine Rowland - 1980
Mark Castro - 1992
Diosdado Mondero - 1993

Life Size Figure made by
Mark Castro - 1991 - USA

Christmas Tree Ornaments on the left - right. The middle item is a 13″ tall Wooden Candle Holder - all of the items were made by Richard Taddei - 1988-1990 - USA

6′ tall Wood and Canvas Sculpture
by Jennifer Borton
1990 - USA

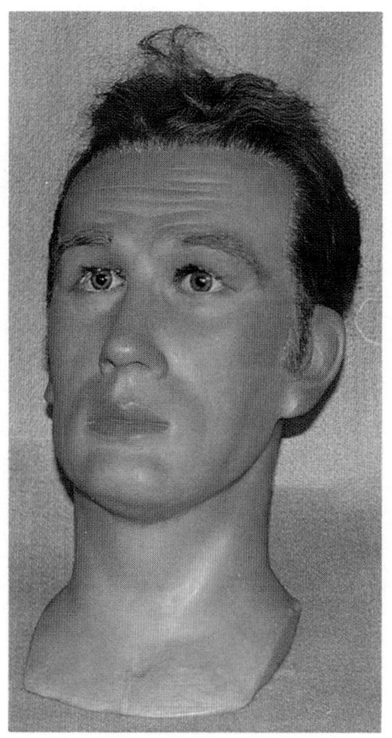

Original Way Head from
the Coney Island Wax
Museum - USA - 1958

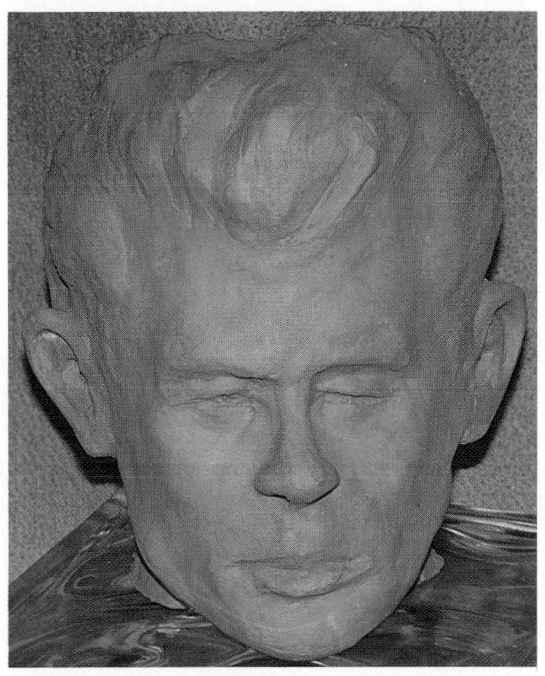

Clay Bust
by Morris Bennett - USA - 1988

Hook Rug 30″ x 44″
by Jim Schutter - USA - 1990

PORSCHE 550 SPYDER

There are rarities, and then there are rarities. When he died behind the wheel of his brand new Porsche racer, Dean established that car as one of the most morbidly desired collectibles of all time.

Hollywood car customizer George Barris, who had detailed the Spyder for Dean, bought the twisted wreckage shortly after the accident. Barris parted out the engine and drive train to other racers and loaned the the twisted aluminum body to a traveling highway safety exhibit. The Porsche allegedly brought bad luck to everyone who came near it. A mechanic at Barris's shop broke his leg when the car fell on him. Drivers using parts from the Spyder were injured or killed in accidents. A truck driver transporting the car was killed when it fell on him after a collision. Grabby patrons of the safety exhibit cut themselves while attempting to tear souvenirs from the wreckage. One of the favorite stories is that, in late 1959, in Detroit, the car fell from its mounting onto a teenage boy. Supposedly, the boy was decked out in jeans, t-shirt, and a red jacket just like Dean's character in Rebel Without a Cause.

Following that mishap, the car was taken out of circulation and put into storage. The next year, Barris was persuaded to loan it out for a display in Miami. Surprisingly, everything went smoothly. Depending on who is telling the story, the wreckage was then loaded into either a truck or a train car for shipping back to Los Angeles. When the shipment reached its destination, all seals on the compartment were intact, but there was no car inside. It has never surfaced.

Several companies have produced Spyder replicars, and devoted fans have gone to great length to recreate near-perfect facsimiles of Dean's car. But the original, one-of-a-kind and unseen for almost 40 years, is unchallenged as the most sought after, yet allusive, of all Dean collectibles.

Books

James Dean should perhaps be the recipient of a posthumous award for promoting literacy. It seems that virtually everyone who ever met the young actor has been inspired to write his or her own version of the Dean story. Because he playeed different roles for different people, the various interpretations are often contradictory. But therein lies the truth of the man. Above and beyond all else, Dean was always an actor. He enjoyed pushing the limits, testing those around him and observing their reactions. These books provide an interesting chronicle of the results he achieved. No two people may tell the stories the same way, but that doesn't necessarily make those tellings any less true. The total number of full-fledged biographies is now in the mid-twenties. Add to those the books and memoirs in which Dean plays a secondary role, and you've got the nearly three hundred volume list presented here. Taken as a whole, these books comprise the ultimate Dean biography.

Listed side by side in this chapter are accounts and mentions of Dean both contrived and legit. That the fiction is not separated from the non-fiction could rightfully be taken as an editorial comment. Several of the "biographies" are little more than fiction, regardless of where a librarian would shelve them, while some of the novelizations seem to hit closer to the mark. Although much of what is written about Dean is unsubstantiated rubbish, there are some exceptional works, like those by David Dalton and Val Holley, that stand like tent poles supporting an otherwise sagging lot.

The first real biography of James Dean was written by his friend and roommate Bill Bast in 1956. The book is largely limited to the times Bast and Dean spent together, a fact that defines both its weakness and its greatest strength. Bast actually knew Dean, and was one of the very few people to spend time with him in New York, Los Angeles, and Indiana. Difficult to find in any form, this book is one of the Holy Grails of Dean collectors in its original hardcover, one of a very few from the 1950s. For years the Bast book stood alone, although in the late fifties Dean characters made appearances in novels by T. T. Thomas and Walter Ross. Books devoted exclusively to Dean were few and far between in the 1960s and into the early 1970s, but that lull ended forever in 1974.

That year, David Dalton and Venable Herndon released very good biographies in quick succession, and a Dean craze was born in the publishing industry. Ron Martinetti and Dean's friend John Gilmore presented their versions of the tale the following year. In the late 70s and early 80s, photographers Roy Schatt, Dennis Stock and Sanford Roth each released pictorial collections. Dalton got back into the mix in 1984 with one of the most beautiful books devoted to any motion picture actor, *American Icon.* In the wake of Dalton's second book, other publishers rushed to press with their own photo-intensive overviews.

The 1990s are so far proving to be a mixed bag. A string of biographers have focused their books on Dean's sex life, real and imagined, each seemingly trying to outdo the others with the most sordid details. Meanwhile, Val Holley and Donald Spoto have contributed two of the better books yet written on Dean.

As the fiftieth anniversary of his death approaches, and with Dean's friends Christine White and Elizabeth "Dizzy" Sheridan among those with books in progress, the boon in the world of James Dean literature seems to be moving strongly into the new millennium.

Special Care for Books

Althought books should for the most part be cared for in the same way as any paper item, there are a few considerations unique to this category of memorabilia. Each book is itself a collection of paper items. As such, deterioration problems are multiplied with each page. A minor flaw can set off a chain reaction, since damaged pages cannot be removed and separated from those that are undamaged. Acid-free tissue inserts can help slow the spread of deterioration if it is detected early, but by and large this is a problem without a complete solution.

Another unique concern is that the various materials used to create a book react differently to moisture. As with any item that is not uniform in composition, it is possible that some oparts may respond differently than others to the same conditions. A warping of the cover boards is a common symptom of this problem, as tensions between papers, cloth and binding materials are altered. Careful observation should help you settle upon an appropriate environment for your collection.

Remember also that books need to breathe. While impurities in the air can be harmful, air itself does little damage to a book. In fact, it is important to make sure air circulates around books and bookcases, maintaining a balanced climate with no stagnant areas. Books should be opened from time to time so that air can circulate through their pages. Store books loosely on shelves, supported by bookends if necessary. Bookcases should be smooth and free of sharp edges and corners. Steel shelving with a smooth baked enamel finish is ideal. If wood is to be used, it is important that it be thoroughly sealed. Triple coating with a polyurethane varnish that does not contain formaldehyde should do the trick.

Under no circumstances should bookmarks, papers, flowers or other acidic material be left in a book's pages. If there are smudges or pencil marks in a book, remove them with an art eraser, working gently from the center of the page toward the edge. If possible, clean the book between the pages with a soft brush to remove all accumulations of dirt and grit. Grit will act as an abrasive in the gutter, damaging the sewing and the binding. A simple dusting is usually maintenance enough for a book's exterior. A few drops of rubbing alcohol on a paper towel can work wondrs on glossy dust jackets or covers, but can cause irreversible damage if used on the wrong surface. Experiment with common books before jeopardizing your collection.

As with other types of collectibles, condition of books is all-important. It is a simple but true book dealers' adage that "Good copies get better, but poor copies don't." Even a relatively rare and valuable item loses much of its worth if the copy is a mess. A collectible book is clean and free of stains, pages not dog-eared, with no scribbling or underlining of text. Covers are clean, not showing wear at the edges, corners not bent or bumped. The spine will be straight whether viewed from top or bottom. If the book was issued with a dust jacket, it should be free from stains and tears, with crisp color and clean folds.

East of Eden
by John Steinbeck
Viking Press - 1952
Hardcover

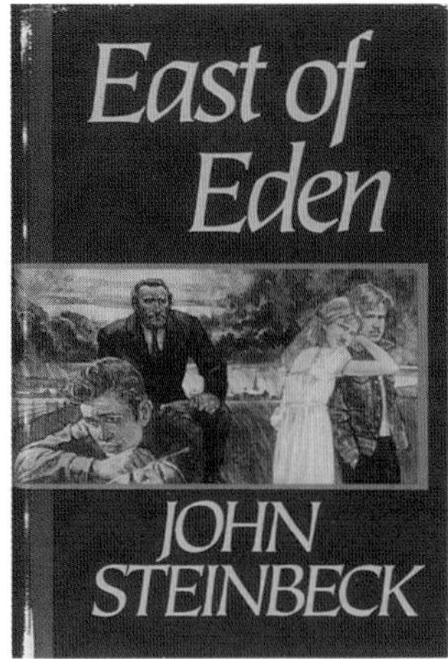

East of Eden
by John Steinbeck
Viking Press - USA
No Date - Post 1970

Rebel Without A Cause
by Robert M. Lindner
Grune & Stratton - 1944
USA, Hardcover

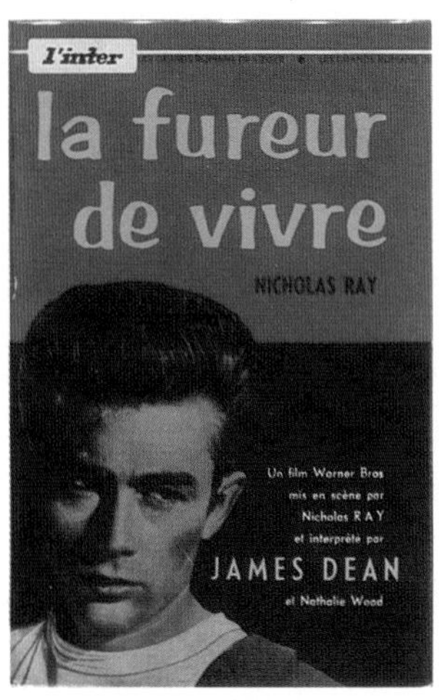

La Fureur De Vivre
by Nicholas Ray
Intercontinentale Du Livre
France - 1956, Hardcover

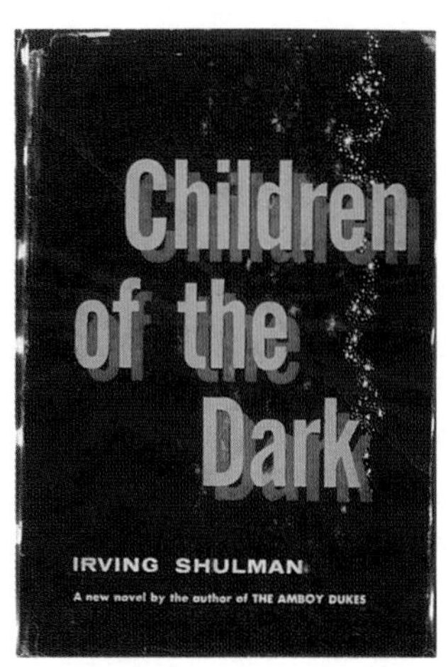

Children of the Dark
(based on Rebel without a Cause)
by Irving Schulman
Henry Holt & Co. - USA
1956 1st Ed. - Hardcover

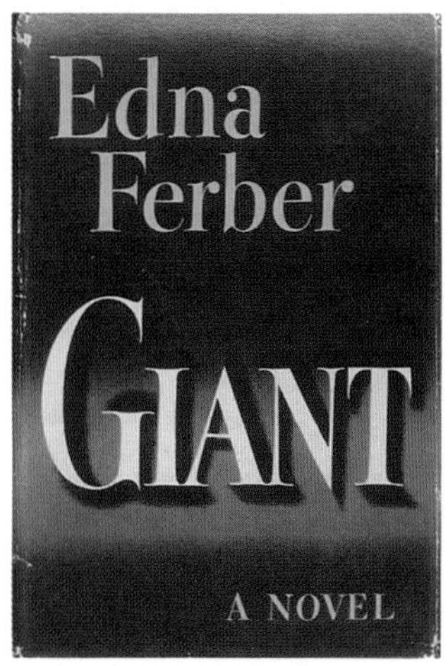

Giant
by Edna Ferber
Doubleday - 1952
Hardcover

Giant
by Edna Ferber
Doubleday & Co. - 1952
USA, Hardcover

Giant
by Edna Ferber
Gollancz Books - England
1957 - Hardcover

The Immortal (a novel)
by Walter Ross
Simon & Schuster - 1958
USA, Hardcover Cover by
Andy Warhol

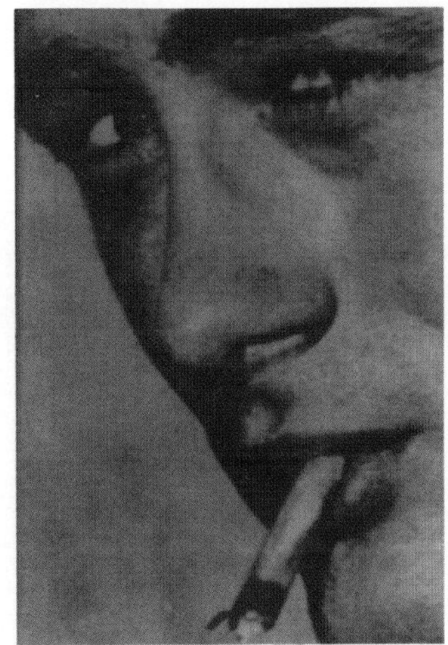

The James Dean Story
by Ronald Martinetti
Carol Publishing Co.
USA - 1995 - Hardcover

James Dean: The Biography
by Val Holley
St. Martins Press
USA - 1995 - Hardcover

Rebel The Life and Legend
of James Dean
by Donald Spoto
Harper Collins Publisher
USA - 1996 - Hardcover

James Dean
A Bio-Bibliography
by David Hofstede
Greenwood Press
USA - 1996

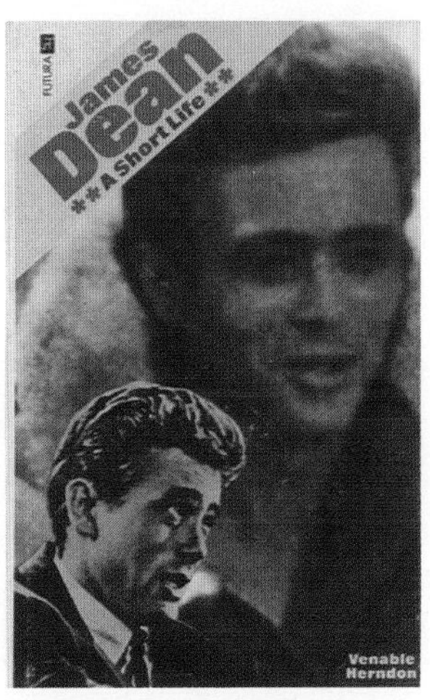

James Dean A Short Life
by Venable Herndon
Futura Publications
England - 1974 - Hardcover

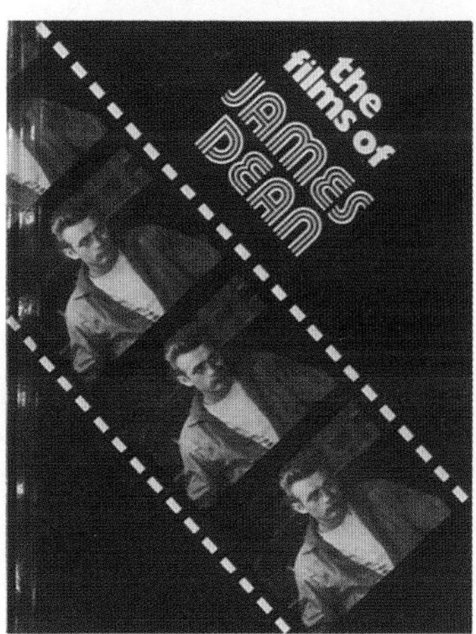

The Films of James Dean
by Mark Whitman
Greenhaven Press
England - 1978

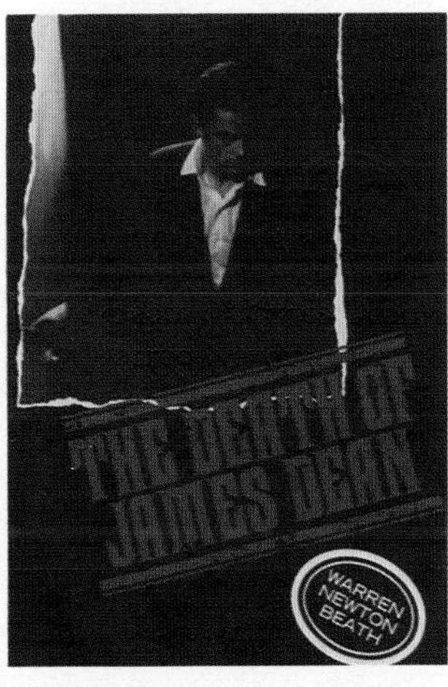

The Death of James Dean
by Warren Newton Beath
Sidgewick & Jackson - 1986
England - Hardcover

The Death of James Dean
by Warren Newton Beath
Grove Press - 1986
USA - Hardcover

The Unabridged James Dean
His Life and Legacy from A to Z
by Randall Riese
Contemporary Books - 1991
USA, Hardcover

James Dean
by Bahia Verlag
Romequanite, Germany
1984

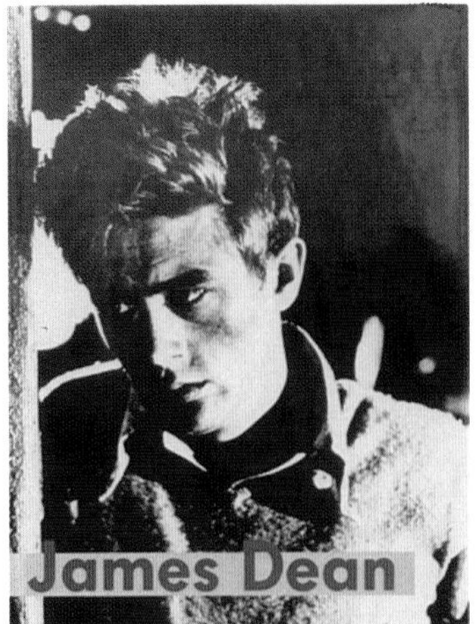

James Dean:Footsteps of a Giant
by Wolfgang Fuchs
Germany - 1989

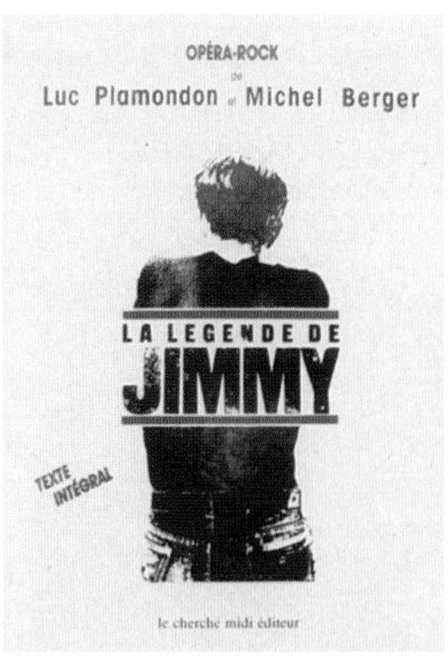

La Legende De Jimmy
le cherche midi éditeur
Play France - 1990
Hardcover

James Dean In His Own Words
by Neil Grant
USA - 1991 - Hardcover

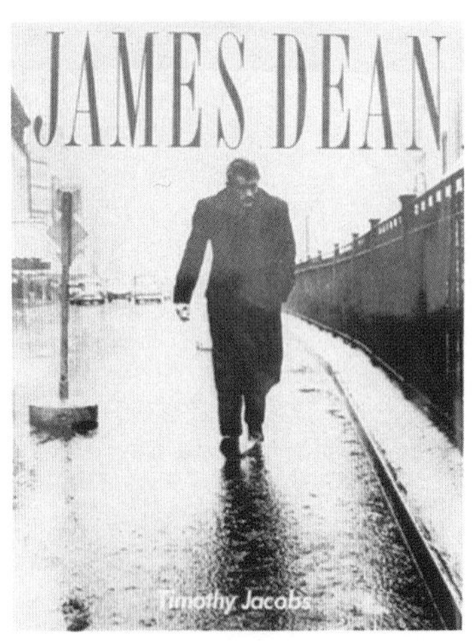

James Dean
by Timothy Jacobs
Mallard Press
USA - 1991

James Dean Tribute To A Rebel
Publications International Ltd.
by Val Holley/David Loehr
USA - 1991 - Hardcover

James Dean Boulevard of Broken Dreeams
by Paul Alexander Little, Brown, & Co.
England - 1994 - Hardcover

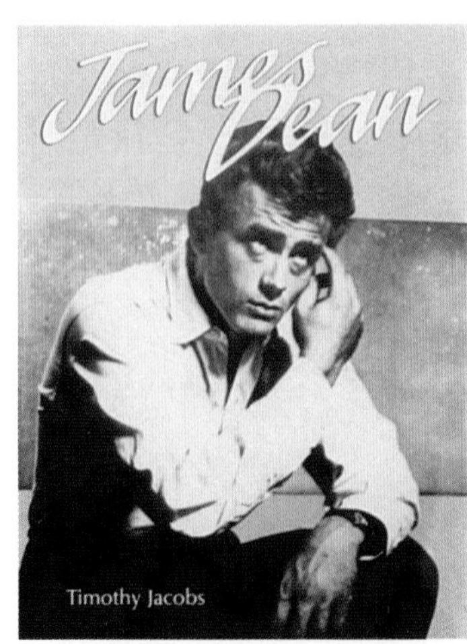

James Dean
by Timothy Jacobs
JG Press
USA - 1994

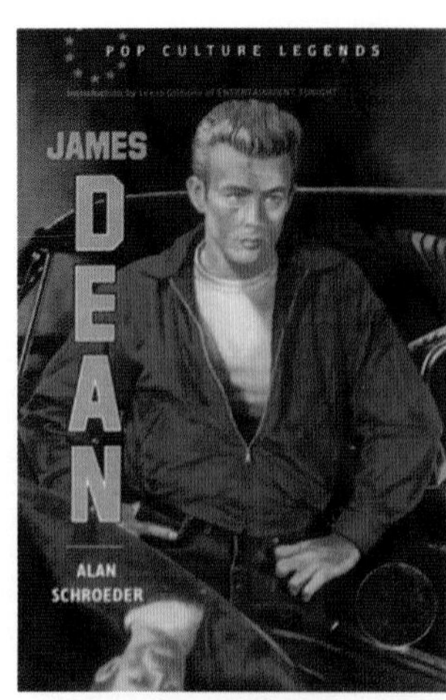

James Dean
by Alan Schroeder
Chelsea House Publisheers
USA - 1994 - Hardcover

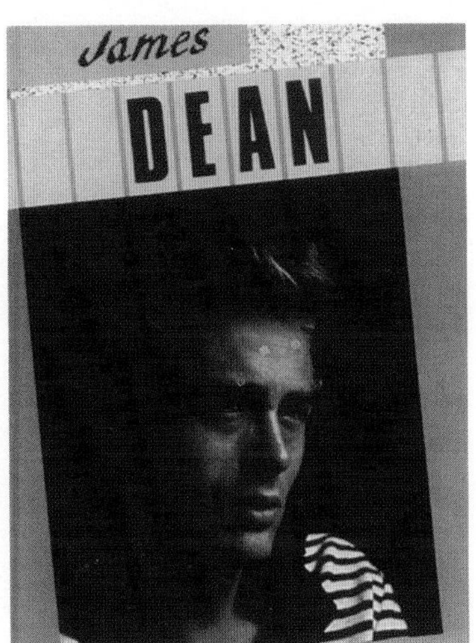

James Dean
Spain - 1985

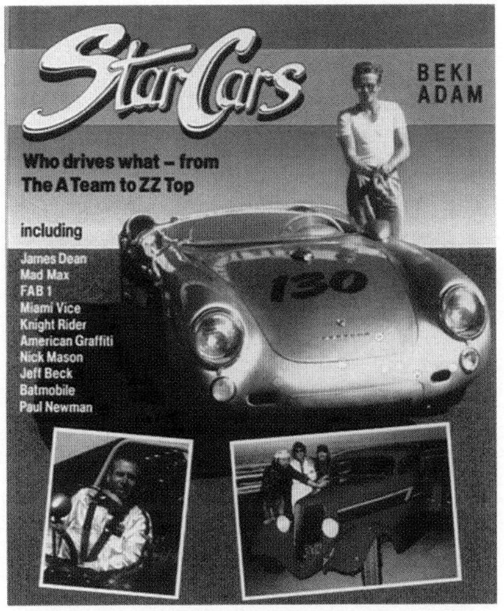

Star Cars - Osprey Publication
United Kingdom - 1987 - Hardcover

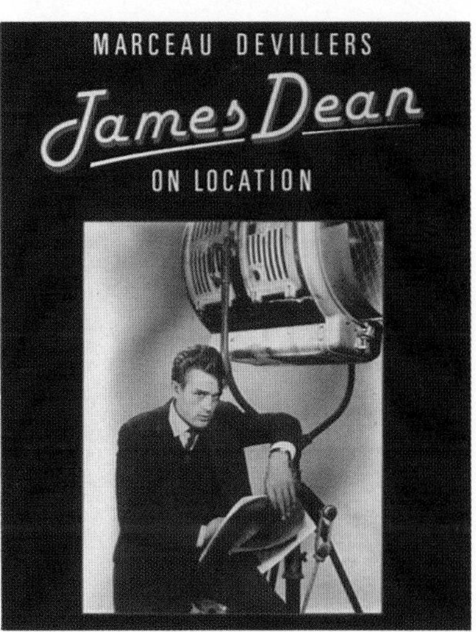

James Dean on Location by
Marceau Devillers - England - 1987

James Dean Behind The Scenes
Edited by Leith Adams
and Keith Burns
USA - 1990 - Hardcover
1992 - Softcover

James Dean
by Marceau Devillers
Chartwell Books
USA - 1994 - Hardcover

James Dean
La Passion Foudroyée
Graton Editeur
Belgium - 1995
Hardcover

James Dean Shooting Star
by Barney Hoskyns/David Loehr
United Kingdom - 1989
Doubleday - USA - 1990

Phil Stern's Hollywood
Photographs,1940-1979
Alfred A. Knopf
USA - 1993 - Hardcover

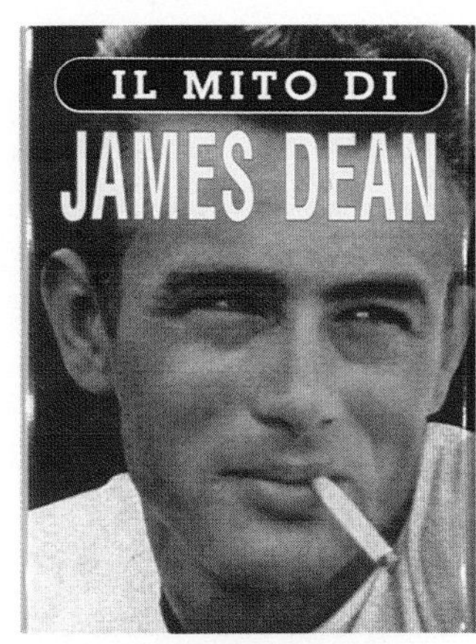

Il Mito Di James Dean
by A. Noble
Gremese Editore - Italy
1997 - Hardcover

Dramatists Play
Service, Inc.
USA - 1954

James Dean
Japan - 1981
Hardcover

James Dean Little Boy Lost
by Joe Hyams
Warner Books
USA - 1992

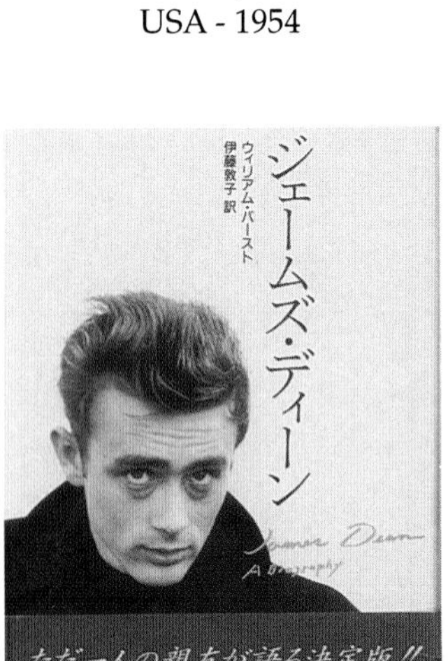

James Dean A Biography
by William Bast
Japan - 1993
Harcover

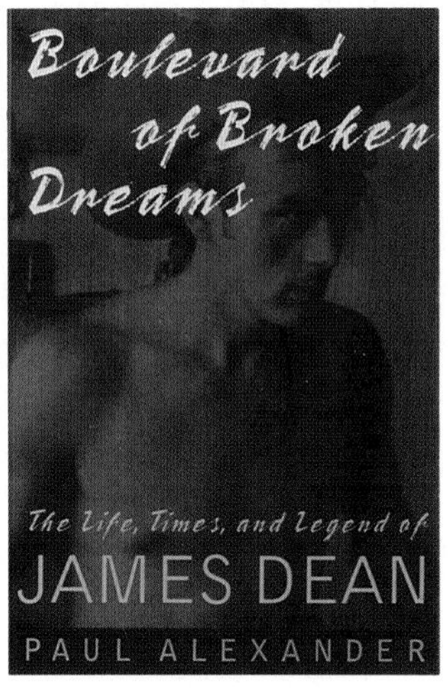

Boulevard of Broken Dreams
by Paul Alexander
Viking Press -USA - 1994

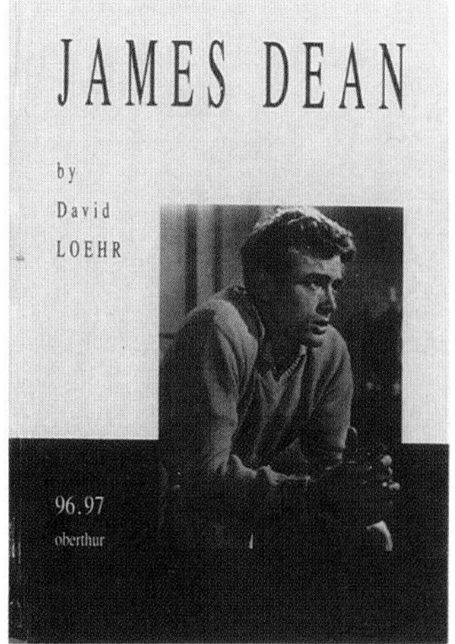

James Dean
by David Loehr
1996 - 97 Diary
France 1996

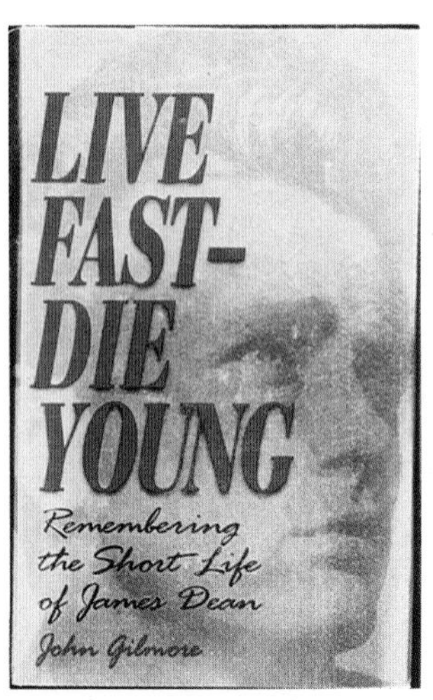

Live Fast-Die Young
Remembering the Short Life of
James Dean
by John Gilmore
Thunders Mouth Press
USA - 1997 - Hardcover

The James Dean Story
by Ron Martinetti
Estonia - 1998

James Dean
Back Creek Boy
by James Courtney
USA - 1990

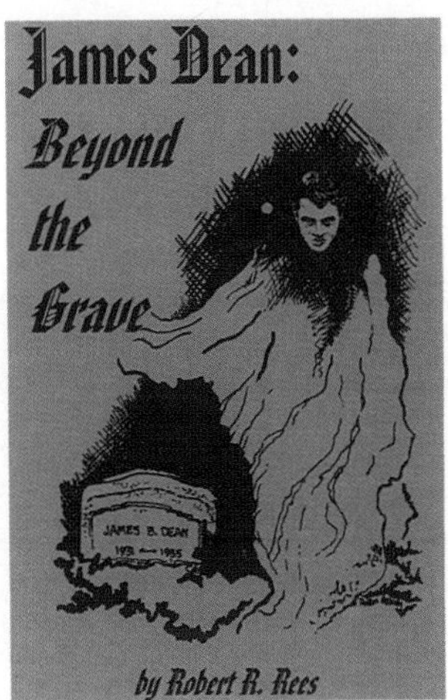

James Dean
Beyond the Grave
by Robert R. Rees
Empire Inc. USA - 1995

James Dean's Trail
One Fan's Journey
by Robert R. Rees
Empire Inc. USA - 1995

Just Like James
by Lou Mathews
Sands - Houghton
USA - 1996

The James Dean Jacket Story
by Don Skiles
Cross Roads Press 1997

Summer was only
Beginning
by D. Mrkich
Commoners' Publishing
Society Canada - 1997

The Ultimate James Dean
Scrapbook!
by American Legends USA - 1996

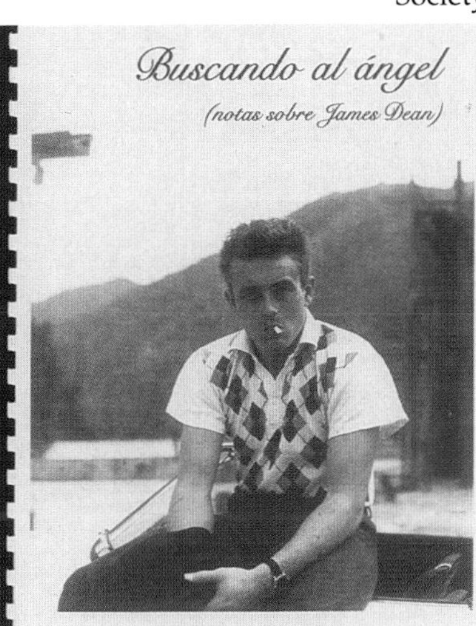

Buscando al ángel
(Notas Sobre James Dean)
Laura Pardini -(Spanish)
USA - 1998 - Limited at 50

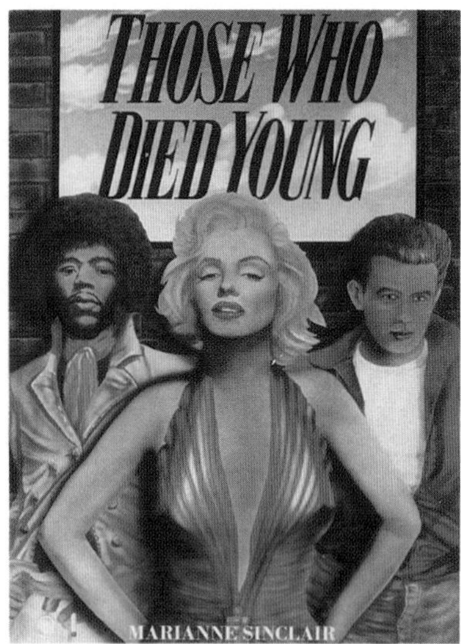

Those Who Died Young
by Marianne Sinclair
Penguin Books - USA - 1979 - Softcover

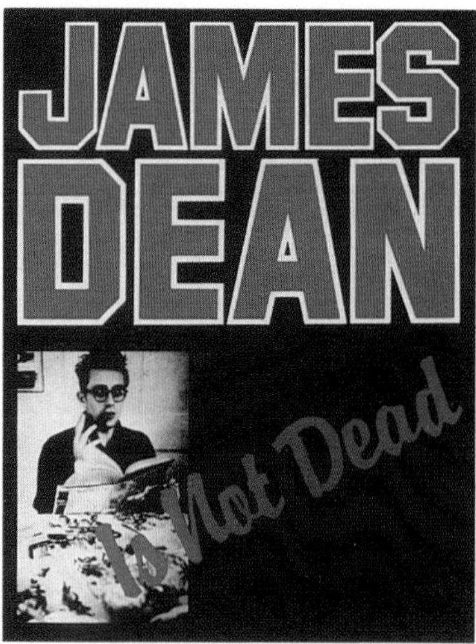

James Dean Is Not Dead
by Steven Morrissey
England - 1983

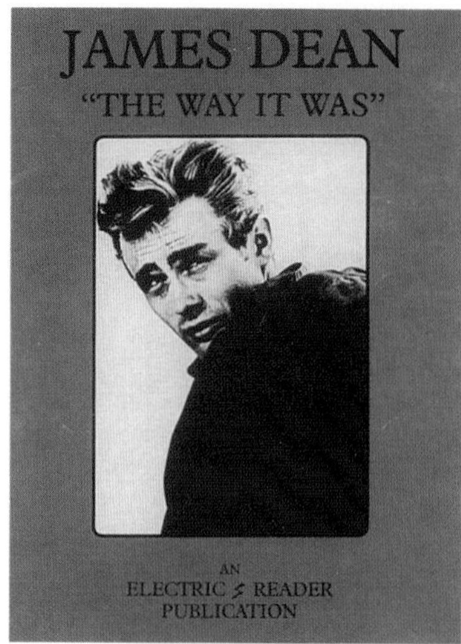

James Dean The Way It Was
Electric Reader Publishing
England - 1983

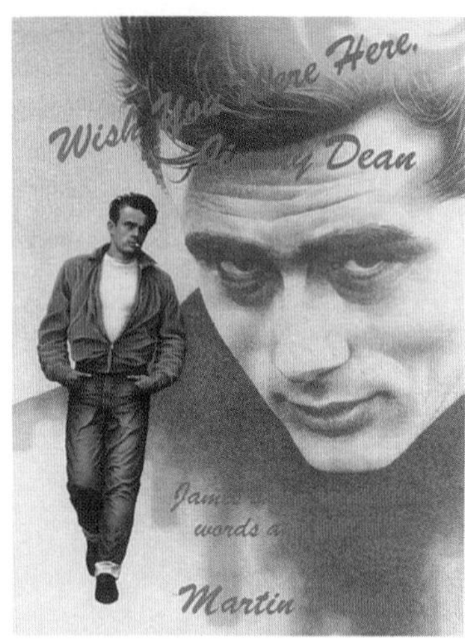

Wish You Were Here, Jimmy
Dean by Martin Dawber
Columbus Books- England-1988

James Dean
Poster Book
Atalanta Press
United Kingdom - 1986

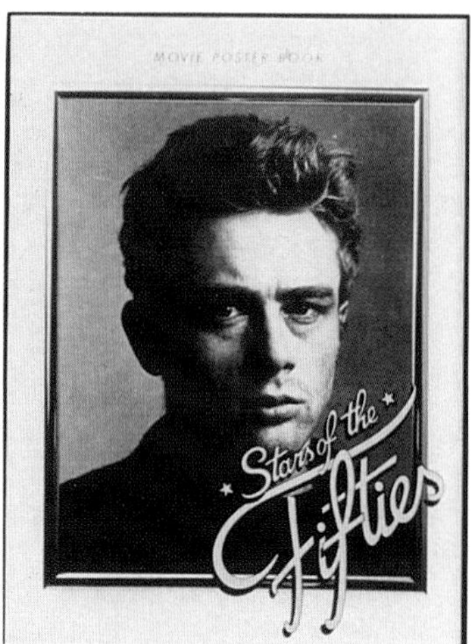

Stars of the Fifties
Octopus Books
United Kingdom - 1986

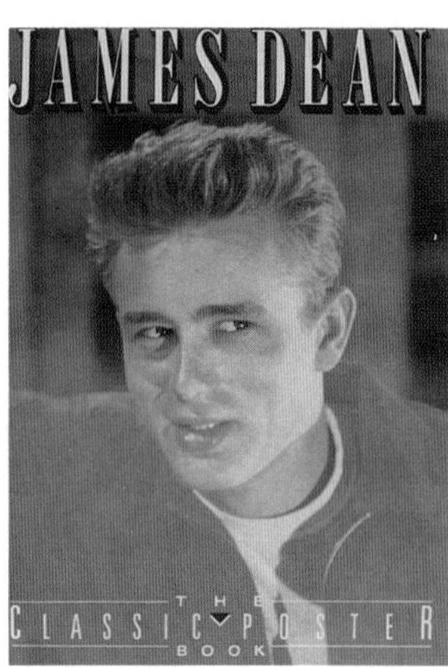

The Classic Poster Book
United Kingdom - 1990

Helnwein Posterbook
by Taschen
Germany - 1992

Mondo James Dean
Edited by Richard Peabody
& Lucinda Ebersole
St. Martins Griffin
USA - 1996

James Dean Shooting Star
by Barney Hoskyns - Virgin Books
United Kingdom - 1990 - Softcover

James Dean L'uomo, L'attore,
La Leggenda
Gremese Editore
Italy - 1993 - with poster

James Dean Horst Königstein
Dressler/Menschen
Germany - 1977

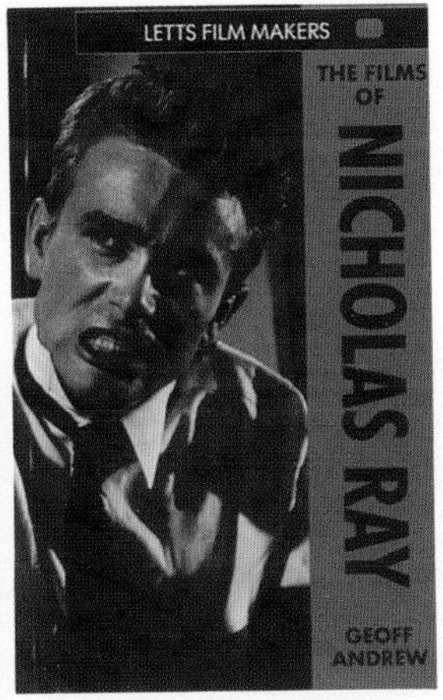

The Films of Nicholas Ray
by Geoff Andrew
Charles Letts Publisher
England - 1991

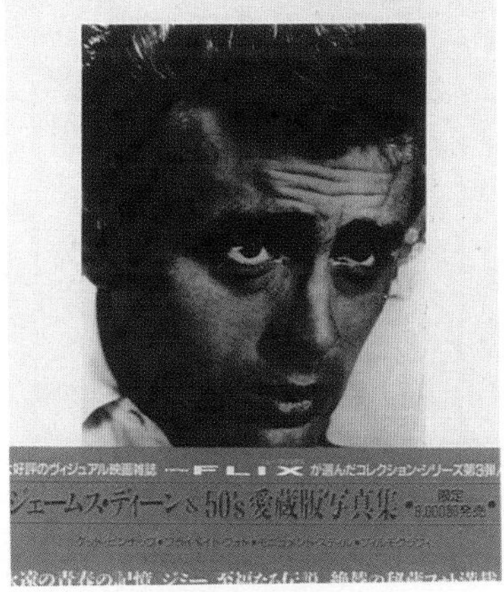

James Dean
Japan - 1991

Shirmer/Mosel Publisher
Germany - 1989

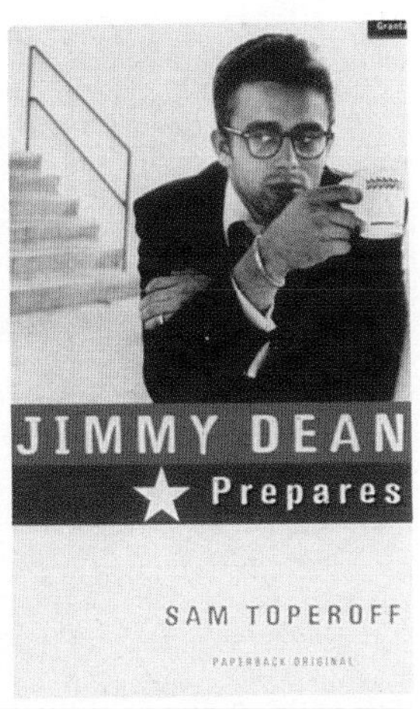

Jimmy Dean Prepares (a novel)
by Sam Toperoff
Grant Books - England - 1997

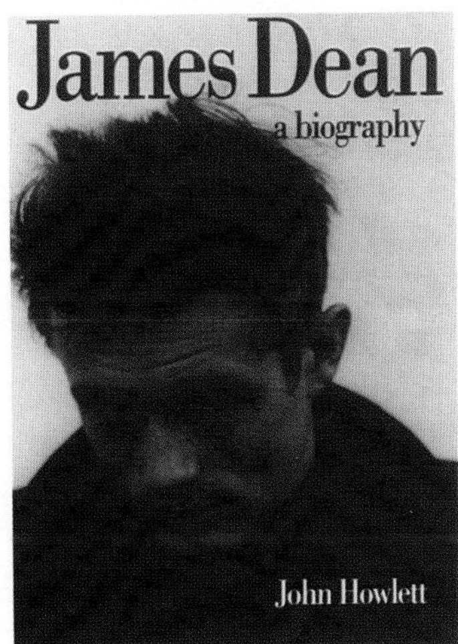

James Dean A Biography
by John Howlett
Plexus Publishing
United Kingdom - 1997

James Dean The Biography
by Val Holley
Robson Books Ltd
United Kingdom - 1995

East of Eden #1
Japan - 1972

East of Eden #2
Japan - 1972

East of Eden #3
Japan - 1972

James Dean A Short Life
by Venable Herndon
Japan - 1974

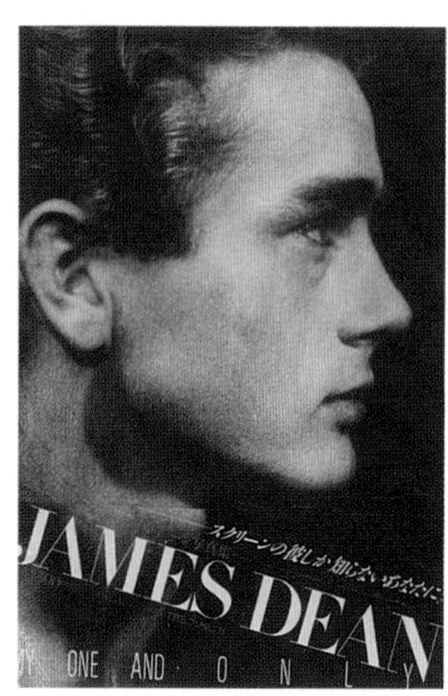

James Dean My One and Only
Japan - 1991

James Dean
Japan - 1979

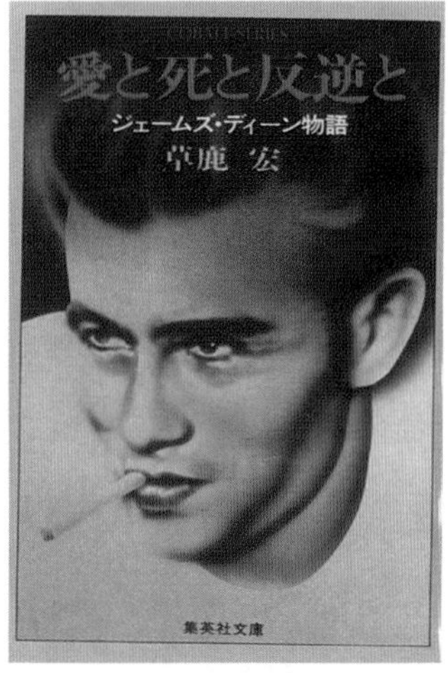

James Dean
Japan - 1977

James Dean
The First American Teenager
Japan - 1977

East of Eden
Japan - 1982

Catalog Jimmy Dean
Japan - 1977

De Majory Bell
Romans #595
Denmark - circa 1955

De Majory Bell
Romans
Denmark - Nov. 21, 1957

James Dean
Argentina - 1957

James Dean
Su Vida y Su Pasion
Argentina - 1957

James Dean
y su tragico destino
Argentina - 1957

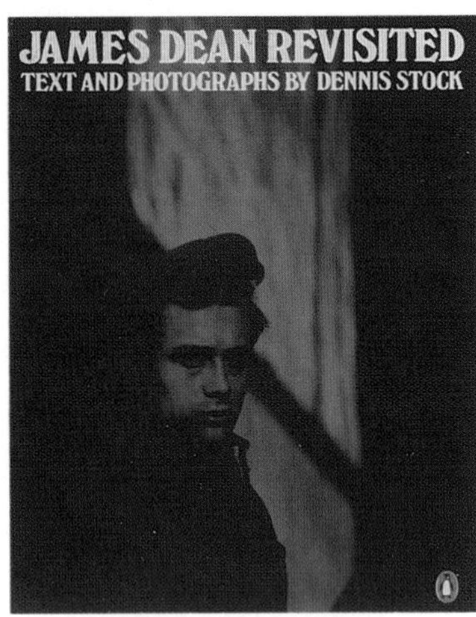

James Dean Revisited
by Dennis Stock
Penguin Books - USA - 1978

James Dean Revisted
by Dennis Stock
Japan - 1979

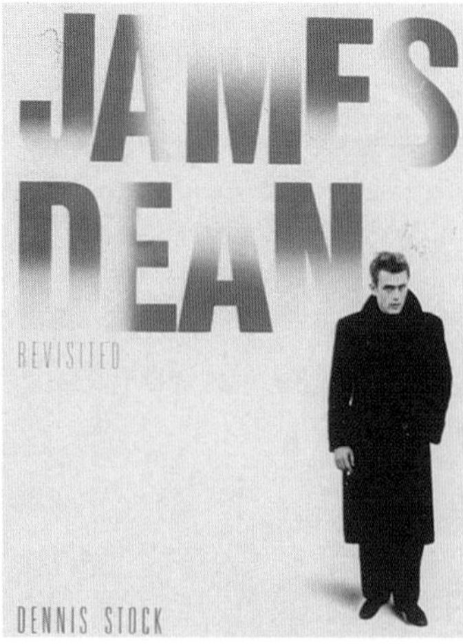

James Dean Revisited
by Dennis Stock
Chronicle Books - USA - 1987

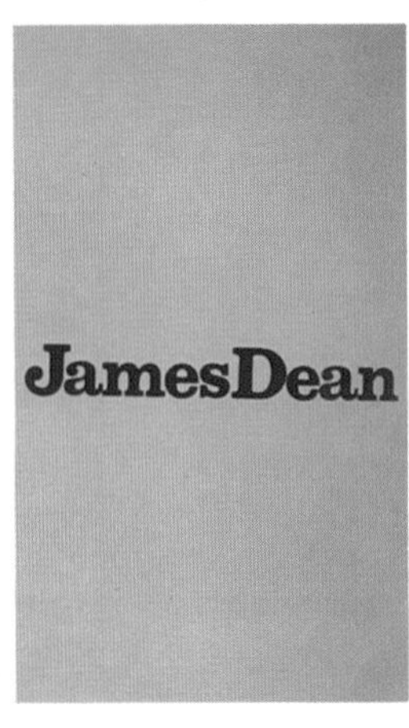

James Dean
Pomegranate Artbooks
Beulah & Sandford Roth
USA - 1983

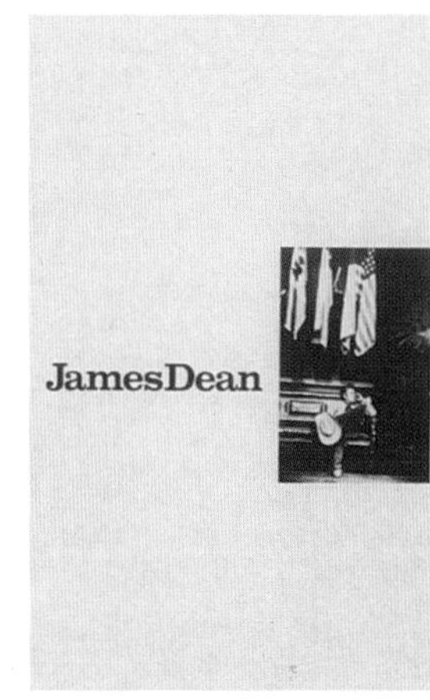

James Dean
Pomegranate Books
USA - 1987

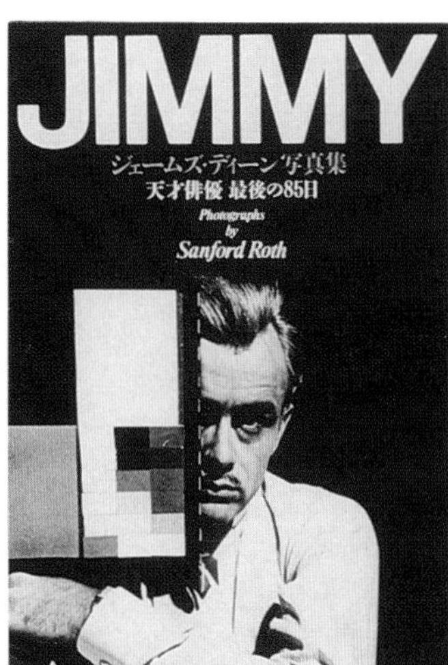

Jimmy
Photographs by S. Roth
Japan - 1983

Screen Pictorial James Dean
Japan - 1983

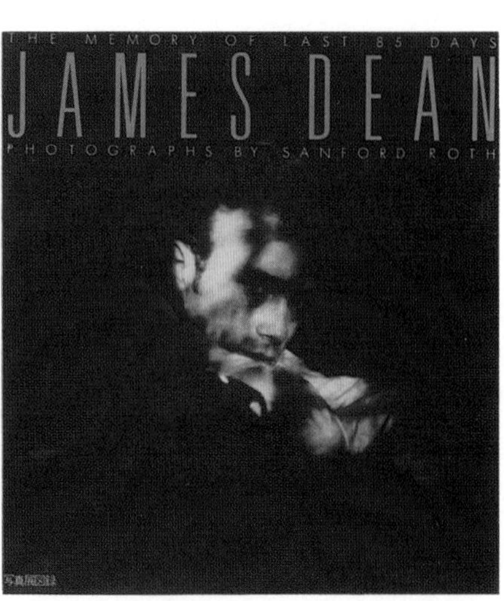

The Memory of the Last 85 Days James Dean
Photographs by Sanford Roth
Japan - 1987

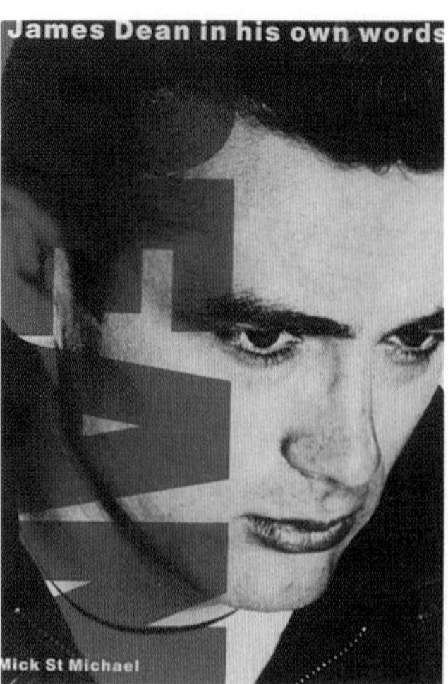

James Dean in His Own Words
by Mick St. Michael
England - 1989

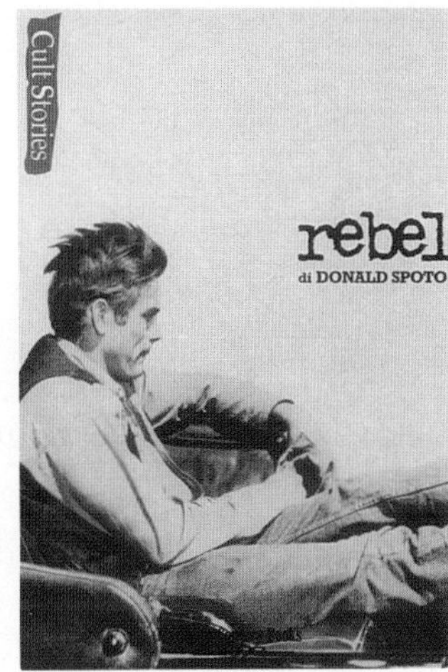

Rebel
by Donald Spoto
Edimar Publishing
Italy - 1996

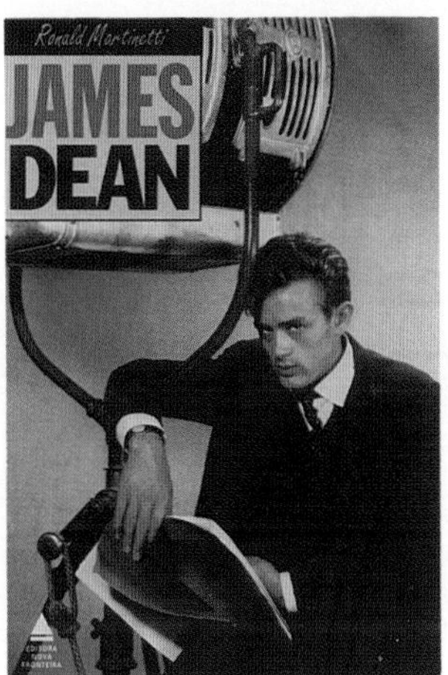

James Dean
by Ronald Martinetti
Brasil - 1996

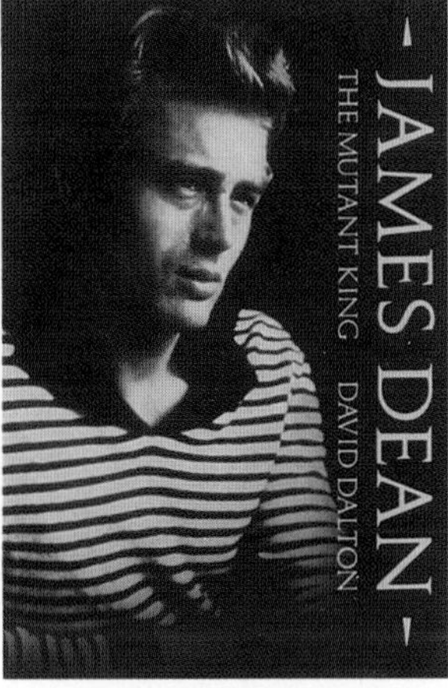

James Dean:
The Mutant King
by David Dalton
Plexus Publishing Ltd.
England - 1974

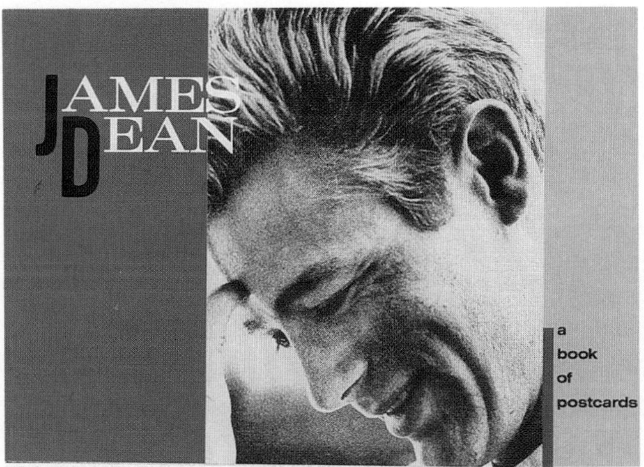

James Dean (Book of Postcards)
Pomegranate Artbooks
USA - 1989

James Dean
by Roger St. Pierre - Anabas Books
United Kingdom - 1985

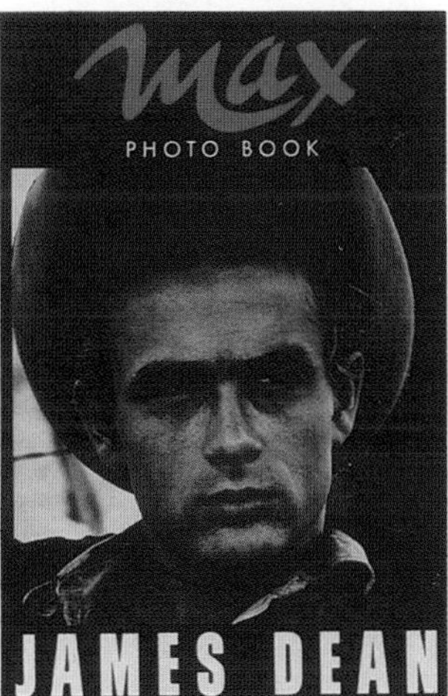

Max Photo Book
James Dean
Italy - 1990

The Films of James Dean
by Mark Whitman
England - 1964

James Dean El Gran Rebelde
by Luis Gasca
Ultramar Editores
Spain - 1988

The Films of James Dean
by Mark Whitman
England - 1974

James Dean
ou Le Mal Devivre
by Yves Salques
France - 1957

James Dean
ou La Vie A Tombeau Ouvert
by Ronald Martinetti
Editions France Empire
France - 1975

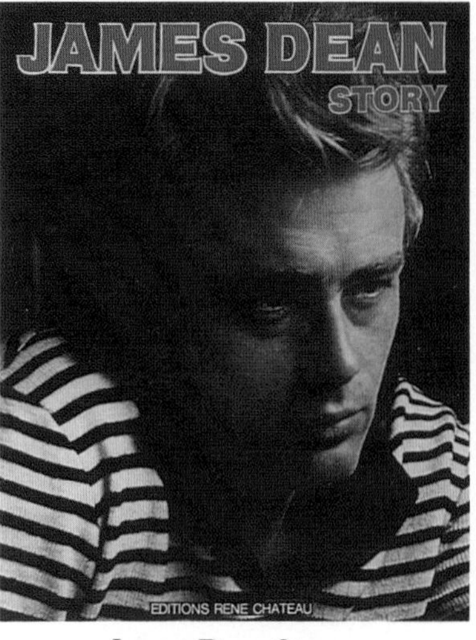

James Dean Story
Editions Rene Cheteau
France - 1975

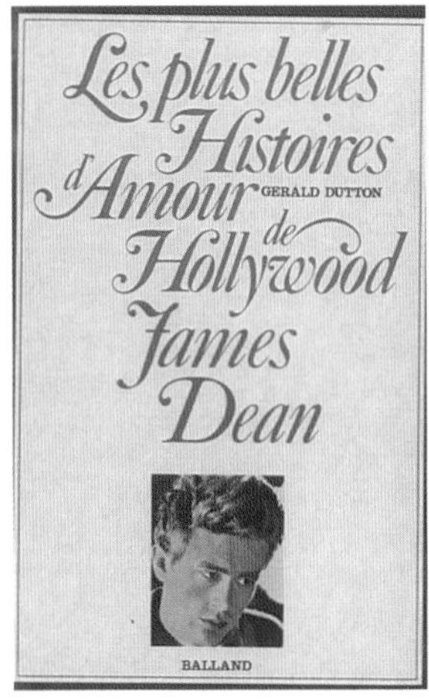

Les plus belles Histoires
d'Amour de Hollywood
James Dean
by Gerald Dutton
Ballard Publishing - France - 1981

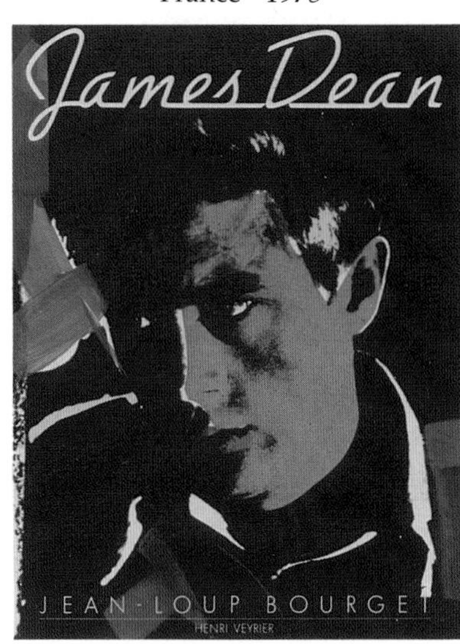

James Dean
by Jean-Loup Bourget
France - 1983

Anna-Maria Pier Angeli
Une Madone a Babylone
by Mariella Righini
Robert Lafont Publishing
France - 1989

Von Fans Für Fans James Dean
Rebell Und Idol
Germany - 1980

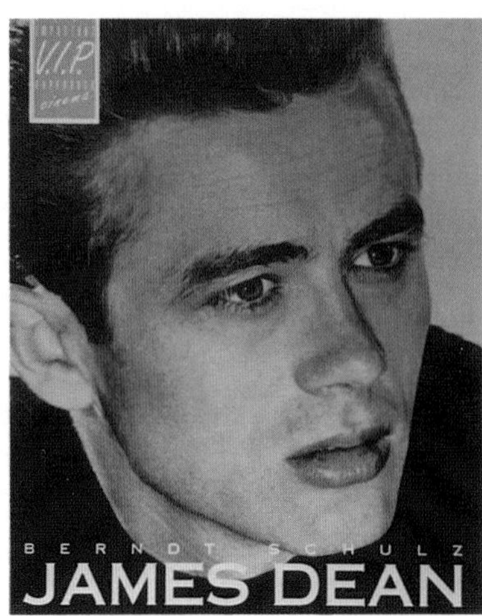

VIP Cinema - James Dean
Berndt Schulz - German - 1992

James Dean
by Paul Alexander
Goldmann Publishing
Germany - 1995

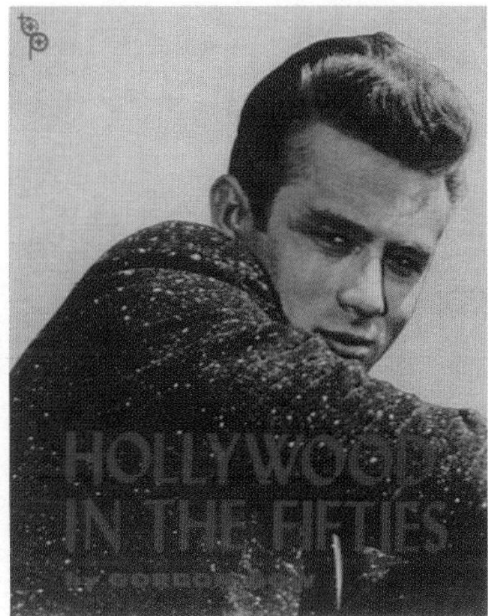

Hollywood In The Fifties
by Gordon Gow
USA - 1971

James Dean The Mutant King
(uncorrected proof)
St. Martins Press - USA - 1974

James Dean The Mutant King
by David Dalton
St. Martins Press - USA - 1983

James Dean
by John Howlett
USA - 1975

James Dean A Portrait
by Roy Schatt
USA - 1982

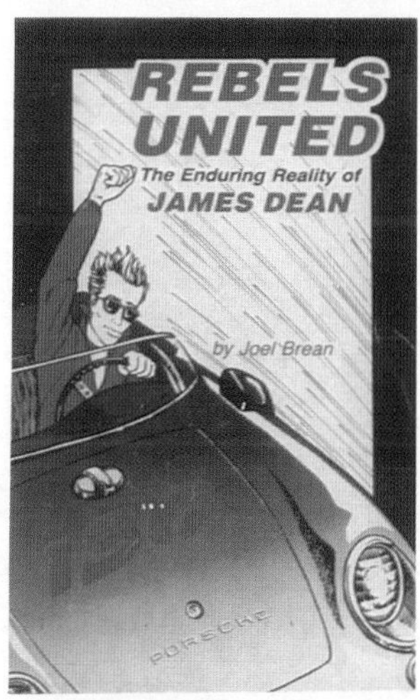

Rebels United The Enduring
Reality of James Dean by Joel Brean
USA - 1984

James Dean American Icon
(uncorrected page proof)
by David Dalton & Ron Cayen
St. Martins Press - USA - 1984

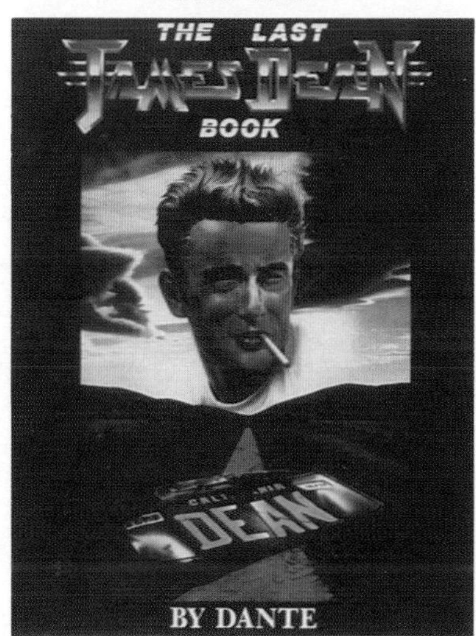

The Last James Dean Book
by Dante
Quill - USA - 1984

James Dean A Portrait
by Roy Schatt
Beufort Books - USA - 1986

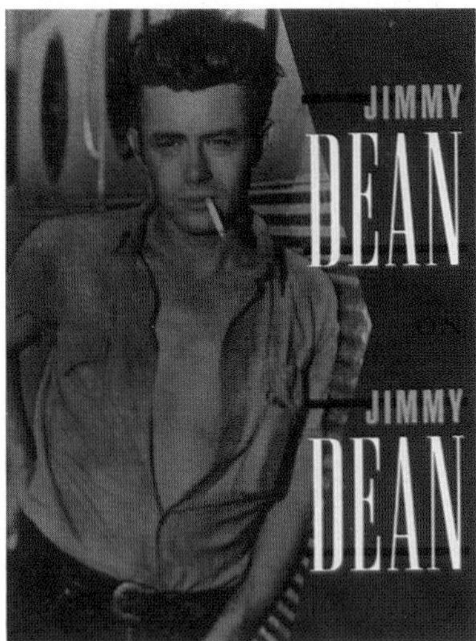

Jimmy Dean on Jimmy Dean
England - 1990

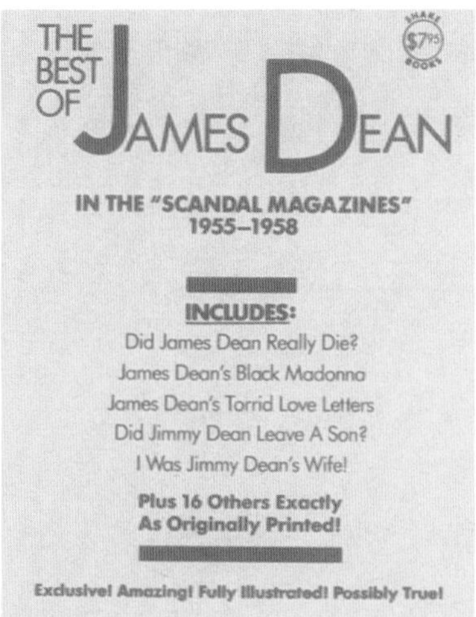

The Best of James Dean in the
Scandal Magazines 1955-1958
Compiled by Alan Betrock - USA - 1990

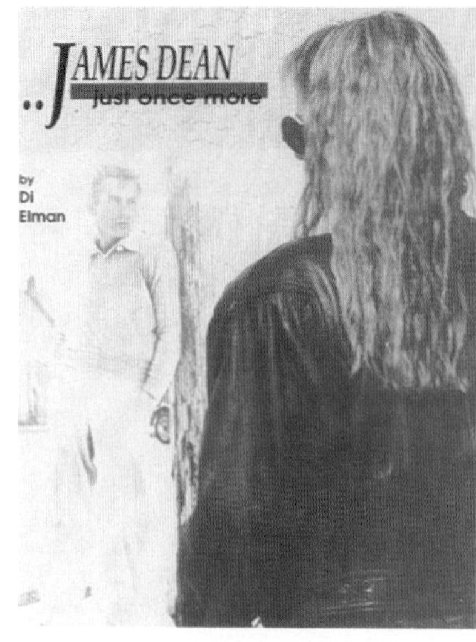

James Dean Just Once More
by Di Elman
Dayenu Productions - USA - 1990

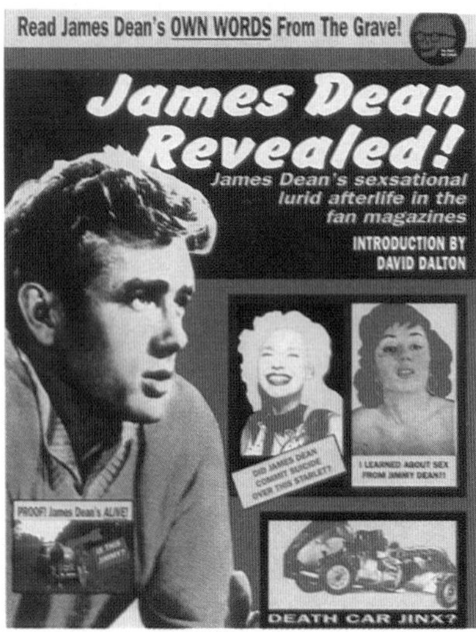

James Dean Revealed
Introduction by David Dalton
USA - 1991

The Man, The Character,
The Legend Deanmania
by Robert Headrick Jr. - USA - 1991

James Dean Tear Out Photo Book
England - 1994

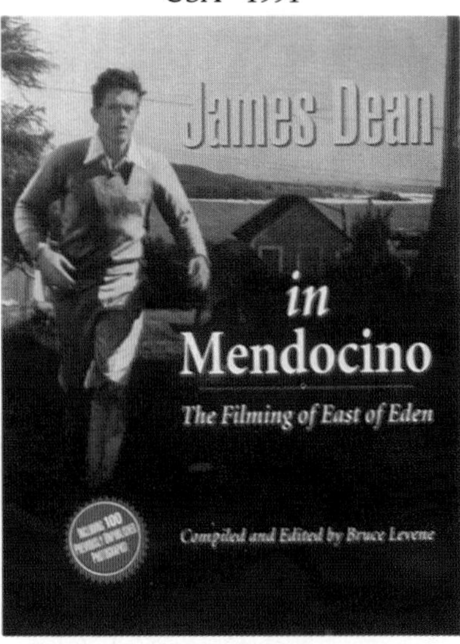

James Dean in Mendocino
The Filming of East of Eden
compiled & edited by Bruce Levine
Pacific Transcriptions - USA - 1994

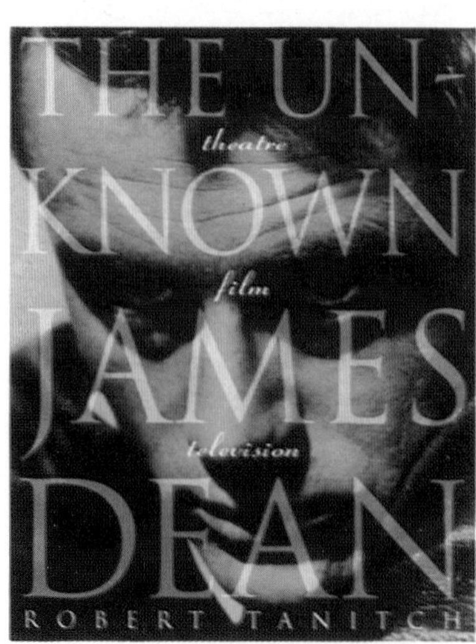

The Unknown James Dean
by Robert Tanitch
England - 1997

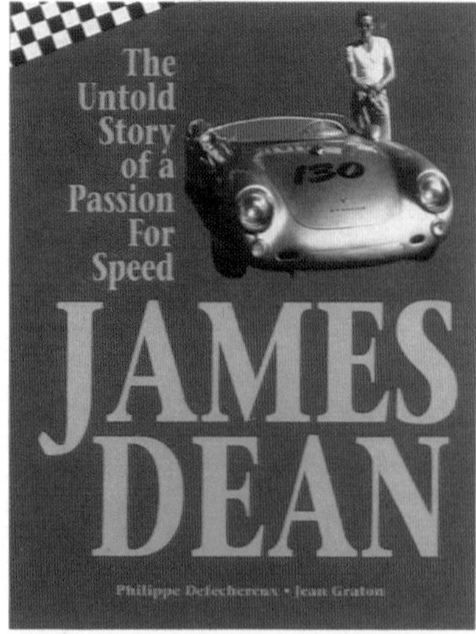

James Dean The Untold Story of A
Passion For Speed
by Philippe Defechereux & Jean Graton
Mediavision Publications - USA - 1996
Softcover - Hardcover

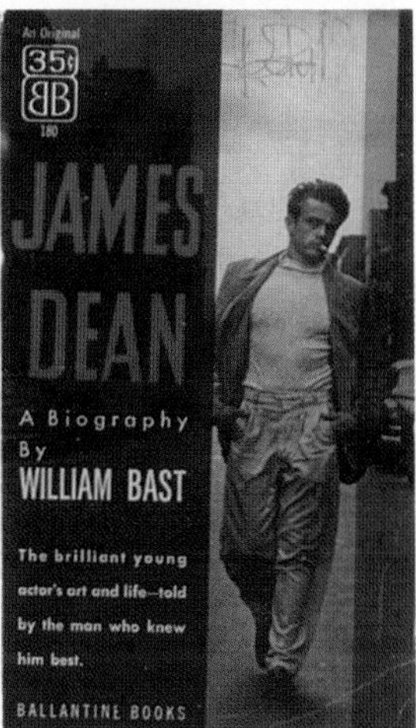

James Dean: A Biography
by William Bast
USA-1956

James Dean: A Biography
by William Bast
Japan - 1984

James Dean o bir asiydi!
by William Bast
Turkey - 1989

The James Dean Story
by Ronald Martinetti
USA - 1975

The James Dean Story
Ronald Martinetti
Carol Publishing - USA - 1995

Die James Dean Story
by Ronald Martinetti
Germany - 1979

James Dean: A Short Life
by Venable Herndon
USA - 1975

James Dean: A Short Life
by Venable Herndon
England - 1974

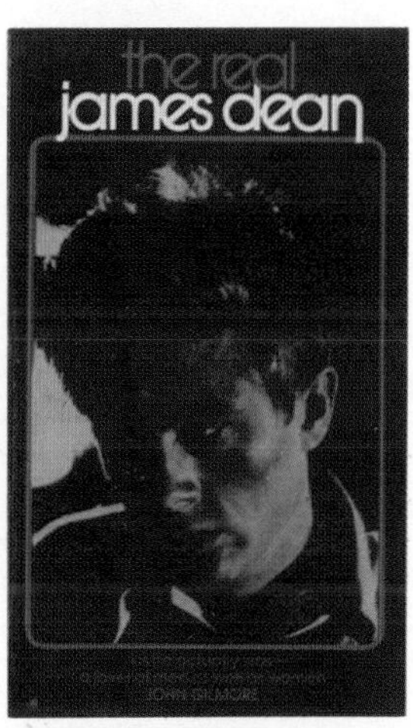

The Real James Dean
by John Gilmore
USA - 1975

James Dean Et Notre Jeunesse
by Xavier Grall
France - 1958

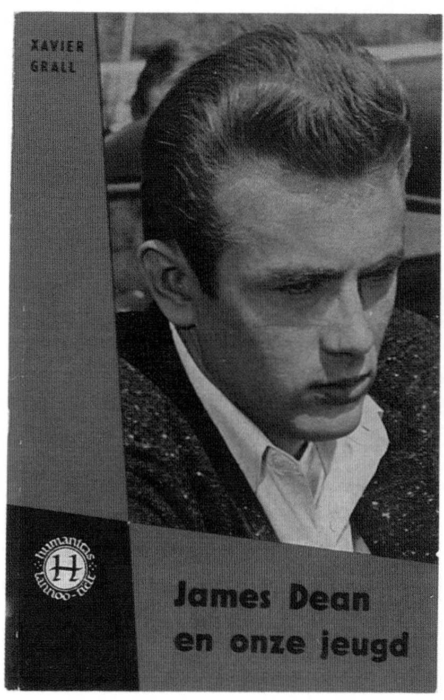

James Dean en onze jeugd
by Xavier Grall
Belgium - 1958

James Dean: Idol einer Jugend
by William Bast
Germany - 1957

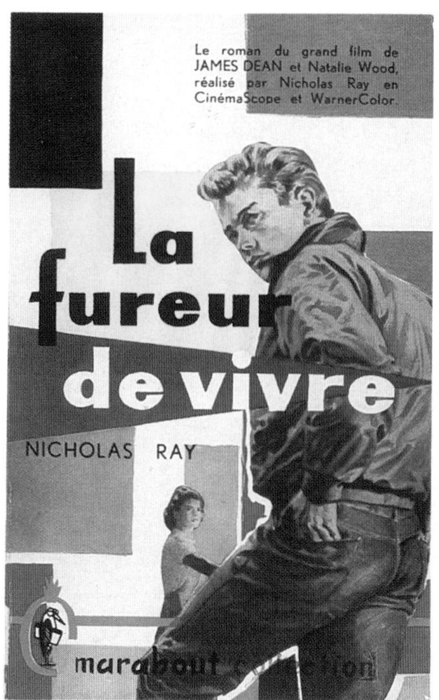

La Fureur de vivre
by Nicholas Ray
Marabout Collection
France - 1956

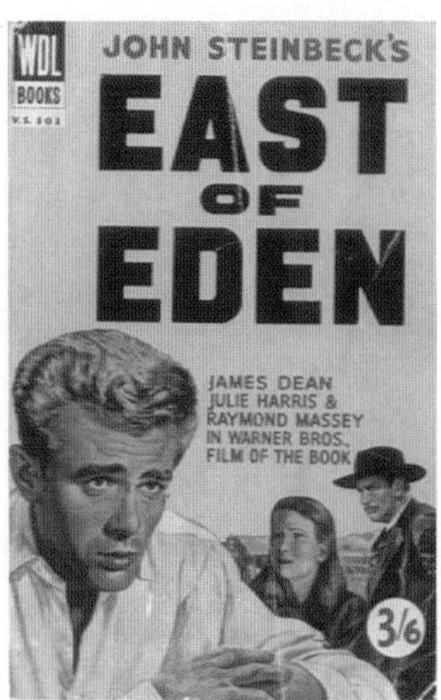

East of Eden by John Steinbeck - WDL Books England - 1959

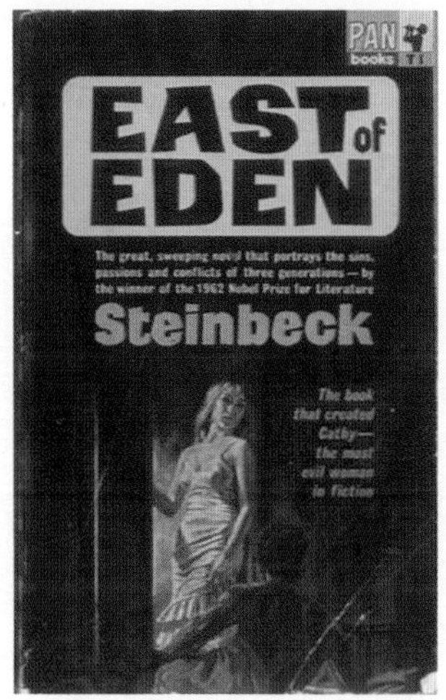

East of Eden
Pan Books LTD
United Kingdom - 1966

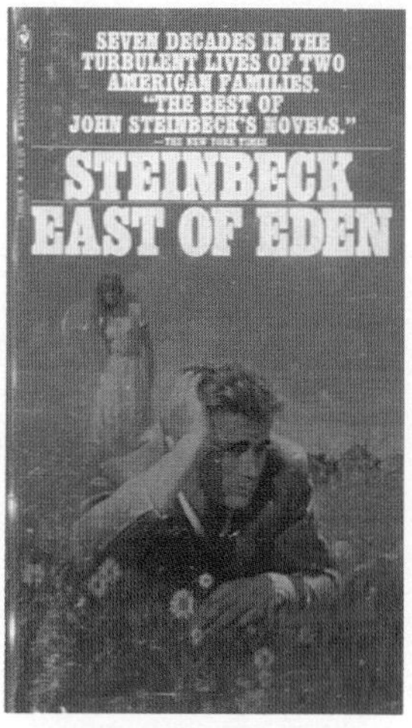

East of Eden
by John Steinbeck - Bantam Books - USA - 1977

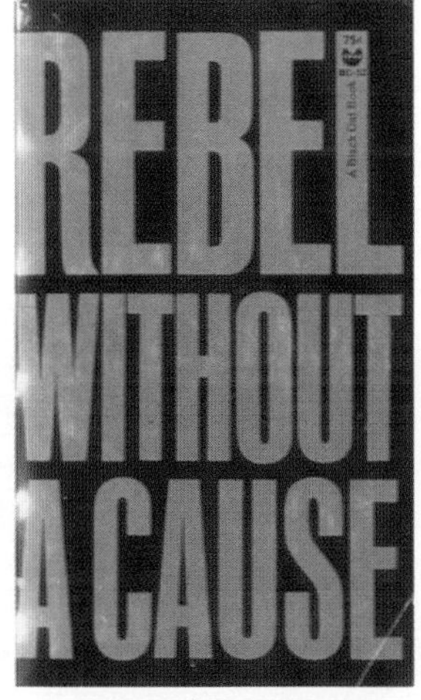

Rebel Without A Cause
by Robert M. Linder
Grove Press - USA - 1944

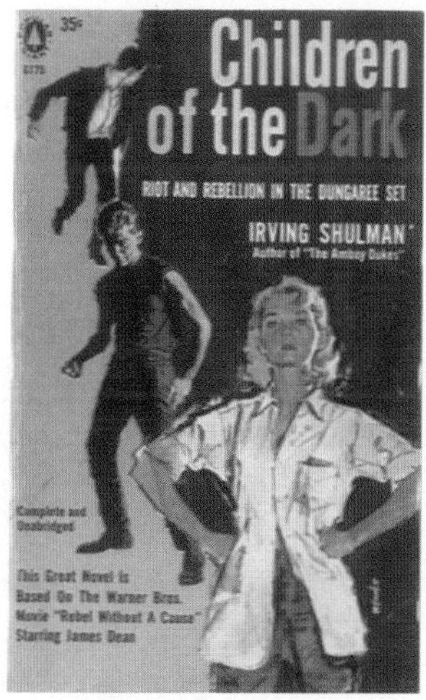

Children of the Dark
by Irving Schulman
Popular Library - USA - 1956

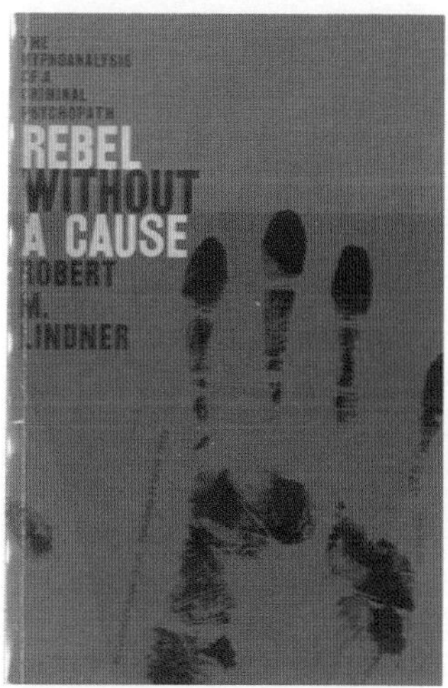

Rebel Without A Cause
by Robert M. Linder
Grove Press - USA - ©1944

Giant by Edna Ferber
Pocket Books Inc. - USA - 1956

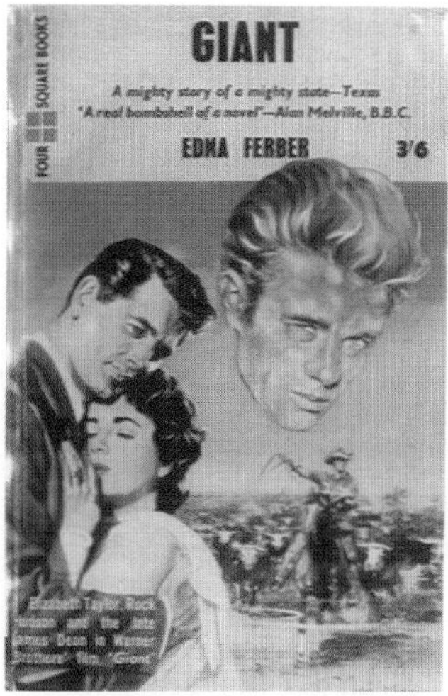

Giant by Edna Ferber
Four Square Books
England - 1957

9/30/55 (A Novel)
by John Minahan
Avon Books - USA - 1977

Rebel
by Royston Ellis
England - 1962

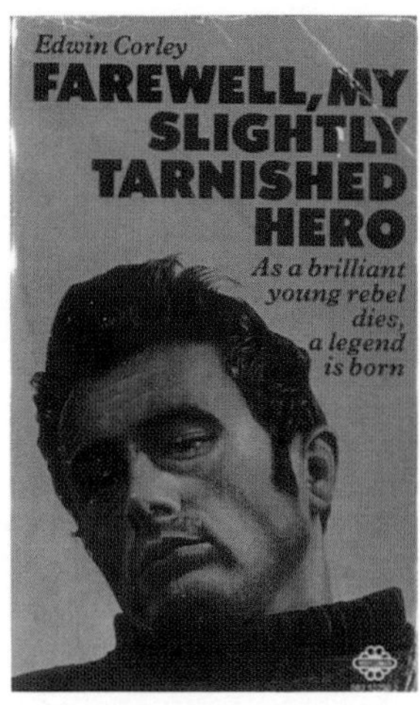

Farewell, My Slightly Tarnished Hero
(A Novel) by Edwin Corley
England - 1974

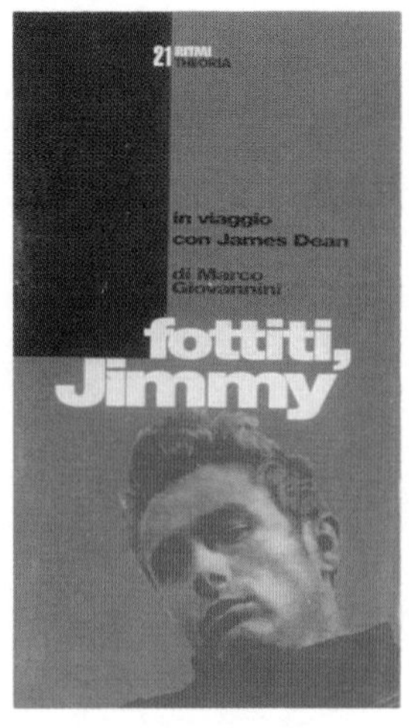

Fottiti, Jimmy
by Marco Giovannini
Italy - 1995

I, James Dean
by T.T. Thomas
USA - 1957

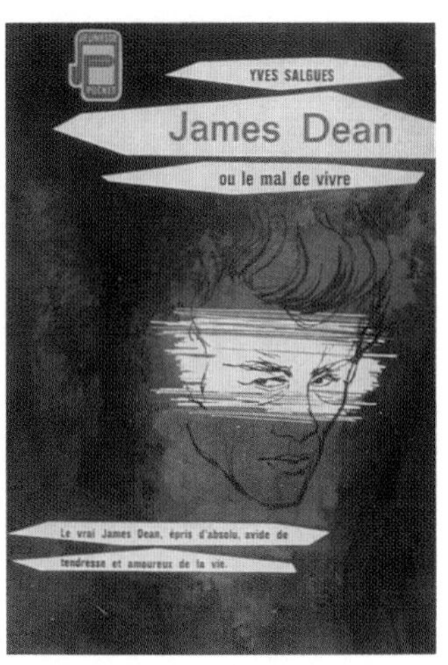

James Dean ou le mal de vivre
Jeunesse Pocket
France - 1957

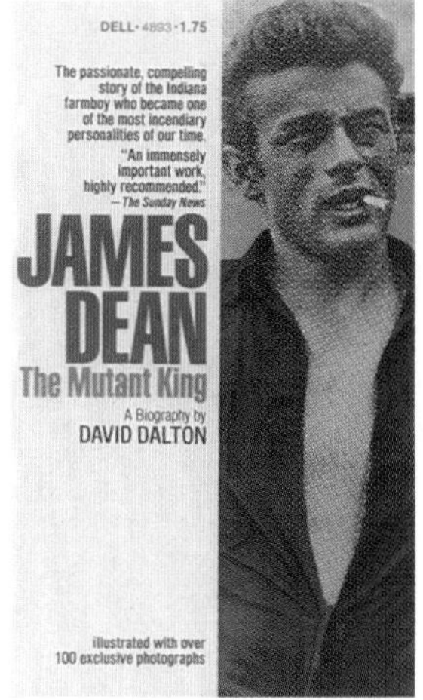

James Dean:
The Mutant King
by David Dalton - USA - 1975

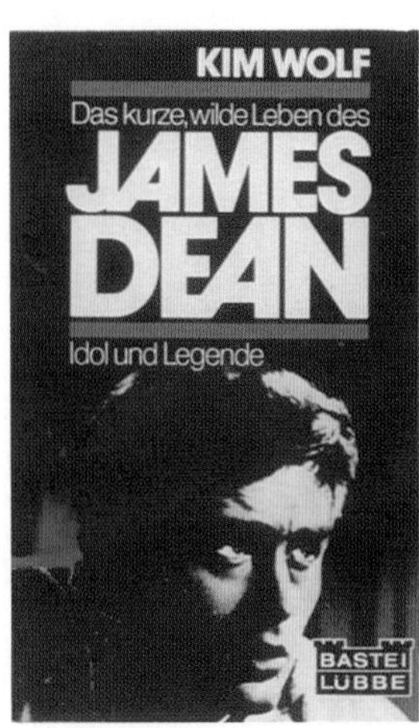

Das kurze, wilde Leben des
James Dean Idol und Legende
by Kim Wolf - Germany - 1979

James Dean Eine Bild-
Biographie by John Howlett
Germany - 1983

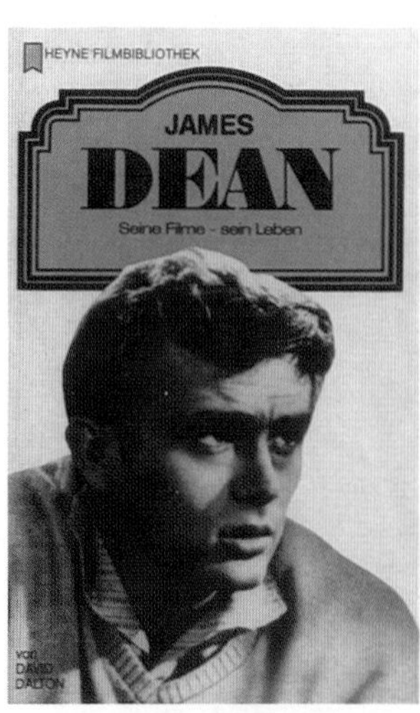

James Dean Seine Filme -
sein Leben
by David Dalton -
Germany - 1984

The Immortal
by Walter Ross
Cover by Andy Warhol
England - 1958

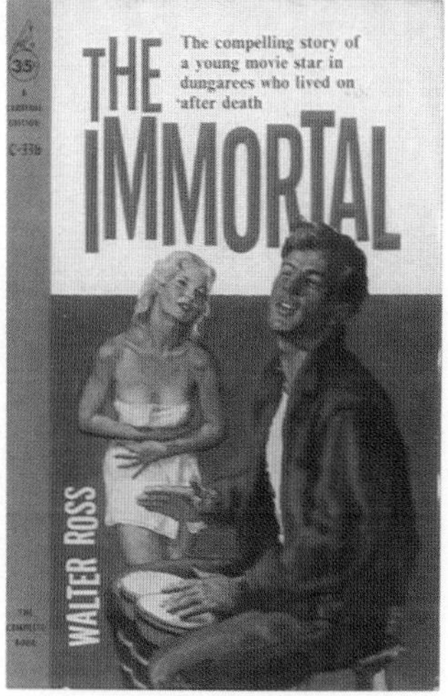

The Immortal
by Walter Ross
USA - 1959

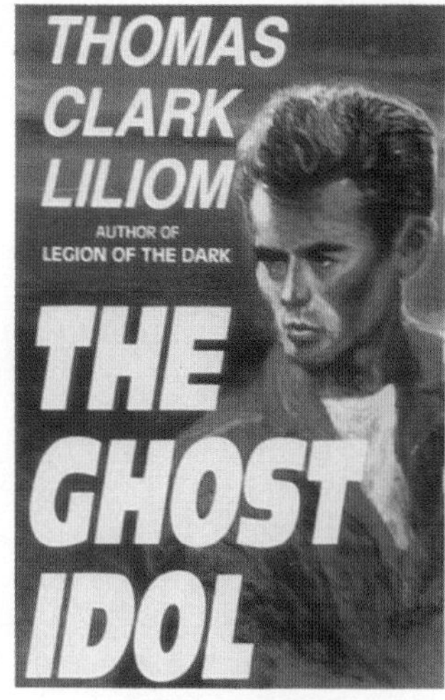

The Ghost Idol
by Thomas Clark Liliom
USA - 1986

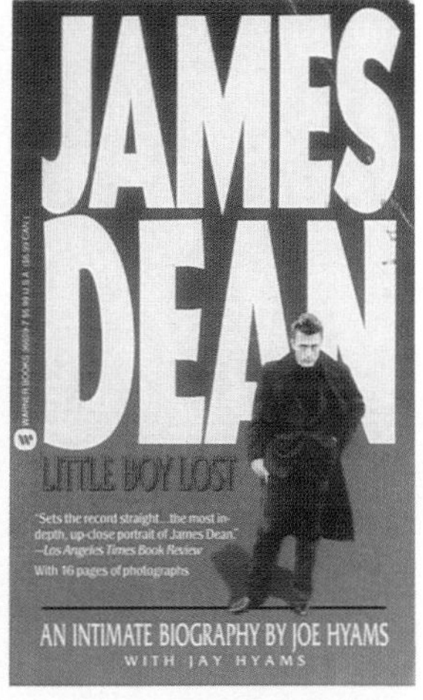

James Dean Little Boy Lost
by Joe Hyams
Warner Books - USA - 1994

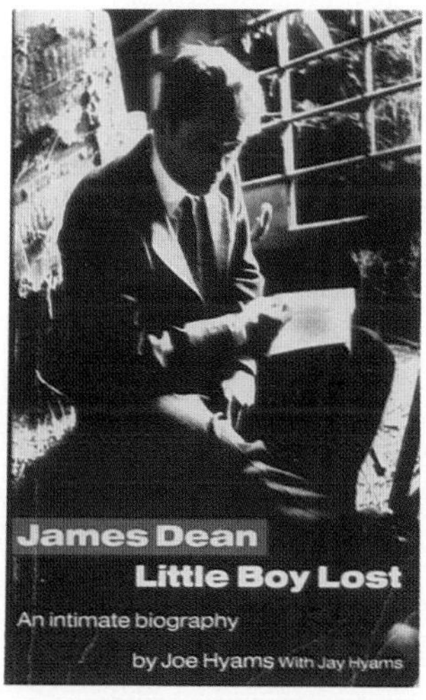

James Dean Little Boy Lost
by Joe Hyams
Arrow Books - United Kingdom - 1992

James Dean
by Antonio Bivar
Brasil - 1983

The Death of James Dean
by Warren Beath
New English Library
United Kingdom - 1988

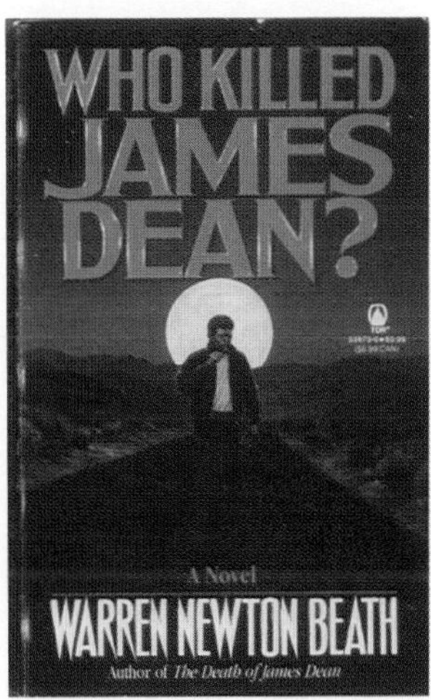

Who Killed James Dean?
by Warren Beath
Ator Book - USA - 1995

James Dean
by Michel Bulteau
France - 1985

Dean Related Books

The following list is limited to books in the English language. All information given indicates the first English edition. With the exception of those singled out in the photo section, most of these volumes can be obtained inexpensively.

Adam, Beki. **Star Cars.** Osprey Publishing, London, 1987.

Adams, Cindy. **Lee Strasberg: The Imperfect Genius of the Actors Studio.** Doubleday, New York, 1980.

Adams, Leith and Keith Burns. **James Dean Behind The Scenes.** Birch Lane Press, New York, 1990.

Adler, Bill. **Elizabeth Taylor: Triumps and Tragedies.** Ace Books, New York, 1982.

Alexander, Paul. **Boulevard of Broken Dreams: The Life, Times and Legend of James Dean.** Viking, New York, 1994.

Allan, John B. **Elizabeth Taylor.** Monarch Books, Derby, Connecticut, 1961.

Alleman, Richard. **The Movie Lover's Guide to Hollywood.** Harper and Row, New York, 1985.

Allen, Steve. **Mark It and Strike It: An Autobiography.** Holt, Rinehart and Winston, New York, 1960.

Allen, William. **Starkweather.** Houghton Mifflin, Boston, 1976.

Andrew, Geoff. **The Films of Nicholas Ray.** Charles Letts, London, 1991.

Andrews, Bart with Brad Dunning. **The Fabulous Fifties Quiz Book.** New American Library, New York, 1978.

Anger, Kenneth. **Hollywood Babylon II.** E.P. Dutton, New York, 1984.

Archer, Joe. **Here Is The Real Story of My Life By James Dean as I Might have Told It To Joe Archer.** Original manuscript on file at Marion (Indiana) Public Library, dated November 24, 1956.

Arens,Axel. **James Dean Photographs.** W.W. Norton Books, New York, 1992.

Astor, Mary. **A Life on Film.** Delacorte Press, New York, 1971.

Astor, Mary. **My Story: An Autobiography.** Doubleday, New York, 1959.

Backus, Jim. **Rocks on the Roof.** G.P. Putnam's Sons, New York, 1958.

Baker, Carroll. **Baby Doll.** Arbor House, New York, 1983.

Barraclough, David. **Hollywood Heaven: From Valentino to John Belushi, The Film Stars Who Died Young.** Gallery Books, New York, 1991.

Bast, William. **James Dean: A Biography.** Ballantine, New York, 1956.

Beath, Warren Newton, **The Death of James Dean.** Grove Press, New York, 1986.

Beath, Warren Newton. **Who Killed James Dean?** Tom Doherty Associates, New York, 1995.

Benedict, Brad. **Fame 2.** Indigo Books, New York, 1984.

Berle, Milton. **B.S. I Love You.** McGraw-Hill Book Company, New York, St. Louis and San Francisco, 1988.

Berlitz, Charles. **Charles Berlitz's World of Strange Phenomena.** Wynwood Publishers, New York, 1988.

Betrock, Alan. **The Best of James Dean in the "Scandal Magazines" 1955-1958.** Shake Books, New York, 1988.

Betrock, Alan. **The I Was a Teenage Juvenile Delinquent Rock 'n' Roll Horror Beach Party Movie Book! A Complete Guide to the Teen Exploitation film, 1954-1969.** St. Martin's Press, New York, 1986.

Blum, Daniel. **Screen World 1955.** Biblio and Tannen, New York, 1969.

Blum, Daniel. **Screen World 1956.** Biblio and Tannen, New York, 1969.

Boddy, William. **Fifties Television.** University of Illinois Press, Urbana and Chicago, 1990.

Boller, Paul F. and Ronald L. Davis. **Hollywood Anecdotes.** William Morrow and Company, New York, 1987.

Bosworth, Patricia. **Montgomery Clift.** Harcourt Brace Jovanovich, New York, 1978.

Brando, Anna Kashfi and E.P. Stein. **Brando For Breakfast.** Crown Publishers, New York, 1979.

Brando, Marlon. **Songs My Mother Taught Me.** Random House, New York, 1994.

Brean, Joel. **Rebels United: The Enduring Reality of James Dean,** Brean-Jones Publishing, 1984.

Brode, Douglas. **The Films of the Fifties.** Citadel Press, Seacaucus, New Jersey, 1976.

Burt, Rob. **Rockerama: 25 Years of Teen Screen Idols.** Delilah Communications, New York, 1983.

Byars, jackie. **All That Hollywood Allows: Rereading Gender in 1950s Melodrama.** University of North Carolina Press, Chapel Hill, 1991.

Carey, Gary. **Marlon Brando: The Only Contender.** St. Martin's Press, New York, 1985.

Carpozi, George, Jr. **That's Hollywood: The Matinee Idols.** Manor Books, New York, 1978.

Cawthorne, Nigel. **Sex Lives of the Hollywood Idols.** Prion, London, 1997.

Ciment, Michel. **Kazan on Kazan.** Viking Press, New York, 1974.

Cole,Toby and Helen Krich Chinoy. **Actors on Acting.** Crown Publishers, New York, 1970.

Collins, Joan. **Past Imperfect.** W.H. Allen, London, 1978.

Conrad, Earl. **Billy Rose: Manhatten Primitive.** World Publishing, Cleveland, Ohio, 1968.

Corley, Edwin. **Farewell, My Slightly Tarnished Hero.** Dodd, Mead adn Company, New York, 1971.

Courrtney, james. **Back Creek Boy.** GEM Group, Kentwood,Michigan, 1990.

Crivello, Kirk. **Fallen Angels.** Citadel Press, Secaucus, New Jersey, 1988.

Cronyn, Hume. **A Terrible Liar.** William Morrow and Company, New York, 1991.

Cunningham, Terry. **James Dean: The Way It**

Dalton, David. **James Dean: The Mutant King.** Straight Arrow Books, Coronado, California, 1974.

Dalton, David and Ron Cayen. **James Dean: American Icon.** St. Martin's Press, New York, 1984.

Dalton, David, Editor. **James Dean Revealed.** Dell Publishing, New York, 1991.

D'Arcy, Susan. **The Films of Elizabeth Taylor.** Greenhaven Press, St. Paul, Minnesota, 1978.

Davis, Daphne.**Stars!** Stewart, Tabori and Chang, New York, 1983.

Davis, Sammy, Jr.**Hollywood in a Suitcase.** William Morrow and Company, New York, 1980.

Davis, Sammy, Jr. and Burt Boyar. **Yes I Can: The Story of Sammy Davis, Jr.** Farrer, Straus, and Giroux, New York, 1965.

Dawber, Martin. **Wish You Were Here, Jimmy Dean.** Columbus Books, London, 19883

Defechereux, Phillippe and Jean Grafton. **James Dean: The Untold Story of a Passion for Speed.** Mediavision Publications, Los Angeles, 1996.

Devillers, Marceau. **James Dean on Location.** Sidgwick and Jackson, Great Britain, 1987.

Dos Passos, John. **Midcentury.** Houghton Mifflin, Boston, 1961.

Douglas, Kirk. **The Ragman's Son.** Simon and Schuster, New York, 1988.

Drake, Albert. **I Remember the day James Dean Died and Other Stories.** White Ewe Press, Adelphi, Maryland, 1983.

Eames, John Douglas. **The MGM Story.** Crown Publishers,New York. 1975.

Earley, Steven C. **An Introduction to American Movies.** American Library, New York, 1978.

Eastman, John. **Retakes: Behind the Scenes of 500 Classic Movies.** Ballantine Books, New York, 1989.

Eells, George. **Hedda and Louella.** G.P. Putnam's Sons. New York. 1972.

Eisenschitz, Bernard. **Nicholas Ray: An American Journey.** Faber and Faber, London, 1993.

Elman. Di. **James Dean: Just once More.** Dayenu Productions, Santa Barbara, California, 1993.

Was. Electric reader, London, 1983.
Ellis, Royston. **The Rebel.** Consul Books,.Great Britain, 1962.

Fehl, Fred,William Stott and Jane Stott. **On Broadway.** University of Texas Press, Austin, 1978.

Feldman, Frayda and Jörg Schellmann. **Andy Warhol Prints.** Ronald Feldman Fine Arts, New York, 1979.

Ferber,Edna. **A Kind of Magic.** Doubleday, Garden City, New Jersey, 1963.

Findler, Joel W. **All-Time favorite Movies.** Longmeadow Press, Norwalk, Connecticut, 1975.

Finlayson, Iain. **Denim: An American Legend.** Simon and Schuster, New York, 1990.

Forman, Brenda and Lloyd White. **Is Your Name James?** Arthur B. Fromer, New York, 1964.

Fox-Sheinwold, Patricia. **Too Young To Die.** Bell Publishing Compnay, New York, 1979.

Frederick, Nathalie. **Hollywood and the Academy Awards.** Hollywood Awards Publications, Beverly Hills, California, 1969.

Fuchs, Wolfgang. **James Dean: Footsteps of a Giant.** taco, West Germany, 1986.

Garber, Marjorie. **Vice Versa: Bisexuality and the Eroticism of Everyday Life.** Simon and Schuster, New York, 1995.

Garfield, David. **A Player's Place.** MacMillan, New York, 1980.

Gates, Phyllis and Bob Thomas. **My Husband Rock Hudson.** Doubleday, Garden City, New York, 1987.

Gilbert, Julie Goldsmith, **Ferber: A Biography.** Doubleday and Company, New York, 1978.

Gilmore, John. **Live Fast-Die Young: Remembering the Short Life of James Dean.** Thunders Mouth Press, New York, 1997.

Gilmore, John. **The Real James Dean.** Pyramid Books, New York, 1975.

Godfrey, Lionel. **Paul Newman: Superstar.** St. Martin's Press, New York, 1978.

Goodman, Ezra. **The Fifty Year Decline and Fall of Hollywood.** Simon and Schuster, New York, 1961.

Goodwin, Doris Kearns. **Wait Till Next Year: A Memoir.** simon and Scuster, New York, 1997.

Gow, Gordon. **Hollywood in the Fifties.** Zwemmer/Barnes, New York, 1971.

Graziano, Rocky with Ralph Corsel. **Somebody Down Here Likes Me Too.** Stein and Day, New York, 1981.

Griffin, Merv with Peter Barsocchini. **Merv.** Simon and Schuster, New York, 1980.

Griffith, Richard and Arthur Mayer. **The Movies.** Simon and Schuster, New York, 1957.
Grobel. Lawrence. **Conversations with Capote.** New American Library, New York, 1985.

Guinness, Alec. **Blessings in Disguise.** Harnish Hamilton, London, 1985.

Hanna, David. **Hollywood Confidential.** Leisure books, New York, 1976.

Harris, Warren G. **Natalie and R.J.** Doubleday, New York, 1988.

Harrison, Ward. **I didn't Know That! Kentucky's Ties to the Stage and Screen.** Butler Books, Louisville, Kentucky, 1994.

Hazelton, Lesley. **Driving to Detroit: An Automotive Odyssey.** Free Press, New York, 1998.

Headrick., Jr., Robert. **Deanmania.** Pioneer Books, Las Vegas, Nevada, 1990.

Hechinger, Grace and Fred M. **Teen-Age Tyranny.** William Morrow and Company, New York, 1963.

Herndon, Venable. **James Dean: A Short Life.** Doubleday, New York, 1974.

Hess, Alan. **Googie: Fifties Coffee Shop Architecture.** Chronicle Books, San Francisco, 1985.

Heymann, C. David. **Poor Little Rich Girl.** Random House, New York, 1983.

Higham, Charles. **Brando: The Unauthorized Biography.** New American Library, New York, 1987.

Higham, Charles. **Warner Brothers,** Charles Scribner' s Sons, New York, 1975.

Hillier, Jim, Editor. **Cahiers du Cinéma: The 1950's: Neo realism, Hollywood, Ne w Wave.** Harvard University Press, Cambridge, Massachusetts, 1985.

Hirsch, Foster. **Pictorial treasury of Film Stars: Elizabeth Taylor.** Galahad, New York, 1973.

Hirschhorn, Clive. **The Warner Bros. Story.** Crown Publishers, New York, 1979.

Hirschhorn, Joel. **Rating the Movie Stars for Home Video-TV- Cable.** Beekman House, New York, 1983.

Hofstede, David. **James Dean: A Bio-Bibliography.** Greenwood Press, Westport, Connecticut, 1996.

Holley, Val. **James Dean: The Biography.** St. Martin's Press, New York, 1995.

Holley, Val. **James Dean: Tribute to a Rebel.** Publications International, Lincolnwood, Illinois, 1991.

Holzer, Hans. **Star Ghosts.** Leisure Books, New York, 1979.

Hoose, Phillip M. **Hoosiers: The Fabulous Basketball Life of Indiana.** Vintage Books, New York, 1986.

Hopper, Hedda and James Brough. **The Whole Truth and Nothing But.** Doubleday, New York, 1963.

Hoskyns, Barney and David Loehr. **James Dean: Shooting Star.** Doubleday, New York, 1989.

Houseman, John. **Front and Center.** Simon and Schuster, New York, 1979.

Houston, Penelope. **The Contemorary Cinema: 1945-1963.** Penguin Books, Baltimore, Maryland, 1963.

Howard, Jean and James Watters.**Jean Howard's Hollywood: A Photo Memoir.** Harry N. Adams, New York, 1989.

Howlett, John. **James Dean: A Biography.** Plexus Publishing, Great Britain, 1975.

Hudson, Rock and Sara Davidson. **Rock Hudson: His Story.** William Morrow and Company, New York, 1986.

Humphreys, Joseph, consultant. **Jimmy Dean on Jimmy Dean.** Plexus, London, 1990.

Hyams, Joe. **Mislaid in Hollywood.** Peter H. Wyden, New York, 1973.

Jacobs, Timothy. **James Dean. Mallard Press, New York, 1991.**

Jacobson, Laurie. **Hollywood Heartbreak.** Simon and Schuster, New York, 1984.

Jones, Lee Editor. **The Fifties.** Pantheon Books, New York, 1985.

Jordan, Rene. **Marlon Brando,** Galahad Books, New York, 1973.

Joseph, Joan. **For Love of Liz.** Manor Books, New York, 1976.

Kael, Pauline. **I Lost At The Movies.** Little, Brown and Company, Boston, 1965.

Kass, Judith M. **Robert Altman: American Innovator.** Popular Library, New York, 1978.

Kazan, Elia. **Kazan: A Life.** Alfred A. Knopf, New York, 1988.

Kelley. Kitty. **Elizabeth Taylor: The Last Star.** Simon and Schuster, New York, 1981.

Kerbel, Michael. **Paul Newman.** W.H. Allen, London, 1973.

Key, Mike and Tony Thacker. **Fins and the Fifties.** Osprey Publishing Limited, London, 1987.

Kinder, Chuck. **The Silver Ghost.** Harcourt Brace Jovanovich, New York, 1979.

Kitt, Eartha. **Alone With Me.** Henry Regnery Company, Chicago, 1976.

Kitt, Eartha. **Confessions of a Sex Kitten.** Barricade Books, New York, 1989.

Kobal, John. **Hollywood Color Portraits.** Aurum Press, London, 1981.

Koszarski, Richard. **Hollywood Directors 1941-1976.** Oxford University Press, New York, 1976.

Kreidl, John. **Nicholas Ray.** Twayne, Boston, 1977.

LaGuardia, Robert. **Monty; A Biography of Monty Clift.** Arbor House, New York, 1977.

Lamparski, Richard. **Lamparski's Hidden Hollywood: Where the Stars Lived, Loved, and Died.** Simon and Schuster, New York, 1981.

Hymans, Joe. **James Dean: Little Boy Lost.** Warner Books, New York, 1992

Levene, Bruce. **James Dean in Mendocino.** Pacific Transcriptions, Mendoino, California, 1994.

Levant, Oscar. **The Unimportance of Being Oscar.** G.P. Putman's Sons, New York, 1968.

Lewis, Robert. **Method- Or Madness?** Samuel French, New York, 1958.

Libby, Bill. **They Didn't Win the Oscars.** Arlington House Publishers, Westport, Connecticut, 1980.

Liliom, Thomas Clark. **The Ghost Idol.** Pueblo Press, Yukon, Oklahoma, 1986.

Lloyd, Ann, Editor. **Movies of the Fifties.** Orbis Publishing Limited, London, 1982.

Lloyd, Ann, Editor. **70 Years at the Movies.** Crescent Books, New York, 1988.

Lyon, Christopher, Editor. **The International Dictionary of Films and Filmakers.** Macmillan, New York, 1984.

Maddox, Brenda. **Who's Afraid of Elizabeth Taylor?** M. Evans, New York, 1977.

Malone, Michael. **Heroes of Eros: Male Sexuality in the Movies.** E.P. Dutton, New York, 1979.

Martin, Richard and Harold Koda. **Jocks and Nerds: Men's Style in the Twentieth Century.** Rizzoli, New York, 1989.

Martinetti, Ronald. **The James Dean Story.** Pinnacle Books, New York, 1975.

Martinetti, Ronald. **The James Dean Story: A Myth-Shattering Biography of an Icon.** Birch Lane Press, New York, 1995.

Martone, Michael. **Alive and Dead in Indiana.** Alfred A. Knopf, New York, 1984.

Massey, Raymond. **A Hundred Differnet Lives.** Little, Brown and Company, Boston, 1979.

Mathews, Lou. **Just Like James.** Sands Houghton, Los Angeles, 1996.

McBride, Joseph. **Film Makers on Film Making: The American Film Institute Seminars on Motion Pictures and Television.** J.P. Tarcher, Los Angeles, 1983.

McCann, Graham. **Rebel Males: Clift, Brando and Dean.** Rutgers University Press, New Brunswick, New Jersey, 1991.

McCarthy, David. **The Golden Age of Rock.** Chartwell Books, Secaucus, New Jersey, 1990.

McDonogh, Pat and J. Bruce Baumann, editors. **Hoosiers.** Scripps Howard Publishing, New York, 1993.

McGee, Mark Thomas and R.J. Robetson. **The JD Films: Juvenile Delinquency in the Movies.** MacFarland, Jefferson, North Carolina, 1982.

McGilligan, Patrick. **Robert Altman: Jumping Off the Cliff.** St. Martin's Press, New York, 1989.

Mellen, Joan. **Big Bad Wolves: Masculinity in the American Film.** Pantheon Books, New York, 1977.

Michael, Paul. **The Academy Awards: A Pictorial History.** Bobbs-Merrill, Indianapolis, Indiana, 1964.

Millichap, Joseph R. **Steinbeck and Film.** Frederick Ungar Publishing Company, New York, 1983.

Minahan, John. **9/30/55.** Avon Books, New York, 1977.

Moore, Dick. **Twinkle Twinkle Little Star.** Harper and Row, New York, 1984.

Moore, Terry. **The Beauty and the Billionaire.** Pocket Books, New York, 1984.

Morella, Joe and Edward Epstein. **Brando: An Unauthorized Biography.** Crown Publishers, New York, 1973.

Morella, Joe and Edward Epstein. **Paul and Joanne: A Biography of Paul Newman and Joanne Woodward.** Delacourte Press, New York, 1988.

Morella, Joe and Edward Epstein. **Rebels: The Rebel Hero in Films.** Citadel Press, New York, 1971.

Morin, Edgar. **The Stars.** Translated by Richard Howard. Grove Press, New York, 1960.

Morino, Marianne. **The Hollywood Walk of Fame.** Ten Speed Press, Berkeley, California, 1987

Morrissey, Steven. **James Dean Is Not Dead.** Babylon Books, Great Britain, 1983.

The Movie Greats. Ventura Associates, New York, 1982.

Mrkich, D. **Summer Was Only Beginning: A Memoir of James Dean.** Commoners' Publishing Society, Ontario, Canada, 1997.

McCambridge, Mercedes. **The Quality of Mercy.** Times Books, New York, 1981.

Noble, A. **They Died Too Young: James Dean.** Parragon Book Service, Bristol, United Kingdom, 1995.

Norman, Barry. **The Story of Hollywood.** New American Library, New York, 1987.

Offen, Ron. **Brando.** Henry Regnery Company, Chicago, Illinois, 1973.

Oppenheimer, Jerry and Jack Vitek. **Idol: Rock Hudson.** Villard Books, New York, 1986.

Oumano, Elena. **Paul Newman.** St. Martin's Press, New York, 1989.

Pardini, Laura. **Buscando al ángel (notas sobre James Dean).** With English translation. Pamela J. Bixler, Marion, Indiana, 1998.

Parini, Jay. **John Steinbeck: A Biography.** William Heinemann, London, 1994.

Parish, James Robert. **Actors Television Credits.** Scarecrow Press, Toronto, 1973.

Parish, James Robert. **Gays and Lesbians in Mainstream Cinema.** McFarland, Jefferson, North Carolina, 1993

Parish, James Robert. **Great Movie Heroes.** Harper and Row, New York, 1975.

Parker, John. **Five for Hollywood.** Carol Publishing Group, New York, 1989.

Pauly, Thomas H. **An American Odyssey: Elia Kazan and American Culture.** Temple University Press, Philadelphia, Pennsylvania, 1983.

Peabody, Richard and Lucinda Ebersole. **mondo James Dean.** St. Martins Press, New York, 1996.

Pettigrew, Terrence. **Raising Hell: The Rebel in the Movies.** St. Martin's Press, New York, 1986.

Phillips, Gene D. **The Movie Makers: Artists in the Industry.** Nelson-Hall, Chicago, 1973.

Plecki, Gerard. **Robert Altman.** Twayne Publishers, Boston, Massachusetts, 1985.

Price, Nelson. **Indiana Legends: Famous Hoosiers From Johnny Appleseed to David Letterman.** Guild Press of Indiana, Carmel, Indiana, 1997.

Quirk, Lawrence J. **The Films of Paul Newman.** Citadel Press, Seacaucus, New Jersey, 1981.

Rees, Robert R. **James Dean: Beyond the Grave.** Empire, Incorporated, 1995.

Rees, Robert R. **James Dean's Trail: One Fan's Journey.** Empire, Incorporated, 1995.

Rees, Robert R. **Twilight Tales.** Empire, Incorporated, 1996.

Rhode, Eric. **A History of the Cinema: From its Origins to 1970.** Hill and Wang, New York, 1976.

Richie, Donald. **George Stevens: An American Romantic.** Museum of Modern Art, New York, 1970.

Riese, Randall. **The Unabridged James Dean.** Contemporary Books, Chicago, 1991.

Roberts, Monty. **The Man Who Listens to Horses.** Random House, New York, 1997.

Rock and Roll Explosion: Volume One, Story of Rock: The Sound Heard Round the World. S.F. Worthington Associates, New York, 1974.

Rodriguez, Elena. **Dennis Hopper: A Method to his Madness.** St. Martin's Press, New York, 1988.

Ross, Walter S. **The Immortal.** Simon and Schuster, New York, 1958.

Roth, Beulah and Sanford. **James Dean.** Pomegranate Books, New York, 1983.

Roth, Sanford. **The Memory of Last 85 Days: James Dean.** Japan, 1987.

Sarlot, Raymond R. and Fred E. Basten. **Life at the Marmont.** Roundable Publishing, Santa Monica, California, 1987.

Sarris, Andrew, editor. **Interviews with Film Directors.** Bobbs-Merrill, Indianapolis, Indiana, 1967.

Sayre, Nora. **Running Time: The Films of the Cold War.** Dial Press, New York, 1982.

Scaduto, Anthony. **Bob Dylan.** Grosset and Dunlop, New York, 1971.

Schary, Dore. **Heyday.** Little, Brown and Company, Boston, 1979.

Schatt, Roy. **James Dean: A Portrait.** Delilah Books, New York, 1982.

Schickel, Richard. **The Stars: The Personalities Who Made the Movies.** Bonanza Books, New York, 1962.

Schroeder, Alan. **James Dean.** Chelsea House Publishers, New York, 1994

Ray, Nicholas. **I Was Interrupted.** University of California Press, Berkeley, 1993.

Shepherd, Donald. **Jackl Nicholson: An Unauthorized Biography.** St. Martin's Press, New York, 1991.

Sheppard, Dick. **The Life and Career of Elizabeth Taylor.** Doubleday, Garden City, New York, 1991.

Shulman, Arthur and Roger Yourman. **The Television Years.** Popular Library, New York, 1973.

Sinclair, Marianne. **Those Who Died Young.** Plexus Publishing, London, 1979.

Skiles, Don. **The James Dean Jacket Story and Other Stories.** Cross Roads Press, Ellison Bay, Wisconsin, 1997.

Spoto, Donald. **Rebel: The Life and Legend of James Dean.** Harper Collins Publishers, New York, 1996.

St. Michael, Mick. **James Dean: In His Own Words.** Omnibus Press, Great Britian, 1989.

Steen, Mike. **Hollywood Speaks!** G.P. Putnam's Sons, New York, 1974.

Stephenson, Ralph and J.R. Debrix, **The Cinema as Art.** Penguin Books, London, 1967.

Stern, Phil. **Phil Stern's Hollywood Photographs, 1940-1979.** Alfred A. Knopf, New York, 1993.

Stock, Dennis. **James Dean Revisited.** Viking Press, New York, 1978.

Strasberg, Susan. **Bitter Sweet.** Putnam Books, New York, 1980

Stuart, Ray. **Immortals of the Screen.** Sherbourne Press, Los Angeles, 1965.

Tanitch, Robert. **The Unknown James Dean.** B. t. Batsford Limited, London, 1997.

Tanner, Louise. **Here Today . . .** Thomas Crowell Company, New York, 1959.

Tashman, George. **I Love You, Clark Gable, Etc.: Male Sex Symbols of the Silver Screen.** Brombacher Books, Richmond, California, 1976.

Taylor, Elizabeth. **An Informal Memoir.** Harper and Row, New York, 1965.

Taylor, John Russell. **Alec Guinness: A Celebration.** Pavilion Books, London, 1984.

Thomas, Bob. **Marlon: Portrait of the Rebel as an Artist.** Random House, New York, 1973.

Thomas, T.T. **I, James Dean.** Popular Library, New York, 1957.

Thomson, David. **A Biographical Dictionary of Film.** William Morrow and Company, New York, 1976.

Tice, George. **Hometowns: An American Pilgrimage.** Graphic Society Books, Boston, 1988.

Toperoff, Sam. **James Dean Prepares.** Granta Books, London, 1997.

Tornabene, Lyn. **Long Live the King: A Biography of Clark Gable.** G.P. Putnam's Sons, New York, 1976.

Tresidder, Jack. **Heart-Throbs.** Crescent Books, New York, 1974.

Turner, Adrian. **Hollywood 1950s.** Gallery Books, New York, 1986.

Tyler, Parker. **Screening the Sexes: Homosexuality in the Movies.** Holt, Rinehart and Winston, New York, 1972.

Van Doren, Mamie. **Playing the Field.** G.P. Putnam's Sons, New York, 1987.

Vermilye, Jerry and Mark Ricci. **The Films of Elizabeth Taylor.** Citadel Press, Seacaucus, New Jersey, 1976.

Vinson, James, editor. **The International Dictionary of Films and Filmmakers.** St. James Press, Chicago, Illinois, 1986.

Volpe, Dante. **The Last James Dean Book.** William Morrow and Company, New York, 1984.

Von Frankenberg, Richard. **Porsche: The Man and his Cars.** Robert Bentley Incorporated, Cambridge, Massachusetts, 1961.

Walker, Alexander. **Stardom: The Hollywood Phenomenon.** Stein and Day, New York, 1970.

Wallace, Irving, Amy Wallace, David Wallenchinsky and Sylvia Wallace. **The Intimate Sex Lives of Famous People.** Delacourte Press, New York, 1981.

Ward, Baldwin H. **Year: The Annual Picture History.** Year, Incorporated, Wilton, Connecticut, 1956.

The Warner Brothers Golden Anniversary Book. Film and Venture Corporation, New York, 1973.

Waterbury, Ruth. **Elizabeth Taylor: Her Life, Her Loves, Her Future.** Appleton-Century, New York, 1964.

Dean Related Books

Weis, Wlizabeth, editor. **The International Society of Film Critics on the Movie Star.** Viking Penguin, New York, 1981.

Wenders, Wim and Chris Sievernich. **Nick's Film: Lightning Over Water.** Zweitausendeins, Frankfurt, Germany, 1981.

Whitman, Mark. **The Films of James Dean.** Greenhaven Press, New York, 1974.

Wilding, Michael and Pamela Wilcox. **The Wilding Way.** St. Martin's Press, New York, 1982.

Wiley, Mason and Damien Bona. **Inside Oscar.** Ballantine Books, New York, 1986.

Wilkerson, Tichi and Marcia Borie. **Hollywood Legends: The Golden Years of the Hollywood Reporter.** Tate Weaver Publishing, Los Angeles, 1988.

Wilkerson, Tichi and Marcia Borie. **The Hollywood Reporter: The Golden Years.** Coward-McCann, New York, 1984.

Wilkie, Jane. **Confessions of an Ex-Fan Magazine Writer.** Doubleday and Company, New York, 1981.

Winters, Shelley. **Shelley: Also Known as Shirley.** William Morrow and Company, New York, 1980.

Winters, Shelley. **Shelley II: The Middle of My Century.** Simon and Schuster, New York, 1989.

Wood, Lana. **Natalie: A Memoir by her Sister.** G.P. Putnam's Sons, New York, 1984.

Zinman, David. **50 from the '50s.** Arlington House Publishers, New Rochelle, New York, 1979.

Dean Related Books of the Movies

These are the books of James Dean's movies. Linder's psychological study supplied only the title for Dean's second film. Shulman was one of the screenwriters on that project, and turned his draft of the script into a novel the following year. Dean was scheduled to do the film version of Graziano's biography when he died, a role that was then given to Paul Newman.

Shulman, Irving, **Children of the Dark.** Henry Holt and Company, New York, 1956.

Steinbeck, John. **East of Eden.** Viking Press, New York, 1952.

Lindner, Robert. **Rebel Without a Cause.** Grune and Stratton, New York, 1944.

Ferber, Edna. **Giant.** Doubleday, New York, 1952.

Graziano, Rocky with Rowland Barber. **Somebody Up There Likes Me.** Simon and Schuster, New York, 1955.

The Scholarly James Dean

Serious scholars have occasionally focused their attention on James Dean. Tysl's thesis laid the groundwork for the serious study of Dean as a cultural phenomenon, and at 670 pages is the longest of the Dean books. Professor James Hopgood has continued that investigation with excellent pieces in the Ferrante, Rogers and Salamone books. The Lewison text includes a case study of the James Dean Memorial Gallery by Douglas Hausknecht and Kevin Casper.

Ferrante, Joan and Prince Brown, Jr. **The Social Construction of Race and Ethnicity in the United States.** Addison Wesley Longman, New York, 1998.

Ferrante, Joan. **Sociology: A Global Perspective.** Wadsworth Incorporated, Belmont, California, 1992.

Lerner, Max. **America as a Civilization: Culture and Personality** (Vol. Two). Simon and Schuster, New York, 1957.

Lewison, Dale M. **Retailing.** Macmillan Publishing, New York, 1991.

Richards, Jack C., Jonathan Hull and Susan Proctor. **Interchange: English for International Communication.** Cambridge University Press, Cambridge, United Kingdom, 1991.

Rogers, Linda. **Wish I Were: Felt Pathways of the Self.** Atwood Publishing, Madison, Wisconsin, 1998.

Salamone, Frank A. and Walter Randolph Adams. **Explorations in Anthropology and Theology.** University Press of America, Lanham, Maryland, 1997.

Tysl, Robert Wayne. **Continuity and Evolution in a Public Symbol: An Investigation into the Creation and Communication of the James Dean Image in Mid-Century America.** Michigan State University Press, Michigan, 1965.

Plays and Dramatic Readings

During his acting career, Dean participated in many plays and dramatic readings. First edition information is provided here for works released in book form only, though many of the plays have been pulbished in various forms.

An Apple From Coles County Bars.
Chekhov, Anton. **The Sea Gull.**
Dickens, Charles. **Madman's Manuscript.** (adapted from his novel **The Pickwick Papers).**
Duffield, Brainerd, Helen Leary and Nolan Leary. **Mooncalf Mugford.**
Goetz, Ruth and Augustus Goetz. **The Immoralist: A Drama in Three Acts** (based on the book by Andre Gide).
Goon With The Wind.
Jacob, W.W. **The Monkey's Paw.**
Kafka, Franz. **The Metamorphosis.**
Kaufman, George S. and Moss Hart. **You Can't Take It With You.**
Kerr, Jean. **Our Hearts Were Young and Gay** (based on the book by Cornelia Otis Skinner and Emily Kimbrough).
MacKay, Percy. **The Scarecrow** (based on a story by Nathaniel Hawthorne).
Pound, Ezra. **The Women of Trachis** (adapted from Sophocles).
The Romance of Scarlet Gulch.
Shakespeare, William. **Macbeth.**
Shakespeare, William. **Hamlet.**
She Was Only a Farmer's Daughter.
St. Vincent Millay, Edna. **Aria da Capo.**
To Them That Sleep in Darkness.
White, Christine. **Ripping Off Layers to Find Roots.**
Willingham, Calder. **End As A Man.**

Dean himself has also provided inspirations for more than a few playwrights. The following is a partial listing of Dean-themed stage plays.

Graczyke, Ed. **Come Back to the Five and Dime, Jimmy Dean, Jimmy Dean.**
Howlett, John. **Dean.**
Leone, Patricia. **James Dean: A Dress Rehearsal.**
Musical Selections from Rebel: The James Dean Musical
Rowe, Dana and Trevina Kapchan. **Occurance Near the Chalome Creek Bridge.**

Book Collecting Terms

- As issued - in original condition
- Association - copy that belonged to author or someone associated with book.
- Edition - total number of books printed from one set of plates or from one setting of type. Impression or printing refers to the number of copies printed at one time. For collectors, first edition usually means first impression.
- Errata - sheet added after binding, indicating errors.
- Ex-library - marked as formerly part of library collection.
- Foxing - spotting caused by the reaction of moisture to particles in paper.
- Points - differences between one issue of a book and another.
- Provenance - history of ownership.
- Re-backed - book given new spine.
- Sophisticated - book that has had pages added or replaced from other copies.
- Unopened - book in which sheet folds along the edge of pages haven't been cut.
- Variants - copies of a particular edition, different from other editions because of misprints, changes made in printings, or other mistakes.

This Fabulous Century: 1950-1960. Time-Life Books, New York, 1970.

Fact

Stephen Morrissey, lead singer of the British rock group The Smiths, is not only a Dean fan, he is also a Dean biographer. Morrissey's **James Dean Is Not Dead** was released in Britian in 1983.

Rumor

Rumor has it that Morrissey's original title for his book was **James Dead Is Not Dean,** but an overzealous proofreader caught what was assumed to be a mistake and made the "correction."

What Did James Dean Read?

Balderston, John L. **Goddess to a God.**
Bernstein, Joseph M., editor. **Baudelaire, Rimbaud, Verlaine**
The Best Plays of 1950-1951.
The Bible.
The Burns Mantle Best Plays of 1947-1948.
The Burns Mantle Best Plays of 1949-1950.
Casteel, Homer. **The Running of the Bulls.**
Chekov, Michael. **To The Actor.**
Conrad, Barnaby. **The Matador.**
de Cossio, Jose Maria. **Los Toros.**
DeMille, Agnes. **Dance to the Piper**
Gamow, George. **Creation of the Universe.**
Gorchakov, Nikolai M. **Stanislavsky Directs.**
Harris, Larry A. **Pancho Villa**
Heard, Gerald. **Pain, Sex, and Time.**
Hemingway, Ernest. **Death in the Afternoon.**
Honig, Edwin. **Garcia Lorca.**
Kafka, Franz. **Selectred Short Stories of Franz Kafka.**
Kelly, Walt. **I go Pogo.**
La Mure, Pierre. **Moulin Rouge.**
Lane, Carl D. **How to Sail.**
Lawrence, T. E. **Seven Pillars of Wisdom.**
Lumsden, E.S. **The Art of Etching**
Mann, Thomas. **Death in Venice.**
Porter, Katherine Anne. **Flowering Judas.**
Reshevsky, Sammy and Fred Reinfeld. **Learn Chess Fast.**
Riley, James Whitcomb. **The Complete Works of James Whitcomb Riley.**
Saint-Exupéry, Antoine de. **The Little Prince.**
Seton, Marie. **Eisenstein: A Biography.**
Shakespeare, William. **The Collected Shakespeare.**
White, E.B. **Charlotte's Web.**
Wilde, Oscar. **De Profundis.**
Williams, Tennessee and Donald Windham. **You Touched Me!**

The following books were presented by Dean to his friend Bill Bast:

Maurois, Andre. **The Andre Maurois Reader.**
McCullers, Carson. **The Heart is a Lonely Hunter.**
Woolf, Virginia. **Orlando.**

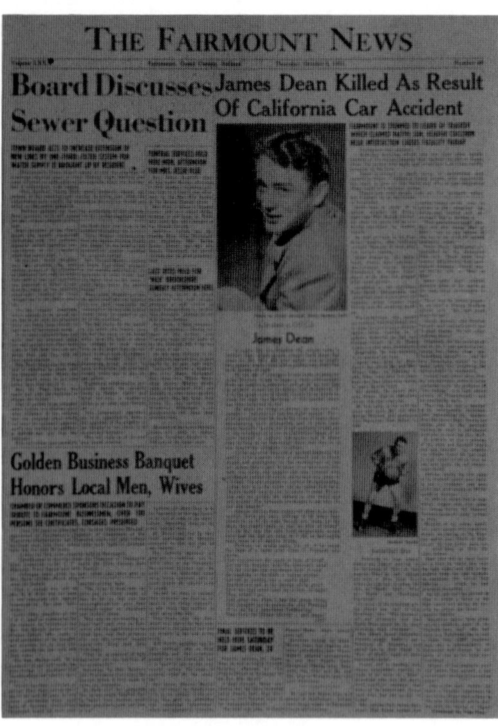
THE FAIRMOUNT NEWS

Board Discusses Sewer Question

James Dean Killed As Result Of California Car Accident

James Dean

Golden Business Banquet Honors Local Men, Wives

The Fairmount News
October 6, 1955

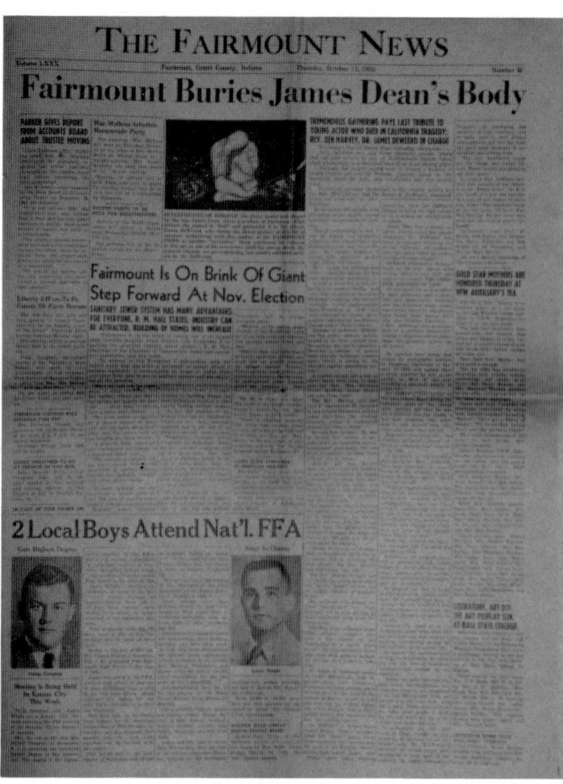
THE FAIRMOUNT NEWS

Fairmount Buries James Dean's Body

Fairmount Is On Brink Of Giant Step Forward At Nov. Election

2 Local Boys Attend Nat'l. FFA

The Fairmount News
October 13, 1955

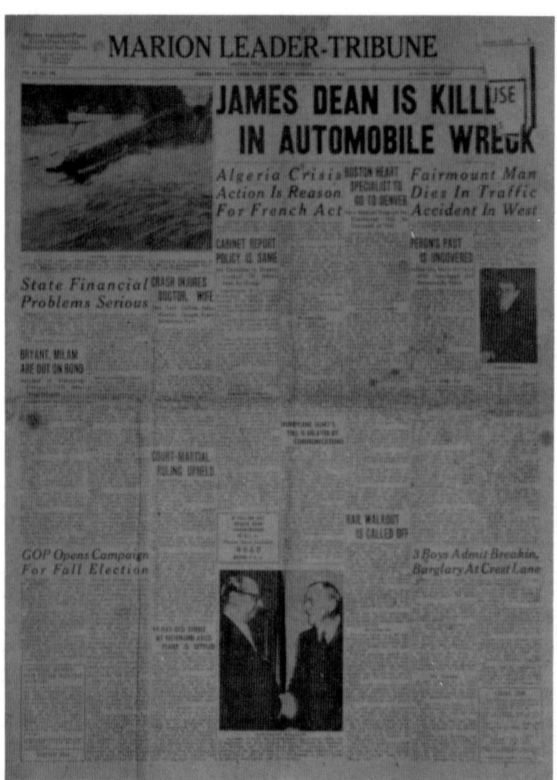
MARION LEADER-TRIBUNE

JAMES DEAN IS KILLED IN AUTOMOBILE WRECK

Algeria Crisis Action Is Reason For French Act

Fairmount Man Dies In Traffic Accident In West

State Financial Problems Serious

GOP Opens Campaign For Fall Election

3 Boys Admit Breakin, Burglary At Crest Lane

Marion Leader-Tribune
October 1, 1955

MARION SUNDAY
CHRONICLE-TRIBUNE

PERFECT CIRCLE PEACE TALKS ARE SLATED

Chronicle Tribune, Marion, Indiana
"Last Rites for James Dean"
October 9, 1955

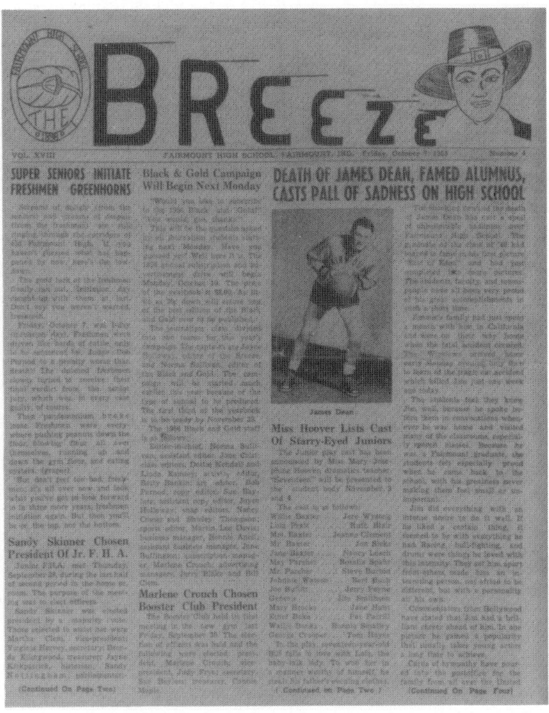
BREEZE

THE

SUPER SENIORS INITIATE FRESHMEN GREENHORNS

Black & Gold Campaign Will Begin Next Monday

DEATH OF JAMES DEAN, FAMED ALUMNUS, CASTS PALL OF SADNESS ON HIGH SCHOOL

Sandy Skinner Chosen President Of Jr. F. H. A.

Marlene Crouch Chosen Booster Club President

Miss Hoover Lists Cast Of Starry-Eyed Juniors

(Continued On Page Two)

(Continued On Page Four)

The Breeze, Fairmount High School
October 7, 1955

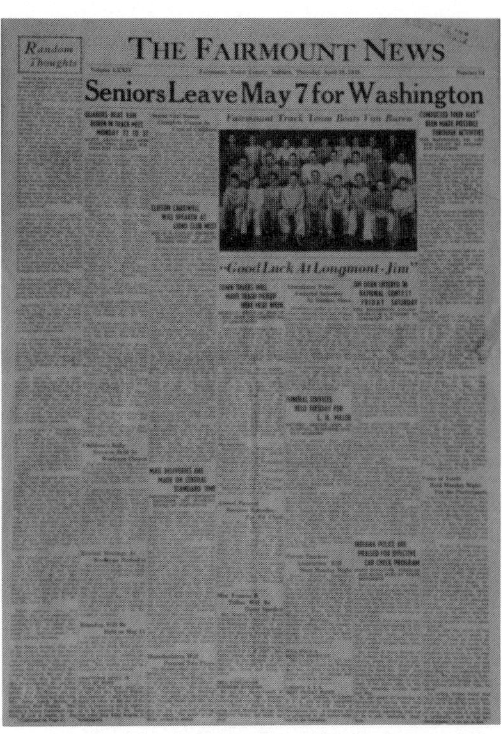
Random Thoughts

THE FAIRMOUNT NEWS

Seniors Leave May 7 for Washington

Fairmount Track Team Beats Van Buren

"Good Luck At Longmont-Jim"

The Fairmount News
April 28, 1949
"Good Luck at Longmont, Jim"

TROJAN NEWS

VOL. XI, NO. 24 LONGMONT, COLORADO THURSDAY, APRIL 28, 1949

National Forensic League Holds All-State Meet In Longmont; City Welcomes Speech Contestants

CITY GOES WESTERN FOR SPEECH MEET

He Is Tournament Manager

COLLEGE FACULTY ACTS AS JUDGES

Six Delegates Represent L. H. S. in National Meet

National Speech Meet Cancels School Friday

Trojan News - Longmont High School, Colorado
April 28, 1949

THE FAIRMOUNT NEWS

C Of C Approves Intersection Light

2,000 Persons Attend Dean Remembrane Service Sun.

Town Board Revamps Controls At City Dump After Protests

Intermediate Girl Scouts Organize Here

Jackets Fall For Quakers 19-13

The Fairmount News
October 4, 1956

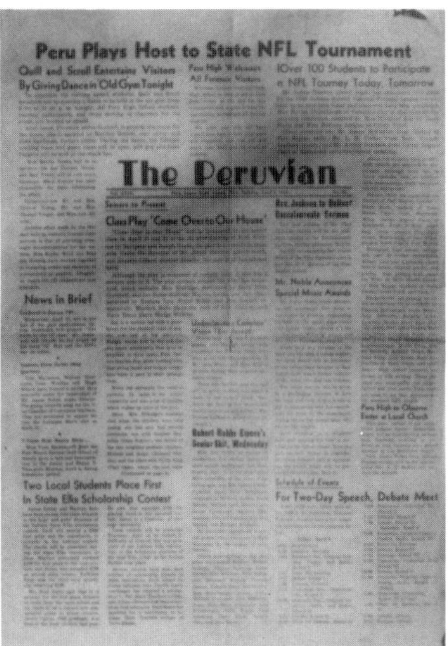

Peru Plays Host to State NFL Tournament

Quill and Scroll Entertains Visitors By Giving Dance in Old Gym Tonight

Over 100 Students to Participate in NFL Tourney Today, Tomorrow

The Peruvian

Class Play 'Come Over to Our House'

News in Brief

Two Local Students Place First In State Elks Scholarship Contest

For Two-Day Speech, Debate Meet

The Peruvian - Peru Indiana High School - April 28, 1949

This article lists participants in the National Forensic League State Tournament. James Dean placed First in the Dramatic Declamation event.

The LONGMONT LEDGER

National High School Speaking Champions Will Be Crowned In Longmont After Finals Saturday Night

Candidates For School Board Posts Speak On The Job Ahead For Schools

The Longmont Colorado Ledger
April 29, 1949

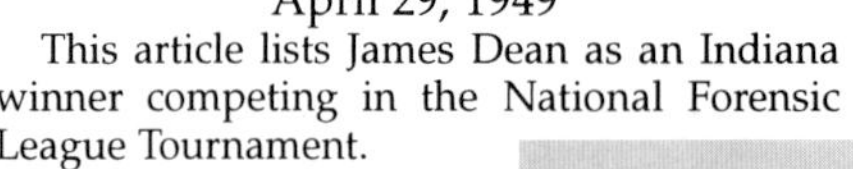

This article lists James Dean as an Indiana winner competing in the National Forensic League Tournament.

THE NEWS-HERALD

James Dean

F.O.G.

LOG

The News Herald, Marion, Indiana
December 4, 1964

Welcome to Longmont National Forensic League

Delegates Flock Into Longmont for National Forensic League Meet

LONGMONT TIMES-CALL

Even a Robin Gets Help in the Spring

TRUMAN HOPEFUL STALIN WILL END BLOCKADE SOON

NAVY READY TO REMOVE AMERICANS

WALKER JURY TO BE IN BOX BY TONIGHT

Tourney Chief

Family of Philippines' First President Slain and Robbed

The Longmont Colorado Times-Call
April 28, 1949

IN MEMORY OF JAMES DEAN

THE FAIRMOUNT NEWS

James Dean Killed As Result Of California Car Accident

Last Rites Will Be

The Fairmount News

This special edition has been reprinted several times since 1956

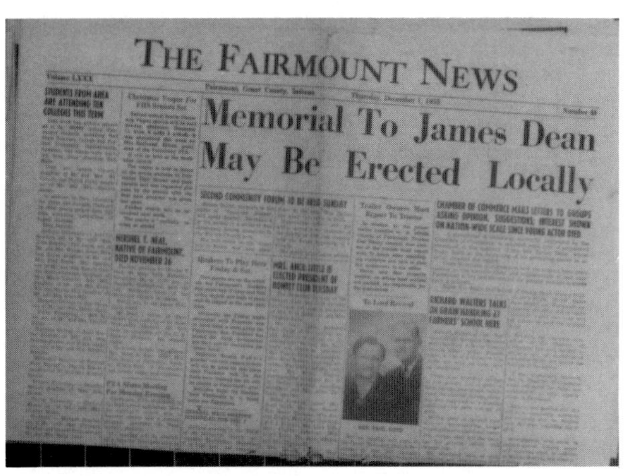

THE FAIRMOUNT NEWS

Memorial To James Dean May Be Erected Locally

The Fairmount News - December 1, 1955

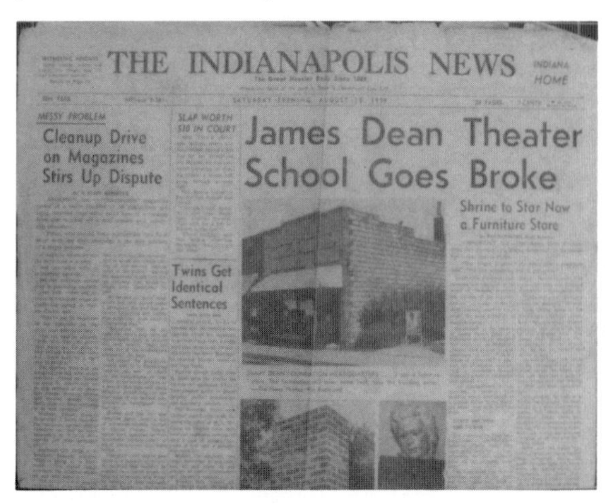

THE INDIANAPOLIS NEWS

Cleanup Drive on Magazines Stirs Up Dispute

James Dean Theater School Goes Broke

Shrine to Star Now a Furniture Store

Twins Get Identical Sentences

The Indianapolis News - August 15, 1959

Newspapers

Chronicle Tribune
JAMES DEAN
COOLER
9/30/55
Fairmount bids farewell to Dean
PG:2 PG:3 PG:4 PG:5 PG:6

Chronicle Tribune, Marion, Indiana - Sept. 25-27, 1992

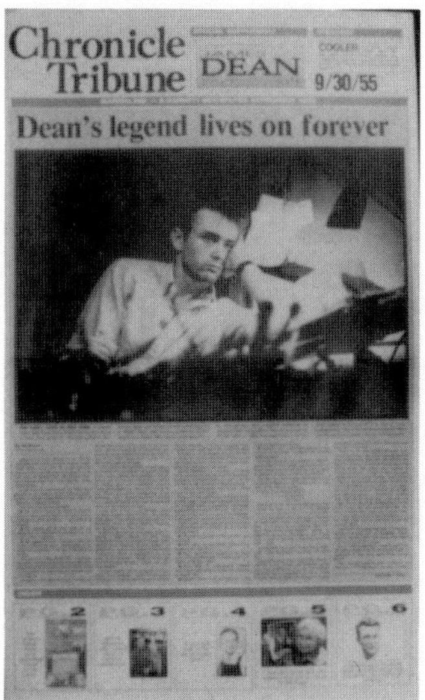
Chronicle Tribune
JAMES DEAN
COOLER
9/30/55
Dean's legend lives on forever

Chronicle Tribune, Marion, Indiana - Sept. 24-26, 1993

Chronicle Tribune
JAMES DEAN
COOLER
9/30/55
JIMMY!
A friend's-eye view of a legend's youth

Chronicle Tribune, Marion, Indiana - Sept. 23-25, 1994

James Dean
A look at James Dean from A to Z

Chronicle Tribune, Marion, Indiana - Sept. 27-29, 1996

James Dean
Fairmount celebrates Dean without its beloved Adeline
Through the looking glass

Chronicle Tribune, Marion, Indiana - Sept. 26-28, 1997

FAIRMOUNT'S
Golden BOY
JAMES DEAN
Chronicle-Tribune

Chronicle Tribune, Marion, Indiana - Sept. 25-27, 1998

LIVING
They love L.A.
James Dean
Legend survives in Fairmount

Ft. Wayne, Indiana Journal Gazette - Feb. 8, 1991

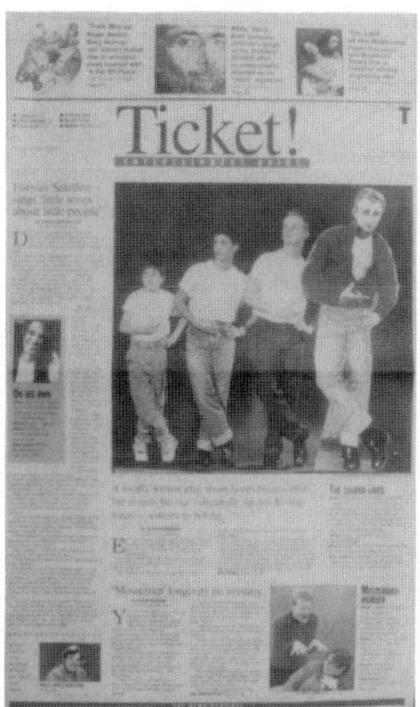
Ticket!

Ft. Wayne, Indiana News Sentinel - Mar. 11, 1993

Weekend
THE DEAN SCENE
Our Picks
Brad Pitt not just a pretty face
'The Age of Innocence' is a delicate feast
Ready for a Mac attack?

Indianapolis Star September 24, 1993

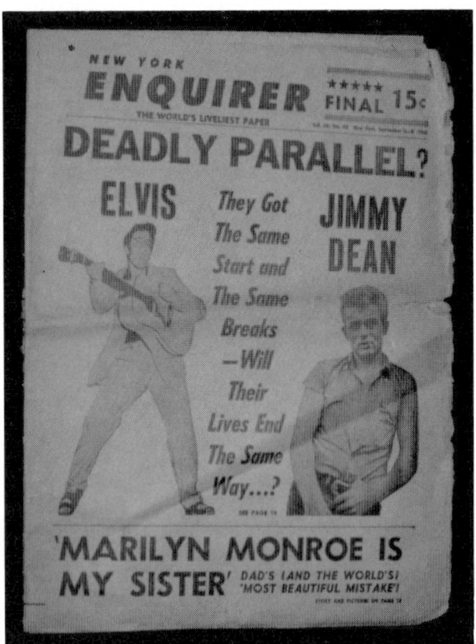

NEW YORK
ENQUIRER
★★★★★ FINAL 15¢
THE WORLD'S LIVELIEST PAPER
DEADLY PARALLEL?
ELVIS
JIMMY DEAN
They Got The Same Start and The Same Breaks —Will Their Lives End The Same Way...?
'MARILYN MONROE IS MY SISTER'
DAD'S (AND THE WORLD'S) 'MOST BEAUTIFUL MISTAKE'

New York Enquirer
September 3-8, 1956

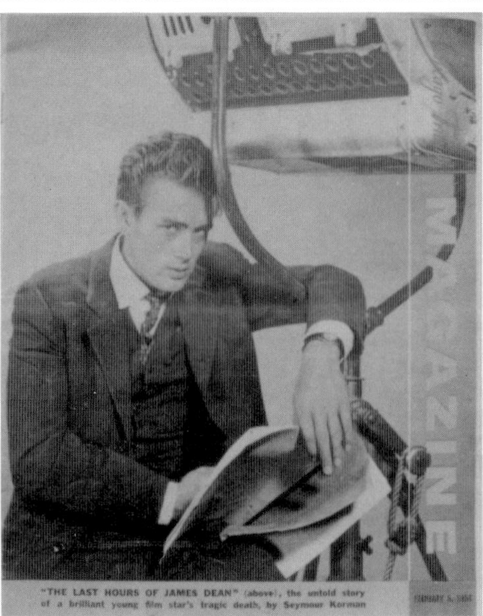

MAGAZINE
"THE LAST HOURS OF JAMES DEAN" (above), the untold story of a brilliant young film star's tragic death, by Seymour Korman

Chicago Tribune Magazine
February 5, 1956

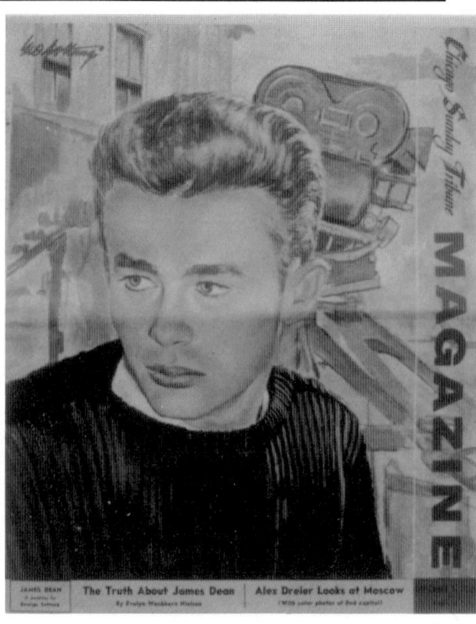

Chicago Sunday Tribune
MAGAZINE
The Truth About James Dean
Alex Dreier Looks at Moscow

Chicago Sunday Tribune Magazine
September 9, 1956

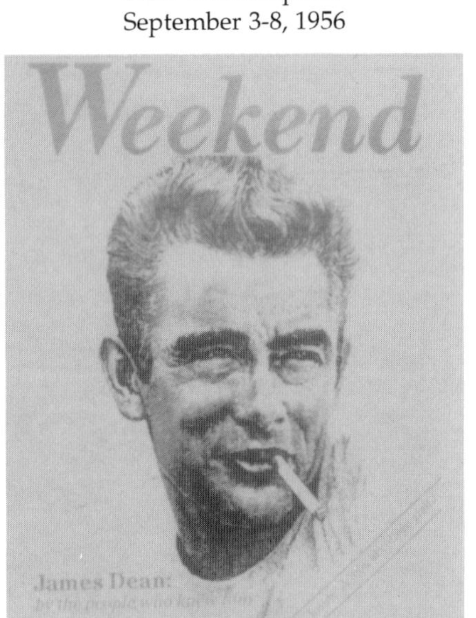

Weekend
James Dean:

Muncie Indiana Weekend
September 10, 1982

THE REPOSITORY
TICKET
ETERNAL COOL
Inside the myth of James Dean

Canton, Ohio Repository
July 29, 1994

CT
Magazine
James Byron Dean

Chronicle Tribune Magazine
Marion, Indiana - September 28, 1980

Friday
REMEMBERING
JIMMY DEAN

New York Daily News
September 28, 1980

Leisure
A quarter of a century later, the world is still awed by the name
JAMES DEAN

New York Daily News - 9-24-95

DAILY NEWS
SUNDAY Spotlight
James Dean's New York
Where to go...
What to see...
4 PAGE ANNIVERSARY SPECIAL

New York Daily News
March 25, 1983

Radio Cinema Television
France - April 15, 1956

Radio Cinema Television
France - March 31, 1957

Amis du film
et de la T.V. (Tout-Ciné)

21 Novembre 1956

MORT AU CINEMA

REBELLES SANS CAUSE ou LA FUREUR DE VIVRE

ENFANTS..

..AU CINEMA

Amid du Film
Belguim - November 21, 1956

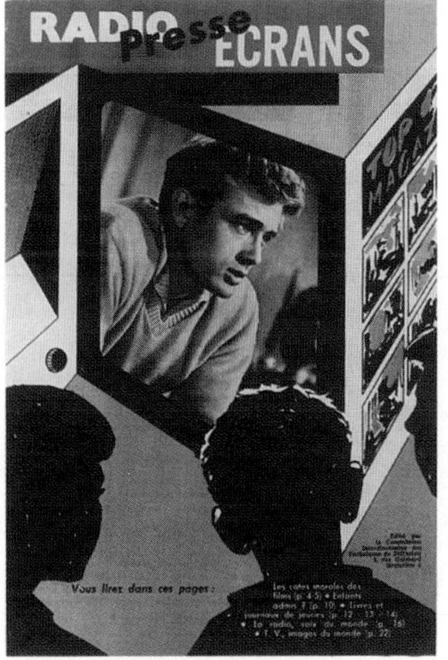

Radio Presse Ecrans
Belgium - 1958

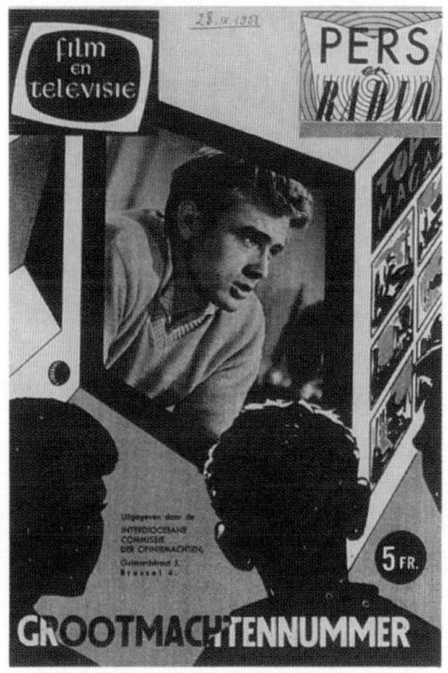

Film en Televisie
Belgium - September 28, 1958

Amis du Film
France - May-June 1957

Ecran - Chile - Sept. 24, 1957

Ecran - Chile - Sept. 20, 1963

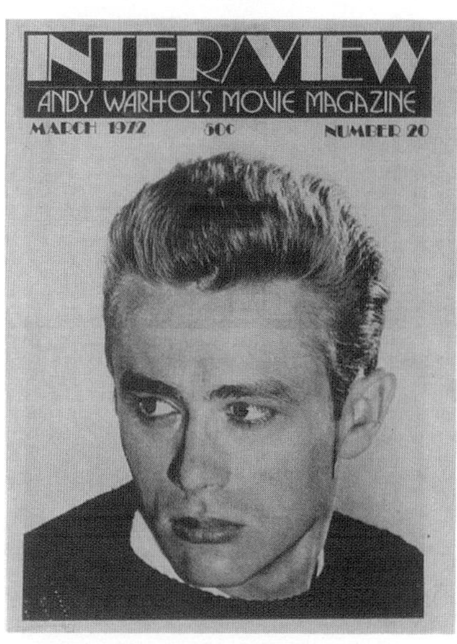

Interview - March 1972

Film Collectors World
December 15, 1978

Nostalgia World #3
USA - 1978

Samedi - Belguim
Sept. 19, 1964

New York Newsday
Sept. 26, 1985

New Musical Express
England - Oct. 20, 1973

Rolling Stone
June 20, 1974 - USA

Performance Monthly
September 1985 - USA

Louisville Times
Feb. 7-14, 1976 - USA

The Fresno Bee
Fresno California
September 24, 1995

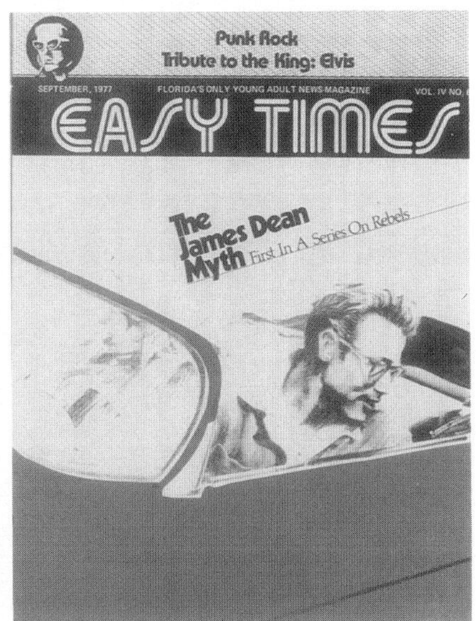

Easy Times
USA - September 1977

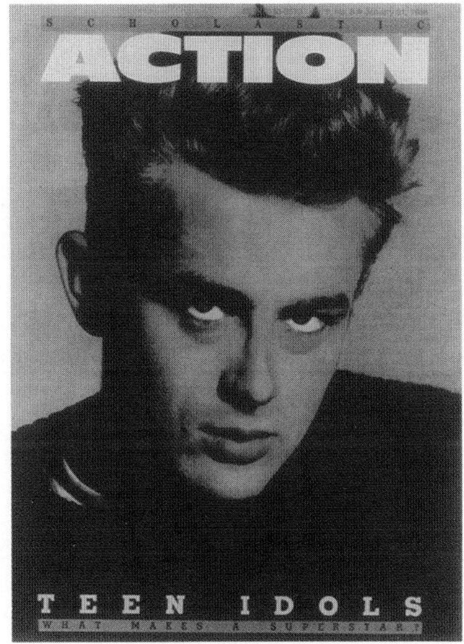

Scholastic Action
USA - January 31, 1986

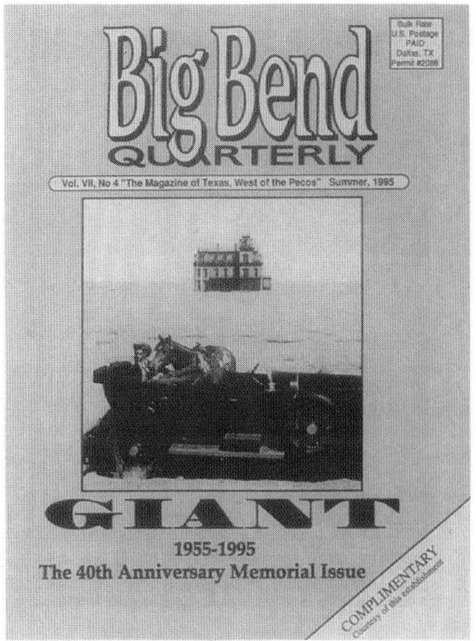

Big Bend Quarterly
USA - Summer 1995

Screen News - Australia - 1957

Hollywood Star Vol. 1 #9
USA - 1977

Yesterday
USA - 1983

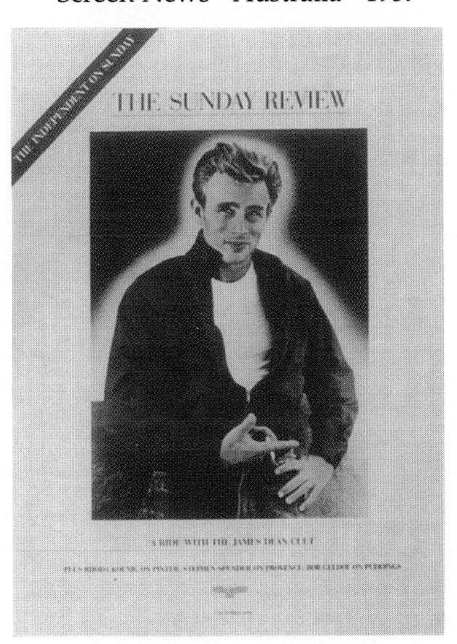

England - Oct. 7, 1990

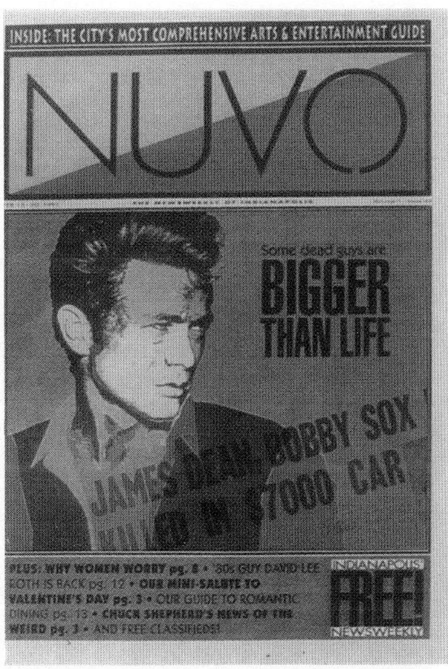

Indianapolis IN - Feb. 13-20, 1991

New York - April 14, 1993

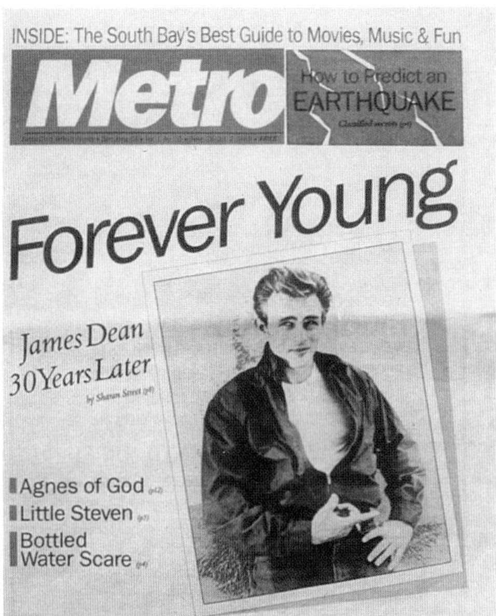
INSIDE: The South Bay's Best Guide to Movies, Music & Fun

Metro

How to Predict an EARTHQUAKE

Forever Young

James Dean 30 Years Later

Agnes of God

Little Steven

Bottled Water Scare

Santa Clara's Metro - Sept. 26 - Oct. 2, 1985

The Fairmount Reporter

Fairmount's James Dean

Nostalgia Shop Opens In Town

The Fairmount Reporter Vol.1 #1
Summer 1992

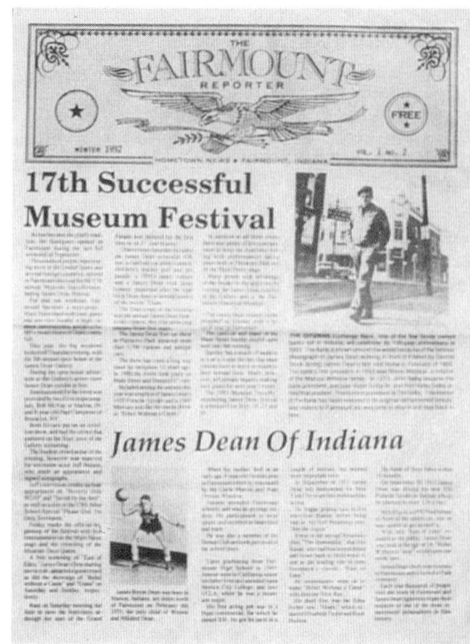
The Fairmount Reporter

17th Successful Museum Festival

James Dean Of Indiana

The Fairmount Reporter Vol. 1 #2
Winter 1992

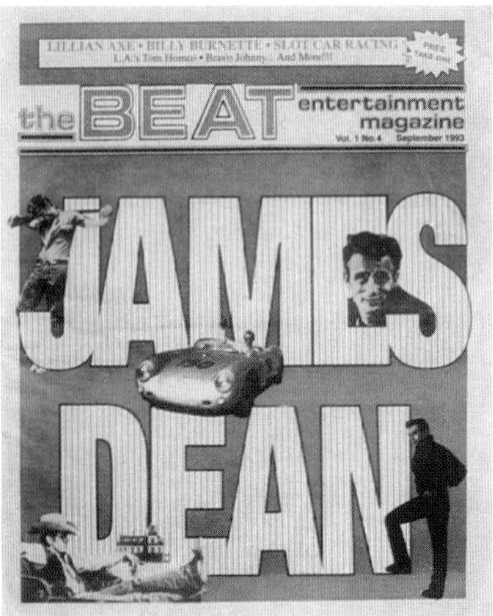
LILLIAN AXE • BILLY BURNETTE • SLOT CAR RACING

the BEAT entertainment magazine

Vol. 1 No. 4 September 1993

JAMES DEAN

The Beat - Highland, IN - Sept. 1993

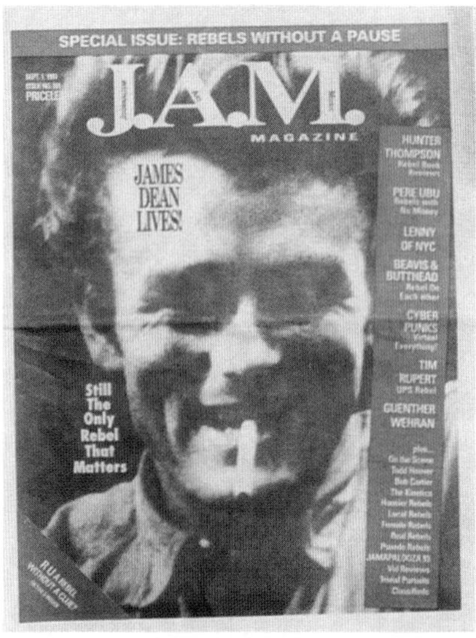
SPECIAL ISSUE: REBELS WITHOUT A PAUSE

J.A.M. MAGAZINE

JAMES DEAN LIVES!

Still The Only Rebel That Matters

J.A.M. Magazine - South Bend, IN - Sept. 1993

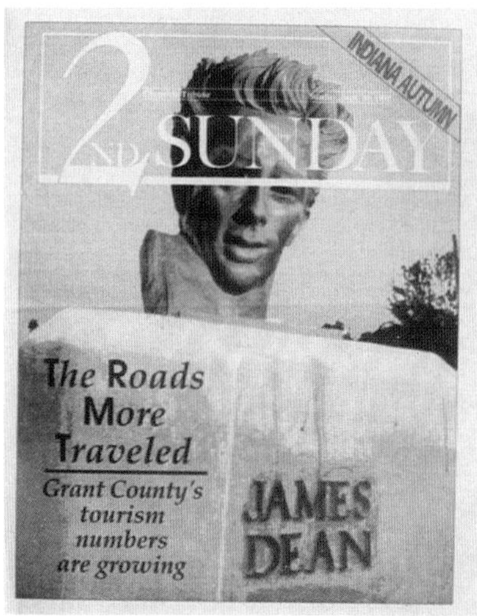
INDIANA AUTUMN

2ND SUNDAY

The Roads More Traveled

Grant County's tourism numbers are growing

JAMES DEAN

Chronicle Tribune - Marion, IN - Sept. 1995

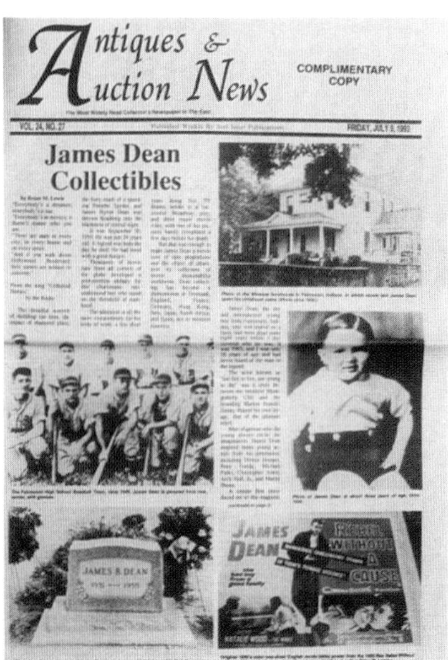
Antiques & Auction News

COMPLIMENTARY COPY

James Dean Collectibles

Antiques Auction News - Mt. Joy, PA
July 9, 1993

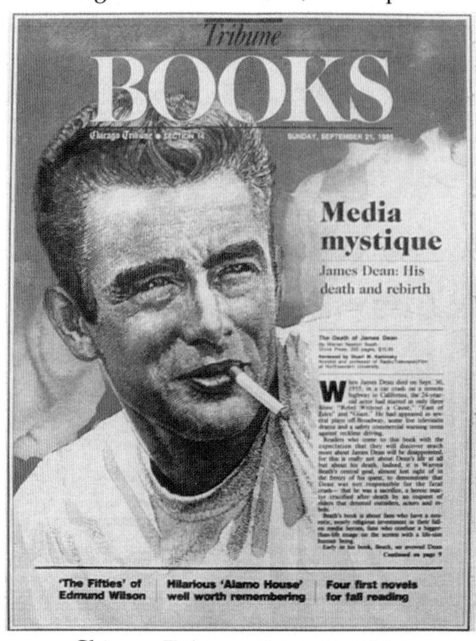
Tribune

BOOKS

SUNDAY, SEPTEMBER 21, 1986

Media mystique

James Dean: His death and rebirth

'The Fifties' of Edmund Wilson

Hilarious 'Alamo House' well worth remembering

Four first novels for fall reading

Chicago Tribune - Sept. 21, 1986

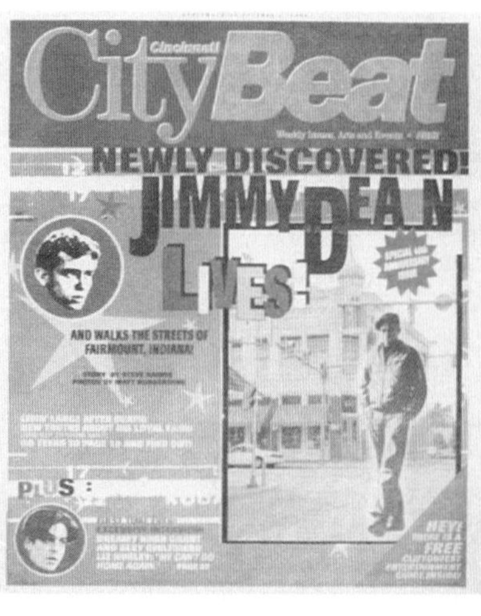
Cincinnati CityBeat

NEWLY DISCOVERED!

JIMMY DEAN LIVES

AND WALKS THE STREETS OF FAIRMOUNT, INDIANA!

PLUS

Cincinnati City Beat - Cincinnati, OH
Sept. 26 - Oct. 2, 1996

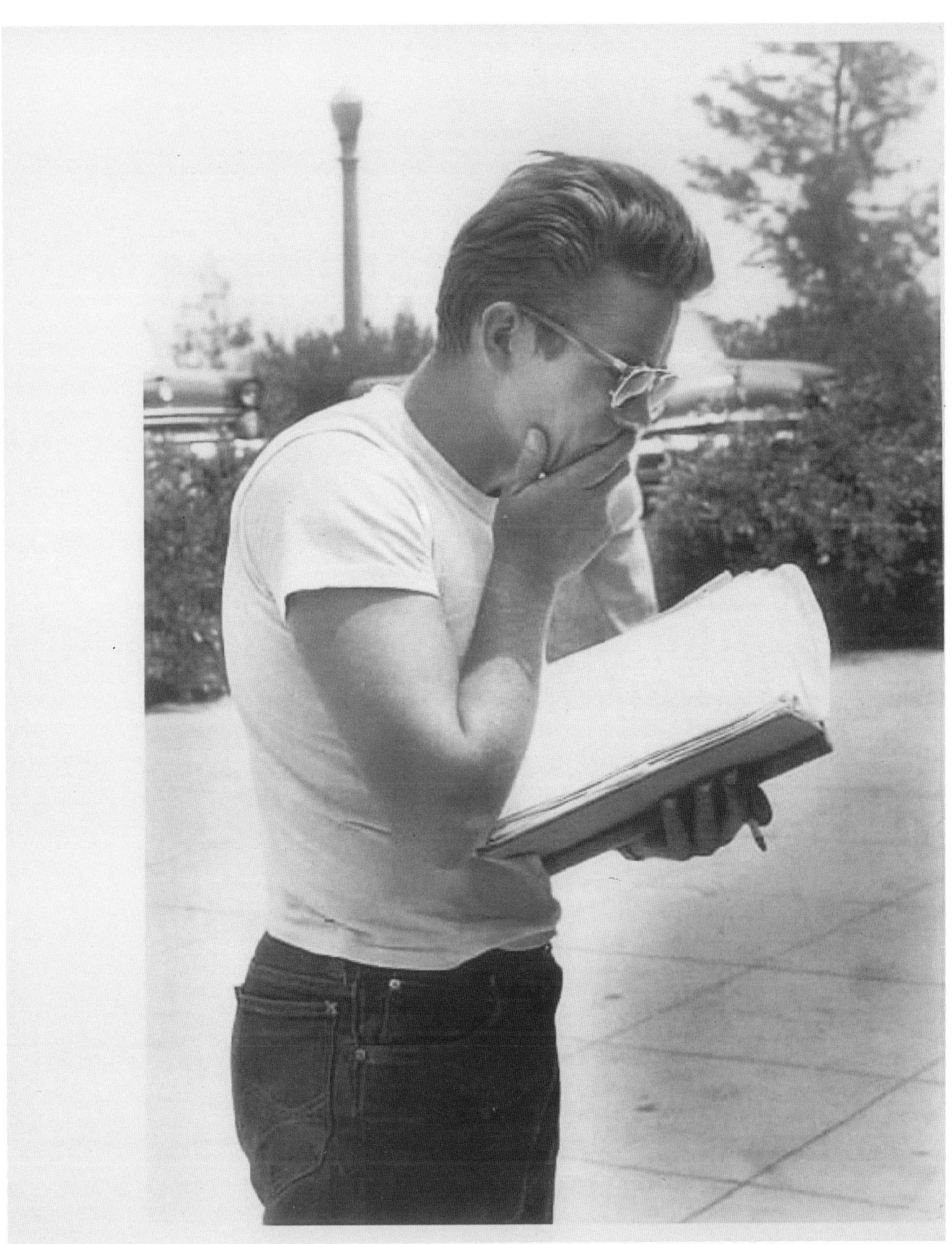

Magazines

"I came to Hollywood to act, not to charm society . . . the objective artist has always been misunderstood. I probably should have a press agent. But I don't care what people write about me. I'll talk to (reporters) I like; the others can print whatever they please."

Speaking to writer Bob Thomas in 1955, James Dean had no way of knowing what the future would hold. Hundreds of thousands of pages have been devoted to his mercurial personality and meteoric career. Praising, condemning, analyzing, hypothesizing, hundreds of writers have indeed printed "whatever they please."

Magazines are one of the favorite Dean collectibles, and with good reason. There are plenty of them. They are colorful and interesting. They don't require a lot of space and are easy to care for. Best of all, even the most expensive can be purchased for prices in the hundred dollar range. For many collectors, magazines offer the perfect combination of challenge and expense. There is plenty of room for variation in a magazine collection. Some choose to limit themselves to photo covers, others to movie fan titles from the fifties or articles about a particular film. Some overly ambitious types expand their focus to include any publication that makes even the slightest reference to Dean.

Of the magazines, a few stand out. The four tribute magazines published in 1956 *(The Real James Dean Story, Jimmy Dean Returns!, Official James Dean Anniversary Book,* and *James Dean Album)* were among the first James Dean collectibles intended specifically as such. Consisting mostly of rehashes of previously published information (or misinformation), they were nontheless "must have" items for any grieving fan. More than four decades later, they form the core of many Dean magazine collections. Another area of particular interest are the articles that appeared during Dean's lifetime. Of these, Dennis Stock's photo-essay that appeared in *Life* (M arch 7, 1955) is by far the best known.

Caring for Magazines

For the most part, magazines should be cared for in the same manner as any other paper collectible. As with books, preservation of magazines is complicated by the impossibility of separating individual pages from each other. The poor quality of paper used in many magazines, especially those from the 1950s, further exacerbates the problem.

Wood pulp paper is full of acidic impurities that break down when exposed to oxygen or ultraviolet light. These papers will often be significantly yellowed after only a few years. In little more than a decade, the paper can be too brittle to fold without breaking.

Protect magazines by placing them in Mylar bags along with a stiff, acid-free backing board. Thus supported, store them upright in boxes, packed tight enough to eliminate leaning. The tops of the bags should be left open. While exposure to air is harmful, prevention of the release of the acids within the paper is much more so.

As with virtually any type of memorabilia, condition of magazines is crucial. Tears, yellowing, dog-eared corners and loose pages or covers all detract heavily from an issue's value. Although many Dean-related magazines are hard to find, very good copies of most do still circulate. Don't settle for a lesser copy unless absolutely necessary.

The bibliographic listing that follows, although the most comprehensive yet assembled, is far from complete. For the most part, the list is limited to English language magazine articles. The newspaper pieces chosen for inclusion are a sampling of the thousands that have been published. Reviews of Dean's performances and articles announcing his death are amoung the primary newsprint items. Undoubtedly the search for items listed here will lead collectors to unlisted articles. But discovery is half the fun. Let the hunt begin.

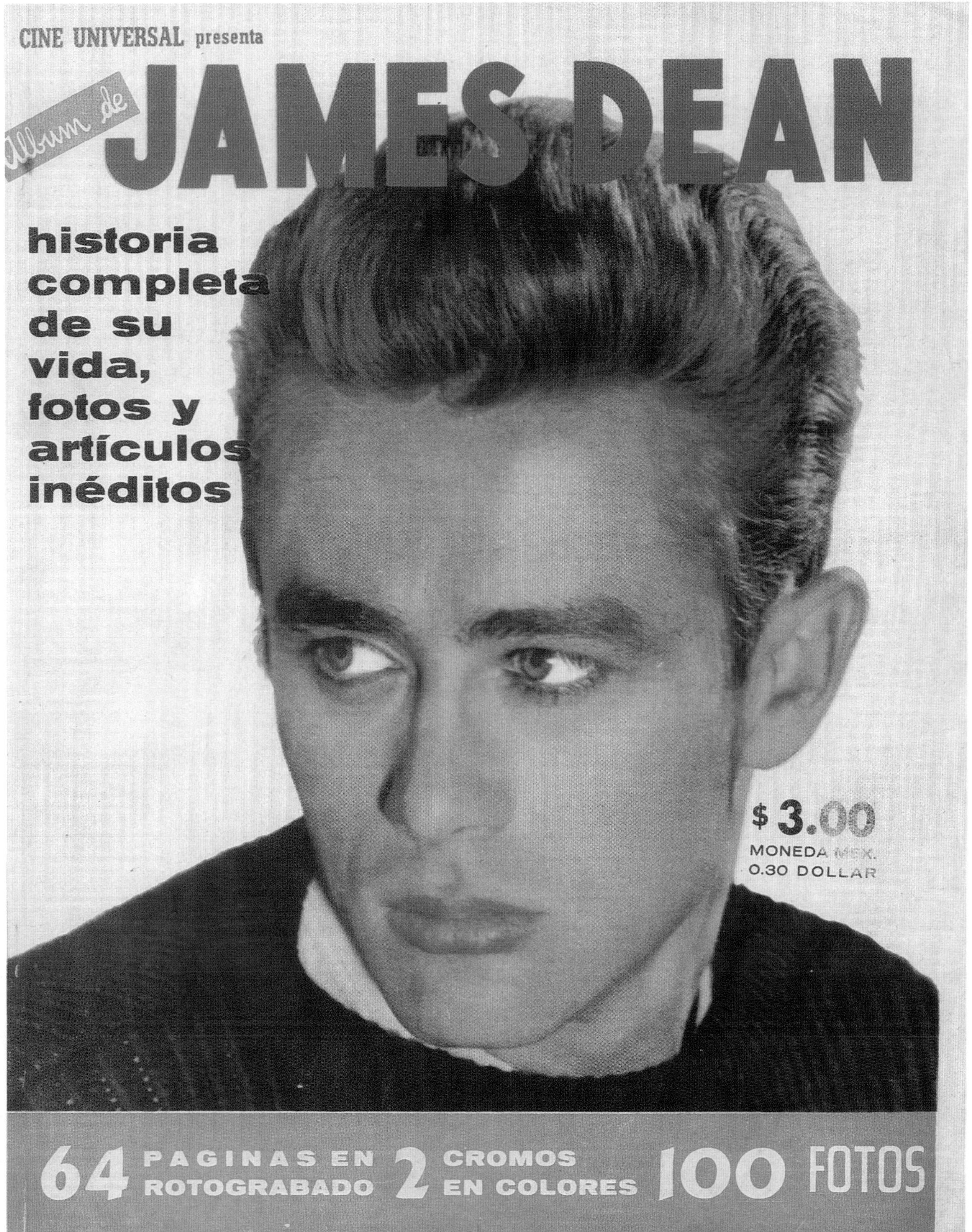
CINE UNIVERSAL presenta
Album de
JAMES DEAN
historia completa de su vida, fotos y artículos inéditos
$ 3.00
MONEDA MEX.
0.30 DOLLAR
64 PAGINAS EN ROTOGRABADO
2 CROMOS EN COLORES
100 FOTOS

Mexico - 1957

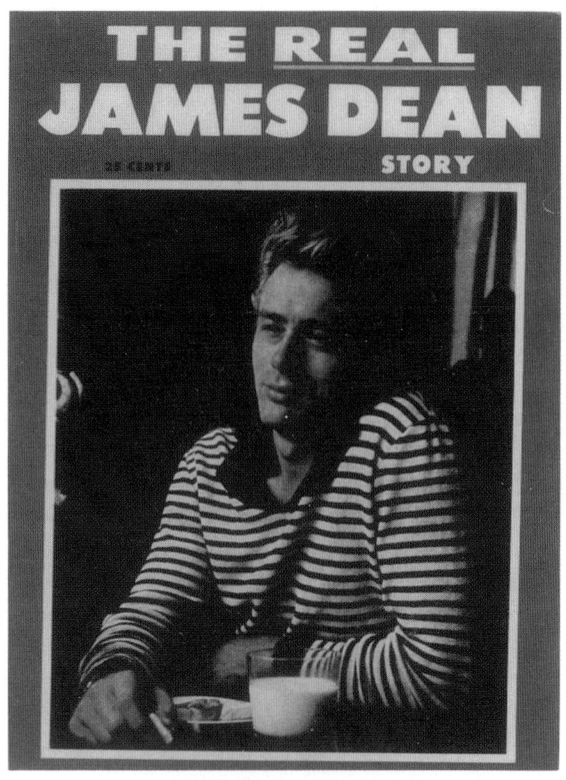

The Real James Dean Story
USA - 1956

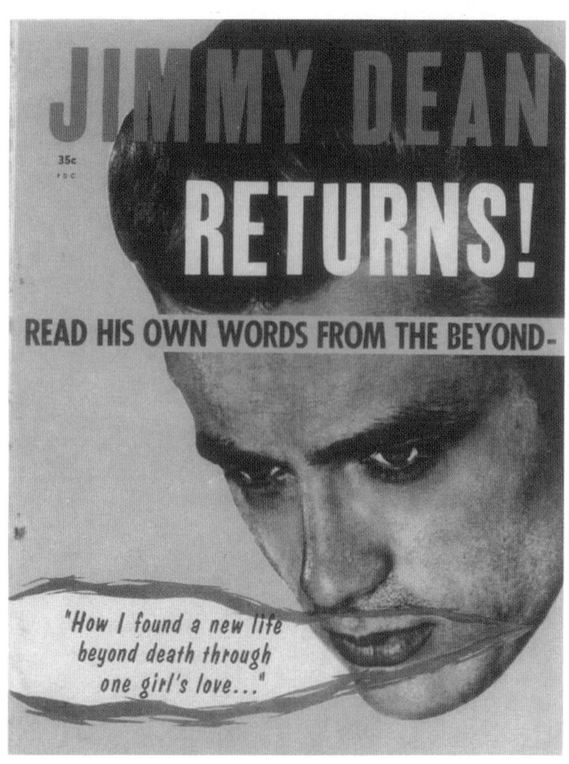

Jimmy Dean Returns!
USA - 1956

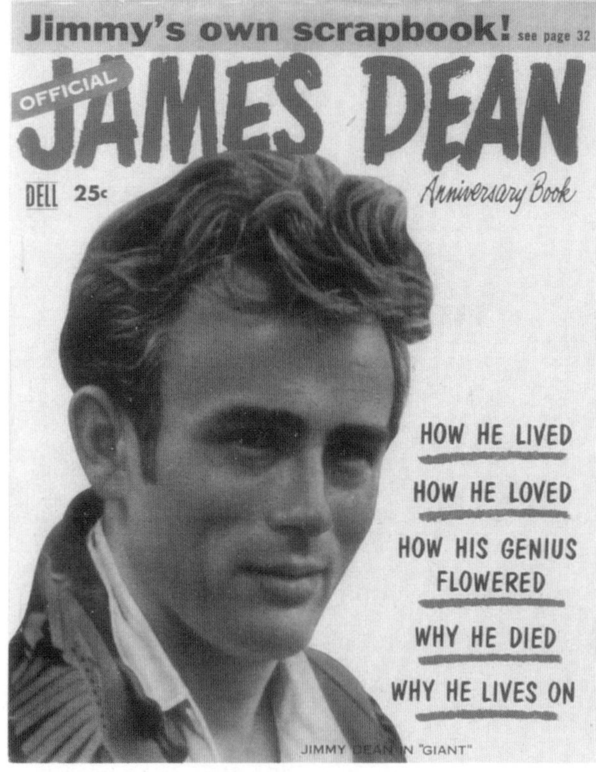

Official James Dean
Anniversary Book
USA - 1956

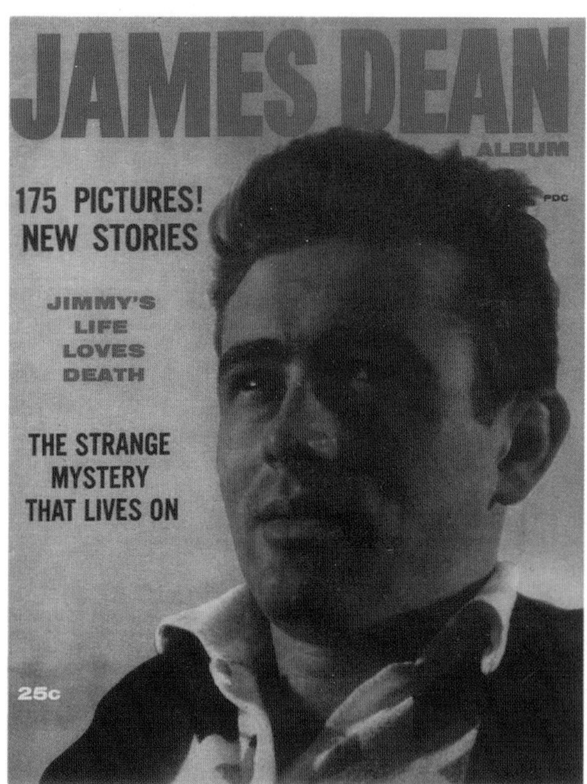

James Dean Album
USA - 1956

Sissi - Vol. 1 No. 15
Spain - 1958

Sissi - Vol. 1 No. 16
Spain - 1958

Sissi - Vol. 1 No. 17
Spain - 1958

Sissi - Vol. 1 No. 18
Spain - 1958

A vida e a morte de James Dean
Portugal - 1957

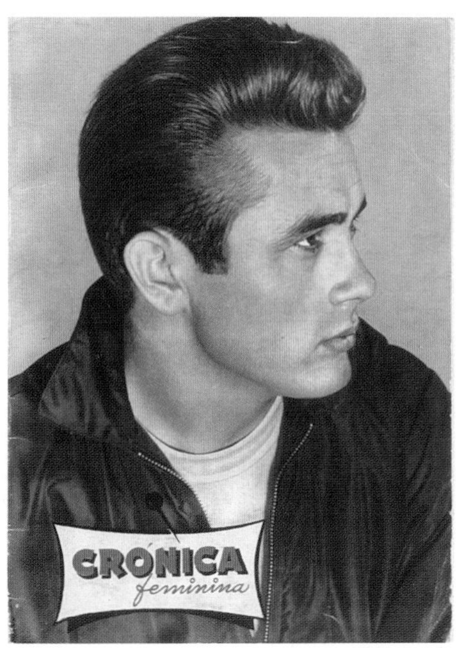

Cronica Feminina
Portugal - December 13, 1956

James Dean non é Morto
Italy - 1957

James Dean El Idolo Que Triunfo Sobre La Muerte
Spain - 1958

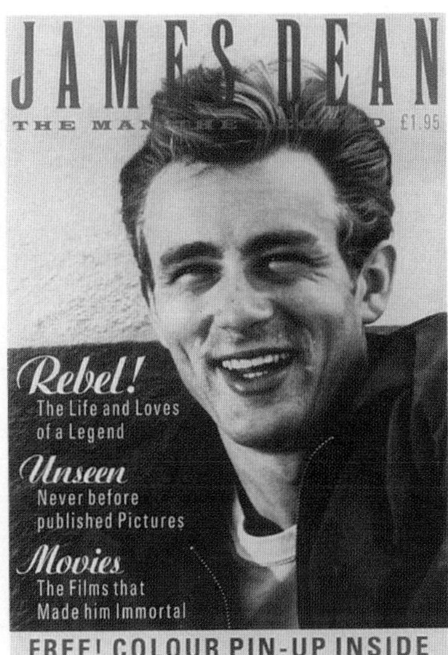

James Dean:
The Man, The Legend
England - 1988

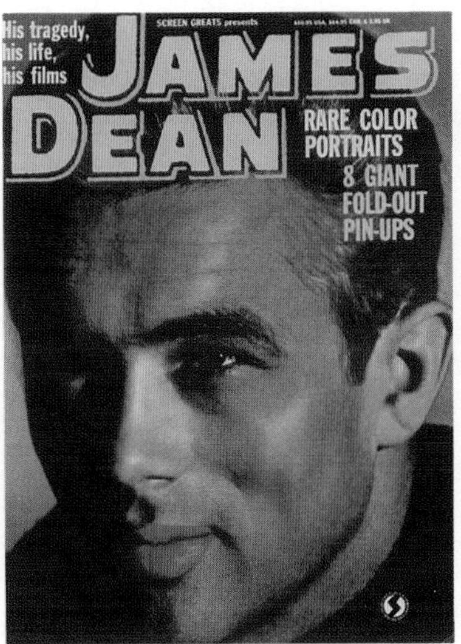

Screen Greats presents
James Dean
USA - 1988

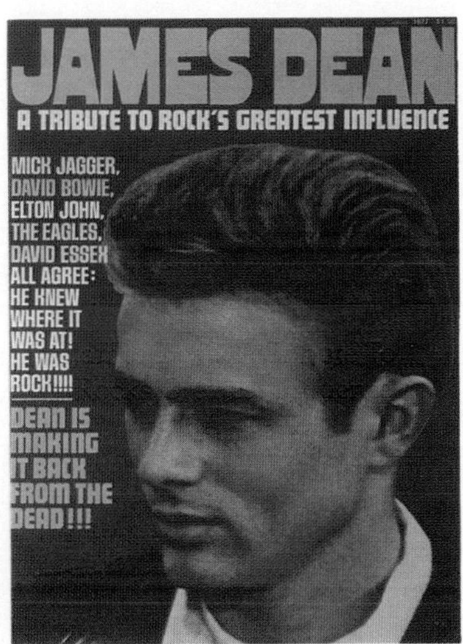

James Dean: A Tribute To
Rocks Greatest Influence
USA - 1977

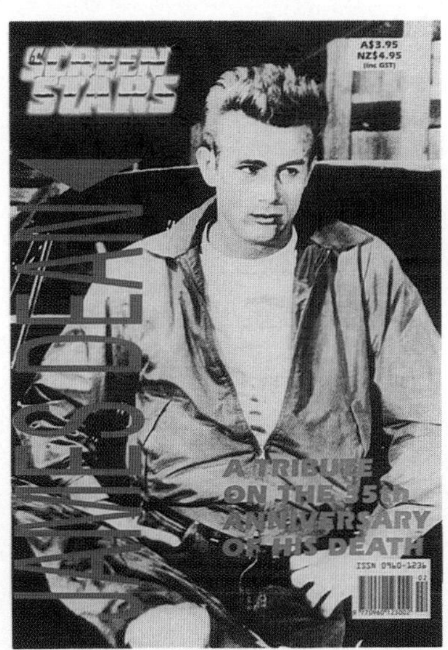

Screen Stars James Dean:
A Tribute on the 35th
Anniversary of His Death
Australia - 1990

Piccadilly
Japan - 1988

James Dean
Sa vie . . . Ses Films . . .
France - 1957

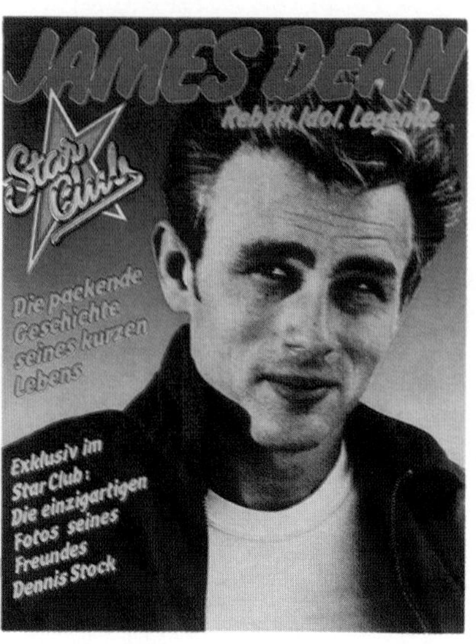

James Dean: Rebell, Idol, Legende
Germany - April 1980

Astros Estrelas
Brazil - 1985

James Dean
Spain - Dec. 20, 1955

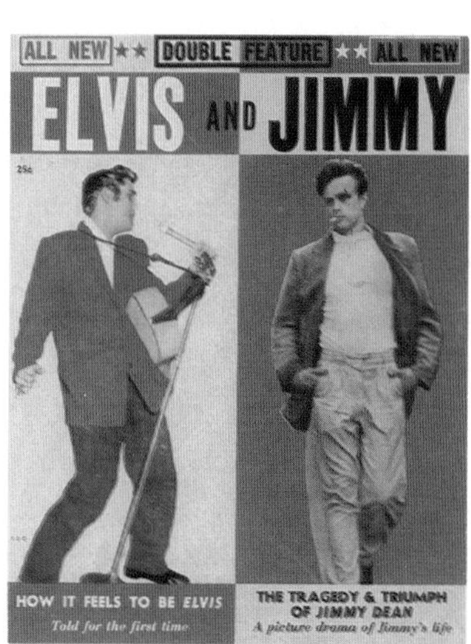

Elvis and Jimmy
USA - 1956

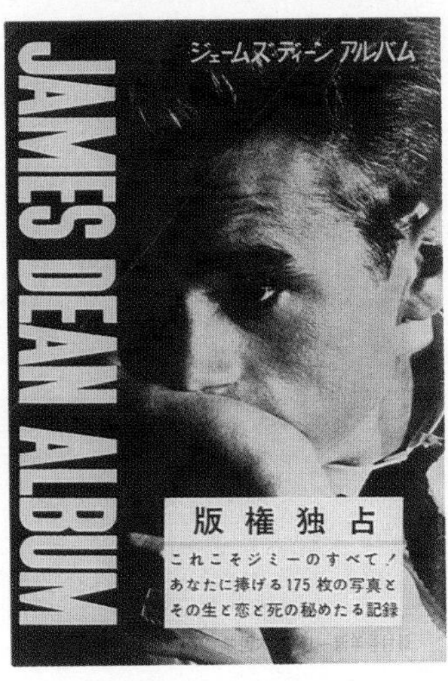

James Dean Album
Japan - 1956

East of Eden
Japan - 1969

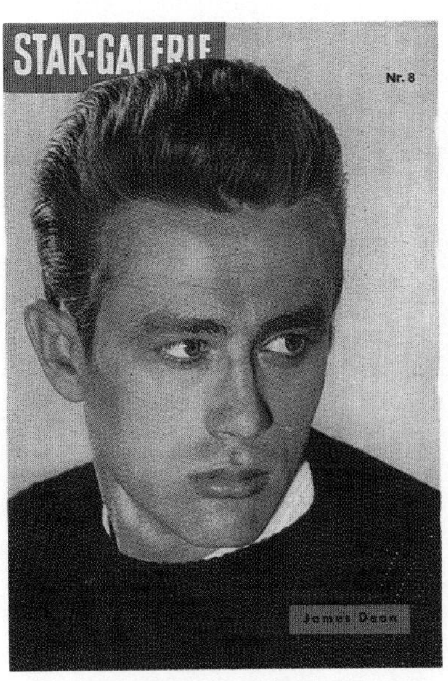

Star-Galerie #8
Germany - 1958

Fans' Star Library #16
England - 1959

Personality Comics
Presents James Dean
USA - 1992

La Vida Apasionante de
James Dean
Spain - 1957

Saturday Review
USA - October 13, 1956

Rave
USA - November 1956

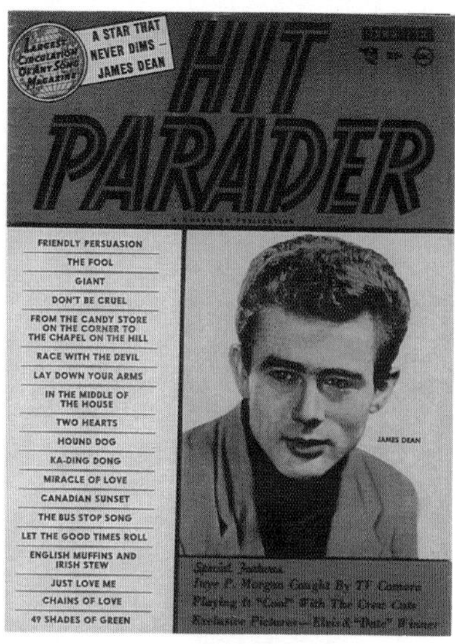

Hit Parader
USA - December 1956

True and Strange
USA - March 1957

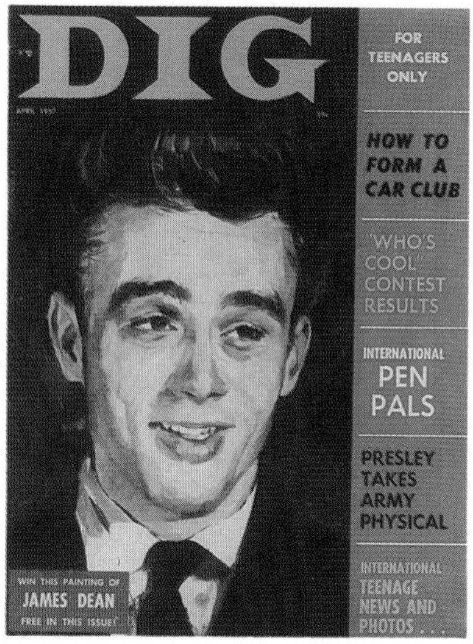

Dig
USA - April 1957

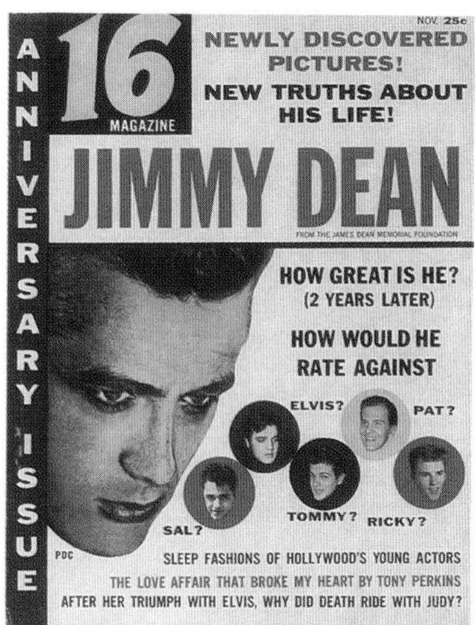

16 Magazine
USA - November 1957

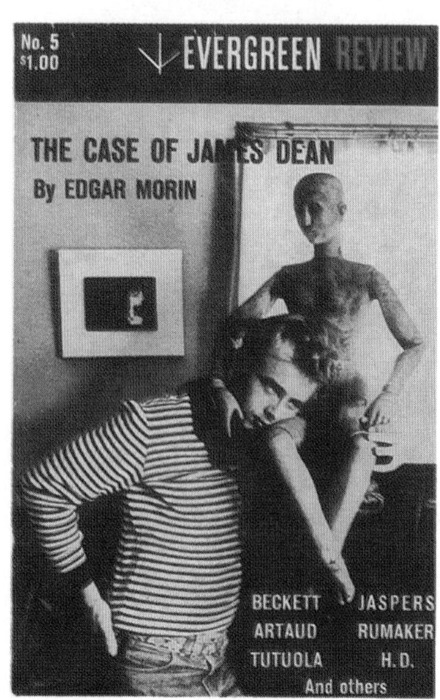

Evergreen Review #5
USA - 1958

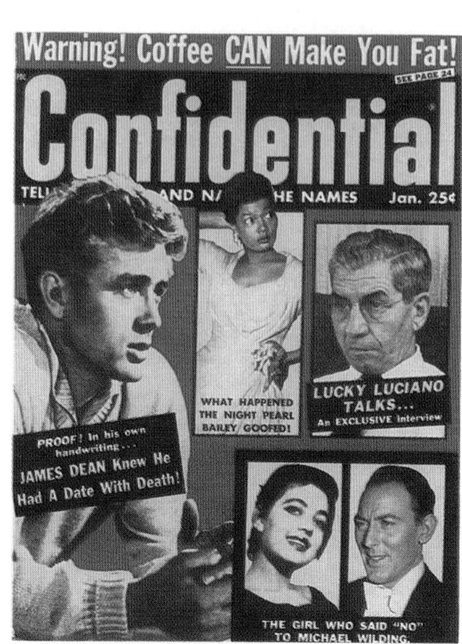

Confidential
USA - January 1958

Dig
USA - August 1962

TV News - Indianapolis, IN
May 6, 1955

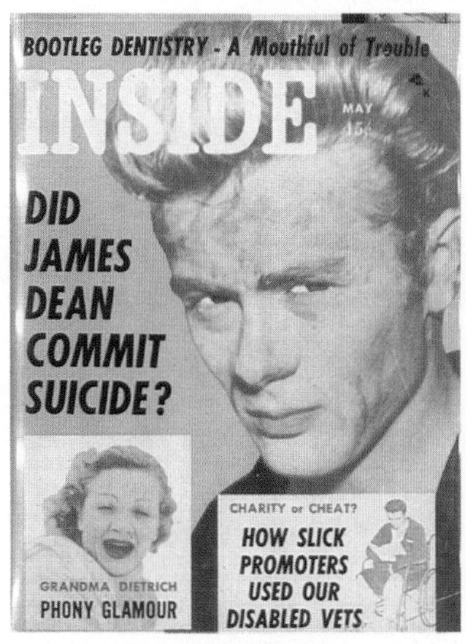

Inside
USA - 1956

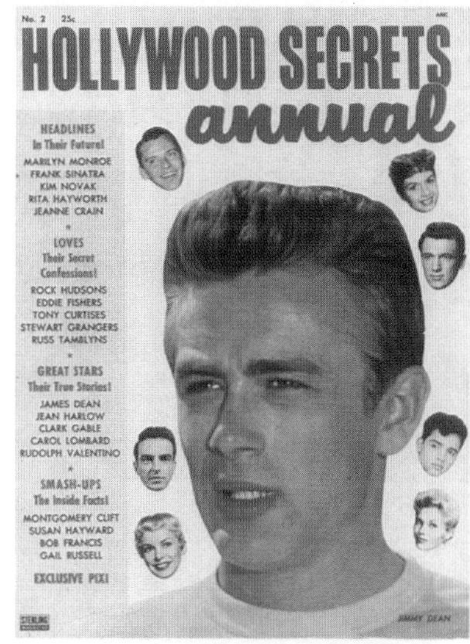

Hollywood Secrets Annual #2
USA - 1956

Off Broadway
USA - June 1956

Movie Stars Parade
USA - May 1956

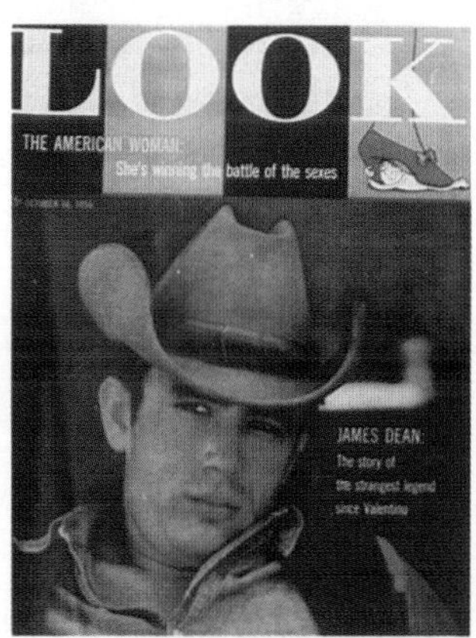

Look
USA - October 16, 1956

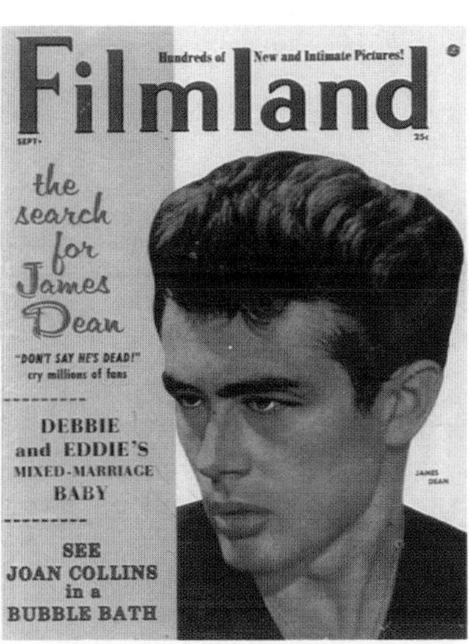

Filmland
USA - September 1956

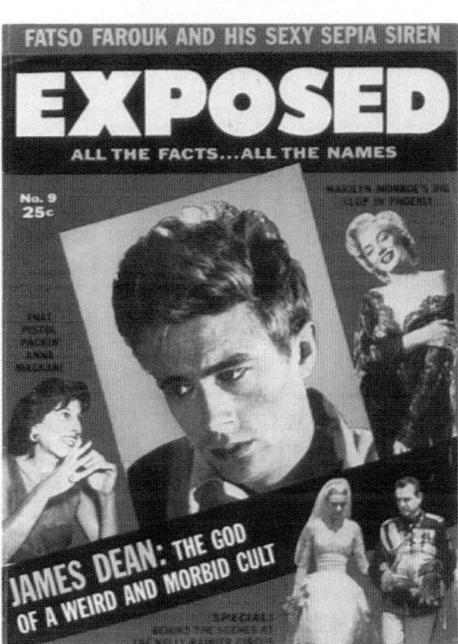

Exposed
USA - September 1956

Cue
USA - September 29, 1956

Screen Facts #8
USA - 1964

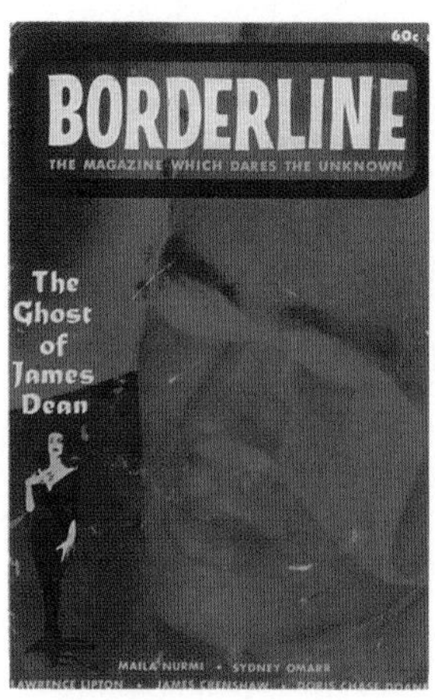

Borderline Vol. 1 No. 4
USA - 1964

Screen Legends
USA - May 1965

Insurgent
USA - May-June 1965

Collecting
USA - April 1996

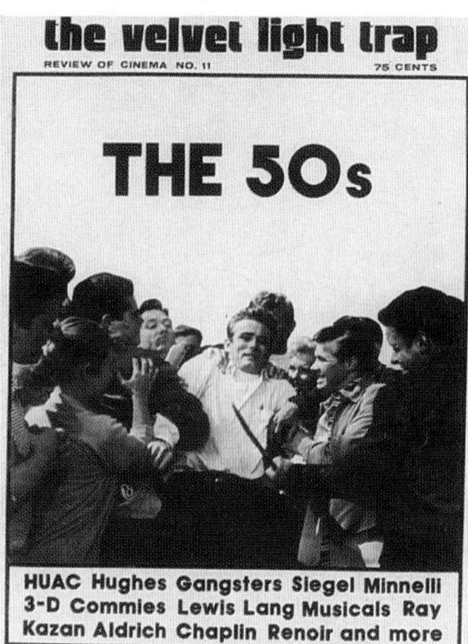

The Velvet Light Trap #11
USA - Winter 1974

Literary Cavalcade
USA - October 1975

Hollywood Studio Magazine
USA - August 1982

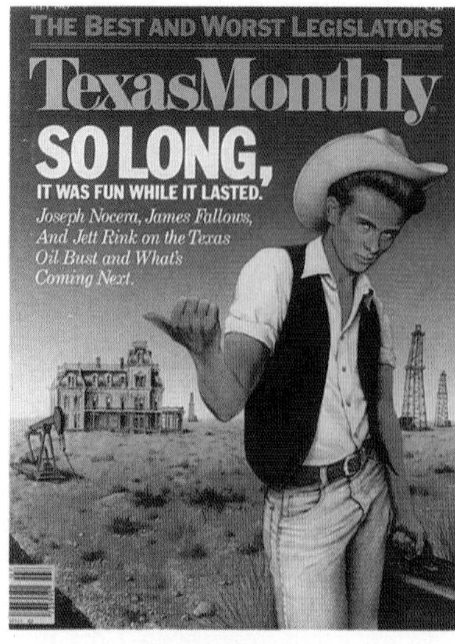

Texas Monthly
USA - July 1983

Hollywood Studio Magazine
USA - May 1984

Hollywood Studio Magazine
USA - September 1987

Hollywood Studio Magazine
USA - September 1986

Hollywood Tragedies
USA - 1985

Remember
USA - October 1995

Houston City
USA - May 1986

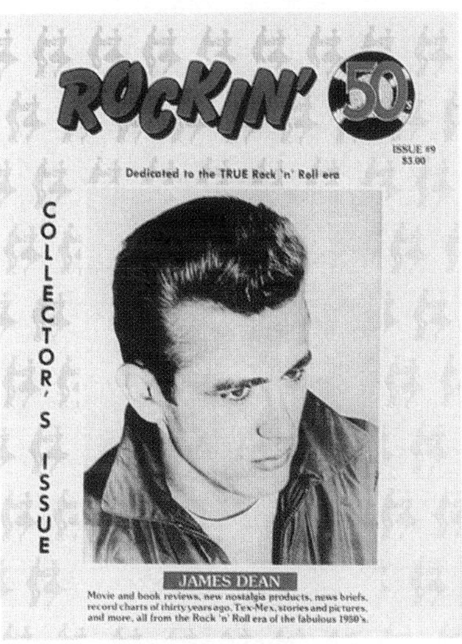

Rockin' 50s
USA - 1987

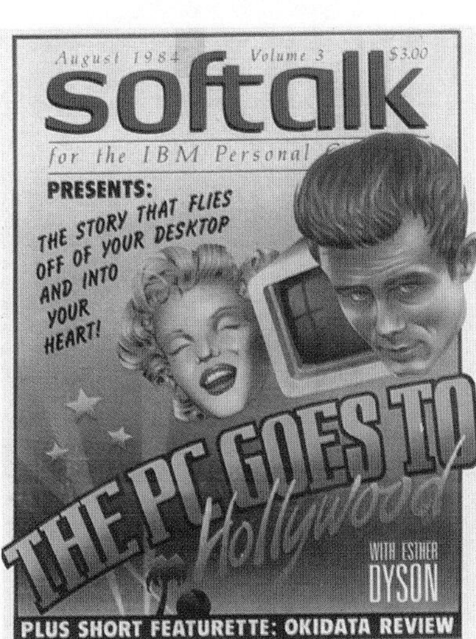

Softalk Vol. 3
USA - August 1984

Indiana Business
USA - February 1988

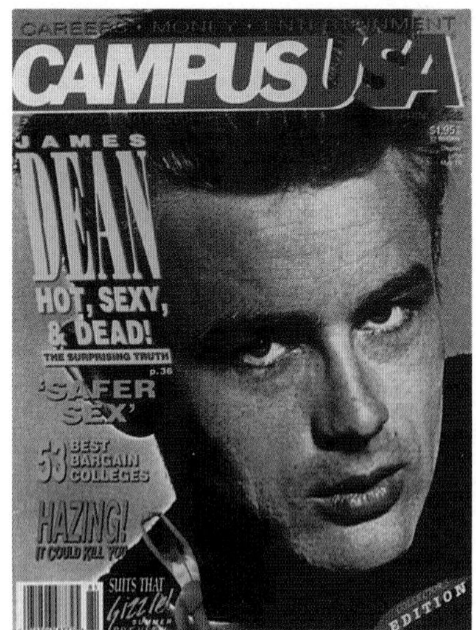

Campus USA
Spring 1988

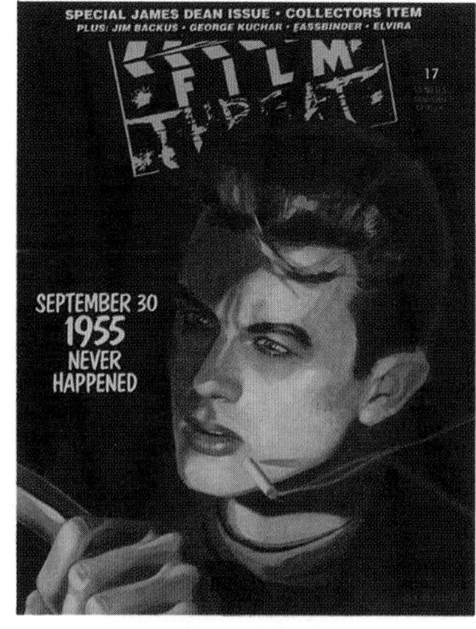

Film Threat #17
USA - 1988

Traces
USA - Fall 1989

Emmy
USA - October 1990

Sh-Boom
USA - June 1990

Exposure
USA - July 1990

The Robb Report
USA - August 1990

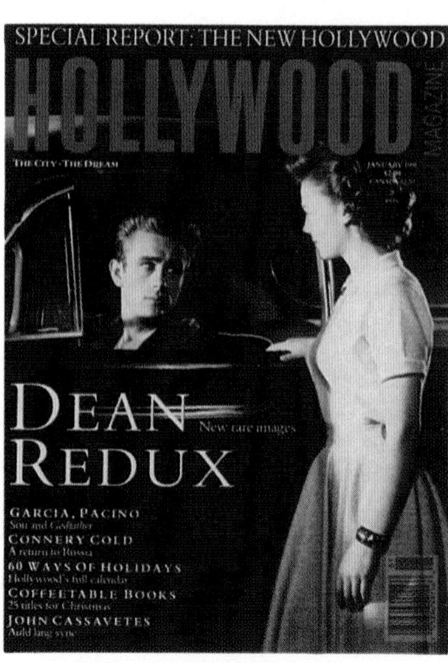

Hollywood Magazine
USA - January 1991

Visa Magazine
USA - July 1991

Spy
USA - March 1992

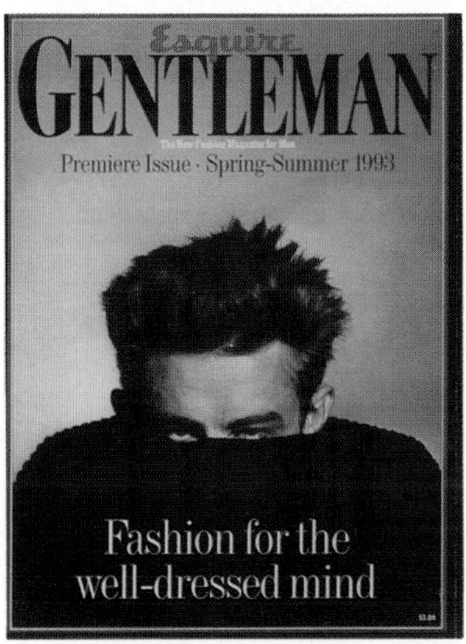

Esquire Gentleman
USA - Spring-Summer 1993

Hollywood Collectibles
USA - April 1994

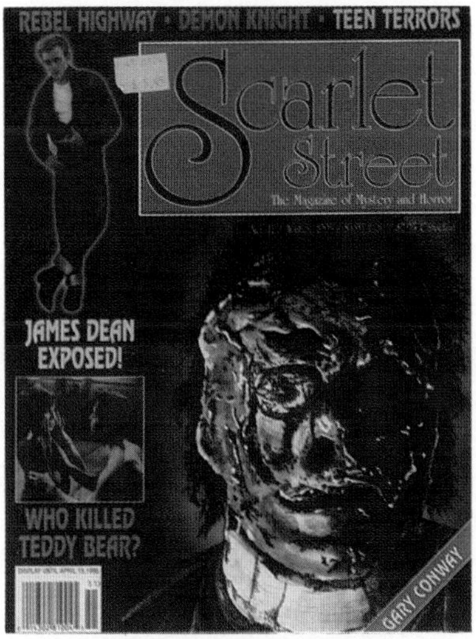

Scarlet Street
USA - Winter 1995

Films of the Golden Age
USA - Fall 1995

Texas Co-op Power
USA - April 1994

MT & Review
USA - Fall 1995

American Movie Classics Magazine
USA - March 1995

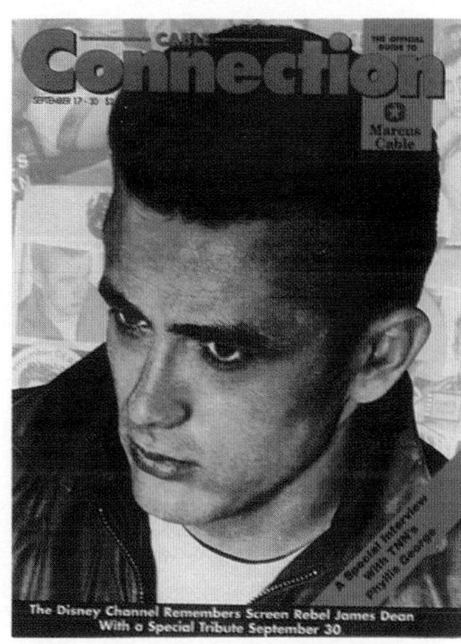

Cable Connection
USA - September 17-30, 1995

Cinemode
France - May 19, 1955

Cinemode
France - September 27, 1956

Cinemode
France - February 14, 1957

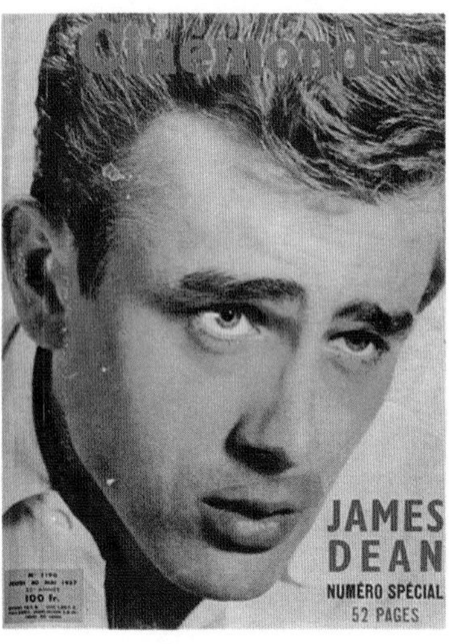

Cinemode
France - May 30, 1957

Paris Match
France - March 30, 1957

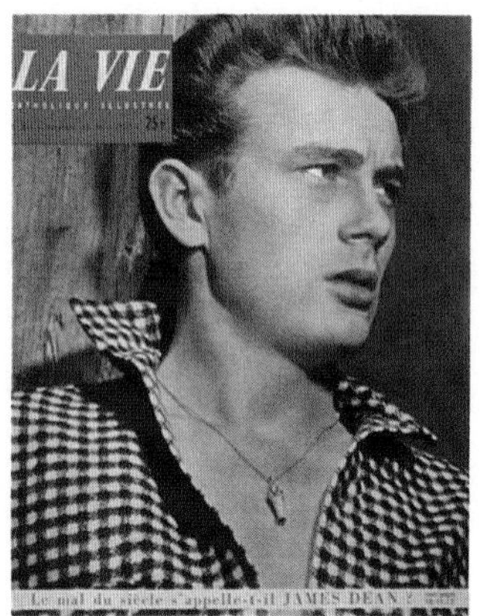

La Vie
France - April 28, 1957

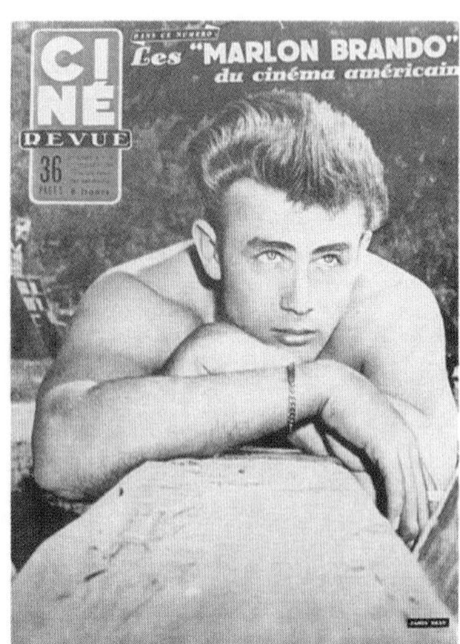

Cine Revue
France - July 1955

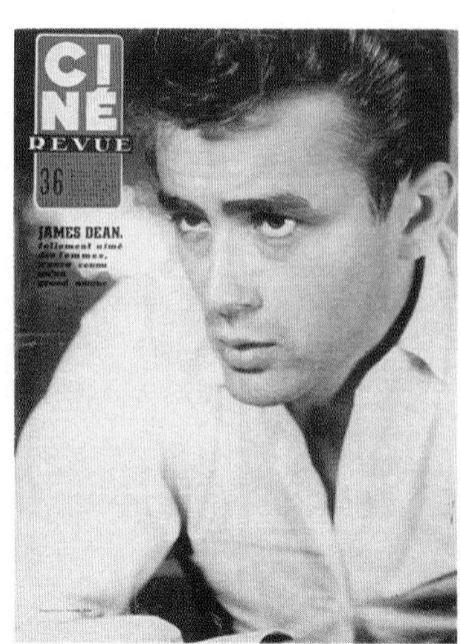

Cine Revue
France - October 21, 1955

Cine Revue
France - September 21, 1956

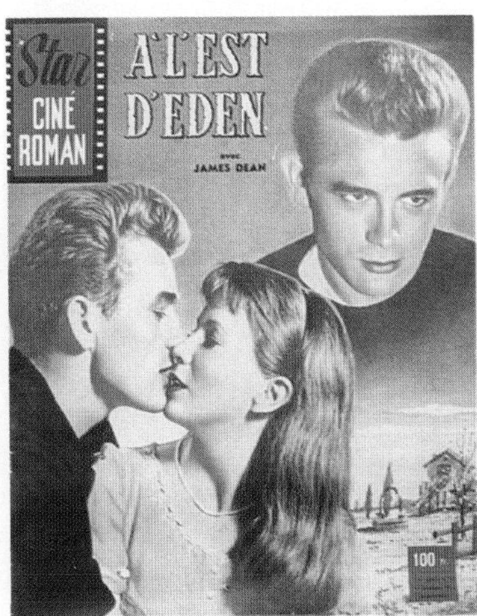

Star Cine Roman
France - December 1, 1957

Star Cine Roman
France - April 1, 1963

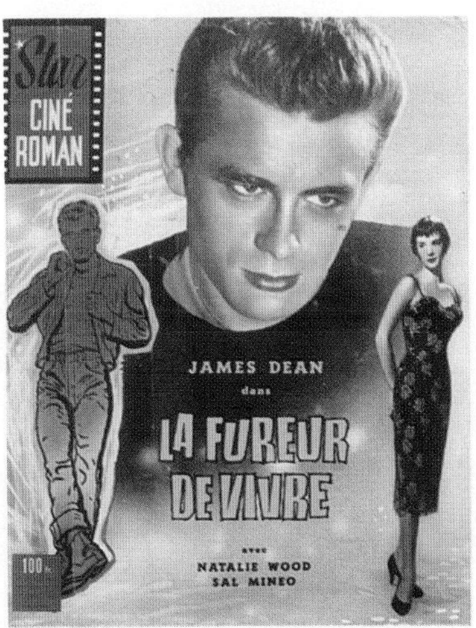

Star Cine Roman
France - November 1, 1958

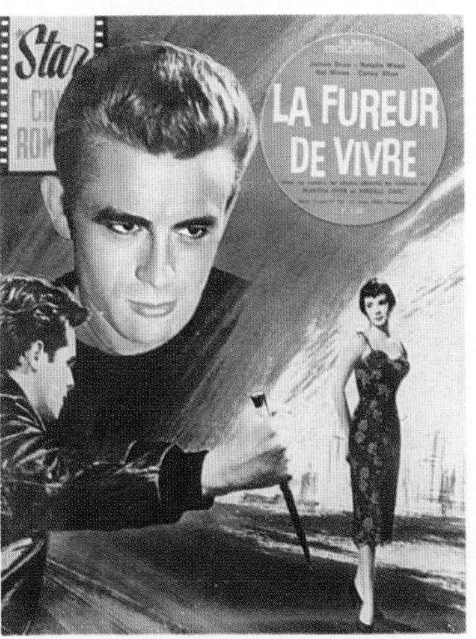

Star Cine Roman
France - March 15, 1963

Star Cine Roman
France - August 15, 1957

Star Cine Roman
France - April 15, 1963

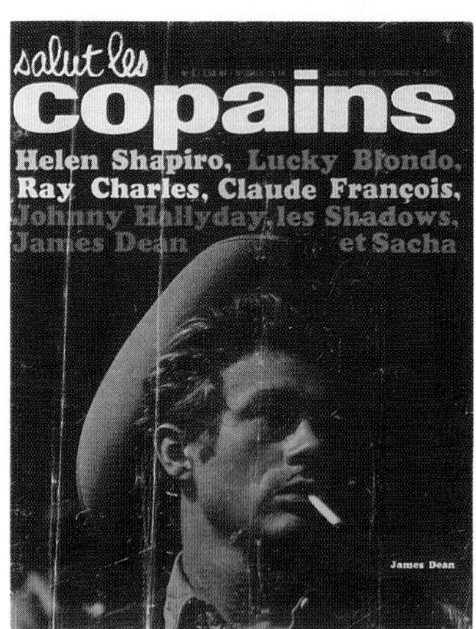

Salut le Copains
France - January 1963

Tele Cine
France - June 1957

Pilote
France - 1982

L'Avant Scene
France - November 1975

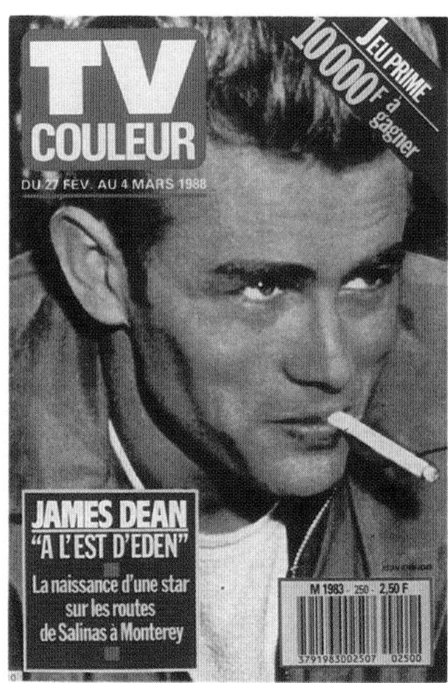

TV Couleur
France - Feb. 27 - March 4, 1988

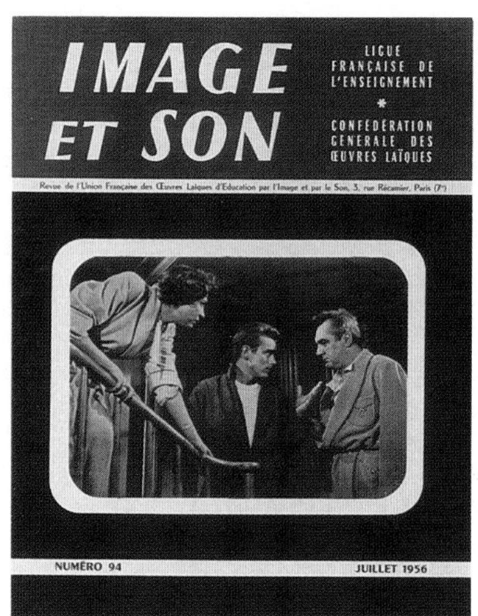

Image et Son
France - July 1956

Disco Revue - France - Dec. 1963

La Methode - France - 1961

Special USA No. 16 - France - 1985

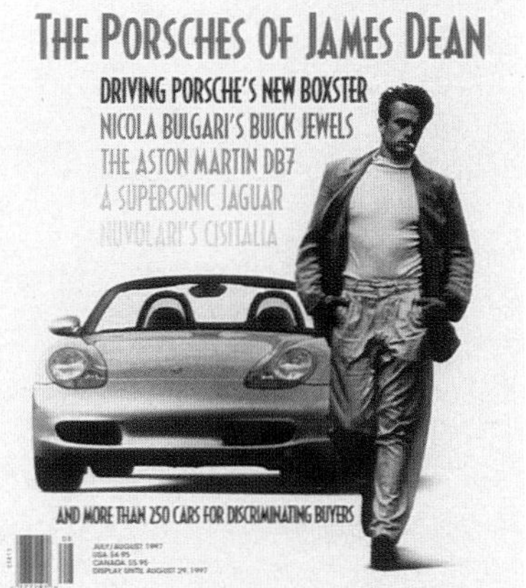

Classic Automobile Register
USA - July-August 1997

Gadfly
USA - May 1998

Official Publication of the
National Forensic League
Rostrum - US - Nov. 1961

L'evropeo
Italy - September 30, 1956

Max
Italy - September 1985

Photo Japon
Japan - May 5, 1986

Brutus Stylebook Special '85
Japan - 1984

Eiga No Tomo
Japan - February 1957

Movie Magazine
Japan - March 1969

Bravo
Germany - May 30, 1959

Bravo
Germany - October 10, 1959

Bravo
Germany - September 3, 1965

Bravo
Germany - September 27, 1965

Bravo
Germany - January 17, 1980

Bravo
Germany - July 24, 1980

Bravo
Germany - October 2, 1980

Bravo
Germany - October 17, 1985

Bravo
Germany - August 19, 1982

Bravo
Germany - March 3, 1957

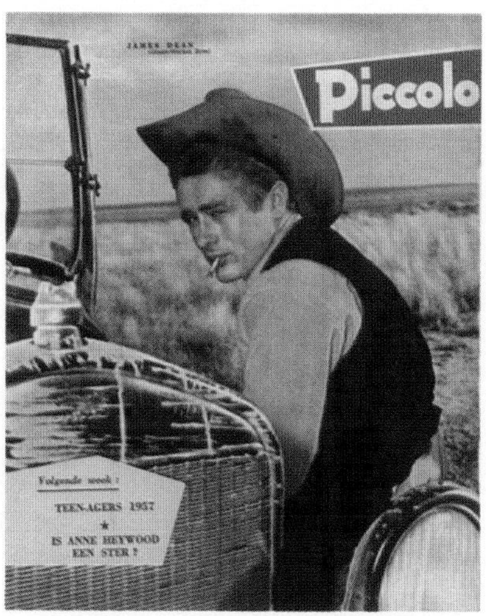

Piccolo
Germany - October 6, 1957

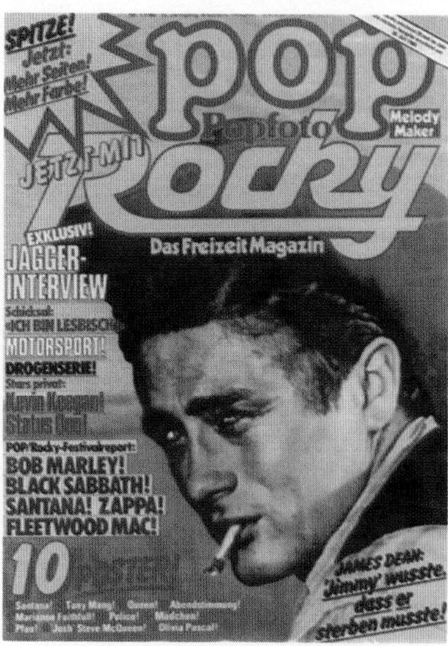

Pop Rocky
Germany - November 1980

Casablanca TV Buch
Germany - Dec. 5-12, 1992

Film Revue
Germany - February 19, 1957

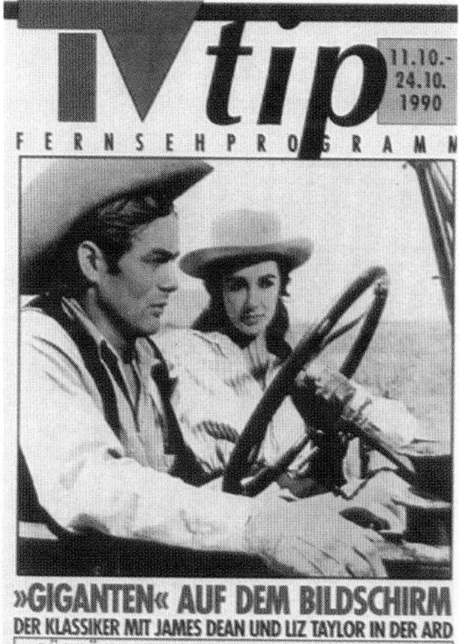

TV Tip
Germany - October 11-24, 1990

Bild & Funk
Germany - April 13-19, 1985

Telexy
Germany - Sept. 21-Oct. 18, 1985

Gong
Germany - August 1992

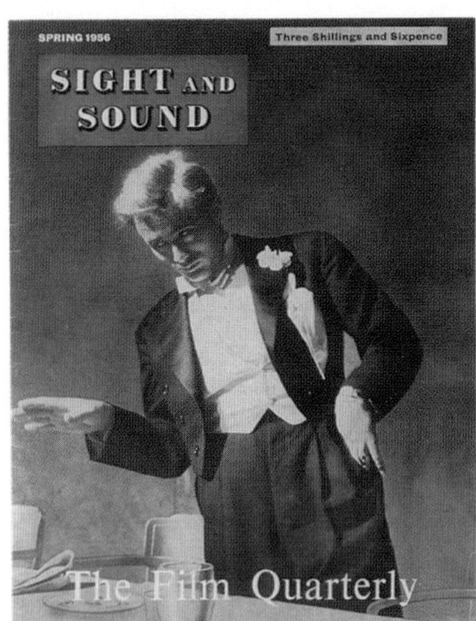

Sight and Sound
England - Spring 1956

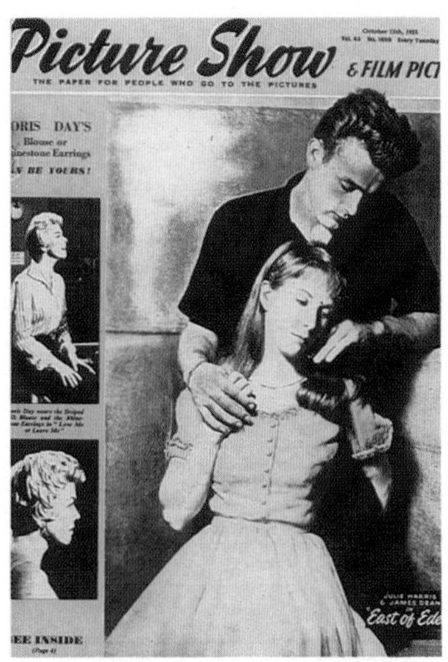

Picture Show & Film Picture
United Kingdom - Oct. 15, 1955

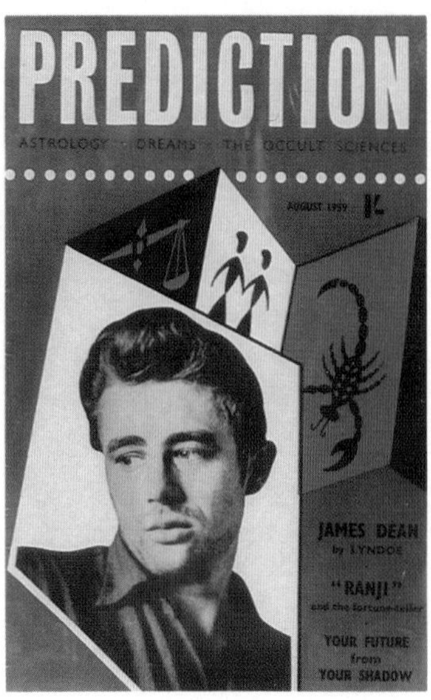

Prediction
England - August 1959

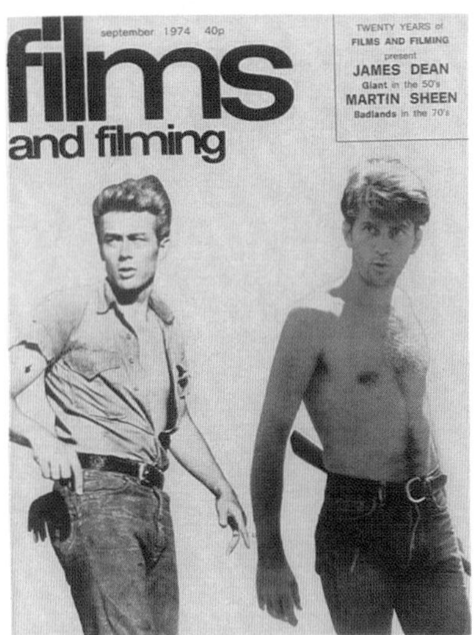

Films and Filming
England - September 1974

Time Out
England - Sept. 26-Oct. 2, 1975

The Movie Scene
England - July 1984

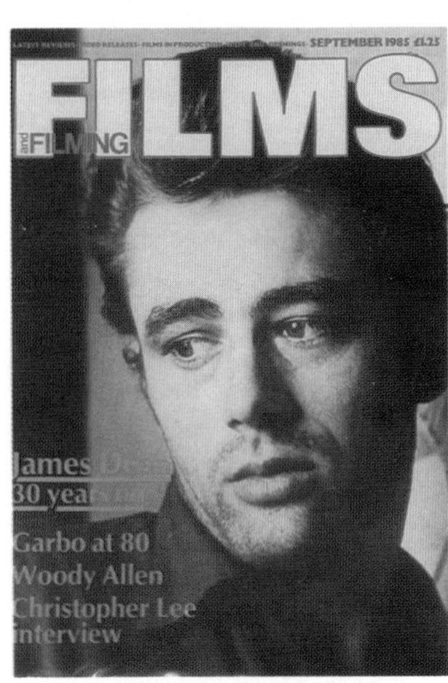

Films and Filming
England - September 1985

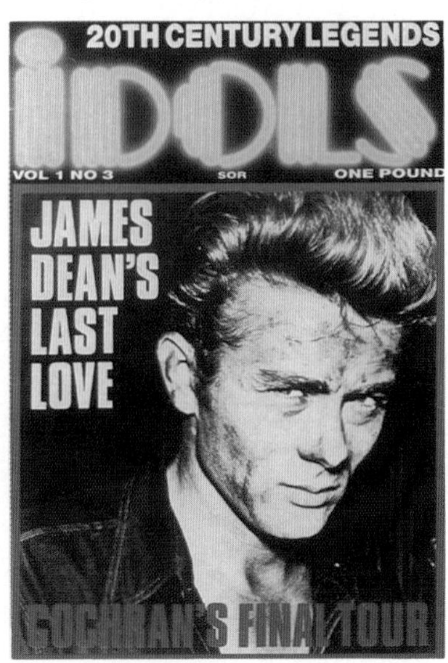

Idols - Vol. 1 #3
England - 1988

Idols - #14
England - April 1989

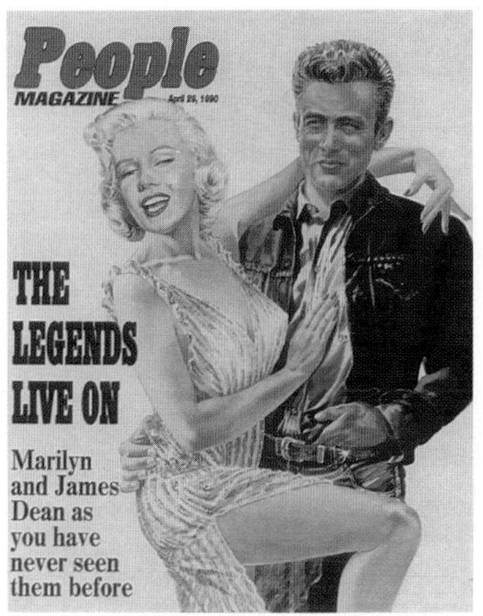

People Magazine
England - April 29, 1990

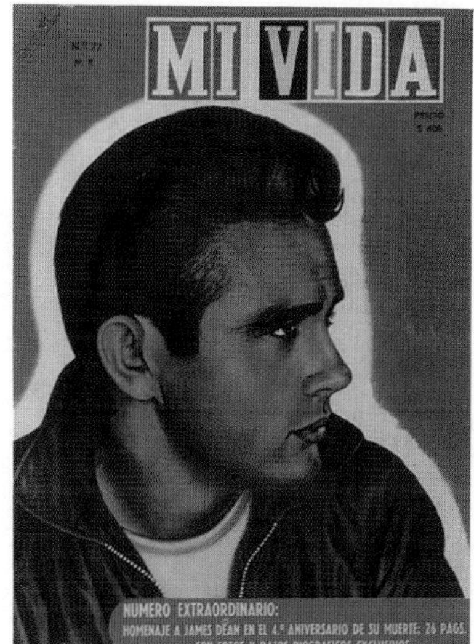

Mi Vida
Chile - September 1959

Leoplan
Argentina - September 1957

EPOCA - #21
Italy - April 1957

Picnic - Vol. 1 #14
Spain - 1958

Katiuscia
Italy - March 1981

Grandes Ciclos TV
Spain - 1990

Escandalos de Hollywood
Spain - 1988

Liberty
Canada - November 1956

Wild West Roman
Belgium - February 27, 1966

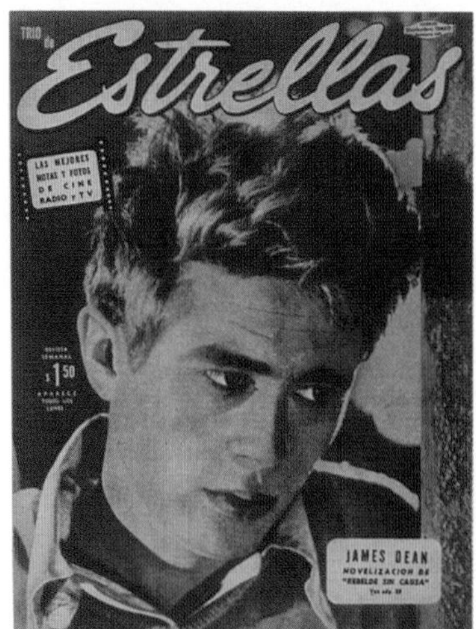

Estrellas
Argentina - July 30, 1956

Estrellas
Argentina - April 17, 1959

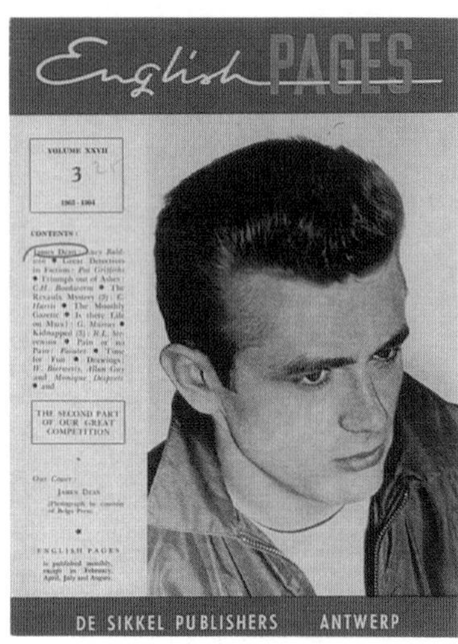

English Pages
Belgium - 1963-64

Cinema
New Zealand - 1957

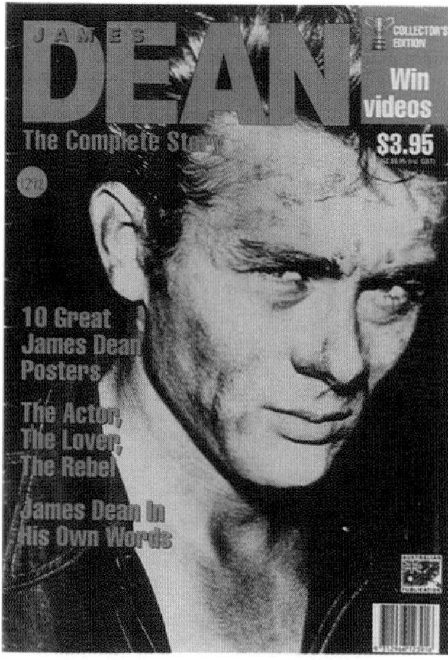

James Dean The Complete Story
Australia - 1992

M.N.E.T. Guide
South Africa - February 1991

Huis Genoot
South Africa - March 7, 1991

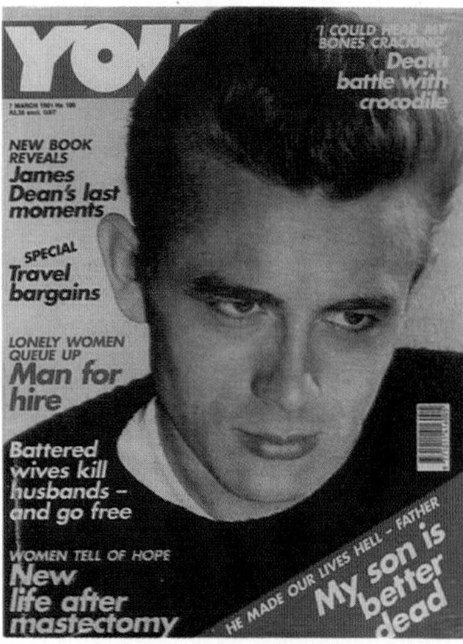

YOU
South Africa - March 7, 1991

Piccolo
Holland - September 30, 1956

Teleknack
Netherlands - March 1997

Damernas Värld
Sweden - May 23-29, 1957

DT Din Tidning - #17
Sweden - 1956

Min Melodi
Sweden - June 1956

Film & TV Guiden
Denmark - Feb. 10-16, 1995

Man
Holland - Jan-Feb 1989

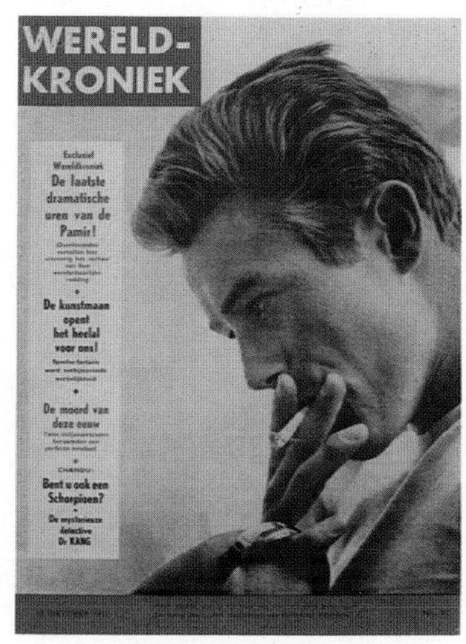

Wereld Kroniek
Holland - Oct. 19, 1957

Wereld Kroniek
Holland - March 9, 1957

Ecrans de France
France - January 1956

Ecrans de France
France - June 1956

Cahiers du Cinema
France - November 1956

Jeunesse Cinema
France - January 1958

TV 8
France - August 4, 1994

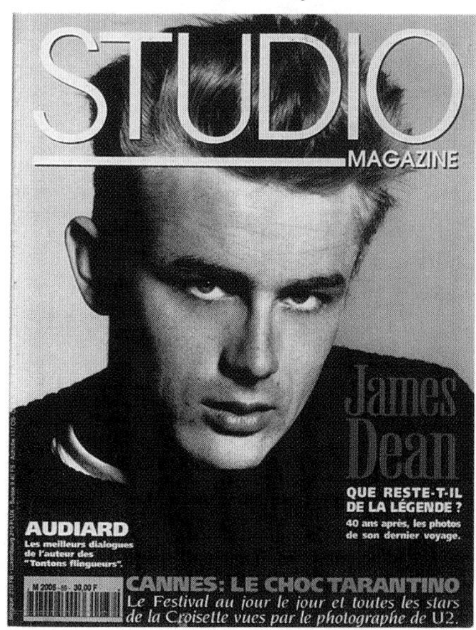

Studio Magazine
France - June 1994

Schweizer Illustrierte
Switzerland - Aug. 25, 1980

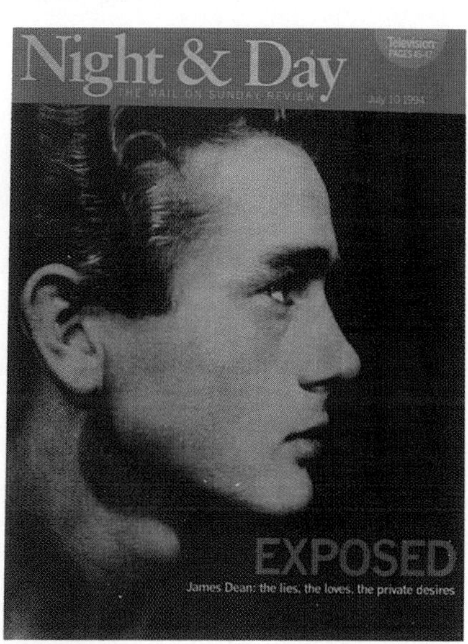

Night & Day
United Kingdom - July 10, 1994

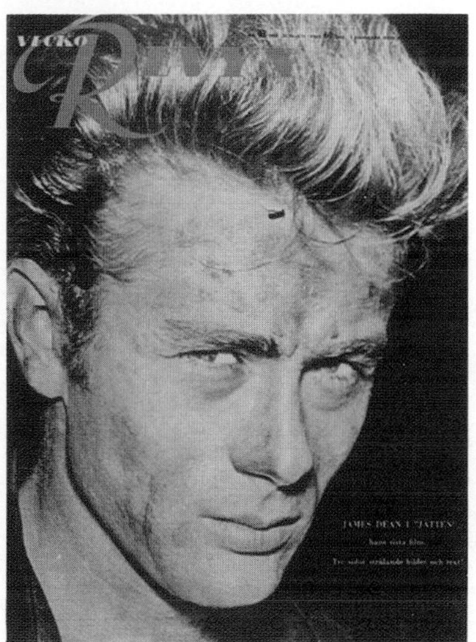

Vicko Revyn
Denmark - October 1956

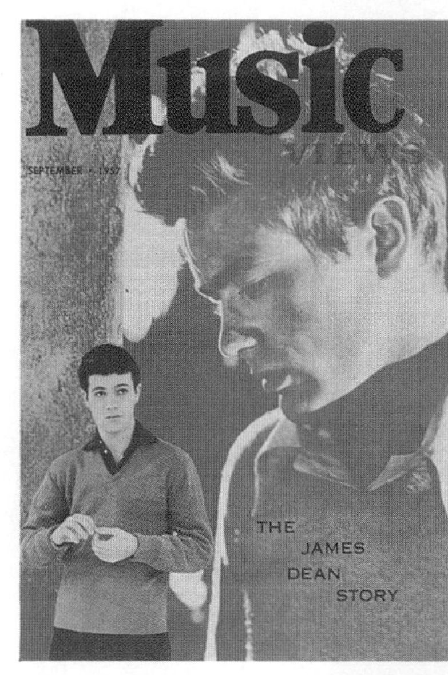

Music Views
USA - September 1957

Mini Tele
Switzerland - August 10, 1995

Flix
Japan - October 1991

Movie Star Photo Supplement to
Empire Magazine - England

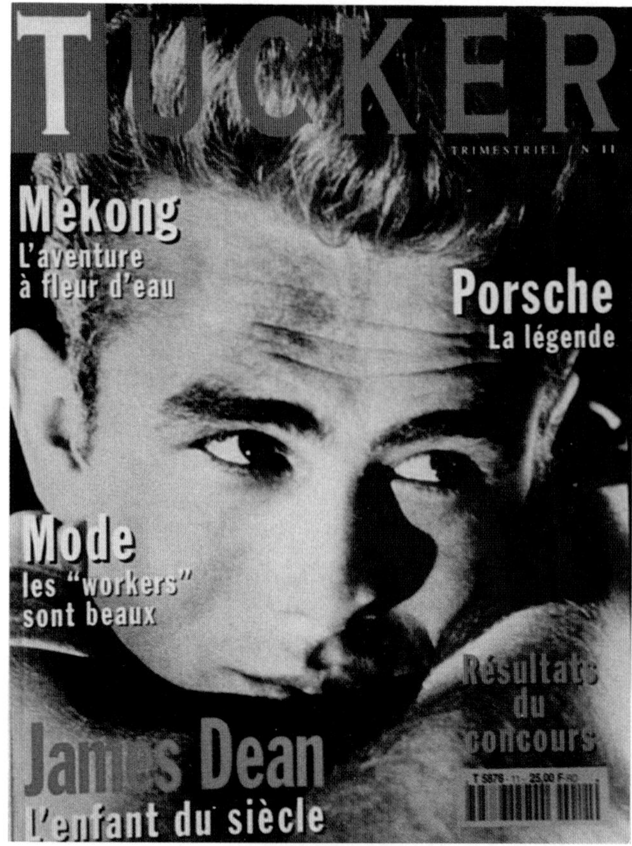

France - 1993

Cicerone
Spain - December 24-30, 1958

Cicerone
Spain - December 8-14, 1958

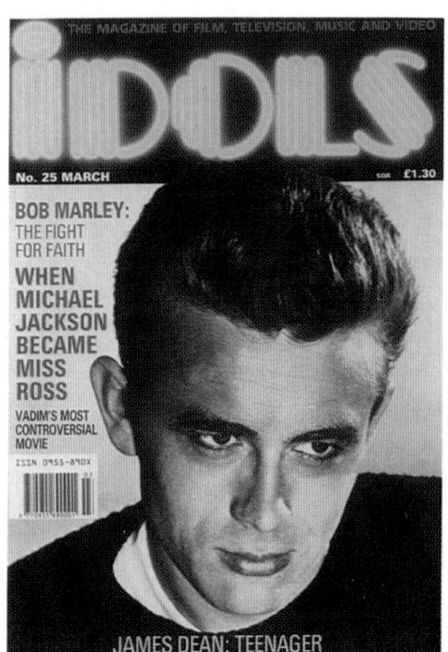

England - March 1990

> *"In a certain sense, I am a (fatalist). I don't know how to explain it, but I have a hunch there are some things in life we just can't avoid. They'll happen to us, probably because we're built that way - - - we simply attract our own fate, make our own destiny."* - - Dean to reporter Jack Shafer

AFTER DARK
May 1969
Lewis, Stephen. "Sal Mineo: Rebel With A New Cause."

February 1976
Hulzenga, Chris. "James Dean and Ferment in the Fifties."

Hulzenga, Chris. "William Bast: Portrait of a Friend."

March 1982
"Giant Rebel"

AMERICA
1977
Keller, Julia. "Mythic Hero in America's Heartland."

AMERICAN ADVERTISING
Summer 1997
Goldfarb, Jeffrey. "Posthumous Pitching."

AMERICAN FILM
December 1982
"The Idolmakers."

October 1985
Bluttman, Susan. "The Dean of Collectors."

Thomson, David. "Rebels Without a Pause."

January-February 1992
Kennedy, Harlan. "The Melodramatists."

AMERICAN MOVIE CLASSICS MAGAZINE
March 1995
Alexander, Paul. "Fall From Eden."

AMERICAN PHOTOGRAPHER
November 1982
Schatt, Roy. "Contact."

THE AMERICAN WEEKLY
July 29, 1956
Capen, Jeanne Balch. "The Strange Revival of James Dean."

AMERICANA ANNUAL
1956
"Obituary - James Dean."

AMTRAK EXPRESS
August/September 1989
Vellela, Tony. "Elia Kazan Looks Forward."

ANDERSON SUNDAY HERALD (Indiana)
August 14, 1993
Delaney, Dave. "Woman Who Claims Dean's Discovery."

ANTIQUES AND AUCTION NEWS
June 9, 1989
Lewis, Brian M. "James Dean Collectibles."

ANTIQUES AND COLLECTING
April 1989
Headrick, Jr., Robert. "Collecting James Dean Memorabilia:
Yesterday, Today and Tomorrow."

ANYTHING GOES
May 1956
Beata, Abby. "Did Jimmy Dean Commit Suicide?"

ARCHITECTURAL DIGEST
April 1996
Spoto, Donald. "James Dean - *The Rebel Without a Cause*
Star's New York Apartment."

AREOPAGUS
Easter 1990
"The Cult of James Dean."

ARETE
November/December 1989
Vaucher, Andrea. "James Dean."

ARTFORUM
February 1989
Hoberman, J. "Believe It Or Not."

AUTOWEEK
December 13, 1993
Moses, Sam. "Retracting Rebel's Route
in a Red 'Retro' Roadster."

Padgett, Nina. "Rebels Without a Clue."

BACKSTREET/THE BOSS MAGAZINE
Fall 1985
King, Wayne. "The Ties That Bind."

BALTIMORE CONCOURS D'ELEGANCE
May 11, 1991
Raskin, Lee. "The Search for the Most
Famous Porsche of All Time."

THE BEAT ENTERTAINMENT MAGAZINE
September 1993
Lounges, Tom. "Jame Dean - The Man Behind The Myth."

BEHIND THE SCENE
January 1957
Dufy, Lisette. "The Other Man
in Vic Damone-Pier Angeli's Life."

BIG BEND QUARTERLY
Summer 1990
"Going Hollywood."

"*Giant* and the Texas Psyche."

"*Giant* Quiz."

BORDERLINE
January 1964
Nurmi, Maila. "The Ghost of James Dean."

BOSTON GLOBE (Massachusetts)
February 9, 1985
Muro, Mark. "Dean of Deanobilia."

August 4, 1996
Wildman, David. "Glimpses of a Fledgling James Dean."

BOSTON HERALD (Massachusetts)
October 24, 1983
Baker, Carroll. "Swept Off Her Feet,
Held by the Magic of Jim Dean."

October 25, 1983
Baker, Carroll. "Sparks, Panties Fly During Wild Bike Run."

BOSTON PHEONIX (Massachusetts)
March 18, 1994
Garboden, Clif. "Picture This."

BOUILLABAISSE
Number 5, 1995
Pell, Ken. "Markie Winslow."

BROOKLYN DAILY EAGLE (New York)
February 9, 1954
Sheaffer, Louis. "Page and Jourdan in Sad Drama
of Abnormal Love."

BUSINESS WEEK
May 8, 1995
Harbrecht, Douglas and Robert Neff.
"Guardian of the Famous and the Dead."

CABLE CONNECTION
September 17-30, 1995
Neal, Jane McGlohen. "James Dean: Live Fast, Die Young, Stay Pretty."

CAMPUS USA
Spring 1988
"James Dean Alive on Campus."

CAR AND DRIVER
October 1985
Yates, Brock. "Far From Eden."

CAR EXCHANGE
April 1980
Howley, Tim. "30 Sept. 55 - The Day James Dean Became a Legend."

CAR LIFE
January 1957
Keyes, E.M. "The Real Reason James Dean Died."

CAVALIER
December 1969
Thompson, James. "James Dean is Alive and Over Thirty and Horribly Scarred."

CHICAGO SUN-TIMES (Illinois)
September 27, 1995
Ebert, Roger. "He Set the Tone for Two Generations of Actors."

Kligman, David. "The Dean Legacy."

CHICAGO TRIBUNE (Illinois)
September 9, 1956
Nielson, Evelyn Washburn. "The Truth About James Dean."

September 29, 1957
Leonard, William. "Hoosier Home Town Re-Lives James Dean's Story."

May 31, 1959
"Future Stars Often Hard to Recognize."

April 21, 1968
McCurdy, Glenn. "James Dean, A Legend Blowin' in the Wind."

September 28, 1980
Dye, John. "James Byron Dean: The Sinister Adolescent."

September 15, 1985
Kart, Larry. "Giant Legacy: The Hero That James Dean Created Still Lives."

September 21, 1986
Kaminsky, Stuart M. "Media Mystique/James Dean: His Death and Rebirth."

CINCINNATI CITY BEAT (Ohio)
October 2, 1996
Constable, Chris. "Remember Dean With a Bang."

Ramos, Steve. "Rebel Without a Pulse."

CINEMA, STAGE AND TV
June 1957
"James Dean: Individualist, Magnificent Actor, Whose Wildest Dreams Came True."

CIRCUS
November 1975
Nelson, Paul. Record review of Warner Brother's album "James Dean."

1977
Goldstein, Toby. "Richard Thomas on 9/30/55."

Wustefeld, Greg. "James Dean: Man and Myth."

CLASSIC & CUSTOM
May 1983
Haynes, Lana. "3rd Annual James Dean Memorial Run."

CLASSIC AUTOMOBILE REGISTER
July - August 1997
Drake, Paul. "The Porsches of James Dean."

COLLECTING
April 1996
Bruhn, Gary. "James Dean: Too Fast To Live . . . Too Young To Die."

COLLIERS
November 25, 1955
Roth, Sanford. "The Late James Dean."

1957 Yearbook
"Obituary - James Dean."

COLUMBUS FREE PRESS (Ohio)
November 1985
Grener, Betsy. "Fans Travel Down James

CONFIDENTIAL
January 1958
Brown, David. "Proof In His Own Handwriting That James Dean Knew He Had a Date with Death."

CORONET
July 1955
Hopper, Hedda. "Young Men of Hollywood."

November 1956
Mitgang, Herbert. "The Strange James Dean Death Cult."

COSMOPOLITAN
March 1955
Parsons, Louella O. "James Dean - New Face With a Future."

October 1956
Honor, Elizabeth. "Hollywood Tragedies."

November 1961
Bocca, Geoffrey. "The Roman Orgy of Movie Making."

CRAWDADDY
February 1976
"Ah, Jimmy, Jimmy: James Dean, Twenty Years On."

March 1978
Braudy, Susan. "Sal Mineo: The Slow Fade."

CREEM
June 1975
"Juke Box Crucifix."

CUE
September 29, 1956
Taylor, Tim. "His Name Was Dean."

CUSTOM CARS
1982
"The James Dean Memorial Run."

CYCLE WORLD
April 1992
Padgett, Nina. "Rebel's Ride."

DALLAS MORNING NEWS (Texas)
December 9, 1998
Woolley, Bryan. "Framing the Wild, Wild West."

DATEBOOK
October 1957
"I Loved James Dean."

THE DELTA (Sigma Nu Fraternity)
Summer 1962
"The Enigma of James Dean."

DETECTIVE DIARY
September 1979
Jackson, Judd. "Sal Mineo's Final Curtain Call."

DIG
June 1956
"Anyone Know Him?"

April 1957
Campbell, Frank. "James Dean."

November 1957
"James Dean Story."

August 1961
"Meet Jack Chaplain."

June 1962
"Dig's Flashback Calendar."

August 1962
Milstead, Janey. "The Miracle of James Dean."

EASY TIMES
September 1977
Thomas, Ross. "Rebels - Inside Dean: His Fantasy, Our Myth."

ELVIS AND JIMMY
1956 *Girl Friend - Boy Friend Corporation*

Cameron, Lou. "The Triumph and Tragedy of Jimmy Dean."

EMMY
October 1990
Bluttman, Susan. "Rediscovering James Dean: The TV Legacy."

ENGLISH PAGES
Volume 27, Number 3, 1963-1964
Baldwin, Lucy. "Three Quarters of an Hour with James Dean."

ENTERTAINMENT WEEKLY
September 28, 1990
"The Dean of Cool"

"The James Dean 35th Anniversary Collection."

O'Tolle, Lawrence. "Rebel, Rebel."

March 26,1993
Gerosa, Melina. "Gold in Black and White."

August 13,1993
Burr, Ty. "Oeuvre Achievers."

October 29,1993
Burr, Ty. "The First Rebel Yell."

ENTERTAINMENT WEEKLY: THE 100 GREATEST MOVIE STARS OF ALL TIME
Fall 1996
Hajari, Nasid. "22. James Dean."

ESQUIRE
December 1956
Mayer, Martin. "The Apotheosis of Jimmy Dean."

October 1958
Dos Passos, John. "The Death of James Dean."

October 1982
Williams, Joy. "Retrospective: *Rebel Without a Cause..*"

EVENING STAR(Washington, DC)
October 1, 1955
"Crash Kills James Dean, Young Hollywood Star."

EVENING SUN (Maryland)
September 30, 1996
Covert, Tony and Shane Warner. "Remembering a Legend."

Thomas, Bob. "Giant Restored: Dean's Final Film 40 Years Later."

EVERGREEN REVIEW
Summer 1958
Morin, Edgar. "The Case of James Dean."

EXCELLENCE
November 1995
Colman, David. "Rubble Without a Pause: James Dean's Crash."

May 1996
Colman, David. "Replicars, Replistars - *James Dean: Race With Destiny.*"

Thoms, Hal. "Filming the Race with Destiny."

EXPOSED
September 1956
Rutledge, Rhett. "James Dean: The God of a Weird and Morbid Cult."

EXPOSURE
July 1990
Sawahata, Lesa. "Stern Snaps Back: The Re-Development of Photographer Phil Stern."

Wiley, Mason. "It's a Wonderful Death: Our Magnificent Obsession with All-Star Stiffs."

THE FAB 50s
Volume One, 1979
"James Dean: The Lost One."

FAIRMOUNT NEWS
February 26, 1948
"Quakers Draw Trojans in Opener."

April 14, 1949
"F.H.S. Studens Win State Meets."

April 28, 1949
"Fairmount Track Team Beats Van Buren."

"Good Luck at Longmont - Jim."

"Seniors Leave May 7 for Washington."

April 7, 1955
"Dean's 'Eden' Proves to be Powerful."

October 6, 1955
"James Dean Killed as a Result of California Car Accident."

October 13, 1955
"Fairmount Buries James Dean's Body."

October 1955 *Special Issue*
"In Memory of James Dean."

October 4, 1956
"2,000 Persons Attend Dean Remembrane (sic) Service Sun."

FAMILY CIRCLE
April 1955
"The Reel Dope: *East of Eden.*"

FANS' STAR LIBRARY
Number 16, 1959
"The Late James Dean."

FILM CAREERS
Fall 1963
Ringgold, Gene. "Elizabeth Taylor."

FILM LIFE
October 1955
Maynard, John. "James Dean: But He's So Young!"

February 1956
Gray, Phyllis. "The Three Loves of Elizabeth Taylor."

Tusher, Bill. "Strictly Confidential."

April 1956
Tusher, Bill. "Strictly Confidential."

June 1956
West, Woody. "Film Life's Strictly Confidential."

"Who Can Take His Place?"

November 1956
"Jimmy Dean's Happiest Moments."

Limke, Helen. "Somebody Up There Like Me, Too."

FILM REVIEW
October 1955
Muir, Davina. *"East of Eden."*

October 1956
Noble, Peter. "Can You Beat the Expert?"

January 1957
"ABC Chatter: The Late James Dean."

Noble, Peter. "Can You Beat the Expert?"

March 1957
Bradford, Philip. "Giant."

August 1957
"ABC Chatter."

Hardie, Elizabeth. "Julie Harris Talks About James Dean and the Method."

FILM THREAT
Number 17, 1988
Caldwell, Tim. "Dean's Influence: An Interview with William F. Nolan."

"Film X-tras: Jim Backus."

Gore, Chris. "Confessions of a Deanophile."

Gore, Chris. "Interview with James Dean: Questions I Wish I Could Ask Him."

Gore, Chris. "James Dean: A Legend in Life Finally Meets Death - A Tribute to an Incredible Man."

Gore, Chris. "James Dean's Hometown."

Gore, Chris. "September 30, 1955 Never Happened."

Thompson, Jim. "James Dean Death Cult."

"Vampira Versus Elvira."

FILMLAND
September 1955
"Hollywood Tattletale."

Walker, Della. "Almost a Lawyer."

September 1956
"Hollywood Tattletale."

"The Search for James Dean."

December 1956
"The James Dean Story: Can It Be Told?"

FILMS AND FILMING
February 1956
"Rebel Without a Cause"

May 1964
Bean, Robin. "Great Films of the Century: *East of Eden.*"

October 1965
Bean, Robin. "Dean - Ten Years After."

January 1966
"Success Begins at Forty."

November 1967
Godfrey, Lionel. "Because They're Young: Part Two."

September 1974
"In Camera: Twenty Years On."

October 1975
"James Dean: The First American Teenager."

August 1977
McVay, Douglas. "Cult Movies? *Rebel Without a Cause.*"

September 1985
Pettigrew, Terrence. "James Dean: The Rebel Saint 30 Years On."

FILMS OF THE GOLDEN AGE
Fall 1995
Lewis, Brian M. "James Dean: 50s Legend Lives On in the Word of Collectibles."

"Tribute to James Dean."

FORT WAYNE JOURNAL-GAZETTE (Indiana)
February 8, 1991
Heithaus, Harriet Howard. "James Dean: Legend Survives in Fairmount."

September 24, 1993
Vagelatos, Alex. "City Man Enjoys Life as Look-Alike for James Dean."

FORT WAYNE NEWS-SENTINEL (Indiana)
March 11, 1993
Derringer, Alan. "Remembering a Rebel."

FRAUDS
April 1957
"Why They Made A Saint of James Dean."

FRESNO BEE (California)
September 24, 1995
Pollock, Dennis. "James Dean."

FURY
June 1957
Roller, Alfred G. "How the Ghouls are Picking at the Bones of James Dean."

GADFLY
May 1998
Dalton, David. "James Dean, Osiris Morphing."

"Who Was James Dean?"

GLOBE
April 13, 1993
"James Dean was a Slowpoke Driver."

GOTHIC
Number 2, 1989
Coffino, Michael. "The Duke of Dean."

GRANADA HILLS NEIGHBOR
February 14, 1991
Chun, J. "The Persisting Legend of James Dean."

GUIDE
Volume 3, Number 4, 1990
"Dean's Birthday Remembered on Feb. 10th."

HAVOK AND WOLVERINE: MELTDOWN
Volumes 1-4, 1989
Comic with thinly masked James Dean character.

HEAR HOLLYWOOD
July 1957
"Please Don't Call Me Jimmy."

September 1957
"At Last - The Voice of Jimmy."

HEAR THE VOICE OF HOLLYWOOD
August 1956
Sturmond, Carol Archer. "We'll Never Forget You . . . "

November 1956
"Hollywood Rumor Mill."

"Hollywood's Whispering About."

"Listen, Hear."

"Out on a Limb."

Sturmond, Carol Archer. "Hollywood's Greatest Tragedies."

HEAVY METAL
January 1984
Matena, Dick. "Rebel Without a Cause."

HEP CAT'S REVIEW
August 1957
"News Tidbits."

Phillips, Susan. "James Dean Lives in our Hearts."

HIGH TIMES
April 1981
Wilmington, Mike. "James Dean: An Appreciation."

HIT PARADER
December 1956
"The Late James Dean."

"Lyrics to *Giant*."

HOLLYWOOD ALBUM OF LOVE
Volume 1, Number 1, 1961
"Hollywood's All-Time Greatest Love Scenes."

"*Rebel Without A Cause*."

Volume 2, Number 1, 1961
"Love Tragedies That Shocked Hollywood."

"What Natalie Wood Could Teach Hollywood About Love."

HOLLYWOOD COLLECTIBLES
April 1994
Mohr, Jim. "A Collector Remembers James Dean."

HOLLYWOOD DREAM GIRL
Number 1, 1955
"Actor Turns Photographer."

HOLLYWOOD LIFE
September 1957
"Jimmy Dean."

HOLLYWOOD LIFE STORIES
Number 5, 1955
"Melancholy Genius."

HOLLYWOOD LOVE AND TRAGEDY
November 1956
"Jimmy Dean's Last Miles."

Lewis, Benjamin. "Jimmy Dean's Hidden Heartbreak."

Number Two, 1957
"Jimmy's Film Farewell."

"Stop Those Attacks on Jimmy Dean's Memory."

HOLLYWOOD MAGAZINE
December 1990 - January 1991
"Dean Redux."

HOLLYWOOD MOVIE PARADE
November 1956
Johnson, Hildegarde. "It's Time to Tell the Truth About Jimmy Dean."

HOLLYWOOD PICTURE LIFE
Winter 1955-1956
"Space Getters."

HOLLYWOOD REBELS
Number 1, 1957
"James Dean: Why Parents Fear Him."

HOLLYWOOD REPORTER
December 5, 1951
"*Fixed Bayonets* Preem Sold Out."

June 10, 1986
Reynolds, Mike. "Licensing Yesteryear."

September 18, 1991
Vittes, Laurence. "Forever James Dean."

HOLLYWOOD SCREEN PARADE
November 1957
Sands, Joy. "Pier Angeli's Tragic Love Jinx."

December 1963
Elwood, Roger. "The Devil Inside Terence Stamp."

HOLLYWOOD SECRETS ANNUAL
Number 1, 1955
"James Dean: This Year's Greatest Discovery."

Number 2, 1956
"Hollywood's Great Stars: Their True Stories."

"A Story of Youth Eternal."

HOLLYWOOD STAR CONFIDENTIAL
Number 1, 1979
"Never Before Published Dean Photos."

HOLLYWOOD STARS
August 1955
Todd, Pinky. "Rebel With a Cause."

August 1956
Eardley, David. "Hollywood's Next Jimmy Dean?"

HOLLYWOOD STUDIO MAGAZINE, THEN AND NOW
February 1977
Kendall, Robert. "The Fateful Night I Met Sal Mineo and James Dean."

August 1982
Agan, Patrick. "James Dean: The Rebel Who Wouldn't Die."

Haspiel, James Robert. "The Legendary James Dean."

Kendall, Robert. "James Dean Collecting is Now World-Wide."

O'Dowd, Brian. "Studio Co-Workers Remember Dean."

May 1983
O'Dowd, Brian. "James Dean Tribute."

May 1984
O'Dowd, Brian. "James Dean: The Lonely Rebel."

Tillotson, Jerry. "James Dean: End of the Cult Gods."

May 1985
Jacobson, Laurie. "Sal Mineo: Victim Without a Cause."

September 1985
O'Dowd, Brian. "James Dean: In His Own Words."

O'Dowd, Brian. "James Dean: 30 Years Later the Legend Keeps Growing."

December 1985
O'Dowd, Brian. "James Dean - John-Erik Hexum: The Good Die Young."

September 1986
O'Dowd, Brian. "Sal Mineo and James Dean: Friendship with a Cause."

June 1987
"30 Sexiest Stars."

September 1987
O'Dowd, Brian. "James Dean: The Day He Died!"

March 1989
O'Dowd, Brian. "The James Dean Dedication."

August 1990
Headrick, Robert J. "Collecting James Dean Memorabilia."

HOLLYWOOD TRAGEDIES
1985
Kline, Elmer L. "Sal Mineo."

Miron, Charles. "James Dean."

"Natalie Wood."

HOME AND AWAY
July/August 1996
Ashley, Bob. "Touring Along Indiana's I-69."

HORIZON
September 1958
Brustein, Robert. "The Cult of Unthink."

HORSE SENSE
June 1957
Barton, Andrew. "James Dean's Own System."

HOUSTON CITY
May 1986
Milburn, Douglas and Jan Short. "Houston Babylon."

HUSH-HUSH
January 1957
Gotram, Mike. "Did James Dean Commit Suicide?"

IDOLS
Volume 1, Number 1, 1987
Simmons, Carl. "The Small Screen Dean."

Volume 1, Number 2, 1988
"James Dean and the Vampire Lady."

Volume 1, Number 3, 1988
"James and Ursula."

"That'll Be the Day."

April 1989
"Dean Scandals."

INDIANA BUSINESS
February 1988
Salzmann, Ed. "Licensing a Legend."

INDIANAPOLIS MONTHLY
June 1992
"Roadside Attractions: The James Dean Gallery."

February 1993
Hensley, Dennis E. "Star Pupil."

INDIANAPOLIS NEWS (Indiana)
August 19, 1983
Mannweiler, David. "Utmost Dean Disciple."

May 29, 1987
Mannweiler, David. "Dean's Hold is Growing."

February 8, 1988
Mannweiler, David. "Another Dean Special."

September 2, 1991
Thomas, Bob. "Legend Lives On In 'Unabridged' Biography."

INDIANAPOLIS STAR (Indiana)
December 9, 1956
"A Living Memorial to James Dean."

December 10, 1967
Brennan, Lynne. "The Legend of Jimmy Dean."

September 22, 1985
Beasley, Michael and John Hawn. "Dean Tales Fact or Fiction? By Now, It's Hard to Tell."

September 16, 1988
Brescia, Julie. "Come Back to Fairmount, Jimmy Dean, Jimmy Dean."

September 24, 1993
Ford, Lynn. "The Dean Scene."

INSIDE
April 1957
"The Unvarnished Truth About James Dean."

September 1957
"Did James Dean Commit Suicide?"

INSIDE HOLLYWOOD
Volume 1, Number 2, 1956
"James Dean: Cause or Causes Unknown."

"Pier and Vic: A Close Call for Master Perry."

INSIDE STORY
February 1957
Dufy, Lisette. "The Amazing James Dean Hoax."

March 1960
Sansoni, John. "The Screaming Horror That Haunts the Stars."

INSURGENT
May-June 1965
Rosebury, Celia. "Rebel With a Cause - Ten Years After."

INTERNATIONAL PRESS BULLETIN
Number 5, 1966
White, Christine Lamson. "James Dean: Prelude to a Legend."

INTERVIEW
March 1972
"James."

O'Brien, Glenn. "Interview with Elia Kazan."

JACKIE
December 14, 1985
"The Older Generation Have God - We Have James Dean."

J.A.M.
September 1, 1993
Smith, John A. "East of South Bend."

JAMES DEAN: A TRIBUTE TO ROCK'S GREATEST INFLUENCE
1977 *Tempest Publications*

May, Christopher. "James Dean: A Tribute to Rock's Greatest Influence."

JAMES DEAN ALBUM
1956 *Ideal Publishing Corporation*

"The Boy Who Refuses to Die."

"The Deepening Mystery of Jimmy Dean."

"The End . . . Or the Beginning."

Ginsberg, Henry. "His True Greatness."

"His Living Legacy: *East of Eden, Rebel Without a Cause, Giant.*"

"His Searching Heart."

"Jimmy Dean Fact Sheet"

"Jimmy's Home Town."

"Jimmy's Moods."

Linet, Beverly. "What Made Jimmy Run?"

Packard, Alice. "The Real Jimmy Dean."

Rowland, Ruth C. "What Jimmy Dean's Death Did To Hollywood."

"September 30, 1955."

"The Short, Tragic Life of Jimmy Dean."

"Those Who Loved Him."

"The Untold Story of Jimmy Dean's Last Days."

"Where Jimmy Found Peace."

JAMES DEAN: THE COMPLETE STORY
1992 *Federal Publishing Company*

Gillespie, Mary. "James Dean: The Complete Story."

JAMES DEAN: THE MAN, THE LEGEND
1988 *Dennis Oneshots, Limited*

Patterson, Jane. "James Dean: The Man, The Legend."

JIMMY DEAN RETURNS
1956 *Rave Publishing Corporation*

"Jimmy Dean Returns."

JURIS
Fall 1990
Rigsby, Chuck. "Rebel With a Cause."

KIT CAR
November 1987
Pettitt, Joe. "James Dean's Last Drive."

September 1989
"D is for Dynamite."

Eggington, Bob. "The Technic Spyder 550 Replica is a Whole Lot of Fun.

LADY CHURCHILL'S ROSEBUD WRISTLET
Volume 2, Number 1, 1998
Bills, Joe. "Hollywood's Masterpiece: James Dean."

LIBERTY
November 1956
Willett, Bob. "James Dean: The Star Who Won't Stay Dean."

LIFE
March 7, 1955
Stock, Dennis. "Moody New Star: Hoosier James Dean Excites Hollywood."

July 30, 1956
"A Fine Part for Pier."

September 24, 1956
Goodman, Ezra. "Delerium Over Dead Star."

October 15, 1956
"Giant."

LITERARY CAVALCADE
October 1975
"East of Eden."

LONGMONT LEDGER (Colorado)
April 22, 1949
"National High School Speaking Champions Will Be Crowned in Longmont After Finals Saturday Night."

April 29, 1949
"Nation's Best High School Speakers Compete Here."

"Speech Meet to Bring Nation's Best to Longmont."

May 6, 1949
"National Champs."

"Parade of Champions."

LONGMONT TIMES-CALL (Colorado)
April 27, 1949
"Special Program Will Open National Speech Meet Thursday Night."

April 28, 1949
"Delegates Flock into Longmont for National Forensic League Meet."

April 29, 1949
"Human Interest Events Spark Speech Tourney."

April 29, 1949 continued
"National Speech Contests Get Underway; Competition Terrific."

April 30, 1949
"Champions Shape Up as Speech Meet Contests Push Into Finals Here."

"Students are Treated to 'Wild West.'"

May 2, 1949
"Girl Champion Wins Despite Terrific Odds."

"Six States Share Honors in Speech Competition."

LOOK
January 11, 1955
Ellis, George and Jack Hamilton. "I Perdict."

April 5, 1955
"Movie Review: *East of Eden."*

October 16, 1956
Scullin, George. "James Dean: The Legend and the Facts."

LOS ANGELES
April 1996
Spoto, Donald. "The Lost Boy."

LOS ANGELES EXAMINER (California)
October 1, 1955
Sutherland, Henry. "James Dean, Bobby Sox Idol, Killed in $7000 Car."

LOS ANGELES MIRROR-NEWS (California)
October 1, 1955
"Film Star Killed in Crash."

Williams, Dick. "'Crazy Kid' Death Was Feared."

LOS ANGELES TIMES (California)
October 1, 1955
"Film Star James Dean Dies in Auto Crash."

February 16, 1976
Shales, Tom. "The Recurring Myth of Dean."

December 18, 1977
Hillinger, Charles. "Town Where James Dean Died Gets A Memorial."

Rosenman, Leonard. "Jimmy Dean: Giant Legend, Cult Rebel."

February 8, 1978
Rosenfield, Paul. "The Dawning of *Sept. 30, 1955."*

February 8, 1981
Owen, Gene Nelson. "The Man Who Would Be 50 - A Memory of James Dean."

September 29, 1983
Seager, S.E. "Driving in the Shadow of James Dean."

July 7, 1985
Broeske, Pat H. "From the James Dean Archives."

September 29, 1985
Christon, Lawrence. "Seeing Ourselves in James Dean."

Zahn, Debra. "Rebel With an Agent."

September 30, 1985
Taylor, Clarke. "Elia Kazan Ponders the James Dean Image."

April 30, 1995
Natale, Richard. "Dean Bio's Got a Firm Foundation."

August 17, 1995
Harvey, Steve. "Only in L.A."

June 25, 1996
Bernstein, Shaon. "Still Pushing the Envelope."

September 28, 1997
O'Neill, Ann W. "On The Road."

November 13, 1998
Natale, Richard. "Old Story, New Troubles."

LOWDOWN
January 1957
Taussig, Perry. "Revealed! James Dean's Torrid Love Letters."

May 1957
Raleigh, Joel. "The Girl James Dean Was Going to Marry!"

MARION CHRONICLE - TRIBUNE (Indiana)
October 9, 1955
"Last Rites for James Dean Held Saturday in Fairmount - 3,000 Attend Services."

September 28, 1980
Dye, John. "Jame Byron Dean: The Sinister Adolescent."

March 22, 1987
"A Visit with James Dean on Stage."

September 13, 1992
Smith, Sherie. "David Loehr and James Dean: The New Guy in Town Takes on the Local Legend."

February 8, 1993
Galloway, Laura A. "Deaners' Bring Annual Revel Without a Pause."

MARION LEADER-TRIBUNE (Indiana)
October 1, 1955
"James Dean is Killed in Automobile Wreck."

MARKETING NEWS
March 29, 1993
Miller, Cyndee. "Some Celebs Just Not Reaching Their Potential - And They're Dead."

METRO
September 26 - October 2, 1985
Street, Sharon. "Deanmania: 'I'm A Fan, Not A Fanatic."

Street, Sharon. "James Dean: A Legend Beyond His Time."

MIRABELLA
November 1990
Hopper, Dennis. "James Dean."

MNET GUIDE
February 1991
"James Dean in *East of Eden, Rebel Without a Cause, Giant.*"

MODEL
February 1989
O'Keefe, Linda. "Bad Boy Finds Good Home."

MODERN MAN
Annual Number 4, 1955
Borgeson, Griff. "100-Mile-An-Hour Sports Cars."

MODERN MATURITY
September-October 1994
Tennesen, Michael. "Rebel With a Cause."

MODERN SCREEN
March 1955
Cronin, Steve. "Three to Love."

Parsons, Louella. "I Nominate for Stardom."

May 1955
Epstein, Florence. "New Movies."

Zeitlin, Ida. "The Way of a Bride."

June 1955
Epstein, Florence. "New Movies."

Miller, Laura Owen and Anna Kendall. "James Dean: Smoldering Dynamite."

Parsons, Louella. "The Letter Box."

August 1955
Moore, Richard. "Lone Wolf."

Parsons, Louella. "Good News."

Zeitlin, Ida. "The Bridge is Love."

September 1955
Nelson, Lori. "The Dean I've Dated."

October 1955
Collins, Imogene. "The Secret Love that Haunts Jimmy Dean."

Epstein, Florence. "New Movies."

Parsons, Louella. "The Letter Box."

December 1955
"Appointment with Death."

Connelly, Mike. "This Was My Friend Jimmy Dean."

Januray 1956
"Announcing Modern Screen's Silver Cup Award Winners for 1955."

Stevens, George. "A Tenderness Lost."

Wilkie, Jane. "Seventeen! Cutest Doll They've Ever Seen."

Zeitlin, Ida. "And the Whole World Played Sweet Music."

March 1956
"Goodbye, Jimmy."

"TV Talk."

June 1956
"A Memento from Jimmy Dean."

August 1956
Parsons, Louella. "I'm On My Soapbox."

October 1956
Adams, Nick. "Jimmy's Happiest Moments."

December 1956
"The Inside Story."

McCarthy, Jim. "It's Me, Jimmy . . . "

January 1957
Connolly, Mike. "The Meaning of Jimmy Dean's Last Message."

February 1957
Epstein, Florence. "New Movies."

Nolan, William F. "His Love Destroyed Him . . . "

March 1957
Wills, Beverly. "I Amost Married Jimmy Dean."

October 1957
Epstein, Florence. "New Movies."

Myers, David. "The Last Story About Jimmy."

Schafer, Jack. "What Jimmy Dean Believed."

Wutherich, Rolf. "Death Drive."

March 1958
"The 'Gringo' With Guts."

May 1958
Parsons, Louella. "Louella Parsons in Hollywood."

August 1961
Brewer, Doug. "Horst Buckholz."

April 1965
Bascombe, Laura. "Let's Go . . . To My Place."

May 1976
"Sal Mineo Murdered."

MODERN SCREEN'S HOLLYWOOD YEARBOOK
Number 3, 1960
Parsons, Louella. "The Fabulous Frantic Fifties."

MODERN TEEN
August 1962
"The Legend of James Dean."

THE MORNING TELEGRAPH (New York)
December 5, 1952
Bolton, Whitney. *"See The Jaguar* Fine Until Its Third Act."

MOTION
Winter 1961/1962
Connolly, Ray. "Eden Revisited."

MOTION PICTURE
December 1954
Weller, Helen. "I'm On My Own Now."

April 1955
Gaucher, Claire. "Movies to See."

Kilgallen, Dorothy. "Coast to Coast with Dorothy Kilgallen."

June 1955
Hopper, Hedda. "Under Hedda's Hat."

Kilgallen, Dorothy. "Coast to Coast."

July 1955
Boyd, Lawrence. "Danger, Hot Stuff!"

Kilgallen, Dorothy. "Coast to Coast."

September 1955
Kilgallen, Dorothy. "Coast to Coast."

Nelson, Lori. "The Dean I've Dated."

December 1955
"James Dean."

Motion Picture Continued
May 1956
Cook, Jim. "Jimmy Dean is Not Dead."

Hopper, Hedda. "Under Hedda's Hat."

Keller, John. "Lori Nelson: When Love Takes Over."

August 1956
Graham, Sheila. "Sounding Off."

"Hollywood's Greatest Untold Love Stories."

Wood, Natalie. "It's a Wonderful Whirl."

September 1956
Meltsir, Aljean. "James Dean: His Life and Loves."

October 1956
Hopper, Hedda. "Under Hedda's Hat."

November 1956
Winslow, Marcus and Aljean Meltsir. "You Can Make Jimmy Dean Live Forever."

December 1956
Hopper, Hedda. "Under Hedda's Hat."

Lopez, Vincent. "Listen with Lopez."

Tusher, Bill. "That Shy Smile."

April 1957
"Popping Questions at Natalie."

August 1957
"Especially For You."

November 1958
Hopper, Hedda. "Changing Styles of Hollywood Love."

January 1959
Abeles, Joseph. "Their Passport to Fame."

February 1959
Patrick, Wanda. "The Ghost Who Wrecked Pier Angeli's Marriage!"

May 1961
Denis, Paul. "Where Is Jimmy Dean? Where Are His Friends? Where Is His Memorial? Where Are His Fans?"

April 1965
Atherton, Brian. "The Night Natalie Stole the Show From Liz!"

October 1965
Denis, Paul. "The Tarnished Memory of James Dean."

June 1972
Carpozi, George, Jr. "James Dean: He Never Learned to Compromise - Even With Death."

October 1975
Fitz Hugh, Cliff. "James Dean at 44: Superstar or Has-Been?"

MOTOR TREND
September 1985
Nerad, Jack R. "On the Trail of James Dean."

MOVIE ALBUM
Winter 1955-1956
"Matinee Idols."

Spring 1956
"For Whom the Bell Tolls."

Number Six 1957
"And Now . . . Tomorrow . . . "

"Dean and the All-Time Greats."

"James Dean: A Tradition is Born."

"The Search for Mr. X."

Number Eight 1962
"The Deathless Legend of Jimmy Dean."

Number Nine 1962
"A Tale of Two Legends."

MOVIE AND TV ALBUM
April 1957
"He Didn't Want It This Way . . . "

MOVIE AND TV SPOTLIGHT
December 1956
Johnson, Hildegarde. "The Crazy Capers of Jimmy Dean."

MOVIE COLLECTOR'S WORLD
April 4, 1986
Ruiz, Bob. "The Phenomenon Called James Dean."

MOVIE FAN
April 1958
"Is His Face His Fortune?"

MOVIE LIFE
November 1954
"Lots to See."

Sloan, Lloyd. "Chatterbox."

December 1954
Sloan, Lloyd. "Chatterbox."

March 1955
"Chatterbox."

"Intimate Closeups."

Warfield, John. "Two Hearts in Time."

May 1955
"Move Over, Marlon."

"Mr. X Reports."

July 1955
"Chatterbox."

Tusher, Bill. "The Unpredictable Mr. Dean."

November 1955
"Heading for Heartbreak."

December 1955
"Movie Life of Elizabeth Taylor."

"Mr. X Reports."

"The Untold Story of James Dean's Last Days."

Williams, Dick. "Chatterbox."

March 1956
"The Boy Who Refuses to Die."

May 1956
"James Dean's Greatest Performance."

June 1956
Blythe, Nell. "Jimmy Dean Fights Back From the Grave."

"Hollywood's Greatest Lovers."

July 1956
"Jimmy Dean's Legacy."

Linet, Beverly. "Strange Revelations of the Stars Rival 'Bridey Murphy."

"Why The Heavy Heart, Liz?"

August 1956
Linet, Beverly. "The Secret Happiness of Jimmy Dean."

"The Truth About Liz Taylor's Personal Problems."

September 1956
Adams, Nick. "Jimmy Dean - Why We Loved Him - Part One."

"Meet Sensational Newcomer Carroll Baker - Is She a Female Jimmy Dean?"

October 1956
Adams, Nick. "Why We Loved Jimmy Dean - Part Two."

"The Search for Sal Mineo's Amazing Secret."

Spencer, Lynn. "Will Pier Let Vic Off the Pedestal?"
November 1956
"Jimmy's Farewell to You."

December 1956
"Coming Your Way."

"That Terrific Nick!"

Wood, Natalie. "I Can't Forget Jimmy."

Movie Life Continued
January 1957
Blythe, Nell. "The Untold Story of the Love Jimmy Lost."

Williams, Dick. "News! News! News!"

February 1957
"Will They Cheat Jimmy Again?"

April 1957
"Natalie and Her Men."

May 1957
"Dean's Dangerous Decision."

"Hot Off the Teletype."

"What You Owe Jimmy Dean."

July 1957
"Why They Want You to Forget Jimmy."

August 1957
"A New James Dean?"

September 1957
Williams, Dick. "Hollywood Dateline."

Williams, Jane. "In Loving Memory."

October 1957
Williams, Jane. "Did Jimmy Dean's Spirit Haunt the Studio?"

November 1957
Blyth, Nell. "Does John Saxon Have a Jimmy Dean Complex?"

October 1958
"James Dean: Three Years of Sorrow - Never Forgotten/Never Replaced."

April 1962
"James Dean - Pier Angeli."

July 1963
Maddox, Tex. "Vice and Virtue: Part One: Jack Lord's Rebel Life."

MOVIE LIFE YEARBOOK
Number 20, 1955
"Introducing."

Number 21, 1955
"Top Men in Town."

Number 22, 1956
"In Loving Memory."

"Movie Life of Elizabeth Taylor."

"Movie Life of James Dean."

"Movie Life of Pier Angeli and Vic Damone."

"Sneak Previews."

Number 23, 1957
"In Loving Memory . . . The Jimmy Dean Saga."

"Natalie Wood: Teenager with a Past."

"The Search for Sal Mineo's Amazing Secret."

Number 24, 1958
"The James Dean Legend: Too Soon Forgotten."

MOVIE MIRROR
July 1956
"Jimmy Dean: So Little Time."

February 1957
"A Special Message to James Dean Fans."

May 1957
McCambridge, Mercedes. "In Defense of Jimmy Dean."

Oppenheimer, Peer J. "Hollywood is Talking About . . ."

July 1957
Watkins, Mary Ann. "In Defense of Natalie Wood."

December 1962
Arthur, Fred. "Hollywood's Unhappy Love Stories."

MOVIE MIRROR YEARBOOK
Number 7, 1964
"James Dean: The Faithful Still Believe."

MOVIE PLAY
September 1955
Ransom, Iris Joy. "Is James Dean a Faker?"

"Stars of Tomorrow - Richard Davalos."

January 1956
"Hello, Young Lovers."

Holland, Jack. "Hot Off the Lots."

Leaf, Earl. "Leaf from Hollywood."

Louis, Merry. "The Boy Who'd Like to Be Brando."

May 1956
Thomas, Bob. "Jimmy Dean's Tragic Life and Death."

September 1956
"Portrait in Stone."

MOVIE SCENE
July 1985
"James Dean: 30 Years an Idol . . . A Myth, A Legend, Or Simply a Fantasy?"

MOVIE SCREEN YEARBOOK
Number 2, 1955
"Hollywood at Work: Sound, Sweat and Stevens."

Number 3, 1957
"Hollywood Will Never Forget."

"Hollywood's Academy Awards."

"James Dean: A Special Message to His Fans."

MOVIE SECRETS
August 1955
O'Leary, Dorothy. "The Littlest Rebel."

December 1955
Bailey, Bill. "Brando and Dean: Double Exposure."

June 1956
"The Truth Behind the James Dean Stories."

October 1956
"James Dean: As You Remember Him . . . "

MOVIE SHOW
May 1955
"New Faces: James Dean."

September 1955
"A Rebel Comes Home to Rest."

September 1956
"James Dean: The Man Who Won't Die."

MOVIE SPOTLIGHT
August 1955
Leaf, Earl. "Hollywood Star Forecast."

Marshall, Hope. "Pier: 'I'm on Cloud #9'"

"Move Over Marlon."

December 1955
Ericson, Ruth. "Great Adventure."

Gardner, Hope. "James Dean's Secret Heartbreak."

Rowe, Rob. "Keyhole Konfidential."

October 1956
"The Last Unpublished Pictures of Jimmy Dean."

MOVIE STARS
April 1962
"Can a Child Star Grow Up Happy?"

March 1963
Gaugin, Lorraine. "Rock Hudson Talks! The Truth About Liz Taylor, Jimmy Dean and Me."

MOVIE STARS PARADE
July 1955
Friedrichson, Frank. "James Dean Hates to be Loved."

September 1955
Elliott, Graham. "Passing Parade."

Rowland, Ruth C. "What Jimmy Dean Has Done to Hollywood."

October 1955
Williams, John. "The Strange Love Making of Jimmy Dean."

November 1955
Gordon, Rose. "What's New at the Movies."

"Hollywood's Hit and Run Lovers."

"Confidentially...This is Hollywood."

MOVIE STARS PARADE
December 1955
Elliott, Graham. "Passing Parade."

Friedrichson, Frank. "The Short Tragic Life of Jimmy Dean."

January 1956
Elliott, Graham."Passing Parade."

Williams, John. "Who is the Next Star Marked for Tragedy?"

February 1956
Rowland, Ruth C. "What Jimmy Dean's Death Did to Hollywood."

April 1956
"The Deepening Mystery of James Dean."

May 1956
"The Deepening Mystery of James Dean."

June 1956
"As You Remember Him."

July 1956
Nielsen, Evelyn Washburn. "Secrets from Jimmy Dean's Past."

August 1956
Nielsen, Evelyn Washburn. "What Jimmy Dean's Hometown Can Now Reveal."

September 1956
Preston, Peter. "6 Unsolved Mysteries of Jimmy Dean's Death."

October 1956
"Should Elvis Presley Play Jimmy Dean?"

November 1956
"Last Chance to Vote: Should Elvis Presley Play Jimmy Dean."

Wright, Ben. "Where Would Jimmy Dean Be Today?"

December 1956
Gordon, Rose. "What's New at the Movies."

"Must We Stop Writing About Jimmy Dean?"

January 1957
"Should Elvis Presley Play Jimmy Dean?"

February 1957
"Jimmy Dean's Fight to Live."

March 1957
Michael, Timothy. "The Night that Changed Natalie Wood's Life."

April 1957
"James Dean Memorial Page."

May 1957
"James Dean Memorial Page."

Preston, Peter. "The Girl Tab Couldn't Give Up."

June 1957
Oppenheimer, Peter J. "Is Natalie Wood Betraying Jimmy Dean?"

July 1957
"Your Chance to Follow in Jimmy Dean's Footsteps."

August 1957
Remington, Ann. "James Dean: The Tragedy That Lives On."

MOVIE STARS PARADE
October 1957
"To Treasure Always."

November 1957
Rowland, Steve. "Goodbye, Jimmy Dean."

October 1958
"Six Unsolved Mysteries of Jimmy Dean's Death."

MOVIE STARS/ TV CLOSEUPS
March 1959
"The Boy Who Followed Jimmy Dean to Death."

MOVIE TEEN ILLUSTRATED
Summer 1957
"Jimmy Dean: A Moment in History."

"What Next Baby Doll?"

Fall 1957
"Jimmy Dean Returns."

"Why Are Jimmy Dean Fans Switching to Tony Perkins?"

March 1958
Hammel, Sidney. "Jimmy, We Shall Never Say Goodbye."

MOVIE - TV SPOTLIGHT
December 1956
Johnson, Hildegarde. "The Crazy Capers of Jimmy Dean By His Closest Pals."

MOVIE WORLD
October 1955
"Movie World Memos."

"Speed Demon Dean."

February 1958
"Thanks To You We Will Always Remember..."

July 1962
"The Ghost of James Dean."

January 1963
"The Secret Rites of the James Dean Fans."

MOVIELAND
MAY 1955
"Hollywood Heroes, Heels and He-Men."

"Inside Hollywood."

"Movieland Reviews."

August 1955
"Inside Hollywood."

"Rebel Without a Cause.."

October 1955
"Inside Hollywood."

"Liz on Location."

"Tough Guy or Big Bluff?"

November 1955
"Man of Many Moods."

"People Who Make News."

August 1956
"A Not-So-Perfect Love."

MOVIELAND
October 1956
"The Star Who Never Died."

November 1956
"Has the Jimmy Dean Craze Gone Too Far?"

December 1956
"Inside Hollywood."

Rowland, Ruth. "How Jimmy Dean Still Works Wonders for Others."

February 1957
Owen, Gene. "An Unforgettable Day with Jimmy Dean."

Movieland Continued

March 1957
Asher, Jerry. "Just a Homeboy at Heart."

May 1957
Swisher, Vi. "Thanks for Everything . . . "

1957 Annual
"Does the Legend Betray the Man?"

MOVIELAND AND TV TIME
July 1962
Brown, Fred D. "Studio Whispers."

August 1962
"The Good Old Days."

December 1962
"Jean-Paul Belmondo: He's the French James Dean."

August 1963
"Elvis Hears From James Dean."

MOVIES
October 1955
"James Dean: The Man Nobody Knows."

THE MOVIES
September 1983
Arbus, Amy. "Magnificent Obsessions."

MUSEUM OF TELEVISION AND RADIO REVIEW
Fall 1995
"James Dean on Television: A Myth in the Making."

MUSIC VIEWS
September 1957
"The James Dean Story."

MY GUY
July 6,1989
"James Dean, The Legend."

MY LOVE SECRET
December 1956
"The Real Story of James Dean."

NATIONAL ENQUIRER
November 9,1982
Derek, Sean Catherine. "His Daughter Tells...How John Derek
Risked Death to Win Ursula Andress."

1983
Baker, Carroll. "James Dean used to Make Natalie Wood Feel Like Dirt."

NATIONAL EXAMINER
October 31,1989
Turner, John. "Rock Hudson Murdered Cult Star James Dean!"

NATIONAL STAR
September 21,1974
Dangaard, Colin. "James Dean Lives Again."

September 28,1974
Dangaard, Colin. "A Movie Giant Who Cried For Love."

NEW MUSICAL EXPRESS
October 20, 1973
"This Man Started It All."

NEW REPUBLIC
February 4,1957
Astrachan, Sam. "The New Lost Generation."

NEW YORK
November 8,1976
Marlowe, Derek. "Solilioquy on James Dean's Forty-Fifth Birthday."

May 1, 1978
Haskell, Molly. "The Nifty Fifties."

New York Continued
February 1,1982
Allen, Jennifer. "Cher and Altman on Broadway."

NEW YORK DAILY MIRROR
December 5, 1952
Mortimer, Lee. "*See The Jaquar* Opens at the Cort."

NEW YORK DAILY NEWS
December 4,1952
Chapman, John. "*See the Jaquar* Lovelyto See and Hear, But It Makes No Sense."

September 28,1980
Haun, Harry. "A Quarter of a Century Later, the World is Still Awed by the Name James Dean."

March 25,1983
Hinckley, David."Remembering Jimmy Dean."

January 1, 1984
Baker, Carroll. "Making Natalie Cry."

November 2, 1986
McCormack, Ed. "Rebels Without a Clue."

September 24, 1995
Reidel, Michael. "James Dean's Walk on the West Side."

NEW YORK ENQUIRER
September 3-8, 1956
Miller, John J. and Gene Coughlin. "Destiny?
Will Elvis' Life Follow Same Dedly Parallel as Dean's?"

NEW YORK EVENING NEWS
December 4, 1952
Field, Rowland. "Bit of Melodrama."

February 9, 1954
Field, Rowland. "Sees Immoralists."

NEW YORK HERALD-TRIBUNE
December 4, 1952
Kerr, Walter F. "See The Jaquar."

June 16,1953
"Theater de Lys Revives *The Scarecrow* Tonight."

June 17, 1953
Kerr, Walter F. "Theater de Lys Presents Revival of *The Scarecrow."*

NEW YORK JOURNAL-AMERICAN
December 4,1952
McClain, John. "Play is Baffling and Confusing."

April 14,1952
Parsons, Louella D. "Dean to Play Graziano Role."

NEW YORK NEWSDAY
September 26,1985
Robins, Wayne. "The Perennial Adolescent."

NEW YORK POST
December 4, 1952
Watts, Richard, Jr. "Two on the Aisle."

September 23,1985
Maychick, Diana. "James Dean's Still a Giant."

NEW YORK TIMES
December 4, 1952
Atkinson, Brooks. "At the Theatre."

June 17,1953
Atkinson, Brooks. "First Night at the Theatre."

February 9, 1954
Atkinson, Brooks. "First Night at the Theatre."

March 13,1955
Thompson, Howard. "Another Dean Hits the Big League."

December 16,1956
Thompson, Howard. "Stage to Screen with Eli Wallach."

New York Times Continued
March 17,1957
Gould,Helen. "Peregrinating Perkins."
October 6, 1957
Robinson, Douglas. "Rising Southern Star."
April 2, 1978
Maslin, Janet. "Richard Thomas-Playing the Worshipper and Not the Hero."
April 5, 1978
Masin, Janet. "He Was Obsessed With James Dean."
April 12, 1990
Alexander, Ron. "The Fame Lives On (In Fact, It Lives Here)."

NEW YORK WOMEN'S DAILY WEAR
December 4, 1952
Dash, Thomas R. *"See The Jaguar."*

NEW YORK WORLD-TELEGRAM & THE SUN
December 4, 1952
Hawkins, Williams. "*Jaguar* Has Obsure Spots."

NEWSWEEK
October 10, 1955
"Transition."
November 7, 1955
"A Moving Performance."
June 18, 1956
"Star That Won't Dim."
April 17, 1976
Ansen, David. "Rebel With a Cause."
Summer/Fall 1990 Special Issue
Leerhsen, Charles. "This Year's Role Model."

NIGHT AND DAY: THE MAIL ON SUNDAY REVIEW
July 10, 1994
Alexander, Paul. "Girls, Prepare For a Shock!"

NOSTALGIA WORLD
Number 3, 1978
Sullivan, Dennis F. and Wayne Jones. "The James Dean Story."
December 1980
"James Dean Revisited."

OFF BROADWAY
June 1956
Corley, Edwin. "James Dean."

OFFICIAL JAMES DEAN ANNIVERSARY BOOK
1956 *Dell Publishing Company*
"A Boy at Home: Photos of Dennis Stock."
"The Accomplishments of James Dean."
"The Actor at Work . . . And a Play: Photos of Sanford Roth."
"The Footprints of a Giant."
"The Girls Who Followed in the Wake of Love."
"Jimmy Dean's Journey Toward a Place Called Love."
"Jimmy's Own Scrapbooks."
"The Little Things That Make a Myth."
"The Man Behind the Legend."
"New Faces: James Dean."
Parsons, Louella. "I Nominate for Stardom: Jame Dean."
"Portrait of the Actor in a Big Town: Photos of Roy Schatt."
"We Who Live On."

OLD CARS
February 8, 1977
Howley, Tim. "Somewhere West of Laramie: A Legend Is Born."
October 15, 1992
Howley, Tim. "So, You Thought 1955 Was a Good Year? Some Thoughts on Motorsports Disasters and James Dean."

OLD HOLLYWOOD
Volume 1, Number 1, 1956
"You Remind Me of Someone I Know . . ."

ON THE QT
March 1957
Miller, Roger. "Was Jimmy Dean a Psycho?"
April 1957
Ashendon, Larry. "Did Jimmy Dean Leave A Son?"
September 1957
"Letters to the Editor."
March 1958
"My Death Drive with James Dean."

ORIGINAL COOL
August - September 1995
Smallwood, Sue. "A Passage to Indiana in Search of James Dean."

OUT
September 1996
Martin, Richard and Deb Schwartz. "Dean of Style."

PACIFIC STARS AND STRIPES
April 9, 1956
Ricketts, Al. "On the Town."
December 8, 1956
"Dean Story Told by Kin Documentary."
March 4, 1957
"Dean Wins '56 Actor Award."
March 11, 1957
Drake, Hal. "Soldier Played Role in James Dean Legend."

PAGEANT
October 1956
Dixon, Daniel. "Darling Jimmy Dean . . . "

PAPER
September 1988
McCormick, Carlo. "James Dean Goes Home."

PARADE
May 15, 1955
Shearer, Lloyd. "Dizzy? Not This Dean."

PEOPLE MAGAZINE
April 29, 1990
Housego, Mike. "The Legends Live On and On."

PEOPLE TODAY
October 1956
"Jimmy Dean: A Cult is Born."

PEOPLE WEEKLY
October 13, 1980
Shaw, Bill. "Dead 25 Years, James Dean is Given a Touching Hometown Tribute by Nostalgic Fans."
November 12, 1990
Dougherty, Steve and Vicki Sheff. "With A New Wife, Son and Movie, Uneasy Rider Dennis Hopper Hopes To Find the Hot Spot Back on Top."

PERFORMANCE MONTHLY
September 1985
Jones, Julie R. "James Dean: America's Misunderstood Son."

PERSONAL ROMANCES
April 1957
"I Was Jimmy Dean's Wife."

PERSONALITY CLASSICS COMICS
Number 4, 1992
"James Dean."

PHILADELPHIA INQUIRER (Pennsylvania)
May 27, 1988
Lloyd, Jack. "Stepping Out:
'Lost in the '50s' Takes a Three-Day Trip in Time."

PHOTOPLAY
March 1955
Muir, Florabel. "Hollywood Whispers."

Ott, Beverly. "Honeymoon on the Heavenly Side."

Skolski, Sidney. "That's Hollywood for You."

May 1955
Graves, Janet. "Let's Go to the Movies."

Higginbotham, Ann. "Photoplay Recommends: *East of Eden.*"

July 1955
Gwynn, Edith. "Hollywood Party Line."

Service, Faith. "Determined Davalos."

Skolski, Sydney. "Demon Dean."

Skolski, Sydney. "That's Hollywood for You."

November 1955
Gwynn, Edith. "Hollywood Party Line."

Skolski, Sidney. "That's Hollywood for You."

Wood, Natalie. "You Haven't Heard the Half About Jimmy Dean."

December 1955
York, Cal. "Inside Stuff."

January 1956
Graves, Janet. "Let's Go To The Movies."

Hunt, Evelyn H. "To James Dean."

March 1956
"Announcing Photoplay's Award Winners of 1955-56."

Dean, Emma Woolen. "James Dean - The Boy I Loved."

Gwynn, Edith. "Hollywood Party Line."

June 1956
"Readers Inc. . . ."

September 1956
Bast, William. "There Was A Boy."

York, Cal. "Inside Stuff."

October 1956
Bast, William. "There Was A Boy, Part Two."

York, Cal. "Inside Stuff."

November 1956
Bast, William. "There Was A Boy, Part Three."

"Photoplay Sneak Preview - *Giant.*"

"The Truth Behind Those Suicide Rumors."

York, Cal. "Inside Stuff."

January 1957
"Love Me Tender."

"The Rebels."

"Suicide? I Say No . . . And Here's Why."

York, Cal. "Inside Stuff."

October 1957
Graves, Janet. "Let's Go To The Movies."

"Natalie Wood Reviews *The James Dean Story.*"

"Over The Editor's Shoulder."

"Readers Inc. . . . "

Sheridan, Dizzy. "In Memory of Jimmy."

Annual 1957
"No One Will Take His Place."

June 1958
Christy, George. "Exposed."

Photoplay Continued
November 1958
Hoffman, Jim. "Can Dean Stockwell Shake Off The Jimmy Dean Jinx?"

Annual 1959
"Rising Stars."

May 1961
Gautschy, Dean. "Announcing the Engagement and Forth-
coming Marriage of Troy Donahue to Lili Kardell."

September 1963
Meltsir, Aljean. "Jimmy Dean, Marilyn Monroe: Life After Death.

November 1967
Waterbury, Ruth. "The Day the Great Ones Died."

June 1972
Tweedle, Tony. "The Legend of James Dean."

July 1979
"Out of the Pages of Photoplay."

PHOTOPLAY (British)
November 1956
"Everybody's Saying It . . . Keep Your Eyes on Photoplay . . ."

December 1956
"The James Dean Life Story: He Meets Kazan . . . "

PHYSIQUE ILLUSTRATED
June 1963
"Jumping Jehosophat! Take a Long Look."

PICTURE PAGEANT
October 1956
Dixon, Daniel. "Darling Jimmy Dean . . . "

PICTURE SHOW
August 4, 1955
"Previews - *East of Eden.*"

PICTURE SHOW AND FILM PICTORIAL
August 6, 1955
"East of Eden."

PICTUREGOER
March 12-19, 1955
"This Is The Year of New Stars - They've Made It."

May 25 - June 2, 1956
"You've Proved the Cynics Wrong."

June 16-23, 1956
Austin, Guy. "Dateline Hollywood - No Thanks for This Memory."

July 30 - August 6, 1955
"Gloom, Gloom, Gloom - But New Boy Dean Will Shake You."

December 22-29, 1956
Mellor, William C. "The James Dean I Knew."

December 30 - January 5, 1957
"Oh, No! Not Presley as Dean."

December 1-7, 1957
"The James Dean Story."

December 7-14, 1957
"Why Kazan Made Him a Star."

December 14-21, 1957
"He Astounded Hollywood."

PIX ANNUAL
Fall 1958
Lindahl, John. "My Death Drive With James Dean."

PLAYBOY
November 1982
Carlinsky, Dan. "Celebrity High."

THE PLAYERS
Fall 1964
Leaf, Earl. "Natalie Wood Grows Up - Painfully."

Summer 1965
Allen, Robert L. "James Dean - Is the Legend Fading?"

POPULAR HOT RODDING
January 1995
Padgett, Nina. "James Dean Remembered."

POPULAR PHOTOGRAPHY
July 1962
Roth, Sanford H. "The Assignment I'll Never Forget."

POPULAR SCREEN
December 1959
"We Still Remember."

PREDICTION
August 1959
Lyndoe, Edward. "Death His New Nativity: The Incredible Legend of James Dean."

PREMIERE
September 1993
Alexander, Paul. "Cause Without a Rebel."

PREMIERE SPECIAL
Winter 1991
"A New Age."

"Premiere's 100 Years of Moviemaking."

PRESERVATION
January/February 1999
Weeks, Linton. "Back Home In Indiana."

PREVIEW SUPER SPECIAL
June 1978
Lewis, Flanzy. "Natalie Wood."

PRIVATE LIVES
June 1957
"Jimmy Dean's Alive!"

PRIVATE LIVES AND PUBLIC AFFAIRS
October 1955
"Is James Dean a Dandy?"

PROBE THE UNKNOWN
June 1973
Jacques, Stephen. "The Mysterious Road of James Dean's Death Car."

PSA MAGAZINE
May 1984
McCann, Clark. "Rebel Run."

RAVE
May 1956
"Did James Dean Really Die?"

November 1956
"James Dean Tells His Life Story 'In His Own Words."

January 1957
Carter, Lynne. "I Was a Friend of Jimmy Dean."

April 1957
Carter, Lynne. "I Learned About Love From Jimmy Dean."

"Natalie Wood: Red Hot Rebel with a Cause."

"Why Jimmy Won't Win Any Oscars."

September 1957
"Why Jimmy Dean is a Living Lie."

REAL
July 1957
Thomas, T.T. "I, James Dean."

THE REAL JAMES DEAN STORY
1956 *Fawcett Publications*

"Behind the Scenes."

Cook, Jim. "Jimmy Dean Is Not Dead."

"East of Eden."

The Real James Dean Story Continued
"Giant."

Hinkle, Bob with Mark Flanders. "My Friend Jimmy."

Hopper, Hedda. "For Jimmy Hedda Was . . . A Friend, A Fan, A Fighter."

Jocobi, Ernst. "The Lonely One."

"James Dean's Life Story in his Own Words."

Mineo, Sal as told to Larry Thomas. "The Dean I Knew."

Nelson, Lori. "The Jimmy Dean I Dated."

"Rebel Without a Cause"

"The Star They'll Never Forget."

Tate, Kathryn. "The Man Behind the Legend."

"This Was His Greatness."

"The Women In His Life."

REDBOOK
September 1956
Hyams, Joe. "James Dean."

REEL CAROLINA
February 1996
Nelson, Connie. "A Legend For All Times."

REMEMBER
October 1995
Rees, Robert. "Rebel With a Cause."

"Souvenirs: Deanabilia."

REPORTER
December 13, 1956
Weales, G. "Movies: The Crazy, Mixed-Up Kids Take Over."

THE REPOSITORY (Canton, Ohio)
July 29, 1994
Kane, Dan. "James Dean: Rebel Without a Pause."

THE REPUBLIC (Columbus, Indiana)
November 13, 1988
Colurso, Mary. "James Dean: His So-Cool Image Didn' Die With Him."

THE ROBB REPORT
August 1990
Smith, Ron. "The Star , The Car - And the Curse that Linked Them."

ROCK HUDSON
1956 *Star Stories Incorporated*

Ardmore, Jane. "How Rock Met the Challenge of Jimmy Dean."

ROCKIN' 50s
December 1987
Rees, Robert. "Spotlight on James Dean."

ROCKY MOUNTAIN NEWS (Colorado)
September 28, 1996
Anthony, Ted. "King of Cool."

ROD AND CUSTOM
May 1956
"Rebel With a Reason."

August 1989
Cook, Terry. "New Jersey News: Unheralded Eastern Events."

ROGUE FOR MEN
February 1957
Phillips, Michael. "Behind the Mask of James Dean."

ROLLING STONE
March 15, 1973
Flattery, Paul. "Adam Faith: Ex-Pop Idol a TV Star."

July 5, 1973
Grover, Lewis. "Paul Newman: Portrait of the Artist at 47."

Rolling Stone Continued

June 20, 1974
Dalton, David. "The Making of a Celluloid Rebel."

November 1, 1979
Vallely, Jean. "Martin Sheen: Heart of Darkness."

November 16, 1980
Zavatsky, W. "Epitaph For a Rebel: Reflections on the Life and Death of James Dean."

May 26, 1983
"Bad Boy Sean Penn: The Next James Dean. . . "

RONA BARRETT'S GOSSIP
October 1974
Leaf, Earl. "The Way They Were - James Dean."

April 1977
Modderno, Craig. "Natalie Wood: 'Nothing Means More to Me Than My Husband and My Children."

ROSTRUM
November 1961
"James Dean."

SAN FRANCISCO CHRONICLE (California)
November 13, 1955
"Preview of the Week: *Rebel Without a Cause.*"

SATURDAY EVENING POST
August 1985
Stuller, Jay. "Legends That Will Not Die."

SATURDAY REVIEW
October 13, 1956
Alpert, Hollis. "It's Dean, Dean, Dean."

August 3, 1957
Knight, Arthur. "Celluloid Monument: *The James Dean Story.*"

November 30, 1957
"The Way of Life We Call America."

SCARLET STREET
Winter 1995
Hatch, George. "Who Killed Teddy Bear?"

Lilly, Jessie. "Night Rebel Jack Grinnage."

Rees, Robert. "Vampira Remembers Jimmy."

Sullivan, Drew. "The Mysteries of James Dean."

Valley, Richard. "Character Actress Ann Doran."

SCHOLASTIC ACTION
January 31, 1986
"Teen Idols."

SCREEN
February 1955
"James Dean: He's New . . . And Independent."

August 1955
"Screen Whispers."

December 1955
"He's No Carbon Copy."

February 1956
Archerd, Armand. "Screen Whispers."

Connolly, Mike. "The Strange Case of James Dean."

SCREEN ALBUM
May - July 1955
"He Found the Cycle-Logical Way to Stop Traffic."

August - October 1955
"To Repair a Broken Heart - An Oil Filter."

"Youth Has a Holiday."

Screen Album Continued
November - January 1955-56
"Confessions of a Successful Neurotic . . ."

"Lots of Little Romances Don't Equal One Love."

"The Eyes of Texas Are Upon Her."

February - April 1956
"Milestones."

"Screen Album's Oscars To . . . "

SCREEN FACTS
Number 8, 1964
Ringgold, Gene. "James Dean."

SCREEN GREATS PRESENTS JAMES DEAN
1988 *Starlog Press*

Hanna, David. "James Dean."

SCREEN HITS ANNUAL
Number Ten, 1955
"East of Eden."

Number Eleven, 1956
"Jimmy Dean in *Rebel Without a Cause.*"

SCREEN LEGENDS
May 1965
Ringgold, Gene. "James Dean: His Life and Legend."

SCREEN LIFE
November 1955
Stewart, David. "He's Not Marion . . . He's Himself."

September 1956
"Jimmy Dean's Last Photos."

Marsh, Paul. "Hollywood Headlines."

August 1957
"Remember Me?"

"Somebody Else Has Taken His Place."

September 1966
"After Ten Years - Is the Legend Finally Dead?"

SCREEN STARS
November 1955
Archerd, Armand. "Confidential Gossip."

Canfield, Alice. "Intimate Hollywood."

Canfield, Alice. "What Makes Jimmy Run?"

September 1956
Adams, Nick. "The James Dean I Knew."

November 1956
Canfield, Alice. "Intimate Hollywood."

"The Immortal Dean."

March 1957
Canfield, Alyce. "Intimate Hollywood."

"Leave Him To Heaven."

Smith, Lillian. "On the Screen."

"What Presley Really Wants - Another Jimmy Dean?"

May 1957
Adams, Nick. "Hollywood's Mixed-Up Blabbermouths."

SCREEN STARS: JAMES DEAN
1990 *Screen Stars*
Humphires, Patrick. "James Dean."

SCREEN STORIES
March 1955
"East of Eden."

"James Dean - A Bluff Pays Off."

Screen Stories Continued
April 1955
Skolsky, Sidney. "Sidney Skolsky Reports."

October 1955
"Jimmy Dean in *Rebel Without a Cause.*"

Skolsky, Sidney. "Sidney Skolsky Reports."

November 1955
Skolsky, Sidney. "Sidney Skolsky Reports."

February 1956
"The Revolt of Liz Taylor."

May 1956
"The Jimmy Dean Film Festival."

June 1956
"Beginning the Jimmy Dean Film Festival: *East of Eden.*"

July 1956
Connolly, Mike. "Last Minute News From Hollywood."

"Jimmy Dean in *Rebel Without a Cause.*"

September 1956
"The Jimmy Dean Film Festival: *The Unlighted Road.*"

"The Question Box."

November 1956
"Giant."

"Jimmy Dean: Two Memories."

Stevens, George. "The Actor Jimmy Dean."

SCREENLAND PLUS TV-LAND
July 1955
Dayton, Mark. "James Dean: Excitement for the Lovelorn."

September 1955
"Marlon Brando: From T-Shirt to Bow Tie."

O'Leary, Dorothy. "Hollywood Love Life."

May 1956
"James Dean: In Memorium."

Maynard, John. "Can Gossip End Her Career?"

SCREENPLAY
April 1965
Webster, Alan. "The James Dean Story Screenplay Waited 10 Years to Print."

SEVENTEEN
July 1957
Miller, Edwin. "James Dean: Bigger Than Life."

September 1962
Winters, Shelley. "The Lonliest Years of My Life."

THE SHEET MUSIC EXCHANGE
August 1984
Johnson, Bob. "The Sheet Music of James Dean."

SHEILA GRAHAM'S HOLLYWOOD ROMANCES
Number 7, 1955
"Can Dean Forget Mrs. Damone?"

Number 11, 1957
"Elizabeth Taylor Searched For a Lover . . . And Found a Father."

"He Wasn't a God, He Was a Man, And He Died."

"Hollywood's Love-Legends."

"Pier Angeli: The Search for Happiness is Never Ending."

SHEILA GRAHAM'S HOLLYWOOD YEARBOOK
Number 7, 1956
"Hollywood's Year of Tragedy."

"Milestones."

SHOW BUSINESS ILLUSTRATED
February 1962
"Elia Kazan."

Morgan, Al. "New Breed of Screen Lover."

SIGHT AND SOUND
Spring 1956
Houston, Penelope. "Rebels Without Causes."

Summer 1956
Lassally, Walter. "The Cynical Audience."

Autumn 1956
Ray, Nicholas. "Story into Script."

Winter 1956-1957
Houston, Penelope. *"Giant."*

Spring 1957
Houston, Penelope. "Hollywood in the Age of Television."

Summer 1957
Anderson, Lindsay. "Ten Feet Tall."

Autumn 1957
"The James Dean Story."

Summer 1958
Gillett, John. "Cut-And Come Again!"

Winter 1959 - 1960
Dyer, Peter John. "Youth and the Cinema."

Spring 1960
Dyer, Peter John. "Youth and the Cinema."

Autumn 1961
Houston, Penelope and John Gillett. "Conversations with Nicholas Ray and Joseph Losey."

SILVER SCREEN
December 1955
Jamison, Jan. "Genius or Jerk?"

Annual 1957
"Hollywood's Biggest Stories: James Dean."

16 MAGAZINE
May 1957
"Editor's Notebook."

November 1957
"Jimmy's Awards."

Johnston, Les. "How Great is Jimmy Dean Today?"

Worth, Frank. "Don't Print That Photo!"

March 1959
"Jimmy the Kid."

November 1959
"A Tribute to Jimmy."

SONG HITS
December 1956
"Paying Tribute to James Dean."

SOUND STAGE
February 1965
Gaugin, Lorraine. "Sound Stage on Stage."

SPORTS CAR ILLUSTRATED
July 1955
Mourning, Jim. "Palm Springs."

SPY
March 1992
Rudnick, Paul. "Everybody's a Rebel."

STAR
October 8, 1985
Wutherich, Rolf. "The Day I Rode With Jimmy Dean to His Death."

April 23, 1991
Parker, John. "Elizabeth and Rock and Natalie and Jimmy and Monty."

STAR MAGAZINE
November 1957
"His Last Chance."

"The Truth About James Dean."

"The Truth Behind Sal's Stardom."

STAR MOVIE MAGAZINE
Yearbook - January 1956
Oppenheimer, Peer J. "Here's Glamourtown!"

Oppenheimer, Peer J. "Inside Rock Hudson: The Secret Self."

"Rebel - And Giant, Too."

THE STORY OF THE MOVIES
Number Nine, 1974
"The Rebel Hero."

STREET RODDER
May 1981
Carter, Geoff. "Street Rodders Remember James Dean."

SUPPRESSED
April 1957
"The Star That Elvis and Jimmy Made."

June 1957
"Money From The Grave."

TAKE ONE
January 1977
Alpert, Barry. "Two for Nicholas Ray."

Cocks, Jay. "Director In Aspic."

Goodwin, Michael and Naomi White. "Nicholas Ray: Rebel!"

TEEN
June 1957
Lund, Allen: "Teen Talent Search."

TEEN CIRCLE
February 1966
Colbert, Suzanne. "Is Paul Peterson Another Jimmy Dean?"

TEEN LIFE
April 1957
"The Man Who Dared Everything: James Dean."

TEENAGE REVIEW
February 1957
Winters, Gail. "Two Men and a Myth."

TEMPO
November 13, 1956
"Why They Still Worship James Dean."

TEXAS CO-OP POWER
April 1994
Macias, George. "Marfa - Contrast, Intrigue, and the Ghost of a *Giant* Past."

TEXAS MONTHLY
July 1983
"Ask Jett Rink."

THE THEATRE
February 1961
Houghton, Norris. "Moscow's Bobby-Sox Idol."

THEATRE ARTS
August 1953
Nash, N. Richard. *"See The Jaguar."*

THRASHER
November 1989
Indiana, Tanya. "Wander Indiana."

TIME
March 21, 1955
"East of Eden."

October 10, 1955
"Milestones."

September 3, 1956
"Dean of the One-Shotters."

Time Continued
October 22, 1956
"The New Pictures - *Giant.*"

November 26, 1956
"The Dean Cult."

February 23, 1998
Lopez, Steve. "American Scene: James Dean All Over Again."

December 14, 1998
Skow, John and James Willwerth. "Horse of a Different Color."

TIME INTERNATIONAL
October 10, 1994
Corliss, Richard. "Show Business."

TIME OUT
September 26 - October 2, 1975
"Live Fast, Die Young."

TOMMY SANDS MAGAZINE
1957 *Bartholomew House*

TRACES OF INDIANA AND MIDWESTERN HISTORY
Summer 1989
"Grant County's Own."

Fall 1989
Breen, Ed. "James Dean's Indiana: The Stage Along Sand Pike."

Nall, Adeline as told to Val Holley. "Grant County's Own."

TRUE STRANGE
March 1957
DeKolbe, Robert. "James Dean Speaks From The Grave."

TRUMP
March 1957
"Giants."

TV AND MOVIE SCREEN MAGAZINE
November 1955
"Star Chatter."

Tusher, Bill. "The Girls in James Dean's Life."

September 1956
Heller, Richard. "Jimmy Dean: The Story He Wanted to Tell."

"Reader's Corner."

June 1957
Holland, Jack. "More in Love Than Ever."

November 1959
Kahn, Stephen. "Sal Mineo: I Still Remember James Dean."

TV GUIDE
May 26 - June 1, 1956
"The Unlighted Road."

June 5 - June 11, 1993
James, Clive. "TV and the Fan Game."

TV MOVIE FAN
September 1957
Hamilton, Tom. "Stardust Scuttlebutt."

Stevens, Bill. "Is James MacArthur the New James Dean?"

TV MOVIE MEN
Number One, 1959
"Must the Hottest ALovers Be Bachelors?"

TV NEWS
May 6, 1955
"From Hoosier Boy to Video Star."

TV - RADIO LIFE
May 1956
Bigsby, Evelyn. "He Had A Little Boy Lost Quality."

"Unlighted Road."

TV STAR ANNUAL
Number Three, 1957
"TV Memories of Jimmy Dean."

TV STAR PARADE
November 1956
"Television's Memories of Jimmy Dean."

TV TIMES
August 14-20, 1976
"Giant."

Lanning, Dave. "Portrait of a Rebel as Middle-Aged Giant."

20/20

March 1990
Guilliatt, Paul. "Rebel Within a Clause."

UNCENSORED
September 1956
"The Truth About Those James Dean Whispers."

March 1957
"The Romance James Dean Couldn't Kill."

US
August 20, 1990
Frascella, Larry. "Brief Encounters."

October 15, 1990
O'Toole, Lawrence. "Saint James: Rebel Without Claws."

VANITY FAIR
September 1984
"James Dean: American Icon."

August 1987
Rosenbaum, Ron. "Riding High: Dennis Hopper Rides Back."

VARIETY
February 10, 1954
Bolton, Whitney. *"The Immoralist* An Outstanding Example of Theatrical Courage."

"Play on Broadway."

August 31, 1977
"9/30/55"

THE VELVET LIGHT TRAP
Winter 1974
Collins, Gary. "Kazan in the Fifties."

VIDEO TIMES
September 1985
"Legend Without a Pause."

VISTA
October 1989
"Celebrity Fax of the Month: James Dean's Trousers Without a Cause."

VOGUE
February 1955
"The Next Successes."

September 1988
Haskell, Molly. "Rebel With A Shrine."

WASHINGTON POST
September 30, 1956
Klibanoff, Hank. "The Dean Obsession."

WEEKEND (Muncie, Indiana)
September 10, 1982

WFMT PERSPECTIVE
October 1961
Fielder, Leslie A. "The Fear of the Impulsive Life."

WHERE ITS AT
February 27, 1978
Billanti, Dean. "Film: *September 30, 1955."*

WHISPER
February 1956
Schaeffer, Sam. "James Dean's Black Madonna."

April 1956
"James Dean's Fans Speak Their Minds."

August 1956
Schaeffer, Sam. "The Girl James Dean Left Behind."

December 1956
Morris, Tina and Sam Schaffer. "James Dean vs. Elvis Presley."

February 1957
Schaeffer, Sam. "How James Dean Got an Oscar."

December 1957
Schaeffer, Sam. "James Dean: Ghost of Polonio Pass."

WHO'S WHO IN HOLLYWOOD
Volume 1, Number 10, 1955

WORCESTER TELEGRAM (Massachusetts)
July 25, 1993
Carnes, Gloria. L. "James Dean: The Roots of This Rebel Without a Cause Are in the Indiana Heartland."

YOU
September 29, 1985
Pettigrew, Terrence. "James Dean: Blueprint for a Rebel."

PAGE 14
All are $20-30 each

PAGE 15
All are $20-30 each

PAGE 16
All are $20-30 each

PAGE 17
All are $20-30 each

PAGE 18
Top Left: $85
Top Right: $120
Bottom: 1. $60 2. $35
3. $120 4. $120

PAGE 19
All are $20-60 each

PAGE 20
All are $40-60 each

PAGE 23
All are $80-140 each

PAGE 24
All are $60-80 each

PAGE 25
All are $40-80 each

PAGE 26
All are $40-80 each

PAGE 27
All are $40-80 each

PAGE 28
All are $20-40 each

PAGE 29
All are $10-20 each

PAGE 30
All are $60-80 each

PAGE 31
All are $60-80 each

PAGE 34
All are $5-10 each

PAGE 35
Top: $40
Middle Left: $50
Middle Right: $20
Bottom Left: $180-250
Bottom Right: $65

PAGE 36
Top: $25
Bottom: $85

PAGE 37
Top: $60
Bottom: $25

PAGE 38
All are $12-20 each

PAGE 39
All are $12-20 each

PAGE 40
All are $4-8 each

PAGE 41
All are $4-8 each

PAGE 42
All are $20-30 each

PAGE 43
All are $2-6 each

PAGE 44
All are $35-55 each

PAGE 45
Top Photos are $15-25 each
Bottom are $8-12 per set

PAGE 46
All are $12-24 each

PAGE 47
Trading Card - $20-30

PAGE 48
All are $25-35 each

PAGE 49
All are $25-35 each

PAGE 50
All are $10-20 each

PAGE 51
All are $10-20 each

PAGE 52
Top Left: $10-12 each
Top Right: $2-4 each
Bottom Left: $12-18 each
Bottom Right: $75-85

PAGE 53
Top: Pencil Holders $18-22 ea
Bottom: $4-18 each

PAGE 54
All are $4-20 each

PAGE 55
All are $8-20 each

PAGE 56
All are $6-10 each

PAGE 57
All are $14-18 each

PAGE 58
All are $14-18 each

PAGE 59
All are $12-16 each

PAGE 60
Top Left: $120-160
Top Right: $200-300
Mid. Left: $20-30
Mid. Right: $30-40
Bottom: $40-60

PAGE 61
All are $20-30 each

PAGE 62
All are $40-80 each

PAGE 63
All are $40-60 each

PAGE 64
All are $10-20 each

PAGE 65
All are $10-40 each

PAGE 66
All are $10-20 each

PAGE 67
Top Left: $30
Top Right: $5
Mid. Left: $10
Middle: $35
Mid. Right: $15
Bottom: $6-10

PAGE 68
All are $20-60 each

PAGE 69
Coins & Medallions: $5-10 ea
Plaque: $80-100

PAGE 70
Mid. Left: $120-140 ea
Mid. Mid.: #30-40
Mid. Right: $35
Bottom Left: $140-160
Bottom Mid.: $15-25
Bottom Right: $180-200

PAGE 71
All are $25-35 each

PAGE 72
All are $50-150 each

PAGE 73
All are $3-30 each

PAGE 74
All are $5-10 each

PAGE 76
$400-500

PAGE 77
$400-500

PAGE 78
$175

PAGE 79
$300-500

PAGE 80
All are $20-30 each

PAGE 81
All are $50-120 each

PAGE 82
All are $40-120 each

PAGE 83
Stetson Hats are $120-160 ea.
All others are $5-15 each

PAGE 84
Top: $180-300
Middle: $100-180
Bottom: $60-100

PAGE 85
Top: $150
Mid. Left: $65
Mid. Right: $30-40
Bottom: $60-80

PAGE 86
All are $35-65 each

PAGE 87
Top: $65-85
All others are $35-45 each

PAGE 88
All are $20

PAGE 89
Catalog $10

PAGE 90
All are $30-60 each

PAGE 91
All are $10-30 each

Price Guide

PAGE 92
Top: $140
Middle: $15-25 each
Bottom: $25-35 each

PAGE 93
All are $20-30 each

PAGE 94
Top Left: Socks, France $20
Tote Bag & Shoes $60-80
Top Right: $65
Bottom: $10-20 each

PAGE 95
All are $12-20 each

PAGE 96
All are $25-35 each

PAGE 97
All are $10-25 each

PAGE 98
All are $20-30

PAGE 99
All are $20-30

PAGE 100
Top Left: $20-30
Top Right: $2-3
Mid. Left: $10-15
Mid. Right: $15-20
Bottom Left: $10-15
Bottom Right: $8-12

PAGE 101
Top Left: $5-10 each
Top Right: $10-20
Mid Left: Table Lamp $30
Globe Lamp $35
Triangle Lamp $55
Mid Right: $20-25 each
Bottom Left: $5-10 each
Bottom Right: $6-10 each

PAGE 102
Top Left: $40-60
Top Right: $85-100
Bottom Left: $12
Bottom Right: $15

PAGE 103
Top: $6-8
Middle: $10-15
Bottom: $25 each

PAGE 104
Top: $65
Bottom: $500 each

PAGE 105
Top Left: $65
Top Right: $35
Bottom: $350

PAGE 106
Top Left: Clay Art $65
Small Statue $200
Statue/Red Jacket $160
Image Co. $200
Diana Young $400
Top Right: $45
Bottom Left: $55
Bottom Right: $22

PAGE 107
Top Left: $60-80
Top Right: $600
Bottom Left: $30
Bottom Right: $40-50

PAGE 108
All are $20-60 each

PAGE 109
Zippo's $80-120
All others are $10-25

PAGE 110
All are $20-35 each

PAGE 111
All are $20-35 each

PAGE 112
All are $5-30 each

PAGE 113
All are $10-40 each

PAGE 114
All are $30-60 each

PAGE 115
Top: $160
All others are $40 each

PAGE 116
Top Left: $20-30
Top Right: $5-10
Bottom Left: $10-15
Bottom Right: $25-35

PAGE 117
Top: $20-25
Middle: $15
Bottom: $3

PAGE 118
All are $10-30 each

PAGE 119
All are $20-40 each

PAGE 120
All are $25-45 each

PAGE 121
All are $25-45 each

PAGE 122
Top: $60-80
Bottom: $30-40

PAGE 123
Top: $200-250

PAGE 124
All are $10-20 each

PAGE 125
Top: $80
Bottom: $30

PAGE 126
All are $30-50 each

PAGE 127
All are $30-50 each

PAGE 128
All are $40-50 each

PAGE 129
Top Left: $65
Top Right: $80
Middle: $45
Bottom: $15-20

PAGE 130
All are $10-30 each

PAGE 131
All are $35-50 each

PAGE 132
All are $20-60 each

PAGE 133
All are $25-40 each

PAGE 134
Top: $60-80 a roll
Bottom: $25-35

PAGE 135
All are $5-15 each

PAGE 136
All are $15-25 each

PAGE 137
All are $4 each

PAGE 138
All are $10-35 each

PAGE 139
All are $5-25 each

PAGE 140
All are $15-25 each

PAGE 141
All are $10-20 each

PAGE 142
All are $10-15 each

PAGE 143
All are $10-25 each

PAGE 144
All are $10-20 each

PAGE 146
All are $40-60 each

PAGE 147
All are $60-80 each

PAGE 148
All are $5-10 each

PAGE 149
All are $5-15 each

PAGE 150
All are $10-15 each

PAGE 151
All are $10-15 each

PAGE 153
All are $40-60 each

PAGE 154
All are $40-60 each

PAGE 155
All are $60-100 each

PAGE 156
All are $30-80 each

PAGE 157
All are $20-30 each

PAGE 158
All are $20-30 each

PAGE 159
$80

PAGE 160
All are $40-60 each

PAGE 161
All are $40-80 each

PAGE 162
All are $20-60 each

PAGE 163
All are $60-80 each

PAGE 164
All are $20-30 each

PAGE 166
Top Left: $140
Top Right: $140
Bottom Left: $140

PAGE 167
All are $180-240 each

PAGE 168
All are $60-80 each

PAGE 169
All are $60-80 each

PAGE 170
All are $60-80 each

PAGE 171
All are $80-120 each

PAGE 172
All are $10-25 each

PAGE 173
All are $20-30 each

PAGE 174
All are $50-60 each

PAGE 175
All are $30-60 each

PAGE 176
All are $30-40 each

PAGE 177
All are $20-25 each

PAGE 178
Top Row: $200-300 each
Middle Row: $100-200 each
Bottom Row: $60-100 each

PAGE 179
All are $180-250 each

PAGE 180
Top Left: $350-450
Top Right: $800-1000
Bottom Left: $250-350
Bottom Right: $600-800

PAGE 181
All are $175-275 each

PAGE 182
Top: $1000-1500
Bottom: $400-600

PAGE 183
Top: $6000-8000
Bottom Left: $400-600
Bottom Right: $400-600

PAGE 184
Top Left: $600-800
Top Right: $300-400
Bottom Left: $300-400
Bottom Right: $300-400

PAGE 185
Top: $600-800
Bottom: $300-400

PAGE 186
Top Row: $200-300 each
Bottom Row: $100-180 each

PAGE 187
Top: $80
Bottom: $60

PAGE 188
Top: $600-800
Middle: $800-1200
Bottom: $200-300

PAGE 189
Top Left: $250-350
Top Right: $250-350
Bottom Left: $150-200
Bottom Right: $600-800

PAGE 190
All are $150-250 each

PAGE 191
All are $150-250 each

PAGE 192
All are $150-250 each

PAGE 193
All are $150-250 each

PAGE 194
$800-1200

PAGE 195
Top Left: $600-800
Top Right: $250-350
Bottom Left: $150-200
Bottom Right: $80-120

PAGE 196
Top Left: $200-300
Top Right: $80-120
Bottom Left: $80-120
Bottom Right: $350-450

PAGE 197
Top Left: $250-300
Top Right: $250-300
Bottom Left: $100-150
Bottom Right: $100-150

PAGE 198
Top Row: $60-80 each
Bottom Row: $350-450 each

PAGE 199
All are $600-800 each

PAGE 200
All are $150-250 each

PAGE 201
All are $150-250 each

PAGE 202
All are $250-350 each

PAGE 203
All are $250-350 each

PAGE 204
Top Row: $400-600 each
Bottom Row: $150-200 each

PAGE 205
Top Left: $600-800
Top Right: $600-800
Bottom Left: $600-800
Bottom Right: $100-200

PAGE 206
Top Left: $600-800
Top Right: $100-200
Bottom Left: $800-1000
Bottom Right: $100-120

PAGE 207
Top Left: $150-200
Top Right: $200-300
Bottom Left: $400-600
Bottom Right: $80-120

PAGE 208
All are $250-350 each

PAGE 209
All are $250-350 each

PAGE 210
Top Left: $150-200
Top Right: $10-15
Mid. Left: $35-50
Mid. Right: $60-80
Bottom Left: $40-60
Bottom Right: $100-120

PAGE 212 & 213
All are $150-200 each

PAGE 214 & 215
All are $250-350 each

PAGE 216 & 217
All are $150-200 each

PAGE 218 & 219
All are $150-200 each

PAGE 220 & 221
All are $40-80 each

PAGE 222
All are $100-200 each

PAGE 224 & 225
All are $40-80 each

PAGE 226 & 227
All are $60-120 each

PAGE 228 & 229
All are $40-80 each

PAGE 230 & 231
All are $30-40 each

PAGE 232 & 233
All are $40-50 each

PAGE 234 & 235
All are $30-40 each

PAGE 236
All are $50-60 each

PAGE 237
All are $50-80 each

PAGE 238
All are $80-100 each

PAGE 239
All are $50-80 each

PAGE 240
All are $20-50 each

PAGE 244
Yearbook - $400-500

PAGE 245
Yearbook - $400-500

PAGE 246
Yearbook - $500-600

PAGE 247
Yearbook - $600-800

PAGE 248
Yearbook - $1500-3000

PAGE 250
Yearbook - $2000-3000

PAGE 252
Yearbook - $300-400

PAGE 253
Yearbook - $300-400

PAGE 254
Yearbook - $300-400

PAGE 255
Log of Memories - $3000-4000

PAGE 256
All are $1000-2000 each

PAGE 257
All are $80-120 each

PAGE 258
Top: $800
Bottom: $1500-2000

PAGE 259
Top: $1500-2500
Bottom: $1500-2000

PAGE 260
Top: $2000-3000
Bottom: $3500-4500

PAGE 261
House Lease - $8000-10,000

PAGE 262
All are $20,000-25,000 each

PAGE 263
All are $12,000-15,000 each

Wardrobe - for reference only

PAGE 271
Feeding Instructions
$6000-8000

PAGE 272
Top: $1000-1500
Bottom: $1500-2000

PAGE 273
Top: $2000-3000
Bottom: $150-250

PAGE 274 & 275
Eulogy - $500-600

PAGE 276
Top Left: $150-200
Top Right: $1500-2000
Middle: $80-120
Bottom: $40-60

PAGE 277
Top Left: $800-1000
Top Right: $600-1000
Bottom Left: $1000-4000
Bottom Right: $4000

PAGE 278
Top Left: $300
Top Right: $300
Bottom Left: $1000
Bottom Right: $500

PAGE 279
Top Left: $600
Top Right: $500
Bottom Left: $160
Bottom Right: $60

PAGE 280
Brochure - $60-80

PAGE 281
Top: $400-500
Middle: $60-100
Bottom: $40-60

PAGE 282 & 283
All are $80-120 each

PAGE 284
Top: $150-250
Middle: $600-800
Bottom: $800-1200

PAGE 285
Top Left: $120-160
Top Right: $140-160
Mid. Left: $20-30
Mid. Right: $150-200
Bottom: $40-60

PAGE 286
Top Left: $40-80 each
Top Right: $3000-4000
Bottom: $80-120

PAGE 287
Top Left: $700
Top Right: $2000
Bottom Left: $180
Bottom Right: $600

PAGE 290
Top Left: $200-400
Top Mid.: $30-40
Top Right: $40-50

PAGE 290 CONTINUED
Mid. Left: $150-200
Middle: $80-120
Mid. Right: $60-120
Bottom Left: $80-120
Bottom Mid.: $150-200
Bottom Right: $350-500

PAGE 291
Biography - $600-800

PAGE 292
Top Left: $80-100
Top Mid.: $120-160
Top Right: $60-80
Mid. Left: $30-40
Middle: $40-60
Mid. Right: $20-30
Bottom Left: $120-140
Bottom Mid.: $120-140
Bottom Right: $60-80

PAGE 293
Top Left: $25-35
Top Mid.: $25-35
Top Right: $25-35
Mid. Left: $50-60
Middle: $65-85
Mid. Right: $35-45
Bottom Left: $30-40
Bottom Mid.: $35-45
Bottom Right: $45-65

PAGE 294
Top Left: $65-75
Top Mid.: $30-40
Top Right: $35-45
Mid. Left: $30-40
Middle: $30-40
Mid. Right: $65-85
Bottom Left: $30-40
Bottom Mid.: $30-40
Bottom Right: $20-25

PAGE 295
Top Row: $35-45
Mid. Left: $35-45
Middle: $20-30
Mid. Right: $35-45
Bottom Left: $55-75
Bottom Mid.: $45-55
Bottom Right: $15-20

PAGE 296
Top Left: $40-50
Top Mid.: $55-75
Top Right: $20-30
Mid. Left: $45-55
Middle: $25-30
Mid. Right: $15-20
Bottom Left: $25-35
Bottom Right: $30-40

PAGE 297
Top Row: $15-20
Mid. Left: $15-20
Middle: $25-30
Mid. Right: $15-20
Bottom Left: $20-30
Bottom Right: $60-80

PAGE 298
Top Left: $25-35
Top Mid.: $80-120
Top Right: $25-35
Mid. Left: $35-45
Middle: $30-40
Mid. Right: $35-45
Bottom Left: $25-35
Bottom Mid.: $25-35
Bottom Right: $15-20

PAGE 299
Top Left: $50-60
Top Mid.: $50-60
Top Right: $75-85
Mid. Left: $15-20
Middle: $40-50
Mid. Right: $15-20
Bottom Left: $25-30
Bottom Mid.: $25-30
Bottom Right: $30-35

PAGE 300
All are $40-60 each

PAGE 301
All are $90-120 each

PAGE 302
Top Left: $50-60
Top Mid.: $60-70
Top Right: $35-45
Mid. Left: $60-70
Middle: $45-55
Mid. Right: $65-75
Bottom Left: $80-100
Bottom Mid.: $65-85
Bottom Right: $45-55

PAGE 303
Top Row: $35-45 each
Mid. Left: $20-25
Middle: $25-35
Middle Right: $25-30
Bottom Left: $45-60
Bottom Mid.: $35-45
Bottom Right: $35-45

PAGE 304
Top Left: $150-200
Top Mid.: $45-65
Top Right: $65-85
Mid. Left: $45-55
Middle: $50-60
Mid. Right: $45-55

PAGE 304 Continued
Bottom Left: $80-100
Bottom Mid.: $40-50
Bottom Right: $35-40

PAGE 305
Top Left: $45-60
Top Mid.: $160-200
Top Right: $15-20
Mid. Left: $40-60
Middle: $65-85
Mid. Right: $60-80
Bottom Left: $160-200
Bottom Mid.: $50-60
Bottom Right: $45-60

PAGE 306
Top Left: $30-40
Top Mid.: $25-30
Top Right: $35-45
Mid. Left: $20-25
Middle: $35-40
Mid. Right: $15-20
Bottom Left: $20-25
Bottom Mid.: $30-40
Bottom Right: $15-20

PAGE 307
Top Left: $80-120
Top Mid.: $45-50
Top Right: $40-50
Mid. Left: $35-45
Middle: $10-15
Mid. Right: $45-50
Bottom Left: $40-50
Bottom Mid.: $50-60
Bottom Right: $40-50

PAGE 308
All are $150-200 each

PAGE 309
Top Left: $60-80
Top Mid.: $25-30
Top Right: $15-20
Mid. Left: $25-35
Middle: $35-45
Mid. Right: $20-25
Bottom Left: $10-15
Bottom Mid.: $60-80
Bottom Right: $20-25

PAGE 310
Top Left: $50-60
Top Mid.: $40-60
Top Right: $10-15
Mid. Left: $80-120
Middle: $80-120
Mid. Right: $25-35
Bottom Left: $25-35
Bottom Mid.: $25-35
Bottom Right: $35-40

PAGE 311
Top Left: $85-120
Top Mid.: $45-65
Top Right: $25-30
Mid. Left: $10-20
Middle: $15-20
Mid. Right: $35-40
Bottom Left: $25-30
Bottom Mid.: $15-20
Bottom Right: $35-45

PAGE 322 & 323
All are $150-200 each

PAGE 324
Top Left: $150
Top Mid.: $150
Top Right: $40-50
Mid. Left: $150
Mid. Right: $20-30
Bottom Left: $60
Bottom Right: $60

PAGE 325
All are $5-15 each

PAGE 326
Top Row: $60-100 each
All others are $20-30 each

PAGE 327
All are $40-80 each

PAGE 328
All are $10-35 each

PAGE 329
Top Left: $15-20
Top Mid.: $15-20
Top Right: $10-15
Mid. Left: $45-55
Middle: $30-40
Mid. Right: $15-20
Bottom Left: $20-25
Bottom Mid.: $15-25
Bottom Right: $15-20

PAGE 330
All are $10-15 each

PAGE 333
Magazine - $180-250

PAGE 334
All are $80-140 each

PAGE 335
All are $140-160 each

PAGE 336
All are $100-140 each

PAGE 337
All are $45-65 each

PAGE 338
Top Left: $45-55
Top Mid.: $65-75
Top Right: $50-60
Bottom Left: $45-55
Bottom Mid.: $80-100
Bottom Right: $120-160

PAGE 339
Top Left: $140-160
Top Mid.: $65-75
Top Right: $60-80
Bottom Left: $85-100
Bottom Mid.: $20-30
Bottom Right: $85-100

PAGE 340
All are $60-100 each

PAGE 341
All are $60-100 each

PAGE 342
Top Left: $40-50
Top Mid.: $40-50
Top Right: $80-100
Mid. Left: $40-50
Middle: $15-20
Mid. Right: $40-50
Bottom Left: $40-50
Bottom Mid.: $25-35
Bottom Right: $25-35

PAGE 343
All are $25-35 each

PAGE 344
All are $25-35 each

PAGE 345
All are $20-35 each

PAGE 346
All are $100-140 each

PAGE 347
All are $100-140 each

PAGE 348
All are $35-55 each

PAGE 349
Top Left: $10-15
Top Mid.: $10-15
Top Right: $40-50
Mid. Left: $60-80
Middle: $35-45
Mid. Right: $35-45
Bottom Left: $35-45
Bottom Mid.: $120-160
Bottom Right: $80-120

PAGE 350
Top Row: $60-80 each
Middle Row: $35-55 each
Bottom Row: $25-35 each

PAGE 351
Top Left: $60-80
Top Mid.: $60-80
Top Right: $35-45
Mid. Left: $15-20
Middle: $80-100
Mid. Right: $15-20
Bottom Left: $20-25
Bottom Mid.: $20-25
Bottom Right: $20-25

PAGE 352
Top Row: $45-65 each
Middle Row: $40-50 each
Bottom Row: $30-40 each

PAGE 353
Top Left: $25-35
Top Mid.: $80-120
Top Right: $80-100
Mid. Left: $25-35
Middle: $80-100
Mid. Right: $25-35
Bottom Left: $20-30
Bottom Mid.: $30-35
Bottom Right: $45-55

PAGE 354
Top Left: $35-45
Top Mid.: $75-85
Top Right: $70-80
Mid. Left: $45-55
Middle: $60-80
Mid. Right: $35-55
Bottom Left: $20-30
Bottom Mid.: $20-30
Bottom Right: $20-30

PAGE 355
Top Left: $80-100
Top Mid.: $20-25
Top Right: $80-100
Mid. Left: $80-100
Middle: $80-100
Mid. Right: $20-25
Bottom Left: $30-40
Bottom Mid.: $75-85
Bottom Right: $75-85

PAGE 356
Top: $70-80 each
Middle: $75-85 each
Bottom: $25-35 each

PAGE 357
Top: $40-50 each
Middle: $65-85 each
Bottom: $35-45 each

PAGE 358
Top Row: $25-35
Bottom Left: $120-140
Bottom Mid.: $120-140
Bottom Right: $30-40